HISTORY AND HERESY: A HOLY PLACE

B. WATERS

Creative Spirit Publishing

Copyright © 2021 B. Waters

Cover design by: B. Waters

Library of Congress Control Number: 2018675309
Printed in the United States of America

CONTENTS

Title Page
Copyright
Preface
CHAPTER I: IN THE BEGINNING 1
CHAPTER II. A NEW COVENANT 29
CHAPTER III. THE LIFE OF JESUS 101
CHAPTER IV. THE CRUCIFIXION AND ITS AFTERMATH 129
CHAPTER V: JEWISH WAR AND INDEPENDENCE 178
CHAPTER VI. ROME 186
CHAPTER VIII. COUNCILS AND CONTROVERSIES 249
CHAPTER IX. RELICS OF THE SAINTS 277
CHAPTER X. SAINTS AND SINNERS 295
CHAPTER XI. THE BIRTH OF ISLAM 327
CHAPTER XII. A HOLY PLACE 369

PREFACE

In the year 2000, I had a sudden and unexpectedly passionate interest in Mary Magdalene (as author Margaret Starbird notes, 2000 is MM in Roman numerals). It was simply time. Something in me said that there was so much more to the Magdalene's story than what we had been told. I had a deep knowing, as did many others, that the slandering of her character was not proof of her sinfulness, but rather of her power and her gifts – in a time when Feminine power was becoming more and more greatly diminished, and intuition and other divine gifts were being vilified and demonized. Doors were opening in the early 2000's to new insights and revelations about her important role in early Christianity. From the beginning of my research, there was a faint whisper of intuition and guidance to "restore the woman, restore the world." This focus was, at first, directed to Mary Magdalene, however, eventually it seemed to apply more generally to the Divine Feminine, her place in religion, and in the greater world.

This book has taken nearly 15 years to write. Indeed, it has been a labor of love, dedication and seeking to understand the deeper truths of Christian history. It is not meant to be a concrete teaching, but rather a fluid exploration of truths. It is not meant to strictly define, but to make people think, to question a variety of beliefs, and the teachings that they have accepted as their own definitive truths in the past.

There are deep questions that arise when you begin to lay out a patchwork of the history of Christianity from various sources: Bible verses next to Quranic verses, hagiographies next to folk tales, hymns and prayers next to satire and cynicism. The puzzle pieces will never fit together satisfactorily – many of the pieces have been altered, so that you end up with gaping holes in some places, and elsewhere awkwardly overlapping bits. The greater image may be elusive like the modern op-art images that seem to suggest unrecognizable patterns, until the viewer softens their gaze and suddenly sees the image hidden within the image. You have the capability to have "eyes that see" - the choice is yours. In any case, it is always up to you – as St. Paul said to "Prove all things." Each of us must take responsibility for our own beliefs and accepted "truths."

I have tried to respect that everyone is entitled to their own beliefs, while also giving a discerning overview of many of the twists and turns within, and among, the teachings and histories of these three faiths. There are questions that can't be ignored. Each perspective, whether from opposing religions or factions within a particular faith has their own ideas about what is true.

I intentionally leave many things for the readers to sort out for themselves. I hope that other writers will follow up with their own research, ideas, and interpretations. Perhaps others will find a better placement for some of the ill-fitting puzzle pieces in this book. Some sections are written as prose, for the freer literary expression of ideas. I chose to use the modern historical notations of "CE" (current era) and "BCE" (before current era), rather than AD and BC. I have also chosen to use numerical notations of centuries (i.e., 1st century, 2nd century), rather than spelling them out. I leave the original notations used in any quoted material. In quotes, I have left the bracketed information that was added for clarification or missing words. I also use brackets for my own clarifications of quoted material. And at times, I have used italics in quoted material for emphasis.

I have, generally, put the source material for quotes from the Bible, the Quran and other ancient texts in parentheses next to the text, with more modern citations as endnotes at the back of the book.

This is a time of great change on the planet. Are we willing to rise to new levels of consciousness – to live from the heart? To fully embody our souls? It was for these very times that the seeds of Christ consciousness were planted 2000 years ago. These are the times. Best to you in your journey, and to all people of all faiths and beliefs. May we find that we can live together in Peace.

~ Dedicated, With Love,

to All Seekers of Truth ~

CHAPTER I: IN THE BEGINNING

EVE

Eve...the Mother of Humanity,
with her husband, Adam,
made the source of Original Sin.
The woman, in the first "Holy Place",
eating the fruit of the forbidden tree,
accused of knowing (judging)
good and evil (duality),
in the paradise garden.
Her husband followed her lead.
When God asked him what he had done,
Adam blamed the woman, who
"gave me of the tree, and I did eat."
The woman blamed the serpent.
But, didn't God create the serpent?

What metaphors within the story?
In much of the *Midrashim*, rabbinical
commentary on the Hebrew scriptures,
the rabbis discussed their (male, of course)
perceptions of the nature of women.
Some were positive descriptions, some
were negative. However, married life
was encouraged, and men were cautioned
against remaining alone and depriving
themselves of marital blessings
(unlike the eventual teachings
of its offspring, Christianity).
Some rabbis emphasized that Eve
came from Adam's rib, that she should
not be above him or below him -
that she was created from close to
his heart, and should walk beside him
as his beloved partner.

St. Paul made the man the origin of sin,
"Sin entered the world through one man
and death through sin, and in this way
death came to all people, because all sinned."
The first sin made necessary the
acceptance of Jesus as savior,
"For as in Adam all die, so in Christ
all will be made alive."
Perhaps the story initially represented
Human frailty and imperfection –
free will choice.

A century or so after Paul, Tertullian,
the North African, early apologist (misogynist)
for the Christian faith, had a different take.
He wrote in the 2nd to 3rd century:
"And do you not know that you are
(each) an Eve? ...You are the devil's gateway:
you are the unsealer of that (forbidden) tree:
you are the first deserter of the divine law..."
He proclaimed that death itself was *her* fault,
and because of *her* sin, even the son of God
had to die – for the redemption of her sin.
Such a stance was reflected in some
degree within rabbinical satire
about a certain woman and her son.

Biblical metaphor: The creation of the world
in seven days – what was a day when
the waters of the firmament had not yet been
separated from the waters of the earth?
When light and dark still mingled.
A measure of time, yes, but there was not
yet a 24-hour division of days –
even of day from night.
Seven days, seven billion years?
Who knows? "A time, and a time, and
a half of a time". Poetic license.

So, one woman – the culprit in
The Fall from Grace? An allegory.

Before the Diaspora – an old story,
a folktale, an oral tradition to explain
human suffering – a metaphorical footnote.
After, a rabbinical perspective,
An allegory "resurrected",
confirmed by Jewish sage-scribes
and concretized in the traditions.
This – and Tertullian's misogynistic stance
came after the destruction of the Holy City
by Hadrian in the early 2nd century.
A woman. What woman?
Highly honored before the end
of the Bar Kochba Revolt of 132 CE –
Her tomb on the Mount of Olives,
directly across the Cedron Valley from the
Temple Mount, towards Bethany.

The Jewish Independence: three years
of Jewish autonomy. Success, glory, freedom!
When Christianity was still a part of Judaism,
However different – revolutionary even,
still a part of the Jewish faith and people.
The Jews had overcome Rome –
Nothing was impossible! Tolerance was easy.
And after: the Temple razed to the ground.
Jerusalem in ruins. Hadrian's destruction of all
that they had built over centuries.
All that they had struggled for.
Freedom, independence and then...
complete and utter devastation.
Jewish exile from the Holy City.
Gone the hub of Jewish life –
the Temple and the Holy of Holies.

The Temple, itself, representing the
Garden of Eden, its doors symbolizing
the very gates of paradise.
When Adam and Eve were cast out
of the Garden, God placed cherubim
East of Eden to "guard the way to
the tree of life." (*Genesis* 3:24)

A metaphor for the Jewish people -
cast out of their Holy Place?
The doorway to heaven now sealed?

A people in mourning.
Christian exile, too – they were still one.
A sweeping blow from Hadrian's hand,
And now persecution, starvation, brutal
suffering such as cannot be described.
A way of life destroyed -
The Temple life, and the oral tradition:
Interpretation, and argument,
but freedom to decide, turned into
synagogues, and rabbinical texts.
The renouncing of Messianism.
The story in the *Torah,*
in *Genesis (Bereshit)* - a bitter history.
Allegories became allegations.
His-story. Harsh satire and blame
(Though not as harsh as with Lilith.)
Metaphor solidified.

After Triumph – despair.
The Jews, scattered on the winds.
The Holy Places of both
Judaism and Christianity in ruins.
Woman blamed for the Fall
(of the Holy Temple?)
What woman? A Mary.
Which Mary? Ah, there's the rub.
Too many convoluted twists and turns
to easily make sense of it all.

And the Romans did their part -
Damnatio memoriae? Almost certainly!
Didn't Constantine "damn the memory"
of his own once-beloved son?
Rub his name off the monuments,
out of the books, out of history?
Never to be mentioned – on point of death.
How much more, by past imperials,
the enemy of the Romans?

A "king of kings" to rival the divine royals?
And his divine counterpart
to his mission.
Names that could not be spoken
became many names and alter egos.
Testaments written, each with its own slant
as record of hidden identities and hidden truths.

How odd that it was Rome that
initially restored her name –
the emperor's mother, Helena,
designated the first feast day of the
legalized Roman Catholic faith
as the "Memory of Mary".
Romans, eventually, praised her -
raised her a bit beyond the pale!
Emperors had declared their own divinity,
Why not a Byzantine "Mother of God"?
Ascetic monks – the Simple Monks -
battled such egregious error!
Traveled to Constantinople to decry the term.
How could a human being be the mother
of the eternal beingness?
A debate that still reverberates.
In many ways, the woman...
her name, her true story, remains
unredeemed – unrestored.

ADAM'S RIB

In Rabbinical exegesis, there are different opinions about how Eve was created. *Gen.* 2:21 states that "He took one of his ribs." In a plain, and literal sense, this is the removing of one of Adam's ribs with which to create Eve. One exegetical opinion interprets *zela* (rib) as "side," as in (Ex. 26:20) "and for the other side wall [*zela*] of the Tabernacle"; hence, God created Eve from Adam's side. According to this opinion, God removed something from Adam when He created Eve. Rabbis frequently draw analogies between the creation of a family and the erection of the hallowed Tabernacle. Comparing Eve's creation with the construction of the Tabernacle imparts sanctity to woman.

As with Plato's description in *Symposium* of man as originally being one androgynous being, or *monad,* male and female, that was cut in two, there are various Rabbinical sources that say that God created an androgynous being, and divided it, forming a back for Adam and a back for Eve (*Gen. Rabbah* 8:1); a similar story appears in the early Babylonian literature. According to this interpretation, Adam's creation did not precede that of Eve – they were created together, like all the other creatures that were created male and female.

Based on the statement in *Gen.* 5:2 in which "male and female He created them," some derive that Adam/Eve was created androgynous. A similar notion is that Adam was created two-faced, as it is said (*Psalms* 139:5): "You hedge [or, formed] me before and behind" (this creature had a face in front and another behind, one of a male, and the other of a female).

The creation of Eve is simply as an act of separation, just as the creation of the upper and lower waters and of light and darkness were acts of detachment between two elements that were previously one. Thus, the joining together of the two sexes in copulation represents the original perfection that existed during the time of the Creation, thus enabling us to understand the praise of marriage in Judaic teachings, which asserts that a man is incomplete without a wife (*Gen. Rabbah* 17:2).

In the 12th century text, *Guide for the Perplexed,* Maimonides speaks of Divine secrets within the *Torah,* the first five books of the Hebrew Bible. He describes how Adam and Eve were one being that was then divided in two: "The unity of the two is proved by the fact that both have the same name, for she is called *ishah* (woman), because she was taken out of *ish* (man), also by the words, 'And shall cleave unto his wife, and they shall be one flesh' (ii. 24). How great is the ignorance of those who do not see that all this necessarily includes some [other] idea [besides the literal meaning of the words]?"[1]

PARDES – THE ORCHARD

The Hebrew word, *Pardes,* of Persian origin, means "The Orchard." In Christianity, it is Paradise – the Garden of Eden. But there is also, PaRDeS, acronym (a bit of wordplay) for Jewish exegesis, related to the layers upon layers of meaning in scriptural texts, requiring study of the *Torah* on many levels:

Peshat (simple) - Direct meaning,
Remez (hints) - Hidden, symbolic meaning,

Derash (inquire, seek) - Inquiry and study of the scriptures,
Sod (secret) - Through study, esoteric meanings," mystery-revelation."[2]

Each type of PaRDeS study is meant to inspire deeper insights into the meaning of a text (which should not contradict the simple meaning). *Peshat* means the plain or contextual meaning of the text. *Remez* is the allegorical meaning. *Derash* includes the metaphorical meaning, and *Sod* represents the hidden meaning.[3] It is apparent from these guidelines, that there is intended to be deeper understanding than simply the literal interpretation of scriptural text. This would also apply to rabbinical writings, which are filled with pun and satire. They are meant to be considered carefully for the deeper meaning. The four types of study can overlap, for instance, when legal discussion of a verse is influenced by mystical interpretations or when a "hint" is determined by comparing a word with other instances of the same word.

Within Rabbinic literature, such as the *Talmud* and *Midrashim*, *Halacha* is Jewish legal discussion and ruling, while *Aggadah* (or *Haggadah*) is Jewish theological/narrative discussion.[4] The exoteric methods of *Peshat*-Simple, *Remez*-Hinted and *Derush*-Homiletic exegeses methods, can be used in either context.

THE ALEPH AND THE TREE OF LIFE

The Alphabet of Rabbi Akiva (*Akiba*) is a *midrash,* that is to say, an ancient Jewish exegetical commentary, on the letters of the Hebrew alphabet. In this work, Akiva, the 2nd century sage or *tanna* (highly respected Jewish rabbi) gives esoteric meanings for each letter, which are used in study and meditation to give deeper layers of meaning to scriptural texts. Two versions of this midrash are known to exist. In the first version, the letters are introduced from the last to the first. Each letter makes claims for why they should be the first letter of the alphabet. They contend with each other for the honor of being designated in the role of being the first, the beginning of creation (*bereshit*).[5]

Only the *aleph* makes no boastful claim. The *aleph* is noted by the Most High for its modesty. Its meaning denotes the oneness of God. For its humility, the *Aleph* is assured that it is the chief of all letters, and that it shall have its place at the beginning.[6]

In the second version, the meaning of *aleph* is, "Thy mouth learned truth", suggesting not only truth, but also including connotations of the praise of God, as well as (*imrah*) - the creative Word of God, a phrase which Christians used to describe Jesus. Or it might even be seen as a reference to God Himself as *Aleph*, the first, the Prince and Prime of all existence.[7] In some variants, the *aleph* looks more like the letter "N", and in others, more like the letter, "X". which may be pertinent in discussions of X as the symbol of Christianity.

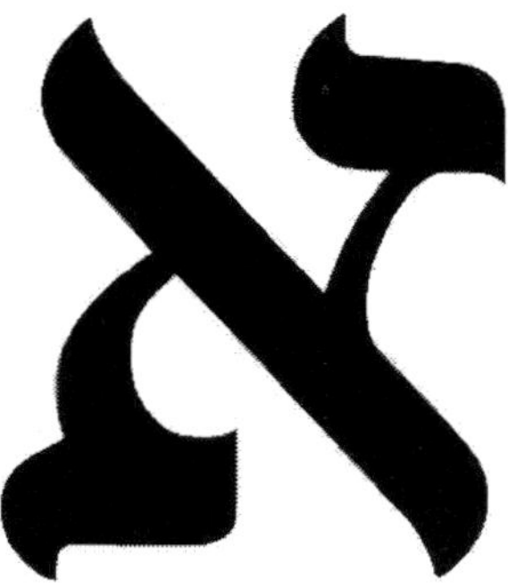

Plate 1: The Aleph

Rabbi Akiva used the *aleph*, the first letter in the Jewish alphabet as a metaphor to describe the intricate esoteric understanding of God in Judaic teachings. In his discussion on the *aleph*, Akiva emphasized the unity of the waters (above) and the waters (below), as representing Divine transcendence (the nature and power of God) and Divine immanence (God's presence in the material world). Unity is the key of the teaching – as well as a caution against judgment.

Mystical literature (*Zohar* I, 26b and *Tikunei HaZohar* 40), adds to the story: "The ancient Saba (an old man) stood up and said (to Shimon bar Yochai), "Rabbi, Rabbi! What is the meaning of what Rabbi Akiva said to his students, "When you come to the place of pure marble stones, do not say, "Water! Water! lest you place yourselves in danger, for it is said, 'He who speaks untruths shall not stand before My eyes.'" (*Babylonian Talmud Hagigah* 14b)[8]

The old man makes reference to *Genesis* 1:6, "*There shall be a firmament between the waters and it shall separate between water (above the firmament) and water (below the firmament).*" Since the Torah describes the division of the waters into upper and lower, why should it be problematic to mention this division in the context of the Holy Place, and why did Rabbi Akiva warn them, "...do not say, 'Water! Water!' "?

The Holy Lamp (Shimon bar Yochai) asks for clarification from the old wise one for the *chevraya* (students or disciples) who don't understand. The ancient Saba answered, "Rabbi, Rabbi, Holy Lamp. Surely the pure marble stones are the *yud* - one the upper *yud* [horizontal dash] of the letter *aleph*, and one the lower *yud* of the letter *aleph*. Here there is no spiritual impurity, only pure marble stones, so there is no separation between one water and the other; they form a single unity from the aspect of the tree of life, which is the *vav* (diagonal line) in the midst of the letter *aleph*. In this regard it states, 'and if he take of the Tree of Life (and eat and live forever)'. "[9]

This allegory is meant to highlight the idea of the place of the White Marble - the Holy Place - as the place where heaven and earth, the above and below, connect. To cause separation here would be to commit a devastating error, akin to the error of Adam and Eve.

The story of Adam and Eve puts forth that they were cast out of the garden for eating the fruit of the Tree of the Knowledge of Good and Evil. But the greater caution, some would say, is that if they ate the fruit of the Tree of Life, they would become immortal, and God-like.

The more in-depth meaning involves the complicated connections with the Tree of Life configuration in Jewish teachings. The *sefira* of *chochma* is called *yesh*. It is spelled with the letters *yud-shin* in Hebrew. The lower *chochma* is called *shai* [*malchut*/kingship], spelled *shin-yud*. These are the same letters, but in reverse – a kind of mirroring. When both words are combined, they form the word *shayish* — *shin-yud-shin* (the yud of each uniting into one), which means "marble".[11]

The various strokes of the letter *aleph* are explained by Akiva in a simple manner:

> "The *shayish* is the place of the marble,
> the Holy Place.
> The *Aleph* is unity: Above reflecting below.
> The *yud* of Wisdom (Divinity) from which the
> light of the Divine descends,
> and the *yud* of Kingship (Creation), from which
> the light of the Creation ascends,
> through the *vav*, the diagonal line of Compassion
> that unifies the two into wholeness,
> symbolized in the letter *Aleph*."[10]

Brown-Driver – Briggs defines *shayish* as: "material of temple." Strong's Concordance gives its simple meaning as: "alabaster." Akiva's description connects the place of the white marble, or alabaster (the Holy Place within the Jewish Temple) to the Tree of Life.

The Tree of Life is a fundamental archetype in many of the world's mythologies, and religious and philosophical traditions, in the form of the sacred tree. In the *Book of Proverbs*, the Tree of life is associated with wisdom: "[Wisdom] is a tree of life to them that lay hold upon her, and happy [is every one] that retaineth her." (*Proverbs* 3:13–18)

The Tree of Knowledge, connecting heaven and the underworld, and the Tree of Life, connecting all forms of creation, are found in the *Book of Genesis* – both forms of the world tree or cosmic tree. *Revelation* 22 speaks of the "pure river of water of life" which proceeds "out of the throne of God". The river feeds two trees of life, one on each side of the river. which "bear twelve manner of fruits" ... "and the leaves of the tree were for healing of the nations" (v.1-2).

The Tree of Life in *Genesis* is distinct from the Tree of the Knowledge of Good and Evil, from which Adam and Eve ate the "forbidden fruit", which resulted in their being cast out of the Garden of Eden. To afterward prevent their access to this tree - the Tree of Life, cherubim with flaming swords were placed at the east of the garden to prevent access to its gifts. (*Genesis* 3:22–24)

In *Genesis* 2:9 and 3:22-24; the Tree of Life is called the source of eternal life in the Garden of Eden. Upon the sin of Adam and Eve, access is revoked, and man is changed from immortal to mortal and driven from the garden. To emphasize this point: Adam and Eve were originally immortal. The Tree of Life then reappears at the end of the bible in the *Book of Revelation*, as a part of a new garden of paradise. Access will then be given, once again, to the garden: those who "wash their robes" (they that do his commandments) ..."have right to the tree of life" (v.14). It says, in *Rev* 2:7, "To him that overcometh will I give to eat of the tree of life, which is in the midst of the paradise of God." Redemption of humanity - and immortality - is attainable, through righteousness, meaning alignment with higher truths, thus reconnecting the Shekinah - the Divine Feminine that was trapped within matter, to God.

The Old Testament stories of the Tree of Life appear also in Christian traditions, where either the *eucharist* or Christ, himself, was equated with it. Augustine of Hippo said that "the tree of life is Christ"[12] and Pope Benedict XVI that "the Cross is the true tree of life."[13] Here, Christ is seen to be the redeemer of fallen humanity. In modern times, one might see this as the Christ Consciousness - accessible to all who follow Jesus' teachings - "these things shall ye do and greater."

In the Jewish mysticism of *Kabbalah*, the Tree of Life might be seen to describe existence, God, or the human psyche. The Kabbalic Tree of Life is drawn in the form of a diagram of interconnected nodes called *Sefirot,* through which the unknowable divine *Ein Sof* manifests all of creation. This "emanationist theology" is deeply embedded in the Torah teachings, and Jewish worship. It represents, in esoteric symbolism, the purpose of creation as unification of Divine and human in the *Sefirot*, restoring harmony to creation.[14]

Thus, the Tree of Life might also be seen to relate to the path to enlightenment within the human body, much like the Hindu diagram of the seven chakra system, and the three channels of energy that are connected to them.

The *Sephirot* – the Divine emanations, are the 10 attributes, through which *Ein Sof* (The Infinite) reveals Itself and continuously creates both the material world and the higher spiritual realms.

Plate 2: The Tree of Life

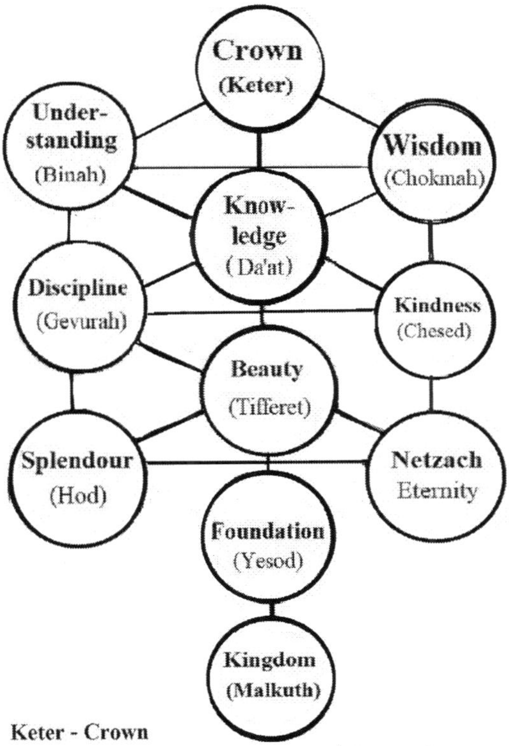

Crown (Keter)
Under-standing (Binah)
Wisdom (Chokmah)
Know-ledge (Da'at)
Discipline (Gevurah)
Kindness (Chesed)
Beauty (Tifferet)
Splendour (Hod)
Netzach Eternity
Foundation (Yesod)
Kingdom (Malkuth)

Keter - Crown
Chokmah - Wisdom
Binah - Understanding
Knowledge - Da'at
Chesed - Kindness
Gevurah - Discipline

Tifferet - Beauty
Netzach - Eternity
Hod - Splendour
Yesod - Foundation
Malkuth - Kingdom

The *Sephirot*, including Wisdom, Compassion and Kingship comprise the dynamic life in God's Persona. In the highest of the Four Worlds (*Atzilut*-Emanation), there is complete unity of the *sephirot* and creation. Apparent separation only pertains, in successive degrees, to the lower Three Worlds and our physical realm. Introducing false separation (through judgment) causes the exile of the Shekinah, the Divine Feminine Presence within creation, from God. One might say, it causes the perceived separation of creation (the material world) from conscious connection to God.

Judging the created human form and persona as not good enough, sinful, causes the perception of separation of human from God. It must be remembered that God, himself, called all of his creation "good."

Moshe Cordovero, Kabbalist (Jewish mystic) of the 16th century, explains Akiva's warning about the "sin of separation" in terms of the *aleph* as it relates to the Tree of Life: "The marble stones represent the letter *yud* [horizontal brushstroke] ...a *yud* at the beginning, and a *yud* at the end...The first is Wisdom, the second Kingship, which is also Wisdom according to the light that returns from Below to Above. The upper is the *yud* of the *Tetragrammaton* (first letter), while the lower is the *yud* of *Adonai* (last letter). The latter is "female waters", and the former is "male waters"...the inner and outer aspects...signified by the top and the bottom *yuds* of the letter *aleph*..."[15] There is a dynamic flow between the Above and Below.

Cordovero describes more fully the mirroring effect within *shayish*, which means "marble": "White 'marble' indicates Compassion, similar to 'waters of kindness'...Wisdom is יש *Yesh* (Being). Kinship is שי *Shay* (reverse of Yesh). Combined they form שיש *Shayish* (marble). The letter ש *Shin* are the dividing emanations. When the two lights combine as "marble", the two *yuds* [the dash on either side] combine as one...These waters are completely pure...Through Compassion the daughter (Kingship) is able to ascend 'to her father's house as in her youth."[16]

The gender associations seem to be reversed: Wisdom or Chokmah, is a feminine term - "For she is the breath of the power of God, and a pure influence flowing from the glory of the Almighty: therefore can no defiled thing fall into her." Likewise, "kingship" would seem to indicate masculinity. The paradox is left unexplained.

Cordavero goes on, "The firmament between them (letter *vav* in the א *aleph*), which is Compassion, unites them...There is no separation other than in a place of spiritual impurity, but 'Here there is no impurity..."[17]

Through the pattern of the Tree of Life flows the mirror-like qualities of Divine transcendence (the nature and power of God) and Divine immanence (God's presence in the material world.) This might also be seen as the unification in descriptions of the relationship of Divine and human in the Christian formulas of the "two natures of Christ" - unity of the waters of above and below, within the body of Christ.

THE HOLY PLACE

A story in the Jewish *Haggadah*:
Rabbi Akiva, revered Jewish sage,
warned of the Holy Place,
the place of the White Marble –
"Don't say water (above), water (below)" –
Take care not to make separation, or hint
of separation, in the Place of the White Marble,
lest the *Shekinah*, the feminine "Indwelling Presence",
become trapped in matter – lest man/woman be cast out,
unable to return until the holy relationship be restored.

After the diaspora, who would listen?
The separation was to be found in the book,
in the teaching, in the mind of a people, of the world.
The woman. Wisdom and Love.
"She who knew the all." (*That* Mary.)
A kind of Eve - blamed for the Fall?

THE FOUR TANA'IM

The *Aggadah* of the four *Tannaim* is a story found in the Babylonian *Talmud*, compiled in the 3rd to 6th centuries CE:

> *Four rabbis, through dedicated practice,*
> *achieved entrance to Pardes, the Orchard.*
> *Ben Azzai gazed and died. "Precious in the eyes*
> *of God is the death of His pious ones".*
> *Ben Zoma gazed and was harmed... "Did you find*
> *honey? Eat only as much as you need,*
> *Lest you be overfilled and vomit it".*
> *Acher cut down the plantings*
> *[the trees – the old teachings?],*

while Rabbi Akiva entered in peace
and departed in peace.
(*Babylonian Talmud Hagigah* 14b)

Many centuries later, Rabbi Schlomo Yitzchaki,12th century head of the rabbinical court at Troyes, also known as Rashi, explained that Ben Zoma lost his sanity. Ben Azzai died from looking at the Divine Presence. Acher's "cutting down the plantings" in the orchard refers to becoming a heretic from the experience. Who was it that became a heretic of Jewish teachings?

Rabbi Akiva (Akiba, Yacub, Jacob, James), in contrast to the previous three, became the leading Rabbinic figure of the Jewish faith in that era – widely praised in the time after the Bar Kochba Revolt.

In this story, each rabbi had a different experience. Rashi explains that they ascended to Heaven by meditating upon the Divine Name, achieving spiritual elevation through ancient Jewish meditation practices. The idea of ascension was intrinsic to Judaic beliefs.

Rabbi Louis Ginzberg insisted that the journey to paradise "is to be taken literally and not allegorically". In contrast, the *Tosafot*, medieval commentaries on the *Talmud*, says that the four sages "did not go up literally, but it appeared to them as if they went up." Might one say, ascended? According to another interpretation, *PaRDeS*, the acronym for the four traditional methods of exegesis in Judaism is meant to imply that these four legendary sages were the four to understand the whole Torah.

ASCENDING AND DESCENDING

Jacob's Pillow – the heavenly stone
that, when Jacob rested his head upon it
gave him visions of Angels,
ascending and descending at *Beth El*,
the House of God, the gate of heaven –
Angels moving between heaven and earth
like the very atoms of material form
moving in and out of material existence.
The Orchard, a metaphor, yes –
accessed through the Holy of Holies:
Heaven, Paradise, from which only
Rabbi Akiva (Jacob, James), the greatest
Jewish sage of all, returned intact.
The other three, not so lucky.

Three, yes, three – a puzzle, a riddle to decipher.
How to see beyond the written his-story?
Unfocus the gaze:
Mary, a "pious one", raised in the Temple
by high priest, Zacharias, father of John.
John, who lived in the desert, on honey
and *akris* (locusts), or was it *enkris* (honey cakes)?
Indeed, the DaVinci Code gave us the Mary/John
connection (isn't that the "other Mary"?)
But who "cut down the plantings"?

Who bypassed Mosaic Law – "An eye for an eye" –
who ended blood sacrifice, created a new teaching,
made a New Covenant:
"Love God with all thy heart and soul
and mind, and love thy neighbor as thyself,
This is the sum of the Law"?
Acher, meaning "the other", but also
the Egyptian word *aker* meaning "light being".
Study, meditation, *sod*, hidden meaning, wordplay, pun.
Is *acher,* the third sage, related to this Egyptian term?
The Messiah, the Christ, the Anointed One –
anointed by the Holy Spirit.
The body ascending, the light descending.
Unity...One.

THE FOUNDATION STONE

The Foundation Stone – the stone "from which flow all the waters of the world" is said to be the "pierced stone" on the Temple Mount, on which rested the Jewish "Holy of Holies". Beneath the Foundation Stone, a cavern, known as the Well of Souls – sometimes claimed to be the traditional hiding place of the Ark of the Covenant.

The Roman-Era midrash *Tanhuma* states:
"As the navel is set
in the centre of the human body, so is the land
of Israel the navel of the world...situated in
the centre of the world, and Jerusalem
in the centre of the land of Israel,

and the sanctuary
in the centre of Jerusalem, and the holy place
in the centre of the sanctuary, and the ark
in the centre of the holy place, and the
Foundation before the holy place,
because from it the world was founded."[18]

The Zohar insists, "The world was not created until God took a stone called *Even haShetiya* and threw it into the depths where it was fixed from above till below, and from it the world expanded. It is the centre point of the world and on this spot stood the Holy of Holies."

Here, again, a nod to the concept of the "above and below" of "the waters and the waters", mentioned by Rabbi Akiva. *Genesis 1* states, "And God said, Let there be a firmament in the midst of the waters, and let it divide the waters (which were above the firmament) from the waters (which were below the firmament). And God called the firmament SCHAMAIM ('there are waters' also translated as 'the Heavens')..."And "God gathered the waters under the heavens...and let the dry land appear...and God called the dry land, the Earth; and the gathering together of the waters, called He the seas."

In the *Zohar,* the place of connection between heaven and earth is the place of the stone, *Even haShetiya* – the especially Holy Place, the place of the White Marble, the Holy of Holies. According to the *Talmud,* it was at the site of the Foundation Stone that God gathered the earth to form into Adam. On this rock, Adam – and later, Cain and Abel, then Noah – offered sacrifices to God. It is said to be the place where Abraham bound and prepared to sacrifice to the Lord his son, Isaac, when the Angel intervened, stayed his hand, and a ram appeared as a substitute sacrifice. In *Genesis 22*, this Holy Place is identified as Mount Moriah which is to say, the Temple Mount.

In *2 Chronicles,* it states, "Then Solomon began to build the temple of the LORD in Jerusalem on Mount Moriah, where the LORD had appeared to his father David. This was the threshing floor of Araunah the Jebusite, the place provided by David," said to be the Foundation Stone upon which King David offered sacrifice. He wanted to build a temple on the spot, but God prevented him from doing so, as David's hands had been "bloodied" by war; thus, his son, Solomon, was left to complete the Temple on the site in c. 950 BCE. Solomon became a fabulously wise and wealthy king, prophet, and messenger of God – his wisdom so sought after that one wonders – did he have use of a prophetic tool such as the one that gave Jacob the vision of angels?

The Old Testament speaks of the building of Solomon's Temple, whose walls, ceiling and floor were first covered in wood: "And he carved all the walls of the house round about with carved figures of cherubim and palm trees and open flowers, within and without. And the floors of the house he overlaid with gold, within and without." (2 Chronicles 3:7, KJV) Such ornamentation and gold covered the doors of olive, and the doors of fir also. These were fitting symbols for the Holy Place - the entrance to Paradise, and the heavenly realms.

It describes an inner room, "And the oracle he prepared in the house within, to set there the ark of the covenant of the Lord. And the oracle in the forepart was twenty cubits in length, and twenty cubits in breadth, and twenty cubits in the height thereof: and he overlaid it with pure gold; and so covered the altar which was of cedar."[19] Some translations put the measurement in feet: 30x30x30 feet. In either case, these measurements describe a cube.

In the oracle also were two great cherubs, about 15 feet tall with a wingspan of 15 feet each, also covered in gold. "The walls of the main room and of the inner room were all decorated with carved figures of winged creatures, palm trees, and flowers. Even the floor was covered with gold." (1 *Kings* 6:23-30, KJV)

Here in the inner room, the "oracle" in the King James Version of the bible, would be placed the Ark of the Covenant which rested upon the Foundation Stone. The Ark, also made of wood and covered in gold, and containing the tablets of Moses, was placed between the cherubim and formed the "Mercy Seat", upon which the power/presence of God, in the form of the *Shekinah* came to rest. (*Exodus* 25:17-22) These cherubim in the inner room are reminiscent of the cherubim with flaming swords who stand guard at the entrance to the Garden of Eden, or paradise, in *Genesis*.

This inner sanctuary, the "Holy of Holies", required the highest purity and integrity. The prophet Isaiah spoke of his purification by an angel holding a hot coal, "And he laid it upon my mouth, and said, Lo, this hath touched thy lips; and thine iniquity is taken away, and thy sin purged." (*Isaiah* 6:7 KJV) The high priest, only after purifying rituals, could enter once a year, with highest intention – representing, interceding for the people, the whole Jewish community.

One of the few Jewish prophets not to have a connection to the Foundation Stone was Moses, perhaps because he was raised in Egypt and wandered the desert with the Israelites for 40 years. However, one might say that the Israelites carried their Holy Place with them in the form of the Ark of the Covenant. Moses experienced another Holy Place on Mount Sinai, where the tablets of the Ten Commandments were given, though that experience might be attributed to the presence of the Ark in the Israelite camp at the base of the mountain.

In *Exodus*, it was required of Moses and the Israelites that the Ark be covered by a veil, and only the high priest, sanctified in preparation, could go in to the tabernacle to give sacrifice on Yom Kippur. On the day of the first raising up of this Holy Place, the "cloud of the Lord" covered the tabernacle (*Exodus* 40:33–40:34). At those times that the Lord would appear in the cloud upon the mercy seat (*kapporet*), the priests were instructed not to enter into the tabernacle (*Leviticus* 16:2). Once the dedication of the Tabernacle had been made, the Voice of God spoke to Moses "from between the Cherubim" (*Numbers* 7:89).

The *Mishnah*, in tractate *Yoma*, confirms the importance of a stone in the Holy of Holies, called *Shetiya*, the crossing point of heaven and earth, which had been revealed by the early prophets – David and others. Some equate this stone with the Foundation Stone, upon which the Ark of the Covenant was placed. In the Second Temple period, when the Ark of the Covenant was not present, it was upon the barren rock of the Foundation Stone that the High Priest, in the yearly Yom Kippur service, offered up incense and sprinkled the blood of the sacrifices.

But was the threshing floor - the pierced stone - actually *even Hashetiyah*, or was there a smaller stone that fit into the pierced stone, a stone that fell from the heavens, a prophetic stone used by Jacob as a pillow that gave him dreams of angels ascending and descending? Was this the stone that marked the crossing point of heaven and earth, and the creation of the world?

THE OLD TESTAMENT

The first significant Jewish Diaspora was the result of the Babylonian Exile of 586 BCE. After the Babylonians conquered the kingdom of Judah, the Jewish population was dispersed or deported into slavery. A large Jewish population were held captive in Babylon. There was another diaspora which followed the Siege of Jerusalem in 70 CE. Another followed the brutal Roman suppression of the Jewish Independence during the Bar Kochba Revolt.

Author Harold Bloom writes, "What is supposed to be the very essence of Judaism - which is the notion that it is by study that you make yourself a holy people - is nowhere present in Hebrew tradition before the end of the first or the beginning of the second century of the Common Era."[20]

This would coincide with events from 135 CE, the ending of the Bar Kochba Revolt, which brought about "the Diaspora," the dispersion of Jews from the Holy City of Jerusalem, and its Temple-centered mode of worship, to a multitude of smaller synagogue-based communities throughout the region.

The earliest teachings of Judaism were called the Oral *Torah*, said to have been passed down from Moses, who lived in about 1300 to 1200 BCE (though some early biblical scholars propose a couple of centuries earlier). A written *Torah* developed from these oral teachings, though the oral traditions continued. At the time of the destruction of Jerusalem and Solomon's Temple in 70 CE, the written *Torah* became important as a unifying element of the faith, when the people could no longer gather in the Temple.

The Jewish *Septuagint* was written, most scholars agree, around the 3rd to 4th century BCE.[21] Further books were translated over the next two to three centuries. It is not altogether clear which was translated when, or where, nor the timeline of revisions, though some were made during this time and later.[22]

The first five books of the *Torah*, also called the "Five Books of Moses", or the *Pentateuch* (meaning "five books/scrolls") are also the first five books of the Bible. These books are: *Genesis, Exodus, Leviticus, Numbers,* and *Deuteronomy*.

In a general overview of the material in each of these books:

Genesis is about the Creation of the earth and human beings, and names the ancestors of the Israelites, mainly Abraham, Isaac, Jacob, and Joseph.

Exodus, describes the sojourn of the Israelites in Egypt, and how they left Egypt. It gives the early history of the people of Israel as a nation, and its laws.

Leviticus includes the laws around sacrificing to God, and the work of the priests, also known as Levites.

Numbers involves the many years that the Israelites wandered in the desert under the leadership of Moses (the title derived from the census that God commanded for the twelve tribes of Israel – the counting of all the men over twenty who were fit to fight) and how the Israelites traveled with the sacred Ark of the Covenant.

Deuteronomy is about Moses's final speech to his people and a summary of the *Pentateuch*. The *Torah* was passed down orally from generation to generation, but was not codified until the 2nd Century C.E.

Over time, new books were added to the collection, and the scope of the Greek Bible became quite large. The *Pentateuch* maintained its pre-eminence as the basis of the canon; but the various *hagiographa* were incorporated into the prophetic collection (out of which the *Nevi'im* were selected). Some of the newer works, such as *Maccabees* and the *Wisdom of Ben Sira*, are not considered to be part of the Jewish canon. Also, the Septuagint version of some works, like Daniel and Esther, are longer than those in the Masoretic Text. It would become the basis of The Old Testament of the Christian Bible.

There is general scholarly consensus that the *Talmud* was written between the 3rd and 6th century CE, though Orthodox Jews insist that it was revealed to Moses, along with the *Torah*, and preserved orally until it was written down. The *Talmud* is thus known as the "Oral Torah," with the first five books of the *Tanakh* designated as the "Written Torah." It is important to understand that the written form of these scriptures could have added teachings or changes to the teachings that were current to the time of their being written down, which would have been well after the time of Jesus, but also after the diaspora, brought about by the Roman crushing of the Jewish Bar Kochba Revolt in 135 CE.

The Talmud includes two parts; the *Mishnah* (200 CE), a written compendium of rabbinic Judaism's Oral Torah; and the *Gemara* (500 CE), a clarification of the *Mishnah* and related rabbinic writings that covers other subjects and expounds broadly on the Hebrew Bible.

Rabbinic Judaism developed alongside the codification of the Babylonian *Talmud* in the 6th century CE, as rabbis, exiled to Babylon, interpreted the written Law.

Approximately half of the books of the Christian scriptures are texts that were written for the Jewish people. This deep, intrinsic connection to Judaism cannot be denied.

The various books of the Bible have been interpreted in many ways down through the centuries, sometimes as literal, historical texts, sometimes as inspired metaphors for concepts that are much broader than a literal history. Many scholars find them to be a mix of history and symbology.

Are we meant to see the Bible as inspired by God, or as the expression of the beliefs of very dedicated, sincere, but still human authors? In modern-day writings, we can sense the difference between the ideologies expressed by a fundamentalist (of any faith) and a mystic. We are aware of the filters of belief systems that put a "spin" on theological discussions. Somehow, we don't allow ourselves the same kind of discernment when dealing with the Holy Scriptures. Yes, there is inspiration in these writings, and there is the human component as well, with error, mistranslation, and deliberate glosses and alterations to consider as real possibilities.

Certainly, you can find a loving message in the Old Testament, similar to the teachings of Jesus. Micah, for instance, writes, "And what does the Lord require of you, but to do justice, and to love kindness, and to walk humbly with your God?" However, there are also shocking stories of incest, rape and pillage, beheadings, and lack of empathy. There is brutality and vengeance – even by the Father God! Some of the most abusive attitudes in the Old Testament are attributed to God toward his "bride", Israel.

In many narratives there is also the possibility that the scribes and priests were seeking an explanation for why certain events like earthquakes or the Great Flood occurred. The destruction of Sodom and Gomorrah was said to have come from God as punishment for sinfulness, specifically, homosexuality. If you approach the Bible literally, then it would seem that, first of all, God is unforgiving, and second of all, that homosexual behavior is sinful. However, the story might be seen as an effort by Jewish priests to explain the destruction of the city by natural events that were then attributed to an angry father God.

The patriarchal stance of the story of Sodom and Gomorrah also gives a clear indication of the diminished value of women within the society of that time and place. When the crowds demanded to have their way with the "two angels" who were visiting with Lot, he offers them his own daughters instead! Lot said to the people, "Please, my brothers, do not act wickedly. Now behold, I have two daughters who have not had relations with man; please let me bring them out to you, and do to them whatever you like; only do nothing to these men, inasmuch as they have come under the shelter of my roof."

Riane Eisler, in her book, *The Chalice and the Blade,* points to this story as the epitome of patriarchal attitudes that insisted that women were possessions to be used as men saw fit.[23] The same cultural stance is demonstrated in the shocking story of the man in *Judges* 19, who, in like manner, gave his concubine to the mob to be used by them, rather than give them the man who was a visitor in his home. By the morning, she was dead.

In a gruesome protest, he cut her body into 12 pieces and sending one piece to each of the 12 tribes of Israel. He protested, but only after the fact; he had abandoned her to her brutal death. It was a protest at the loss of a valuable possession, not a woman with rights.

Are these stories meant to be taken as metaphor or history, allegory or truth? Do we see this as appropriate "sacred" teaching today? Or do we see that the norms of the time period influenced the moral attitudes of the author, and should not be followed as guidelines for present times? In essence, do we allow that "Truth", in theology, in religion, in human belief, is allowed to – no, more emphatically – *should* evolve?

In her book, *Urgent Message from Mother*, Jean Shinoda Bolen gives the story of Abraham as another classic example of patriarchal belief systems. She writes that Abraham's willingness to sacrifice his own son, Isaac, to please God would be unnatural to the mother instinct. She says, "Abraham is praised and blessed because he would kill his son if God ordered it. He is a religious example of unquestioning obedience, which is a military virtue."[24] And it is clear that military virtues like blind obedience and brutal behavior were much admired and promoted in biblical times – a pushback to overturned matriarchal beliefs?

This is not to speak against masculinity – it is simply to say that the patriarchal masculine, without the balance of feminine principles and influence, becomes unfeeling, harsh, dictatorial, and abusive. The action-based, mind-oriented, outward expression of masculine power and will, without the tempering influence of the feminine, inward, heart-oriented qualities of wisdom, compassion, and understanding becomes abusiveness, violence, and, at the extreme end of the spectrum, war. The Bride separated from her Beloved – the *Shekinah* trapped in matter, the separation of matter (and the earthly realms) from God.

Might we attribute the idea of there being a God of vengeance and retribution to high priests who entered the sanctuary in less than the highest purity? Might we see human filters as being at fault in describing a less than purely loving God?

In Judaism, the name of God is often written as "YHWH", leaving out the consonants so that the actual pronunciation isn't clear. In some translations, that name is *Yahweh.* In others, the name is given as *Jehovah.* We know that there are many biblical narratives that express Yahweh's anger with the Israelites in metaphors of brutality to women. Israel's unfaithfulness brings Yahweh's brutal punishment in ways that resemble an abusive husband.

Many authors have noted that the physical abuse by the divine in such passages seems to condone such behavior in humans. Yahweh strips "the virgin daughter of Babylon" in *Isa.* 47:1-4, and helps the Babylonians rape Jerusalem in *Jer.* 13:26. Surely, this is a human interpretation of events, and not a divine one – not the actions of a God of Love.

These metaphors may have been acceptable in cultures of the time. One must consider this as well, matriarchal ideals had been and were being overturned around the region, and beyond. Goddess religions were being toppled far and wide. In the general masculinization of politics, societal norms, and religion, the high priests were consolidating more and more power in their dominion over the people, and may well have used such imagery to oppress women, and keep them "in their place".

In *Lamentations,* Yahweh crushes "the virgin" Jerusalem "as in a winepress" (1:15), and in Ezekiel he tells his wife *Oholibah* (Jerusalem), "I will raise up thy lovers against thee," and they will "strip thee out of thy clothes"; they will take away not only "thy sons and thy daughters" but "thy nose and thine ears," and "thus will I make thy lewdness to cease from thee." (23:22-27) Sharon H. Ringe in *The Women's Bible Commentary,* writes that such imagery in the Bible "seems to bless the harm and abuse with which women live and sometimes die."[25] As Ringe describes it, Yahweh assures his mutilated wife of a brighter tomorrow, much like the stereotypical wife beater who minimizes what he has done and promises not to do it again.[26]

Old Testament writings, however inspired, in general, were written after patriarchal ideas had taken hold, and by men, in an age when women were, more and more, being seen as "property." Such metaphors were influenced by a certain culture (or faction within it), and a certain time period. Men had the power, according to the laws, and women were, basically, chattel. The attitudes of the times seeped into men's interpretations of God's actions. It must be remembered that this is a human interpretation of events.

And yet, it would seem to be more complicated than that. In modern times, women are highly respected within Jewish culture, community, and homes. There is reason to believe that they were also venerated in the society of Jesus' time, maybe in some communities more than others. Women played an important role in Jesus' ministry, perhaps a greater role in the earliest Christian community than is clear to us in modern times.

The worshiping of the Father God was a later development of Judaism; even in the Old Testament, there are traces of an older belief. We see this in the statement, "God created man in his own image, in the image of God he created him; male and female he created them." (*Gen* 1: 27) This indicates that God was, at that time, considered to be both male and female, or at least to resemble both male and female (God was not considered to be human, but to have these human qualities or attributes). God was considered to be indefinable and ineffable. Any human attempts to define God would fall short. However, females were also created in God's image.

Before the patriarchal, monotheistic teachings of the "One God" of Judaism, the Hebrews honored many Goddesses. In an old Jewish folk legend, the maiden, Istehar, pronounced the ineffable name of God (much as the Jewish priests did in their meditations) – in Istehar's case, to escape sexual oppression: "When the angels came to earth, and beheld the daughters of men in all their grace and beauty, they could not restrain their passion. Shemhazai saw a maiden named Istehar, and he lost his heart to her. She promised to give herself to him, if he would teach her the Ineffable Name, by means of which he raised himself to heaven. He assented to her condition, but once she knew it, she spoke the Name, and ascended to heaven, without submitting to the angel. God said, "Because she kept herself aloof from sin, we will place her among the seven stars, that men may never forget her," and she was put in the constellation of the Pleiades." *Legends of the Jews* [27] (In *The Jewish Gates*, it was Istahar, and she was set in the constellation of Draco.)

In patriarchal times, the God of the Old Testament was often described as jealous, vengeful, and judgmental. This lead various sects, including Marcion and his followers, and the Cathars, to conclude that the God of the Old Testament was a lower-level God, a worldly God or *Demiurge* who ranked beneath a higher, all-powerful God of Love, who was the God that they worshipped.

Along with the fire and brimstone of Sodom and Gomorrah, the Great Flood was also depicted as divine vengeance brought about by human sinfulness. God was described in these stories as dictatorial and punishing. But was this, perhaps, the interpretation of powerful, controlling men who turned the tables and made God in their image?

Deuteronomy 7, speaks of how God tells the Israelites to deal with the Hittites, and the Girgashites, and the Amorites, and the Canaanites, and the Perizzites, and the Hivites, and the Jebusites, "seven nations greater and mightier" than Israel. "And when the Lord thy God shall deliver them before thee; thou shalt smite them, and utterly destroy them; thou shalt make no covenant with them, nor shew mercy unto them: Neither shalt thou make marriages with them; thy daughter thou shalt not give unto his son, nor his daughter shalt thou take unto thy son. For they will turn away thy son from following me, that they may serve other gods: so will the anger of the Lord be kindled against you, and destroy thee suddenly. But thus shall ye deal with them; ye shall destroy their altars, and break down their images, and cut down their groves, and burn their graven images with fire." (*Deuteronomy* 7:2-5)

Such behavior would be followed down through the centuries in Crusades, in "Holy Wars" (the ultimate oxymoron) and genocidal campaigns – all in the name of God. The patriarchal persecution of "heretics" would lead to unbelievable brutality. Is it proper to accept such a stance simply because the Church, or a pope declares it to be proper? It comes down to choosing to believe in a God of vengeance, or a God of Love.

The *Nag Hammadi* texts describe Jesus as teaching wholeness through the marriage of opposites – an internal union of the masculine and feminine that brought about the androgyne, the two as one – a concept perhaps reflected in Dan Brown's *Da Vinci Code* (where it is proposed that John/Mary are one). These were the teachings of many Eastern religions, before the time of Jesus. The Nag Hammadi documents are often described as Gnostic, however, in general, Gnosticism is described as duality-based, and these teachings are often about unity, and not duality. Since our understanding of Gnostic beliefs comes mostly from the opposition, it is hard to say what their true teachings were. Descriptions of Gnostic sects were, it seems, every bit as diverse as that of Christian sects, from libertines to ascetics.

In the New Testament, Jesus taught of a Father God that was merciful and forgiving. He spoke of a "New Covenant" because this would be required in order to influence a people who had lived for centuries by the Covenant of Moses. Zealous belief in the Law of Moses would require the giving of a new Law – the Law of Oneness. In truth, it would seem that it was meant to reconnect people with the suppressed feminine ideals of love, mercy, forgiveness, and understanding – to take the lopsided model of "masculine only" and bring in the other half of the equation. In place of hierarchy, separation, and power of the few, it was meant to bring healing and wholeness to all. This was a threat to those in power at the time, who wished to control people through fear.

Jesus taught love, forgiveness, compassion, and understanding. "I and the Father are One." From Jesus' teachings, we are given a sense of God's nature as well. Jesus demonstrated the enlightened path and the embodiment of divinity in human form. He said to his followers, "He that believeth on me, the works that I do shall he do also; and greater *works* than these shall he do; because I go unto my Father." (*John* 14:12) He says that his followers shall do these things and greater – performing prophecy, miracles, and healing, becoming anointed by the Holy Spirit – even becoming a "Christed" being, as Jesus was. In the Upper Room, at Pentecost, hundreds of people received this anointing of the Holy Spirit.

In *Matthew*, in the "Sermon on the Mount," Jesus says, "think not that I've come to destroy the law and the prophets - I've come not to destroy them but to fulfill them." The result of the coming of the messiah was foretold as the end of the Old Covenant of God with Moses and the Jewish people, and the beginning of the New Covenant based on mercy and forgiveness in place of the legalistic ways of judgment and punishment.

In interpreting the bible, along with questions of archaic societal norms, there is the question of literal interpretation versus metaphorical. In some Books of the Bible, the message seems to be straightforward and literal. In others, it seems necessary to interpret the text metaphorically.

The Creation Story in the *Book of Genesis* proclaims, "And God saw everything that he had made, and, behold, it was very good. And the evening and the morning were the sixth day...And on the seventh day God ended his work which he had made; and he rested ..." (*Genesis* 1:31 KJV)

In the *Book of Genesis,* questions arise about many things, including the time period of God's creation of the Earth, and of the first man and woman. Many questions come up regarding metaphoric or literal interpretation. Were Adam and Eve really the first man and woman? What about Lilith, who didn't make it into Christian texts? In later Jewish folklore she was Adam's first wife, demonized for refusing Adam's demand that she must "lie beneath him." She was then described as becoming a ghoulish figure, a shrieking banshee, a child-killer, feared by all – banished to the desert for, essentially, claiming equality with her partner. What metaphor of matriarchal/patriarchal relationship might be hidden in this story? Does she represent a figure from an opposing belief system, such as Christianity?

Is there a metaphor in the story of the banishment of Adam and Eve from the Garden of Eden? Does it relate to the banishment of the Jewish people from Jerusalem and the Temple in 135 CE? What is the "fruit of the Tree of the Knowledge of Good and Evil"? Is it simply a metaphor for the act of judging things as good or evil? Is it meant to be a diatribe against dualistic teachings?

What is the metaphor of Cain and Abel, the jealousy of sibling rivalry that led to the first intentional murder of a human being? Were they meant to represent two sons, or two tribes of people – the farmers of the land and the nomadic shepherds? Was it an allegory of the ongoing tensions between the two lifestyles, after the first agricultural revolution? Does it describe the beginnings of warfare amongst the tribes of the Holy Land – the descendants of the sons of Abraham: Isaac (the Jews) and Ishmael (the Arabs)?

Many writings of the Early Church Fathers make a correlation between Adam and Eve, and Jesus and Mary – some *patristic* writings conflate, or compare, Jesus with Adam. One of the earliest mentions is by Paul, "And so it is written, The first man Adam was made a living soul; the last Adam was made a quickening spirit...The first man is of the earth, earthy: the second man is the Lord from heaven." (1 *Corinthians* 15:45-47)

In many of these writings, the focus is on the contrast: Eve was the cause of man's downfall, while Mary had a redemptive role. In the 3rd century, Irenaeus wrote, "The knot of Eve's disobedience was loosened by Mary's obedience. The bonds fastened by the virgin Eve through disbelief were untied by the virgin Mary through faith." (*Adv. haereses*, 3:22) Eve's story was a Jewish perspective, and Mary's story a Christian one. Was the same feminine figure allegorically demonized in Judaism, after the Bar Kochba Revolt, and praised in Christianity?

The historicity of the story of Jesus and Mary has been debated by modern-day scholars.[28] Some have questioned whether or not the historical documentation supports their factual existence. There are references to Jesus and Mary in various Jewish writings, including the Talmud and Midrashic writings; understandably, they are generally of a derogatory nature, coming at a time when there was great discord between the two belief systems. The community of followers of Jesus began as a Jewish sect, that, while perhaps seen as radical were, none-the-less, not truly separate from Judaism until, perhaps, after the Diaspora of 135/136 CE.

Islam also mentions Jesus and Mary. Muslims believe that Islam is the complete and universal version of earlier revelations. Like the birth of Christianity from Judaic teachings, where Jesus brought a "New Covenant" and teaching, Islam arose from Judaic – as well as Christian – teachings. Muslims honor the prophets Abraham and Moses, and John the Baptist, along with Jesus, and other Christian prophets, while maintaining that previous messages and revelations were corrupted over time. This might be seen to reflect the stance of various Christian sects at the time of Islam's beginnings, who saw a corrupting influence in the "Hellenizing" of the faith.

Muslims consider the Quran to be the "final dispensation from Allah", the true, unaltered, and complete revelation from God. While the eventual "concretized" history of the origins of Islam state that the teachings came directly from God, through the Angel Gabriel to Muhammad, the writings of the Quran essentially reflect the contents of the Old and New Testaments as well as some apocryphal texts that don't appear in the canons of the bible, but were shared with the Arabs in the 6th to 7th centuries by Syriac monks.

Islamic narratives in the Quran speak highly of both Isa and Maryam (the Arabic equivalent of the names Jesus and Mary). However, Islam states that Jesus was a highly revered prophet rather than the son of God. The Quran also states that Jesus was not crucified – that it was only "made to appear so". And, interestingly enough, Islam speaks of only one Mary.

Though some argue that the records of their lives may have been altered over the centuries, it is clear, from a historical perspective, that there is something of substance in the stories of Jesus and Mary. However contradictory about the facts, or negative towards the subject, these references to Jesus and Mary by those of opposing viewpoints, serve to substantiate their factual and historical existence.

* * *

CHAPTER II. A NEW COVENANT

THE GOSPELS

The word "Gospel" is defined as, "Good news; an unquestionable truth; religious doctrine: the written body of teachings of a religious group that are generally accepted by that group." It is funny that we use the term "Gospel Truth" to mean unassailable fact, when the gospels themselves differ. While it is defined as an "unquestionable truth", the truth is that there are discrepancies among the four Gospels, and even more between the Gospels and the *Acts of the Apostles,* also known as the *Book of Acts* or simply, *Acts.*

Early Church Father, Hippolytus, in his treatise on the *Song of Songs*, describes the different perspectives of the four Gospels: "O new manifold forms of the gospel... For to this one has been preached from Matthew the lion as a king; and has been preached by Luke as shoot, as a vine of a priest-teacher. And in the case of Mark, he was announced as the man, as one who suffered need. And in the case of John, he was the eagle flying ascending to heaven according to the word of the blessed John. By this mystery of proclamation the mystery has been made known."

Why is there no "Gospel according to Jesus"? Why did Jesus so often speak in parables, in metaphor instead of in rigid lists of "thou-shalt-nots"? We could say that Jesus was practicing in the manner of his predecessors, the Jewish rabbis and priests of the community in which he was raised, with oral teachings rather than written ones.

The New Testament was not a reiteration of the Old Testament. The New Covenant was the blueprint of a new relationship between humanity and the Divine – a covenant meant to end blood sacrifice of animals, and instill the idea of living from the heart, rather than by the letter of the law. A covenant of mercy rather than punishment, judgment, and vengefulness. The new teachings would step beyond the concrete legalistic ideas of Mosaic Law, and attempt to express the inexpressible. They would be spoken in parables and symbols that went beyond linear thinking.

The messages of the Messiah were not recorded as a written belief system until after the time of Christ – around the time of the writing of the Babylonian Talmud, and perhaps for similar reasons, since Christians also were scattered from Jerusalem to more distant places. What we now call *The New Testament* came into being, roughly in its current form, more than three centuries after Jesus' lifetime, though the gospels are thought to have been written within decades after the death and resurrection of Jesus.

Lactantius, in an early 4th-century treatise wrote: "But all scripture is divided into two Testaments. That which preceded the advent and passion of Christ—that is, the law and the prophets—is called the Old; but those things which were written after His resurrection are named the New Testament. The Jews make use of the Old, we of the New: but yet they are not discordant, for the New is the fulfilling of the Old, and in both there is the same testator, even Christ, who, having suffered death for us, made us heirs of His everlasting kingdom, the people of the Jews being deprived and disinherited ... For that which He said above, that He would make a new testament to the house of Judah, shows that the old testament which was given by Moses was not perfect; but that which was to be given by Christ would be complete." (Lactantius, *Divine Institutes*)

The Gospels of the New Testament were recorded and studied by the elite class of priests, scribes, and scholars. They were translated from Aramaic into Greek, and then into the new language of the conquerors, the Latin of the Romans. Furthermore, although many words are attributed to the one called Jesus, there is not one line of New Testament writing said to have come from the hand of Jesus. As with many oral accounts, the details become obscured, the meaning skewed by the perspective of the one telling the story. Otherwise, how does one explain the multitude of sects in the early centuries, after the time of Jesus, who called themselves Christians? And, specifically, how else does one account for the differing versions of something as simple as who was the first to come to the tomb of Jesus after the resurrection?

The *Gospels of Mark* and *Matthew* state that Mary Magdalene and "the other Mary" were present at the entombment of Jesus. Luke generalizes, saying it was "the women who had come with Jesus from Galilee". These women came with funeral spices, perfumes, and ointments to annoint the body of Jesus, after his death. John mentions no witnesses to Joseph of Arimathea's burial of Jesus other than his assistant, Nicodemus.

Mark says that Mary Magdalene was accompanied to the tomb by Salome and Mary the mother of James, while *Matthew* omits Salome. The *Gospel of John,* 20:3,4 states that Peter and the "other disciple" were heading to the tomb, when the other disciple outran Peter and arrived there first. (When alter egos become problematic, the narrative gets murky.) Many scholars assume that the other disciple is John, but if you ascribe to the revelations in the DaVinci Code, John is Mary Magdalene, which would make her the first to arrive at the empty tomb, though not acknowledged by name.

Luke says that it was, "Mary Magdalene, Joanna, Mary the mother of James, and the others with them", though Peter showed up after them. Paul, in 1 *Cor* 15, takes a completely different stance, saying that Peter was the first to arrive at the tomb. How can we explain these differences if all of the writings are inspired "Truth"?

And again, there is a discrepancy between the gospel versions, and Paul's account of who was first to see the resurrected Christ. In all four gospels, Mary Magdalene is the first one to witness Jesus' Resurrection. *John* and *Mark* state that Jesus' first post-resurrection appearance was to Mary Magdalene alone. In *Matthew*, Mary Magdalene and the other women are returning from the empty tomb when they witness the first appearance of the resurrected Lord. *Luke*, again, generalizes: "two men in clothes that gleamed like lightning" announce the resurrection to "the women" at the tomb. In *Luke* 24:18, it states that Jesus spoke first to Cleophas, when Cleophas and another disciple walked with someone that they later realized was Jesus. Some propose that Cleopas is actually Peter. Mark describes this as occurring after the initial appearance to Mary Magdalene, which the disciples refuse to believe. After this Mary Magdalene fades from the picture – Jesus ascends to heaven, and she is not mentioned again.

In *Corinthians*, Paul's narrative is completely different from the four Gospels, but we must consider Paul's own claim that he was a Roman citizen, as well as having close ties to Luke, whose Gospel was written for the Gentiles. Paul makes no mention of Mary Magdalene at all (not surprising, since, in Roman society, women held a lesser status than men). Instead, he states that Jesus "appeared to Cephas, and then to the Twelve". After this, he appears to James and then, "And last of all he was seen of me also, as of one born out of due time." This seems to be a reference to his vision of Jesus on the road to Damascus, presumably, after Jesus' death and resurrection.

Though there are many traditions within the Church, and folk tales or legends about Mary Magdalene's life after the resurrection, within the Gospels, her fate remains undocumented. She is last seen at the time of the resurrection, and then disappears.

John and *Luke*, previous to the death and resurrection of Jesus, make mention of a "Mary of Bethany," the sister of Martha and Lazarus. One of the great miracles that Jesus was recorded as performing was the raising of Mary's brother, Lazarus, from the dead. Many biblical scholars disagree on whether or not Mary of Bethany was the same person as Mary Magdalene, but scripture does state that "Jesus loved Mary and Martha" as well as Lazarus. Some scholars propose that Mary Magdalene/Mary of Bethany was the Beloved Disciple, while others say that this was John or St. John. Many now propose that these two are one.

In searching out the truth of the history of Christianity, many non-Christians may discount much of the story as told by the Catholic Church. On top of the discrepancies between each of the gospels, the story of the virgin birth, the miracles of walking on water, and turning water into wine, miracle healings, the crucifixion, death, and resurrection, and the ascension into heaven are extraordinary events, and, perhaps, difficult for non-Christians to believe.

We also know that many of these stories weren't written until after the time of Jesus. When you compare the extraordinary stories of Christianity in the gospels with other myths and legends from that time in history, it becomes even harder to find the thread of truth. One must consider the near-certainty of "syncretization," or assimilation of previous religious mythologies into the stories of Christianity, due to the Romans usurping the course of the faith – as evidenced by the many similarities with older stories of pagan Gods and Goddesses.

There are certainly questions that arise when older belief systems are examined: there is a symbolic resemblance of the last supper to the practices of Mithraism or Zoroastrianism, of the virgin birth of Mithras and other God-beings to the narrative of the Nativity, the death and resurrection of Gods like Osiris, Tammuz, and others to the death and resurrection of Jesus. Christianity states that, during the three days between the crucifixion and the resurrection, Jesus descended into hell to minister to the souls imprisoned there, a sequence known as the "harrowing of hell". According to legend, Dionysus and Orpheus, as well as the Goddesses, Aphrodite and Venus, went to Hades or the Underworld and returned.

The scholar Tom Harper, in *The Pagan Christ* states, in reference to the patterns inherent in ancient pagan beliefs: "The divine teacher is called, is tested by the "adversary", gathers disciples, heals the sick, preaches the Good News about God's kingdom, finally runs afoul of his bitter enemies, suffers, dies, and is resurrected after three days. This is the total pattern of the sun god in all the ancient dramas".[29]

Ctesias wrote about the Babylonian god Tammuz: "Trust, ye saints, your Lord restored, Trust ye in your risen Lord; For the pains which Tammuz endured, Our salvation have procured."(*Persika*, c. 400 BCE).

Is it possible that the Mother and Child duo was taken from, or at least reinforced by the stories of Isis and Horus or the teachings of other belief systems which were thriving among the Roman elite at that time? Certainly, the celebration of the birth of the Christ child in late December seems have been a concession to pagan practices of celebrating the solstice, and the return of the light.

Some scholars say that there was an astronomical origin to the belief in salvation by crucifixion. The sun is said to be hung on a cross or "crucified" at the time of the equinoxes. The Spring Equinox, for the Northern Hemisphere, is when life was renewed or "resurrected" by the return of the sunlight and longer days that brought life-giving energies to the earth.

The celebration of Easter is based on older religions honoring Astoris, Astarte, or Oestre (the word "Easter," itself, is derivative of these names). Her lover, Attis, dies and is reborn annually, at the time of the vernal equinox (spring time), when Easter is celebrated. The ancient Isis-Osiris cult and the northern European Saxons had their versions of the goddess of fertility, and springtime rebirth.

So, who were the Gospel writers, and what were their particular perspectives on the story of Jesus' life? William Barclay gives the meaning behind the emblems which symbolize each of the four gospel authors: "...The man stands for Mark, which is the plainest, the most straightforward and the most human of the gospels; the lion stands for Matthew, for he specially saw Jesus as the Messiah and the Lion of the tribe of Judah; the ox stands for Luke, because it is the animal of service and sacrifice, and Luke saw Jesus as the great servant of men and the universal sacrifice for all mankind; the eagle stands for John, because it alone of all living creatures can look straight into the sun and not be dazzled, and John has the most penetrating gaze of all the New Testament writers into the eternal mysteries and the eternal truths and the very mind of God."[30]

The definition of the word "Gospel" as an "unquestionable truth" cannot be considered accurate, since there are discrepancies among all four canonical Gospels. Thus, the other definitions would be more accurate: "religious doctrine" and "the written body of teachings of a religious group that are generally accepted by that group." The reference to "that group" are important to consider, since there were other Gospels that were accepted by certain groups in ancient times, but which were not included in the accepted "canonical Gospels" of the Church after about the 4th century CE.

The four canonical Gospels include: the *Gospel of Mark*, the *Gospel of Matthew*, the *Gospel of Luke*, and the *Gospel of John*. For centuries, *Matthew* was considered to be the first Gospel written, though many now consider it more likely that Mark's gospel was written first.

The different perspectives of each of these gospels might be summed up in a very basic way. *Matthew* was written by a Jewish author for a Jewish audience. This alone gives weight to the idea that *Matthew* was the first Gospel written; there was no Gentile audience at the time. Explanations of events or traditions were not included because they were not needed with a Jewish audience that would understand all that was said.

Mark was written by a Jewish author for a Gentile audience. This would seem to indicate a later text, which was needed when the Gentiles became a bigger part of the faith. Descriptions were given, in *Mark*, to help the reader understand the intricacies of the Jewish faith, while also explaining Christian ideals.

The *Gospel of Luke* was written by a Gentile author for a Gentile audience. *Luke* focused on the humanity of the "Son of Man" and like the chronicles of ancient Greek and Latin writers, attempted to give a history as well as an epic chronology of the life of Christ. It also delineates the "salvation history" of the life of Jesus, and that it was Jesus' mission to be crucified for the forgiveness of mankind's sins.

John, the last of the four canonical Gospels was written from the mystical perspective, and describes and defines the "deity of Jesus."

Three of the four canonical gospels are called the "synoptic gospels", for their similar point of view. These include *Mark*, *Matthew*, and *Luke*. The *Gospel of Mark* was probably written in about 66–70 CE, during Nero's persecution of the Christians in Rome or the Jewish revolt, as suggested by internal references to war in Judea and to persecution.

Mark was traditionally thought to be an *epitome* (summary) of *Matthew*, which accounts for its place as the second gospel in the Bible, after *Matthew*. Many contemporary scholars find reasons to regard it as the earliest of the gospels to have been written, by an unknown author working from a number of sources, and that it was the basis for the later gospels of *Matthew* and *Luke*. However, since the Ebionites (or Evionites), one of the earliest Jewish-Christian sects, used only the *Gospel of the Ebionites*, which was seen to be a truncated and modified version of the *Gospel of Matthew*, it makes more sense that *Matthew* was the original Gospel, perhaps, originally in the form of the Ebionite version of the Gospel.

Mark recounts the ministry of Jesus from his baptism by John the Baptist to his death and burial and the discovery of the empty tomb – there is no genealogy or birth narrative (much like the *Gospel of the Ebionites*), nor, in what is now considered to be the original ending at chapter 16:8, any record of a post-resurrection appearance. It portrays Jesus as a man of wisdom, an exorcist, healer and miracle worker. He is said to be the son of God, but he keeps his identity secret, concealing it in parables so that even the disciples fail to understand. The gospel ends, in its original version, with the discovery of the empty tomb, a promise to meet again in Galilee, and instructions to spread the good news of the resurrection.

R.G. Price writes that *Mark*, much like the writings of the historian, Josephus, the Jewish-turned-Roman historian, was a reaction to the devastation of Jerusalem in the First Jewish Revolt of 70 CE. Josephus, like Mark, was a Jewish author writing for Gentile sensibilities. However, where Josephus gives very little about Jesus and the disciples, *Mark* details their lives in the time leading up to the Revolt. Mark gives an unflattering view of the disciples, very little theology, and no information on the birth or origin of Jesus. Price describes *Mark* as allegory, portraying both Judean Jews and the early Christian apostles as fools who brought destruction upon themselves.[31] Mark's gospel was, then, an alternate version of the story which was also told in the same time period by Josephus.

The longer ending of the *Gospel of Mark*, in *Mark* 16:9 – 20, adds to the narrative the appearance of the resurrected Christ. He makes his first appearance to Mary Magdalene, a high honor, followed by the detail, "from whom seven demons were cast out" – praise, and then what seems to be censure. One must keep in mind that this comes in the longer version of the gospel - narrative that seems to have been added to bring a more hopeful ending to the story. It should also be noted that in Matthew 11:18, Jesus spoke of how the people criticized John the Baptist: "For John came neither eating nor drinking, and they say, He hath a devil." A similar comment is made about Jesus in John 10:20, when Jesus said "I lay down my life, that I might take it again," a power he wielded according to the commandment of his Father (God). "And many of them said, He hath a devil, and is mad; why hear ye him?"

In *Mark* 16, the disciples don't believe Mary's account of the Lord's appearance to her, or the account of others who saw Jesus while on the road. When Jesus finally appears to all the disciples, he chides them for not believing in his resurrection appearance to Mary, and ends by giving them the "Great Commission." Jesus instructs his disciples to go out and share his teachings, "Go ye therefore, and teach all nations..." and then, with little narrative detail, he ascends to the Father in heaven. This is a much more comforting ending than that in the shorter version of *Mark*, where Mary Magdalene and the women with her, "went out quickly, and fled from the sepulchre; for they trembled and were amazed: neither said they any thing to any man; for they were afraid."

It certainly would appear that the longer version of *Mark* included additions to the narrative, perhaps after these details had unfolded, or become part of the oral traditions after the time of Jesus.

In the non-canonical Gnostic *Gospel of Mary,* Peter and his brother Andrew don't believe Mary's account of her, most would say, post-resurrection interaction with Jesus. In this Gospel, it is Levi who chastises the brothers for doubting Mary, and behaving like "the adversaries."

Some scholars believe that the later chapters of *Mark* were added by those who wanted to bring it into alignment with *Matthew* and *Luke*, and that the details of the resurrection, and the Great Commission to the disciples were embellishments to the original text, giving hope and inspiring missionary zeal.

We don't have information from Epiphanius on whether or not the ending of the Ebionite Gospel aligned with the canonical Gospels. One would presume that he would have mentioned if it ended like the shorter version of *Mark* with Jesus' ascension into heaven, and not with the crucifixion scene. However, it could be that the longer version of *Mark* with the details of the crucifixion scene was a later addition even than the time of Epiphanius, which would mean that he would not have noted a discrepancy if the crucifixion was missing from it.

In *A Textual Commentary on the Greek New Testament*, Bruce Metzger writes of the added verses in *Mark*: "Clement of Alexandria and Origen [early third century] show no knowledge of the existence of these verses; furthermore, Eusebius and Jerome attest that the passage was absent from almost all Greek copies of *Mark* known to them." [32] Eusebius and Jerome were Early Church Fathers, 3rd and 4th/5th century, respectively. Epiphanius lived at the end of the 4th century. Jerome compiled the Vulgate version of the bible in 420 CE, seventeen years after Epiphanius died.

The *Gospel of Matthew* is, generally, believed to have been composed between 80 and 90 CE, though some propose as early as 50 to 70 CE. The anonymous author seems to have been a highly educated Jew, intimately familiar with Jewish law – and honored within the Jewish community. Modern scholars who feel that *Matthew* was not the first gospel, generally cite three main sources for this gospel: the *Gospel of Mark*; the hypothetical collection of sayings known as the "Q source"; and material unique to his own community, called "*Special Matthew*", or the "M source".[33]

Matthew contains some 600 of *Mark's* 661 verses and *Luke* also has many commonalities. However, *Matthew* leaves out much of the material that is included in *Mark*. *Matthew* emphasizes Jesus' place in Jewish traditions. There are 220 verses or so, shared by *Matthew* and *Luke* but not found in *Mark*.

Interestingly, the very early Jewish-Christian sect of the Ebionites, the "poor ones", are said to have used only a shorter version of the *Gospel of Matthew*. The heresiologist, Epiphanius, called this abbreviated gospel, "not wholly complete, but falsified and mutilated." The Ebionite

Gospel lacked some or all of the first two chapters of *Matthew*. This would include the infancy narrative of the virgin birth of Jesus and the Davidic genealogy via Solomon. He wrote, "They have removed the genealogies of Matthew ..." (14.2–3).[34]

But perhaps there is more to consider in this absence of the first two chapters that are found in the standard versions of the *Gospel of Matthew*. The version of *Matthew* that the Ebionites used began with the baptism of Jesus, when God spoke from the heavens, "And, behold, a voice from heaven, saying: This is my beloved Son, in whom I am well pleased" (*Matthew* 3:17). The Holy Spirit descends to Jesus in the form of a dove and enters into him. This anointing by the Holy Spirit at the time of his baptism is known as an Adoptionist Christology. It is found in the quotation of *Psalm* 2:7, just as in the "Western text" of *Luke* 3:22, "You are my son, this day I have begotten you," referring to sonship through baptism.

Though it isn't clear how the Ebionite Gospel ended, is it possible that the ending connected with the beginning? Did it end with the same opening of the heavens – with the Transfiguration where Jesus becomes radiant with the light of God, is witnessed to speak with the prophets, and again, God speaks from Heaven, "This is my Beloved Son, in whom I am well pleased... listen to Him."

The Spirit entering into Jesus and the Spirit moving on the face of the water in *Genesis* are seen to relate to the prophecies of Isaiah 61:1 and 9:1, respectively. The idea of Jesus' adopted "sonship" included the belief that Jesus was not born the son of God, but was a mere human, who, by virtue of perfect righteousness, was imbued with the divinity of the eternal Christ through his Baptism in order to carry out the prophetic task for which he had been chosen. Without the nativity, Jesus is not born as "the son of God", but becomes imbued with the sonship at the descent of the Holy Spirit, "the breath of God". We might say that, in the terms of the Jewish faith, he becomes a vessel of the "indwelling presence," the sanctified body that houses the *Shekinah*, the Divine Feminine.

According to Petri Luomanen, and others, the Ebionite Gospel portrays Jesus as having come to abolish the sacrifices rather than substituting for them; thus, the institution of the Eucharist as practiced by Nicene orthodox Christianity does not fit Ebionite beliefs. However, scholars have not reached a consensus on the significance of Jesus' mission as depicted in the Ebionite gospel.[35]

The North African Christian apologist, Tertullian, had an issue with the teachings of Marcion, a Christian leader in Rome in the 2nd century, who apparently also dismissed the Nativity story. He wrote: "Marcion, Who

Would Blot Out the Record of Christ's Nativity, is Rebuked for So Startling a Heresy."[36]

These inconsistencies with later mainstream Christianity are, interestingly enough, found in Muslim beliefs as well. Some may not realize that the Quran is roughly the equivalent of both the Old and New Testaments, along with some apocryphal (non-canonical or unaccepted) stories. It is maintained that these were not translations, however, but are considered to be the new and most accurate dispensation of the word of Allah (God) – just as Early Church Fathers previously claimed that Christianity was the new and most accurate form of the scriptures. This final, pure dispensation is said to have come to Muhammad through the Archangel Gabriel (Jibril).

The nativity does not match with Quranic texts, nor does the crucifixion story. Islam portrays Jesus as a great prophet, but not as the Son of God. It makes sense that these two narratives, as in the Ebionite (Jewish Christian) gospel, are missing from the Quran, in great alignment with Jewish or Judeo-Christian theology as well as Syriac and Nestorian-Christian ideas, in early Islamic beliefs.

Some of the details of Jesus' infancy align with the narrative from the non-canonical *Gospel of Pseudo-Matthew*, as well as other similar texts which may be based on that narrative, such as in the *Gospel of James*, the *Infancy Gospel of Thomas*, and the *Syriac Infancy Gospel* (also, interestingly enough, called the *Arabic Infancy Gospel*).

The Quran states that Jesus was not crucified, though it was made to appear so. This idea shows up in the non-canonical Christian *Gospel of Barnabas,* though that story is dated to the 16th century - long after the Quran was written (which demonstrates how ideas and influence flowed between the two faiths in both directions).

Mark begins with the ministry of John the Baptist, and the baptism of Jesus, and lacks any mention of the birth and early life of Jesus. In its shorter version, it also leaves out the story of the crucifixion, resurrection, and ascension of Jesus. This reinforces the possibility that, in *Matthew* also, the Nativity and genealogy of Jesus, was an add-on to the original text. Perhaps both *Mark* and *Matthew* opened with the narrative of the baptism of Jesus and God speaking from heaven, "This is my beloved Son."

The *Gospel of Luke*, while having much in common with *Mark* and *Matthew*, has its own views. New Testament scholar, Luke Timothy Johnson, notes that, "Luke's account is selected and shaped to suit his apologetic interests, not in defiance of but in conformity to ancient standards of historiography."[37] He states that Luke, "... exercises considerable literary license in his shaping of Paul's portrait, just as he does in his presentation of Jesus and the other apostles."

Some scholars propose that the *Gospel of Luke* was written toward the end of the 1st century, around 80-100 CE. The dating of the writing of *Acts*, also thought to be authored by Luke, can't be before Festus's appointment as procurator (*Acts* 24:27), which, on the basis of independent sources, appears to have occurred between 55 and 59 CE. The date of *Acts* is still in dispute, but an early date (about 63) is gaining support with some scholars.

However, the oldest proof of the *Gospel of Luke* is a fragment dating from the late 2nd century, while the oldest complete texts are the 4th century *Codex Sinaiticus* and *Vaticanus*, both from the Alexandrian family. *Codex Bezae*, a 5th or 6th century Western text-type manuscript that contains the *Gospel of Luke* in Greek and Latin versions, on facing pages, and appears to have descended from an offshoot of the main manuscript tradition, departing from familiar readings at many points. In any case, some form of the Gospel existed in the 2nd century, though perhaps a different form than the complete versions of the 4th century onward. One must always consider the possibility of alterations to the texts, even in ancient times.

Christianity spread throughout the region, as far west as Rome. The movement encountered opposition, which painted Jesus as a revolutionary who was trying to overthrow the Roman government. *Luke* emphasized that Jesus had no quarrel with the Roman government. In *Luke*, Jesus was peace-loving and kind – friend of the poor and the outcast. He had no political intentions, and no intent to interfere with the dictates of the Roman government. As we might expect from the Gentile perspective, Pilate, the prefect of Judaea under Roman Emperor Tiberius, finds no fault in Jesus; he finally consents to the execution of Jesus only at the insistence of the Jews.

Luke's gospel is often said to be the most "readable" of the four gospels. *Acts of the Apostles* which details the travels and ministry of the Apostle Paul, is also attributed to Luke. *Acts* was greatly influenced by the famous epic narratives of Greek literature of the time period, such as the *Iliyad*, and the *Odyssey*. While some scholars consider Luke to be a brilliant historian, others consider the relating of supernatural phenomenon like angels, demons, monsters, etc., to put him outside the bounds of the historical genre.[38] Some propose that his epic depiction was based more on entertainment than fact.

It is generally understood that Luke's purpose in writing the gospel was to persuade; he seems to have taken liberties in trying to do so. Although Luke's writings are seen by some scholars as historical texts, despite the fabulous miracles of Jesus, others see them as an embellished "romance story" in the manner of the Greek epics, with a number of statistical improbabilities, and inconsistencies.[39]

The identity of the author of the *Gospel of Luke* has been much debated; he is described as a physician, and a "companion" of Paul. This term is used in the Quran for the earliest and closest followers of Muhammad. It is also used in the non-canonical Gospel of Philip, for Mary Magdalene, as the companion of Jesus.

Some interpret the details of his descriptions by Paul to indicate that he was a Hellenized Jew, while others consider him to be a Gentile. Because *Acts* focuses greatly on Paul's mission to the Gentiles, his slant is very Roman-friendly (much like the writings of the Jewish-turned-Roman historian, Josephus), and this is the audience to whom Luke caters. We must keep in mind the perspective that *Luke* provides. He is distinguished from Jews (the circumcised) in *Colossians* 4:10-14. He may have been one of the earliest members of the early Gentile Christian community.

None of the Gospels mention the destruction of the Jewish temple in 70 CE. Jesus had prophesied about the temple, " ... the days will come in which there will not be left one stone upon another which will not be torn down." (*Luke* 21:6, *Matt.* 24:1; *Mark* 13:1). This prophecy was fulfilled in the Jewish Revolt of 70 CE, when the Romans sacked Jerusalem and burned the temple. The Romans took the walls apart, stone by stone, to get the gold that had melted in the heat of the fire. It is hard to imagine that such a fulfilment of prophecy by Jesus would not have been recorded, but the story ends before this event.

Acts of the Apostles, which Luke wrote after the *Gospel of Luke*, records a history of the Christian church right after Jesus' ascension. Like *Luke, Acts* also fails to mention the incredibly significant events of the Jewish Revolt of 70 CE, which would have been included in *Acts* had it occurred before *Acts* was written, though it is quite possible that doing so could have been dangerous to the author. This omission is often used as evidence that *Acts* was written prior to the historically important events of 70 CE. *Acts* does not even include the accounts of Nero's persecution of the Christians in 64 or the deaths of [the apostle] James (62), Paul (64), and Peter (65), which provides further evidence that it was written early. However, this omission may be more related to the fact that the author is of Gentile background, and less attuned to the Jewish suffering in these events.

Edward Goodspeed proposes that *The Gospel of Luke* and *Acts* were two installments of one book. He notes that the introduction to each are connected, much in the way that Josephus connected his two-part *Against*

Apion, books I and II, which were written as a refutation of Apion's accusations against Jewish culture and teachings. This refutation includes Josephus' rebuttal to an outrageous polemical accusation that Jews had a tradition of bringing one Greek each year to a great feast (likely the Paschal feast), whereupon he was "fattened up," and then was consumed by the Jews as a "sealing" of the enmity between the cultures. *Against Apion* indicates the hostility to Judeans in antiquity. Josephus responds to both Egyptian and Hellenistic slurs on the Judean people, their origins and character. According to John M. G. Barclay, Josephus' robust defense of his people constitutes the finest example of Judean apologetics from antiquity.

Where Josephus' refutation focuses on the negative relationship with Greek and Egyptian cultures, Luke's writings, in contrast, promote goodwill and conciliation. These two texts both support the values of the Jewish community, and attempted to bring greater understanding between Jews and non-Jews, though the writings of Josephus are derogatory to Jesus ben Ananus, and the writings of *Luke/Acts* glorified the Lord Jesus.

Goodspeed makes the interesting observation that, "... the *Gospel of Luke* does not reach the goal it sets itself-the impartation of the Spirit to the disciples." This is a reference to the time when the *Paraclete* - the Comforter - would come to them, and the disciples would be filled with the Holy Spirit.

He goes on, "The gospel tells them, 24:49, 'I will send down upon you what my Father has promised. Wait here in the city until you are clothed with power from on high.' The fulfillment of this promise does not come until the second chapter of *Acts*." He proposes that, "It is hard to believe that Luke would think his story was told, with such a forecast left hanging in the air unfulfilled. But of course, this is simply the art of the continued story – to foreshadow in one installment something of great importance that is to be related in the next. By these verses Luke links book ii to book i in unmistakable fashion."

Goodspeed says, "Of course, all this would be much clearer if the *Acts* had not been anciently separated from the *Gospel of Luke* when the gospel was gathered into the great quartet of gospels early in the second century. It is the fact that, as we first know these books, *John* comes between *Luke* and *Acts* that obscures their continuity and actually hides it from us."[40]

In *Luke*, the author prefaces his account by stating the purpose of the work, "The first account I composed, Theophilus, about all that Jesus began to do and teach, until the day when He was taken up, after He had by the Holy Spirit given orders to the apostles whom He had chosen." Luke introduces his gospel as having been delivered by "eyewitnesses, and ministers of the word." He states, "It seemed good to me also, having had perfect understanding of all things from the very first, to write unto thee in order, most excellent Theophilus, That thou mightest know the certainty of those things, wherein thou hast been instructed." (Luke 1:1-4)

The introduction in *Acts* begins with, "In my first book, O Theophilus, I wrote about all that Jesus began to do and to teach, until the day He was taken up to heaven, after giving instructions through the Holy Spirit to the apostles He had chosen."

Most scholars believe that *Acts* was written by Luke; many also propose that Theophilus (Grk. "lover of God") was Luke's patron who financed the writing of both *Luke* and *Acts*. Luke addresses Theophilus in a notable manner as "most excellent Theophilus." This term "most excellent" is used in 3 places in Luke: the letter of Lysias to the governor Felix (*Acts* 23:26), an address to Felix by Tertullus (24:3), and Paul's speech to the governor Festus (26:25). Thus, it seems that Theophilus may have been a Roman governor as well.

Theophilus was (coincidentally?) the name of a member of the priestly dynasty of the family of Ananus (also called Ananias or Annas), shortly after the time of Jesus. Theophilus ben Ananus was high priest from 37-41 CE, and would have been known to all at that time. There might be connections between other gospel-authors and this powerful sacerdotal family. Certainly, the high priests and their scribes authored written works in the time period. What is notable is the possibility that the office of the high priest might also have been related to the offices of the Roman government.

Matthew may be an alternate name to that of Matthias ben Ananus, who was high priest in 43 CE. The Hebrew name *Matityahu* was transliterated into Greek as *Mattathias*, which was shortened to *Matthaios* or *Matthias*. The name was Latinized as *Matthaeus*, which became Matthew in English, commonly shortened to *Matt.* in citations. In the same manner, John may be a shortening of the name, Jonathan ben Ananus, who was high priest from 36-37.

The *Gospel of Luke* and *Acts* are closely related. Written by the same author and for the same purpose, both were addressed to Theophilus and the introduction to each states that they were written to document a complete historical narrative of the early Christian movement. Luke not only collected the various narratives, but added his own interpretation so as to make a unified narrative - seemingly, to "harmonize" the various stories and teachings into one cohesive text.

There are also certain contradictions between *Luke* and *Acts*. For example, the gospel seems to place the Ascension on Easter Sunday, immediately after the Resurrection, while *Acts* 1 puts it forty days later. There are similar conflicts within the theology. While it may not rule out the single authorship of *Luke-Acts*, these differences do suggest inconsistency.

Luke certainly mentions Mary Magdalene and Mother Mary, but *Acts* does not. *Acts*, which begins after the death and resurrection of Jesus, mentions many women, but Mary Magdalene has disappeared from the narrative. With *Acts*, Mary, has left and Paul the Apostle, who has not been heard from before, comes on the scene. Paul was called an apostle, but not a disciple. He did not connect with Jesus in person, but only through a vision. He spoke of his teachings as "revelations from Jesus Christ."

It is strange that Luke was said to be "a companion of Paul", but Paul does not appear in Luke's Gospel, only in his *Acts of the Apostles.*Were changes made when the two texts of *Luke* and *Acts* were divided? Or was Acts written when it had become dangerous to mention certain names?

It must be noted that both *Luke* and *Acts* were written by a Gentile writer for a Roman audience (Luke was "of the uncircumcized"), most likely, after the Roman siege of Jerusalem. That is to say, this was a time when the Romans were in charge of the city, and therefore, in some degree, *also of the narrative*. Mary Magdalene, an important woman in the earliest Christian community, would be given no place in a Roman perspective on the faith - at least not in her own identity.

It is believed that Luke made use of at least three different sources: the *Gospel of Mark*, the Q source ("The Sayings of Jesus"), and a third source that is usually designated as "L" to distinguish it from other biographies. Some scholars see connections between *Matthew* and *Luke*, while others claim that there is no proof that Luke knew anything about *Matthew* or made any use of it in his writings.

Luke opens with two Annunciations: the foretelling of the birth of John, the forerunner, and the foretelling of the birth of Jesus. As with the *Gospel of John*, the narrative closely intertwines the lives of John, Mary, and Jesus. *Luke* includes stories that are not recorded in the other Gospels; they would seem to derive from later oral traditions.

Unlike *Mark*, which begins with the Baptism of Jesus, and the Ebionite Gospel, which also seems to do so, *Luke* first recounts the nativity story. He tells of Joseph and Mary's journey to Bethlehem, the birth in a stable, with the infant being wrapped in swaddling clothes and placed in a manger "because there was no room for them in the inn." He tells of shepherds who came to worship the holy infant. After eight days, the child is presented at the Temple (the traditional time for circumcision), and blessed by Simeon and Anna.

Luke also records the only story we have in the New Testament about Jesus' boyhood. When Jesus was twelve years old, he went to Jerusalem with his parents to attend the Feast of Passover. On the way home, when his parents discovered that he was not with them, they returned to the Temple and found him involved in a profound discussion with prominent Jewish rabbis. After the introductory chapters, *Luke* follows the outline of events as they are recorded in the *Gospel of Mark*. However, he does not follow *Mark's* narrative as closely as *Matthew* does. Occasionally, he leaves out some material and substitutes a different narrative. For example, he substitutes a narrative of Jesus preaching in the synagogue at Nazareth in place of his proclamation at the beginning of his Galilean ministry.

The Q Source (from the German: *Quelle,* meaning "source") is a hypothetical written collection of Jesus's sayings (*logia*). Q is a reference to the "common" material found in the *Gospels of Matthew* and *Luke* but not in the *Gospel of Mark*. According to this hypothesis, this material was drawn from the early Church's Oral Tradition, which may indicate that the Islamic *Injil (The Gospel of Jesus*), was likewise the oral tradition of Jesus' teachings. Much of Luke's material on Jesus' teachings is not found in the other Gospels. If he and Matthew both used the same Q source, then *Luke* used more material from it than did *Matthew*. In *Luke* alone we find the parables of the Good Samaritan, the Publican and the Pharisee who went to the Temple to pray, the rich man and Lazarus, the lost coin, the prodigal son, the unjust steward, the rich fool who would tear down his barns and build greater barns in order that he might store his goods.

Chapters 9–18 are often referred to as *Luke's* "long insertion," where he departs from the sequence of events in *Mark* and introduces a section that includes much of the most valued portions of Jesus' parables. In the story of Jesus and the sinful publican, Zacchaeus, who climbs a tree to see the Lord, the publican invites Jesus to be his guest. He says that he will give half his goods to the poor, and repay fourfold anyone that he has taken money from by false means. The people are astounded that Jesus would consent to be the guest of such a man, but Jesus says to Zacchaeus, "For the Son of Man came to seek and to save what was lost." The parables and stories, which may have come from the material known as "the Sayings of Jesus," illustrate essential aspects of Jesus' work. It would appear that these were recorded by someone other than Jesus.

Luke emphasizes the fact that Jesus was a friend not only to Jews but to Samaritans and to people from different races and nationalities. *Luke* makes it clear that Jesus' mission is for all nations, and not just for the Jews. This would be important to the Gentiles, who were becoming more prominent in the faith.

In the introductory chapters of the gospel where *Luke*, like *Matthew*, traces the genealogy of Jesus, the universality of Jesus' mission is reinforced. While *Matthew* traces the ancestry back to Abraham, who is regarded as the father of the Hebrew people; *Luke* traces it back to Adam, the father of all humanity.

Luke describes the events leading to the crucifixion, emphasizing Jesus' innocence of any wrongdoing toward either Jews or the Roman government. He gives an account of the resurrection and Jesus' subsequent appearances to the disciples. Jesus joins two men on the road to the village of Emmaus; they do not recognize Jesus until he sits at a table with them and blesses the meal. Later, Jesus meets with the eleven disciples (with Thomas not present) in Jerusalem and proves his identity, and material form, by showing the wounds of his hands and feet to them. They cook some fish, and Jesus partakes of the food with them, also meant to confirm a bodily resurrection.

In his farewell discourse to the disciples, Jesus instructs them on what they should do. It is similar to the "Great Commission" in *Matthew*, however, Luke's Gospel clearly states that Jesus has conferred upon them the authority to heal, to cast out demons and to perform miracles. They go together as far as Bethany, whereupon, after blessing the disciples, Jesus leaves them, and is carried up to heaven.

Luke,,"a companion of Paul", depicted Christianity as a universal religion, and emphasized that all humans were in need of salvation. Jesus was, for him, the supreme example of what the power of God can do in a human life. Paul has often been referred to as a Christian mystic because of his conviction that salvation comes only by "union with God". Paul does not abandon the apocalyptic conception of the coming of the age's end, but he emphasizes the quality of living that alone can prepare one for the coming of this future event.

Luke was sympathetic to Paul's mystical teaching of the Christ. Luke does not emphasize the nearness of the end of the world, as the other evangelists do. He proposes, as Paul taught, that the Spirit of God dwells in the human heart and mind, as it did in the person of Jesus. Luke makes clear Paul's teaching that the kingdom of heaven is not a distant promise, but can be found in the present through union with God.

Luke highlighted the broad humanitarian character of Jesus' work that was manifested from the first, demonstrated in Jesus' attitude toward the Samaritans and others whom the Jews regarded as their enemies. Jesus commended those who had a humble and contrite heart, whether they were

Jews or Gentiles.

At the time of Luke's writing, the Spirit of Christ was regarded as the guiding factor in the life of the Christian church. Luke said that this guidance was only a continuation of what had been present all along, demonstrated by Jesus' repeated references to the Spirit of God throughout his public ministry. Many of the statements attributed to Jesus were interpreted in light of what had happened already, implying that at least some of his statements were intended as prophecy for the future of the Church.

The *Gospel of John*, also known as the "Fourth Gospel", or simply *John*, is the last of the four canonical gospels in the Christian Bible, written in three layers and finalized sometime between 90 to 100 CE. It traditionally appears fourth, after the synoptic gospels of *Matthew*, *Mark* and *Luke*. John begins with the witness and affirmation of John the Baptist and concludes with the death, burial, resurrection, and post-resurrection appearances of Jesus.

In Chapter 21 of *John*, it states that the book derives from the testimony of the "disciple whom Jesus loved" considered to be John the Apostle (that is to say, himself). The gospel is closely related in style and content to the three surviving *Epistles of John* such that commentators treat the four books, along with the *Book of Revelation*, as a single body of Johannine literature. Many modern scholars do not believe that the apostle John was the author of any of these books.[41] However, it is not definitive.

The discourses in the *Gospel of John* seem to deal with issues of the church-and-synagogue debate that was in full force at the time when the Gospel was written. In this Gospel, more than the others, the community defines itself primarily in contrast to Judaism, which would seem to confirm a late date for its origin. Christianity started as a movement within Judaism, and eventually, Christians and Jews became bitterly opposed, and separated into two distinct faiths. The *Gospel of John* is regarded by many scholars as a 4th-century work, perhaps written to demonstrate more harmony between traditions than actually existed.

Where *Luke* put forth an epic tale, particularly of the ministry of Paul, and his many heroic experiences, *John* reverts to Judaic themes. There are close correlations between the text of the *Gospel of John* and the *Book of Genesis*, which a number of scholars have discussed. *Genesis* 1:1 states, "In the beginning God created the heavens and the earth" (NKJV). *John* 1:1 says, "In the beginning was the Word, and the Word was with God, and the Word was God." These two opening sentences connect the Holy Place of Judaism - the Holy of Holies in the Jewish Temple - to the "Word of God" in the form of Jesus Christ, who, through the overshadowing of Mary by the Holy Spirit, "became flesh and dwelt among us". (*John* 1:1, 14)

These correlations between *Genesis* and *John* can be found throughout the texts, which seem to be an effort to connect the *Gospel of John* to the sacred text of the Jewish *Pentateuch*, and *Genesis* particularly, perhaps a reference to a new beginning with the teachings of Jesus.

Of the four gospels, the *Gospel of John* focuses on the esoteric. It is the teaching of a mystic. Rudolph Steiner writes, "Whereas the three other evangelists relate the exoteric. Saint John relates what he experiences as an initiated seer, who could look into the Spiritual worlds. The writer of the Saint John Gospel wrote from the point of view of an initiate. Whoever looks upon it as a book that one should read and understand in the same way as one reads and understands any other book knows nothing of the *Saint John Gospel*. He alone has knowledge of it who can experience it. Most translators do not render the Spirit of it at all.[42]

And so, we have the *Gospels of Mark* and *Matthew* with decidedly Jewish leanings, *Luke* (as well as *Acts*, also attributed to Luke) with seemingly Gentile (Roman) leanings, and *John* with a new covenant and a mystical new teaching. It is important to understand, that even the Gospels themselves give biased viewpoints on the stories of Jesus, Mary, and John the Baptist.

PSEUDEPIGRAPHY

Paul in his *Letter to the Thessalonians,* said, "Prove all things, we are exhorted, hold fast that which is good." From its earliest days, there were those in the Church who frowned upon the use of "pseudepigraphy," which is the Anglicized form of "pseudepigrapha", from the Greek: *pseudes*, "false" and *epigraphe*, "to write/record/inscribe afterwards." It can mean a falsely attributed written work produced after the supposed author has passed away.

Pseudepigraphy is also defined as "spurious writings," or "writings falsely attributed to biblical characters or times." It can refer, specifically, to "a body of texts written between 200 BCE, and 200 CE, and spuriously ascribed to various prophets and kings of Hebrew Scriptures."

Eusebius quotes Serapion, Bishop of Antioch (190-203), concerning the *Gospel of Peter*: "We receive Peter and the other apostles even as Christ; but the writings [*Pseudepigrapha*] which are falsely inscribed with their names we reject". (Eusebius, *Hist. Eccl.* 6:12) There is often a problem in determining, definitively, which writings are falsely attributed, and, though the church may well have frowned upon it, the use of pseudepigraphy seems to have been quite common throughout the history of the Church. It might even be said that it was rampant in the early writings of the church, when Christianity was outlawed, as well as during periods of schism, during the various crusades, during the Reformation, and through the Renaissance period in Europe.

We must keep in mind that Eusebius of Caesarea, who wrote against pseudepigraphy, was the same Eusebius who stated that it was acceptable to falsify writings for the greater good of the faith.

There is a broader, but related phenomenon in historical writings, which includes, not just falsely-attributed authorship, but also the use of a "nom de plume," or "pen name," including writers who use a false name to hide their identity, and writers who use a false name as a coded message, as well as writers who write under the name of another person to contradict their writings with an opposing argument.

There is the tendency for the *acta* (hagiographies) of the saints, and other writings to be written with metaphor, allegory, symbolism, and hyperbole that is meaningful to a certain audience, and is not factual, but perhaps contain some specific encrypted truth. In Medieval times, we can also add the various forms of writing which became popular with the Troubadour movement, including political and religious satire, which led to a trend of completely fictitious "historical" writings that were written simply to make a political argument.

The Apostle Paul had to deal with false writings even in his time. In 2 *Thessalonians* 2:2 he writes of a "letter seeming to be from us." Elsewhere, he notes, "I, Paul, write this greeting with my own hand. This is the sign of genuineness in every letter of mine; it is the way I write." (2 *Thessalonians* 3:17) He also makes similar comments in 1 *Corinthians* 16:21; *Galatians* 6:11; and *Colossians* 4:18).

There has been heated debate about the authorship of some of the *Epistles of Paul*; the *Pastoral Epistles,* particularly, having questionable authorship. Donald Guthrie demonstrated that, since the work of Baur and Friedrich Schleiermacher, disputes of authorship had called into question the authenticity of all of the letters of Paul.

Most biblical scholars believe that 1 *Peter* was faithfully recorded by Peter's secretary or scribe. But there is great controversy over whether or not Peter actually had anything to do with writing 2 *Peter*. The general consensus among biblical scholars is that it was written by a different author using Peter's name.

F. W. Beare finds 1 *Peter* to also be pseudepigraphical, "There can be no possible doubt that 'Peter' is a pseudonym."[43] (This does beg the question – a pseudonym for whom?) He proposes that the readers of 1 *Peter* "would recognize the pseudonym for what it was – an accepted and harmless literary device, employed by a teacher who is more concerned for the Christian content of his message than for the assertion of his own claims to authority." There is also the possibility that, when Christianity was illegal, on point of death, it was dangerous to write under one's own name.

It may be the case that people of the time period knew what writings were authentic and which were not. It may also be true that no harm was intended in this practice. However, it certainly does complicate the picture in modern times, when the reference points for such matters have either become fuzzy or disappeared altogether.

Often, when a text was known to be falsely attributed, it was prefaced by the term "pseudo", as in "Pseudo-Clementine," or "Pseudo-Apollodorus." Mark Powell suggests that pseudepigraphy was considered an acceptable practice, until, eventually, the abundance of questionable writings, caused the church to take a hard line against its use. In many cases, it was used in the same way that satire and other less-than-factual commentary is used in modern times. People know who is being lampooned, or glorified, and in what manner – though centuries from now, or even 50 years from now, the connotations may be lost to the general public.

The 5th century moralist, Salvian, published *Contra avaritiam* ("Against avarice") under the name of Timothy; he explained in a letter to his former pupil, Bishop Salonius, his motives for doing so. Many of the accepted histories of people from ancient through Medieval times seem to be completely fictitious, with the historical references actually intended as coded satirical diatribes. This type of writing goes back even further than the beginning of Christian writings, and can be seen in rabbinical commentaries, as well as ancient Greek authors.

There can be great loyalty to and heated debate over certain writings, especially those texts belonging to a religious canon. The work itself might have importance to readers beyond, and in spite of, it's commonly accepted pseudepigraphical nature, even though such loyalties do not make the writings authentic or true.

Along with deliberate misdirection, there has also been the false ascription of names of authors to perfectly authentic works, due to poor documentation, or confusion of authorship. So, the incorrect attribution of authorship may give a perfectly authentic text the label of "pseudepigraphy."

In the art world, the attribution of paintings to a certain painter may be debated within scholarly circles, until the artist has been authenticated;

likewise, authenticating the writer of a text is often debated within the discipline of literary criticism. Certainly, that is the case with many biblical texts, as well as apocryphal ones. The *Philosomena*: or *Refutation of All Heresies*, long ascribed to 3rd century author, Origen, was finally, in the 16th century, attributed to Hippolytus.

Along with questions of the authorship of ancient texts, there is also the problem of later additions or alterations to authentic texts. Sometimes a scribe may have made a notation in the margins of an early text which was subsequently incorporated into later copies. This was then used by clergy to "substantiate" their own doctrinal beliefs, and seems to have happened often, when councils and synods made some doctrinal change. Sometimes the meaning of certain words was changed in the translating of the text – perhaps accidentally, perhaps purposefully. Sometimes important sections of ancient texts were deliberately damaged or eradicated, while the rest of the writings remained quite intact, such as with the *Gospel of Mary*, and other apocryphal texts.

Heated debates come up frequently regarding the historical accuracy of written materials from the early centuries, whether it is scriptural texts, or other religious or historical texts. It is necessary, in seeking the truth of the development of Christianity, to keep the phenomenon of pseudepigraphy, and its various political motivations firmly in mind.

Even the names of many of the earliest writers on the subject of Christianity (whether they were Christian apologists, or opponents) seem to be metaphors and symbols – chosen names rather than given names: Origen (so similar to "Origin"), Epiphanius (which comes from "Epiphany", a sudden and striking realization), Eusebius (which comes from "Eusebeia," or "holy ones"), Athanasius (the Immortal One), and Augustine (which means "high, august one," and is the diminutive form of Augustus, as in, "Augustus Caesar"). It must be said that many of the authors of the early writings on Christian theology were not the real names of actual people. Many writings that were attributed to various saints or historical figures were political, polemical, and were skewed to a specific viewpoint.

Then we also have the subjects of these writings: Hypatia (high, supreme one), St. Agnes (holy, sacred one), St. Euphemia...well, you get the picture! Many of the people who were the subjects of early Christian writings, the early saints, particularly, were not real people – or were intended to represent someone else whose name must not be mentioned.

Robert Eisenman, in his book, *James the Brother of Jesus*, persuasively proposes that the confusions, alterations, and obfuscations in many early writings of the church, stem from an effort to cover up the importance, and therefore the identity, of, according to him, the *desposyni*, the "Heirs of Jesus", who he claimed, functioned in Palestinian Christianity as a dynastic model.

Notably, the gospel texts treat Jesus' mother, brothers and sisters either harshly (*Mark* and *John*) or gently (*Luke* and *Acts of the Apostles*), seemingly as an outgrowth of a power struggle over claims to leadership of the Church. Who were the rightful heirs to this dynasty – the family of Jesus, or Peter and the Disciples? Or Paul, who was not an original Disciple of Jesus?

Why did the Synoptic lists of the apostles differ between themselves and between manuscripts of each of the Gospels? Eisenman, very credibly, connects these phenomena with another: the confusion arising among early theologians over the mention of the siblings of Jesus. This issue arises after the dogmatic insistence on Mary's perpetual virginity. As in other instances, the acceptance of a new formula required some "tweaking" of accepted traditions. Conflicting references had to be harmonized with the new dogma, so brothers and sisters became "kinsmen", cousins, step-siblings, etc. And so, characters changed, or were added, and the names multiplied. Eisenman notes that Mary suddenly had a sister named Mary because the mother of James, Joses, and Judas could no longer, reasonably, also be the mother of Jesus.

There is one other highly important possibility: the practice, throughout the centuries, of using various names for one person, particularly, whose name it was dangerous to mention. It is possible that speaking the name of this person, or the true history of this one's life, could mean death. Both male and female names were used, for reasons that may become clearer upon exploring the written histories. Some people attempted to record a clear and accurate theology of this person's teachings; others attempted to contradict it – often by using the same "nom de plume."

The writings of early Christianity cannot be accepted at face value. As Paul suggests, we must, "Prove all things." It is clear that, throughout the history of the church, whether the church frowned on it or not, people were using false names to hide their identity, people were using symbolic names to make a point, and people were "borrowing" the names of actual, historical figures to promote, or to contradict, or demonize, or satirize their message.

The many and varied influences that have shaped the faith from the very beginning, require that scholars be cautious even about taking the Gospels, whether canonical or apocryphal or otherwise, at face value. There is conflicting information in them that can't be reconciled. Sometimes there are gaping holes in the stories; sometimes information from conflicting stories overlaps in such a way that both stories cannot be true.

If you were to read the opinions of the greatest biblical scholars, you would find many arguments about the validity of innumerable gospel quotes. If the truth of the history of Christianity is to be uncovered – you must suspend the weight of centuries of tradition and, instead, weigh the stories in your own heart. You will have to question – yes, question – everything. You will have to soften your focus in order to have the "eyes to see".

APOCRYPHAL TEXTS

Eusebius, in his chronicle, c. 324 CE, states, "One epistle of Peter, that called the first, is acknowledged as genuine. And this the ancient elders used freely in their own writings as an undisputed work. But we have learned that his extant second Epistle does not belong to the canon...The so-called *Acts of Peter*, however, and the Gospel which bears his name, and the *Preaching* and the *Apocalypse*, as they are called, we know have not been universally accepted, because no ecclesiastical writer, ancient or modern, has made use of testimonies drawn from them." (*Ecclesiastical History*, Book 3, Chapter 2)

The term *Apocrypha* is used with various meanings, including "hidden", "esoteric", "spurious", "of questionable authenticity", and "Christian texts that are not canonical". The word comes from the Greek and means "those hidden away." Prior to the adjudication of a set "canon" of biblical texts, and use of the terms "canonical" and "apocryphal", writings were described, in general, as either, *Homologoumena* (authentic) or *Antilegomena* (disputed texts). Most of what is now called the New Testament were *Homologoumena*, or universally acknowledged as authentic, since as early as the middle of the 2nd century.

Eusebius used the term *Antilegomena* to describe Christian scriptures that were "disputed" or literally, "spoken against" before the final determination of the New Testament canon. (*Ecclesiastical History*, Book 3, Chapter 2, c. 325) They were, however, widely read and held in high regard in the Early Church. These disputed texts included the *Epistle of James,* the *Epistle of Jude,* the *Epistle of Barnabas, 2 Peter, 2* and *3 John,* the *Apocalypse of John,* the *Apocalypse of Peter,* the *Gospel according to the Hebrews,* the *Acts of Paul,* the *Shepherd of Hermas,* and the *Didache.* This group is distinct from the *notha* ("spurious" or "rejected writings"), which came to be known as "heretical."

The writings attributed to the apostles circulated among the earliest

Christian communities. Paul's epistles were circulating by the end of the 1st century CE and may well have been the earliest written documents of the Christian faith. Justin Martyr, in the early 2nd century, mentions the "memoirs of the apostles",[44] which Christians called "gospels" and which were regarded as on par with the Old Testament. A four-gospel canon (the *Tetramorph*) was in place by 160 CE, when Irenaeus mentions it. (*Adversus Haereses*, 3.11.8)

The "Muratorian fragment" indicates that, by 200 CE, there was an accepted set of Christian writings similar to the current New Testament, though perhaps not in their current form. By the early 3rd century, Origen of Alexandria, highly honored at the time, was using the same 27 books as in the modern New Testament. Once the canons, or accepted texts, were determined, the terms "canonical" and "apocryphal" came into common use. Where "apocryphal" refers to non-canonical texts, the term *Apocrypha*, usually refers to a specific set of non-canonical Jewish writings.

Canonical texts are those that are accepted in the canons of the Church; apocryphal, or extracanonical texts are considered to be outside the canon of books that are held to be "Sacred Scripture." Many such texts were argued over – and some still are.

The *Book of Susanna*, (*Shoshanna* in Aramaic texts, which means "lily,") is an interesting example of a book that is accepted as canonical by some Christians, and as apocryphal by others. It is included in the *Book of Daniel* by the Roman Catholic and Eastern Orthodox Churches, but is considered apocryphal by Protestants.

SUSANNA

In the musical piece, *Peter Quince at the Clavier*, by Wallace Stevens, he writes:

> "Susanna's music touched the bawdy strings
> of those white elders; but, escaping,
> left only Death's ironic scraping.
> Now, in its immortality, it plays
> on the clear viol of her memory, and makes
> a constant sacrament of praise."

Women are not completely missing from the early history of Christianity. There are the obvious references to Mother Mary and Mary Magdalene – one submissive, holy, and eternally virgin (even after giving birth), one who was "tainted" with the hinted faults of sexuality and waywardness, perhaps even mental instability, or possession – a very dualistic schism of role models for Christian women.

Where power struggles abound, so also do "smear campaigns." If Mary Magdalene had truly been a prostitute, she would not have appeared in the Gospel texts. She would have been long forgotten by the time of their writing. The demonization of Mary Magdalene in a church where women were systematically stripped of their equality, signifies not her sinfulness, but her powerful role in early Christianity.

Though the defined role of women in the church has been a source of friction and dissatisfaction for many women throughout the ages, there are some vivid portraits of courageous women in biblical texts. Some of them seem quite immoral in achieving their goals, displaying deceit and wily machinations, but these women are shown to be strong, decisive, and often, valiant, even heroic! They change the course of history for their families, for their people. They are most certainly not submissive, subservient, or subordinate to men.

However, the story of *Susanna*, who is shown to be an example of the most pious and "proper" Jewish wifely behavior, is of great interest in its contested status of canonical or apocryphal designation. Whenever a text is contested as a source of truth, one may wish to discern the greater intent and purpose for the writing.

There are two Greek versions of the text of *Susanna*. The *Septuagint's* version appears only in the *Codex Chisianus* which purports to be directly derived from the recension of the Septuagint made by Origen, c. 240 CE. The version of Susanna by Theodotion is the one that appears in Roman Catholic bibles, placed at the beginning of *Daniel*.

The first complete version of Hebrew Scripture, known as the *Septuagint*, was written in Greek in the 3rd century BCE in Alexandria. Though it was several centuries after the decline of the great society of Greece, the "Hellenizing" of surrounding cultures made Greek the language of the literate and learned ones of that time. Alexandria was a bustling metropolis in this period, with a huge Jewish population in the city during and after the time of Jesus. So, the story of *Susanna* came out of a bustling city, a melting pot of diverse cultural influences (Jewish and Christian, Greek and Arabic), from a population that was very literate and knowledgeable about the ancient texts of all of these cultures.

Susanna Laing Drake states that, "The earliest surviving version of the story of Susanna is in Old Greek, which scholars date to the late 2nd century, BCE (from 100-135). The second version, which Origen and later church fathers attributed to Theodotion, is dated to the first half of the first century CE, over a century before the time of Theodotion (late second century). Indeed, readings and references to Theodotion additions to *Daniel* occur in several first century texts, including books of the New Testament. The Theodotion version of *Susanna* is longer than the Old Greek; over a third of it contains new material, while a quarter of it repeats the Old Greek verbatim."[45] This revision seems to indicate a need to update the material for the prevailing politics of the time, i.e., after the time of Jesus.

The *Book of Susanna* is considered to be extracanonical, or apocryphal, depending on the point of view. Though it may be historical, it is also a moral tale about obeying God's law. "There dwelt a man in Babylon, called Joachim: And he took a wife, whose name was Susanna, the daughter of Chelcias, a very fair woman, and one that feared the Lord. Her parents also were righteous, and taught their daughter according to the Law of Moses." (*Susanna*, 1:1 KJV)

Susanna is a pious young wife whose beauty attracts the attention of two lecherous old men who secretly lust after her. Upon discovering their mutual interest in her, they contrive a plan to blackmail her into submitting to them. During her accustomed bath in her private garden, the two lustful men send her attendants away, and secretly spy on the lovely Susanna. When she heads home, they accost her, threatening that, unless she agrees to have sex with them, they will claim that she was meeting a young man in the garden.

Though she knows the penalty if she is accused of adultery, she considers death to be the lesser threat to her soul. She refuses to give in to their demands, so they follow through with their threat, and publicly accuse her. At the trial, they give false testimony, whereupon, the council of elders condemn her to death – the penalty for adultery. "O eternal God, who knowest hidden things, who knowest all things before they come to pass, Thou knowest that they have borne false witness against me; and behold I must die, whereas I have done none of these things, which these men have maliciously forged against me."

The stoning of Susanna is about to begin, when a man named Daniel interrupts the proceedings, insisting that, in order to prevent the death of an innocent, the elders should be interrogated. The two men are separated and questioned about details of what they saw. It becomes clear that there is a discrepancy about the tree under which Susanna supposedly met her lover.

The story of Susanna displays the figurative language of rabbinical writings, which include puns, satire, and humor to make a point that will be impressed upon the people. In the Greek text, the puns and wordplay connect the names of the trees cited by the elders, and the sentence imposed by Daniel. The first elder says they were under a mastic (*hupo schinon*), which relates to Daniel saying that an angel stands ready to cut (*schisei*) him in two. The second says they were under an evergreen oak tree (*hupo prinon*); Daniel says that an angel stands ready to saw (*prisai*) him in two. The great difference in size between the shrubby "mastic," and an oak establishes that the elders have made false accusations. The tables are suddenly turned - the lustful elders are put to death, and virtue triumphs.

Susanna, while essentially a morality play, also expresses the intricacies of Mosaic Law. Several laws are brought into the unfolding drama, and commented on, in turn. In essence, the story seems meant to instruct the reader in how to interpret and abide by the law. It also makes a distinction between the behavior of the "daughters of Israel" and the "daughters of Judah." At one point, Daniel says to one of the elders, "... lust hath perverted thine heart. Thus have ye dealt with the daughters of Israel, and they for fear companied with you: but the daughter of Judah would not abide your wickedness." This political perspective puts Judah/ Judea above Israel, and here, already, we see a commentary dividing those of proper sexual morals and those without. It could be that this is a moral commentary on the nature of Judeans compared to Israelites.

In her book, *Slandering the Jew*, Susanna Drake suggests that early Christian writings painted Jewish men, as being "carnal and licentious." This might be seen as Christian propaganda contrasting the "spiritual" Christian from the "carnal" Jew.[46] A number of church fathers such as Justin Martyr, Hippolytus of Rome, Origen of Alexandria, and John Chrysostom portrayed Jewish men as dangerously hypersexual, at times literally seducing, or in this case, blackmailing virtuous Christian women into compliance.

Sextus Julius Africanus did not regard the story as canonical. Origen observed (in *Epistola ad Africanum*) that it was somehow "hidden" by the Jews. (Or was there a hidden meaning?) There are no early Jewish references to the book. Jerome, noting that it is not found in the Hebrew Bible, treated *Susanna* as a non-canonical fable, placing it at the end of *Daniel*. In his introduction, he opined that it was an apocryphal addition because, unlike the original *Book of Daniel*, it was written in Greek, rather than Hebrew. Jerome's comments on its apocryphal nature makes it interesting as a possible later addition to the Old Testament, and the possibility that it has bearing on early Christianity.

The fact that the Greek puns do not translate in a way that would give the same meaning has been cited, by some, as proof that the text never existed in Hebrew or Aramaic, yet, other pairs of words could have given the same effect in Hebrew or Aramaic. The Anchor Bible uses "yew" and "hew" and "clove" and "cleave" to make the pun in English. This issue highlights how the finer details can be lost in the translation of original texts.

If it is, indeed, fable, what is the point of the *Book of Susanna* – a woman wrongfully accused of sinful behavior by two respected elders, whose differing stories indicate that they did not speak the truth? Is it the historical record of actual events, or is it, like so many writings of the time, a metaphor, or a tongue-in cheek diatribe against an opposing philosophy? Are we able to comprehend, at this point in time, what purpose it served in biblical times?

Susanna is not included in the Jewish *Tanakh* and is not mentioned in early Jewish literature. Even its inclusion in the *Septuagint* is debated by early as well as modern-day scholars. If it was part of the original Septuagint (2nd century BCE), it was revised by Theodotion, a Hellenistic Jew (c. 150 CE).

The *Book of Daniel* was written some 600 years before the time of Jesus and early Christianity, the Septuagint was written in the 2nd century BCE. It isn't clear why it would have been inserted into the *Book of Daniel*, centuries after that book was written. However, there are possible reasons why it might have been added to Daniel in 150 CE, less than 20 years after the Bar Kochba Revolt, which, after the early successful push to Jewish Independence, in the end nearly caused Jerusalem and much of Judea to be wiped off the map. It may have been added in 150 CE, in order to make certain points regarding early Christianity.

The 14th century French parchment illumination, called, *Composition of the Holy Scripture,* or *Ci nous dit* (which means "Here we are told"), by an unknown illustrator of the French School, depicts Susanna and the Elders.[47] It shows two men observing a naked woman, who is hidden behind (or within?) what seems to be a large boulder. This detail may be important in the context of later discussions of the women of early Christianity. Certainly, in the 14th century, the story was used as a criticism of "deceitful elders," and, by this artist, seemingly, to hint at deceit within the composition or translation of the scriptures. *Ci nous dit* (Here we are told), resembles, the colloquialism, "So you say."

ST. PETER

In the *Gospel of John,* it says that John "bore record" of one who was greater than him, one whom he called "the Lamb of God." He points him out to Andrew, Simon Peter's brother.

Next, Andrew brings his brother, Simon, and Jesus gives him the name of Cephas. Though originally from Bethsaida in Galilee (*John* 1:44), during the time of Jesus' ministry, Peter lived in Capernaum, at the northwest end of the Sea of Galilee. Here he and his brother, Andrew, worked as fishermen, along with James, and John, the sons of Zebedee. (*Luke* 5:10).

In traditional medieval iconography, Peter is depicted as a balding or white-haired man with a long beard, holding or wearing one or more keys – according to tradition, given to him by Jesus as the symbol of his leadership role in the church. Peter, in the estimation of early Christian scholars is the disciple upon whom Jesus founded his Church – though there is some debate on the subject.

There is another passage regarding the name-change from Simon to Peter. *Matthew* 16:17 – 20 is often cited as evidence that Jesus passed leadership of the early church very specifically to Peter: "I tell you that you are Peter, and on this rock I will build my church, and all the powers of Hell will not overcome it. I will give you the keys of the kingdom of heaven; whatever you bind on earth will be bound in heaven, and whatever you loose on earth will be loosed in heaven." The name, Peter, might be seen as a reference to the Rock, the Foundation Stone, over which was built the Jewish Temple of Solomon.

However, there is an interesting wordplay in the Greek terms used in Matthew's gospel. Jesus would have spoken in Aramaic, where the nickname was *Cephas*. There would have been no gender difference involved in Aramaic, the same word would have been used twice. In the Greek text in which the gospel was written, the wording was, "You are *petros*, and upon *la Petra* I will build my church." *Petros* is interpreted by some to be a kind of familiar nickname, derived from *la Petra,* which is used to denote a large rock. Also, *petros* is the masculine form, while *la Petra* is the feminine, which leads some to believe that Jesus was actually addressing Mary Magdalene as being the large foundation rock upon which He would build His Church. In Pietro Perugino's Renaissance painting, "Christ Delivering the Keys of the Kingdom to Saint Peter", the Renaissance master depicts this scene, with Jesus apparently giving the keys to Peter, but John who stands behind Peter (and Mary Magdalene, in mirrored position opposite him), seems to ask the question in gesture, "Me?"

Some believe that the "rock" in *Matthew* 16:18 is a reference to Christ not to Peter, and that the New Testament Christian Church is therefore, built on Christ and his gospel, death, burial, and resurrection.

The Gospel of Mary, an apocryphal text, not accepted by the Church, has Peter asking Mary to tell the disciples of her vision of, and private dialogue with, the Lord. Much of the most important part is missing, however, it seems to detail Jesus' teachings on how the Soul rises past the "four powers" through *gnosis* (knowing), becoming free from their bonds and returning to eternal rest. After Mary shares her vision, and the hidden wisdoms that Jesus shared with her, the gospel portrays Peter and his brother Andrew in angry outburst, with the two men negating Mary's vision of the Lord. Peter asks, "Did he then speak secretly with a woman, in preference to us, and not openly? Are we to turn back and all listen to her? Did he prefer her to us?" Andrew states outright that he does not believe her. Levi chastises the two brothers for their outburst, "You are behaving like the adversaries." This Gospel – *not* accepted by the early Roman Catholic Church, puts the relationship of Peter and Mary plainly: Mary states that she fears Peter.

Many of the Gnostic sects, which were possibly as diverse as the factions of mainstream Christianity, were based in ancient Greek philosophy. In *Timaeus*, Plato wrote, "It is only males who are created directly by the gods and are given souls. Those who live rightly return to the stars, but those who are 'cowards or [lead unrighteous lives] may with reason be supposed to have changed into the nature of women in the second generation'. This downward progress may continue through successive reincarnations unless reversed. In this situation, obviously it is only men who are complete human beings and can hope for ultimate fulfillment; the best a woman can hope for is to become a man."

One of the statements attributed to Peter in the Gnostic *Gospel of Thomas* is, "Let Mariham go out from among us, for women are not worthy of the life." Mariham is seen to be a reference to Mary Magdalene. Peter is characterized as hot-headed, but these are strong words from a follower of Jesus. In essence he says, "Make Mary leave!" It is an ironic statement by Peter. This outburst is in contrast to the evidence, even in New Testament accounts, that Mary Magdalene's role was important, and even, some would say, integral, to the mission of Jesus.

Jesus responds: "Look, I will lead her that I may make her male, in order that she too may become a living spirit resembling you males. For every woman who makes herself male will enter into the kingdom of heaven." It is an odd exchange between Jesus and Peter – first that Peter should say such a thing, and second, that Jesus should respond in what seems an appeasing manner. Why does Jesus not correct Peter in this dialog? Why does he say that he will make Mary into a man so that she can enter heaven?

Some scholars consider this interaction to be a later addition to the dialog, from the perspective of Gnosticism. Gnostic beliefs have a deep basis in the Hellenistic teachings of the Greek philosophers, therefore, there are some misogynistic tendencies, though it depends on the particular Gnostic sect. Plato clearly held the belief that women were lesser beings than men. And Peter, in this particular non-canonical gospel, holds similar ideas about the value of women.

On the other hand, in the Gnostic *Gospel of Philip* 36, it says, "There were three who always walked with the Lord: Mary, his mother, and her sister, and Magdalene, the one who was called his companion. His sister and his mother and his companion were each a Mary." Mary Magdalene was his companion.

We must always consider the viewpoint of any given ancient text, just as we do in modern times in regards to political factions and the twists and turns that each side takes in presenting their beliefs. Is the account in the *Gospel of Mary* a Gnostic perspective? Is it a faction that opposed Peter? Is it the supporters of Mary Magdalene?

Jesus' response, "I will make her into a man," seems, at first, to conform to the same Hellenistic ideals. However, there is another possible interpretation. There is also reference in the apocryphal *Gospel of Thomas*, to making "the male and female into a single one," which refers to the idea of uniting the opposites as the prerequisite for entering heaven.

In the New Testament, Jesus chastised Peter more than any other person. When Peter began to walk on the water at Jesus' invitation, he doubted, and then sank beneath the waves, while Jesus scolded, "Oh, ye of little faith, wherefore didst thou doubt?" (*Matthew* 14:30-31) When Peter wanted to interfere in Jesus' mission (as described in the New Testament Gospels), albeit by saving Jesus from being crucified, Jesus cried out, "Get thee behind me, Satan (adversary)".

Peter is also not shown in the best light in the apocryphal Gnostic texts. Where others, particularly the female followers of Jesus, are commended for their understanding, Peter is depicted as lacking in that understanding.

Many scholars have cited evidence of conflict among the early leaders of Christianity. James D.G. Dunn describes Peter as a "bridge-man" between the opposing views of Paul and James the Just, the brother of Jesus,[48] but there is evidence that Peter was, in many ways the opponent of Paul, as well as of Mary Magdalene.

Some traditions state that Simon Peter was called "Simon the Zealot" because of his great and fiery zeal for the Lord and His teachings. Some scholars state that Simon the Zealot is not Simon Peter. Certainly, Simon Peter is depicted as hot-headed and willful. "Zealot" was a word often used for one who was fanatical in their beliefs. In the time of Jesus, however, the Zealots were political fanatics known for their anti-Roman politics and agenda.

While some recent books theorize that Jesus was, Himself, a Zealot, that does not seem at all likely. The Zealots wished to do battle with Rome – to fight, and kill the Romans. This was not aligned with Jesus' teachings in any way. It is negated in his chastising of Peter for cutting off the ear of the Roman soldier who was trying to arrest him. (*John* 18:10) Jesus heals the soldier's ear. Jesus might well have been considered a "Radical" in His beliefs and teachings, but not as part of the political movement of the Zealots, or the even more radical *Sicarii*.

At the Last Supper, Jesus reveals that he will be betrayed by one of those present in the room. The disciples are in confusion about his meaning. It is notable that Peter does not ask the Lord directly. He defers to "the disciple that Jesus loved" who was "leaning on Jesus' bosom," to ask the Lord who will betray him. According to the *Da Vinci Code* (based on a similar reference in *The Gospel of Mary*), this disciple, long said to be John, was actually Mary Magdalene, or you might say, Mary/John.

Jesus indicates that his betrayer is the one who dips bread with him. "And when he had dipped the sop, he gave it to Judas Iscariot, the son of Simon Iscariot," whereupon Judas "went out immediately." There are questions about the meaning of "Iscariot," and several theories may be found. One theory is that "Iscariot" identifies Judas, as well as his father, Simon Iscariot, as members of the *Sicarii*. This was a cadre of assassins among Jewish rebels intent on driving the Romans out of Judea. Some historians maintain that, since the *Sicarii* arose in the 40s or 50s of the 1st century, Judas could not have been a member. However, scholars often quibble about the actual date of Jesus' death, and, since the texts were written after the death of Jesus, the term may have been a later reference – a slur on the character of the father and son. Also, since other references make Simon a "Zealot," it seems a very likely connection.

When Jesus speaks at the Last Supper of his imminent betrayal, Peter protests that he will follow him to the ends of the earth. Jesus responds, "Verily I say unto thee, That this night, before the cock crow, thou shalt deny me thrice."

All four New Testament Gospels indicate that, following the Last Supper, Jesus went out to pray (*John* 18:1). *Matthew* and *Mark* identify his place of prayer as the garden of Gethsemane. Jesus was accompanied by

Peter, John, and James the Greater, whom most scholars consider to be the "brother of the Lord." Jesus asked them to stay awake and pray.

While Jesus prays, the men, including Peter, fall asleep. "And He came to the disciples and found them sleeping, and said to Peter, 'So, you men could not keep watch with Me for one hour? Keep watching and praying that you may not enter into temptation; the spirit is willing, but the flesh is weak.' He moved 'a stone's throw away' from them, where he felt overwhelming sadness and anguish, and said 'Father, if you are willing, take this cup from me; yet not my will, but yours be done.' " *Matthew* 26:42-46

What is the temptation of Peter that concerns Jesus? What is the deep anguish that he feels in this situation? Is it his imminent death, which is said to be his very life mission, or is it the betrayal that he knows is heading towards him from his own disciple – his head disciple – Peter, who would deny him three times before dawn?

Then, a little while later, Jesus said, "If this cup cannot pass by, but I must drink it, your will be done!" (*Matthew* 26:42). He repeats this three times, checking on the three apostles, between each prayer and finding them asleep. On the third occasion, he said, "Get up, let us be going; behold, the one who betrays Me is at hand!"

Judas led the soldiers to Jesus, kissing the Lord on the cheek to signify that he was the one they were looking for. "Then seizing him, they led him away and took him into the house of the high priest." Peter followed at a distance. In the middle of the courtyard, people had gathered around a fire. Peter sat down with them. A servant girl saw him seated there in the firelight. "She looked closely at him and said, 'This man was with him.' But he denied it. 'Woman, I don't know him,' he said." A little later someone else saw him and said, "You also are one of them."

"Man, I am not!" Peter replied. About an hour later another asserted, "Certainly this fellow was with him, for he is a Galilean." Peter denied the accusations for the third time, "Man, I don't know what you're talking about!"

Just as he was speaking, the rooster crowed. In *Matthew* and *Mark*, Peter immediately has the awareness of the fulfillment of Jesus' prediction. In *Luke*, though Jesus is in custody, he must be close enough for Peter to see him. At the sound of the cock's crow, "The Lord turned and looked straight at Peter. And Peter remembered the word of the Lord, how he had said unto him, Before the cock crow, thou shalt deny me thrice. And Peter went out, and wept bitterly."

The fragmentary *Gospel of Peter* is an account of the death of Jesus differing significantly from the canonical gospels. It ascribes responsibility for the crucifixion of Jesus to Herod Antipas rather than to Pontius Pilate, and paints the Jews as the persecutors of Jesus. It contains little information about Peter himself, except that after the discovery of the empty tomb, "I, Simon Peter, and Andrew my brother, took our fishing nets and went to the sea."

The first Christians were all ethnically Jewish - Jesus preached to the Jewish people and from among them came his first disciples. Even if certain Jews persecuted Jesus, it must also be seen that his early followers and supporters, essentially, the first Christians were Jewish. However, in the "Great Commission" of Jesus at the Last Supper, he indicates that the beliefs should be taught to the Gentiles (or non-Jews) as well. Jesus said, "Go ye therefore and teach all nations, baptizing them in the name of the Father, and of the Son, and of the Holy Ghost, teaching them to observe all things whatsoever I have commanded you. And lo, I am with you always, even unto the end of the world." (*Matthew* 28:20)

In the "Upper Room" on Pentecost, all the disciples, including Peter, received the gift of the Holy Spirit, which caused them to "speak in tongues." Afterwards, Peter traveled to Mauritania on the Northwestern coast of Africa to preach the Gospel. Some of the earliest and most vitriolic diatribes against women came from "Tertullian" (so like the name of the accuser at Paul's trial, "Tertullus"). Tertullian was a Christian writer/apologist from North Africa in the 2nd to 3rd century CE.

A medieval tradition reports that Peter was imprisoned in the Mamertine Prison in Rome before his execution; that after converting many to the faith, he was tortured and finally crucified.

CLEMENTINE LITERATURE

Clementine literature, also called *Pseudo-Clementine Writings*, is the name given to the religious romance (Hellenistic adventure tale) composed of discourses attributed to the apostle Peter. It includes an account of the circumstances under which Clement (meaning "Mercy"), came to be Peter's traveling companion, as well as other details of Clement's family history. It purports to contain a record made by Clement (in the narrative, identified as both Pope Clement I, and Domitian's cousin Titus Flavius Clemens).

The writings include the *Clementine Homilies* and the *Clementine Recognitions*. In some ways, the Clementine Literature is a parallel to the *Acts of the Apostles,* written by Luke. It contains many of the attributes of Hellenistic epics like those found in *Acts*, including adventurous travels and a shipwreck, though the stories are not as fabulous as those in *Acts*. However, many scholars see the Clementine texts as pro-Petrine, and anti-Pauline, these being the two most prominent factions of the early Church in Rome. The heretical magician in the Clementines, Simon Magus, with all his fabulous claims, is often interpreted, in these writings, to be a reference to St. Paul.

In Professor F.C. Baur's historical theory, Roman Catholicism resulted from the eventual compromises between the Petrine and Pauline factions of the Church, beginning in the late 2nd century. The tradition that Peter and Paul co-founded Rome's Church in the mid-1st -century and were martyred together, is generally regarded as a fiction that was meant to bring together their two factions under one Catholic (universal) faith.

There is much debate among biblical scholars as to the origin of the Clementine writings, and their date of origin. A. C. Headlam proposes that the original form of the Clementines was not one text but rather a collection of works, from one writer. He proposes that the *Book of Elchasai,* a lost prophetic and apocalyptic text, was a likely source for the Clementine material. He finds no antagonism to Paul, and declares the author as being ignorant of Judaism, thus, it would seem, a Gentile. Having determined that the original work was known to Origen, Headlam dates it to the end of the 2nd or the beginning of the 3rd century.[49]

In 1883 Bestmann made the Clementines the basis of an unsuccessful theory which, as Harnack puts it. "claimed for Jewish Christianity the glory of having developed by itself the whole doctrine, worship. and constitution of Catholicism, and of having transmitted it to Gentile Christianity as a finished product which only required to be divested of a few Jewish husks" (*Hist. of Dogma*, I, 310). Such a theory completely ignores Gentile influences on the development of the theology of the Roman Catholic teachings.

Regarding the Clementine Recognitions (R) and Homilies (H), the Catholic Encyclopedia states that, "Uhlhorn in his valuable monograph (1854) placed the original document ... in East Syria. after 150; H. in the same region after 160; R. in Rome after 170. Lehmann (1869) put the source (Preaching of Peter) very early, H. and R. i-ii before 160, the rest of R. before 170."

It goes on, "In England Salmon set R. about 200. H. about 218. Dr. Bigg makes H. the original, Syrian, first half of second century, R. being a recasting in an orthodox sense. H. was originally written by a Catholic, and the heretical parts belong to a later recension."[50]

Montague Rhode James proposes that, although the *Preachings of Peter* are mentioned in the Clementine Recognitions, "... these are to a great extent imaginary, and, if ever they existed, must have belonged to the same peculiar school of thought as the rest of that literature."[51]

Another popular theory based upon the Clementines, proposes that the *Epistle of Clement* to James birthed the notion that Peter was the first Bishop of Rome. This has been asserted by such noted authorities as J. B. Lightfoot, George Salmon, and John Bright. In Cyprian's time (c. 250) it was universally believed that Peter was Bishop of Rome, and that his bishopric was seen as the origin of the papacy. Modern criticism puts the letter of Clement too late to allow this theory to be possible. Hans Waitz places it after 220, and Harnack after 260, others consider that it probably belongs to the 4th century.

In his *Church History,* Eusebius of Caesarea gives a list of the first bishops of Christianity. He gives the first bishop of Jerusalem as being James the Just, the "brother of the Lord", who according to Eusebius, said that he was appointed bishop by the Apostles Peter, St. James (whom Eusebius identifies with James, son of Zebedee), and John. According to Eusebius, Simeon of Jerusalem was selected as James' successor after the conquest of Jerusalem which took place immediately after the martyrdom of James (i.e., no earlier than 70 CE). Flavius Josephus, puts James' first arrest and subsequent release by Procurator Lucceius Albinus in 63 CE, and modern footnotes give that his martyrdom took place some years afterwards, shortly before the destruction of the Jerusalem Temple in 70 CE.

Professor Joseph Langen in 1890 elaborated a new theory. He proposed that, until the destruction of Jerusalem in 135, that that city was the centre of the Christian Church. After the Roman suppression of the Jewish Bar Kochba Revolt, the Church of Rome made a bold bid for the vacant post of pre-eminence. "Shortly after 135 was published the original form of the Clementine romance. It was a Roman forgery, claiming for the Church of Peter the succession to a part of the headship of the Church of James. James indeed had been "bishop of bishops", and his successor could not claim to be more than Peter was among the Apostles, *primus inter pares"* (first among equals).[52] James was the head of the Jerusalem church, however, he was not connected to the Church in Rome, whereas, there are early claims that Peter was.

Langen claims that there was a struggle for primacy between Rome and Caesarea (Psidian Antioch), demonstrated by the introduction of a new edition, R. (Clementine Recognitions), and that Rome won the vacant primacy after the destruction of Jerusalem.[53]

Whether or not Peter was ever bishop of Rome is difficult to ascertain

– though there has long been such a claim, there has also long been scholarly debate on the subject. The account in Eusebius' *Church History*, which Andrew Louth proposes was first published in 313 CE, would seem to make Simeon another name for Simon Peter, as he is generally seen as the first official Pope of the Church. The Fisherman's Ring, worn by the pope, is said to represent Peter's previous occupation; it carries the image of Peter casting his nets from a fishing boat.

Some historians have challenged the traditional view of Peter's role in the early Roman Church. In a critical study, Otto Zwierlein in 2009, concluded that "there is not a single piece of reliable literary evidence (and no archaeological evidence either) that Peter ever was in Rome."[54]

Paul's Epistle to the Romans, from about 58 CE, attests to a large Christian community already in Rome when he arrived there. He does not mention Peter. However, most scholars conclude that Peter was martyred in Rome under Nero.

Jerome, in the same century as Eusebius, records that: "Simon Peter the son of John from the village of Bethsaida in the province of Galilee, brother of Andrew the Apostle, and himself chief of the Apostles, after having been bishop of the church of Antioch and having preached to the Dispersion the believers in circumcision, in Pontus, Galatia, Cappadocia, Asia and Bithynia, pushed on to Rome in the second year of Claudius to overthrow Simon Magus, and held the sacerdotal chair there for twenty-five years until the last, that is the fourteenth, year of Nero. At his hands he received the crown of martyrdom being nailed to the cross with his head towards the ground and his feet raised on high, asserting that he was unworthy to be crucified in the same manner as his Lord...Buried at Rome in the Vatican near the Triumphal Way he is venerated by the whole world."[55]

The inhabitants of Antioch were the first to call Jesus' followers "Christians" (*Acts* 11:26). A legend claims that the Grotto of St. Peter, a "cave church," was dug by the Apostle Peter himself as a place for the early Christian community of Antioch to meet, and was thus, the very first Christian church. Whether or not this is so, a church had been established in Antioch by as early as 40 CE. Antioch became a major center for planning and organizing the apostles' missionary efforts. It was also the base for Paul's earliest missionary journeys.

The Clementine Literature is considered by many to be a Hellenized version of early Christianity in Rome, with some of the drama and excitement of Greek epics like the Odyssey, However, it is not as fabulous in its storyline as that of St. Paul in the *Acts of the Apostles.*

ST. PAUL

In the *Gospel of Luke*, the author writes of Paul, the Jew-turned-Gentile, *Saul-Paul*, who (like Mary Magdalene in the apocryphal *Gospel of Mary)*, had his own vision of the Lord, which is said to have caused his conversion to the faith. Luke was also a Gentile, writing for a Gentile audience. Where Mary Magdalene has been called the "Apostle to the Apostles", Paul called himself the "Apostle to the Gentiles". The term "apostle" is derived from the Greek word *apostolos*, meaning one who is a messenger – not to be confused with a "disciple" (a follower or student who learns from a "teacher"), which, it seems, Paul was not. Traditionally, Jesus is said to have had Twelve Apostles who spread the Gospel after his Crucifixion.

We know that, after several unpleasant interactions with the Jewish community, including their attempt to stone him (as they also attempted with Jesus), Paul turned away from preaching to the Jews and began focusing on converting Gentiles (non-Jews), mostly Roman citizens, to the faith. But we must remember that Jesus, in the Great Commission, told the disciples to go out and preach the word of God to all nations.

Paul's given name was Saul, perhaps after the biblical king, a name which means "asked for, prayed for". King Saul, a Benjamite (as Paul claimed to be) was the first king of Israel. Essentially, the shift from Saul, a biblical Hebrew name, to Paul, which is derived from the Roman family name, Paulus, is a clue to this change from Jewish to Roman Gentile perspective, and, was perhaps also meant to indicate Paul's royal heritage.

In *Acts*, Saul-Paul, is said to have been a tentmaker from Tarsus, one of several important Seleucid cities referred to as "Antioch," He says of himself, "I am a man which am a Jew of Tarsus, a city in Cilicia" (*Acts* 21:39 KJV) Originally named Parthenia, Tarsus was, in Paul's time a very ancient and very populated city in what is now Turkey, bordering on Syria. It was a great seat of learning, with an extensive library; early in its history, it received many Greek settlers. But Paul grew up in Jerusalem. The title of "tentmaker" may have a hidden meaning, perhaps related to the "Tent of the Tabernacle", a structure which protected the Ark of the Covenant, before the Temple was built.

The Ark went missing from the Temple some 600 years before the time of Jesus, when Jerusalem was sacked by the Babylonians.

Paul grew up in Jerusalem in the mid-1st century CE. *Acts* 22:3 gives that he was raised "at the feet of Gamaliel." Since Gamaliel was a leading authority in the Sanhedrin, this statement implies that Paul began not as a Gentile, but a Jew with close ties to the Sanhedrin. Gamaliel advised the Sanhedrin in *Acts* 5:34–39, to "refrain" from slaying the disciples of Jesus, which is in great contrast to his student Saul, who "zealously persecuted the saints."

In *Galatians* 1:13 –14, Paul says, “For you have heard of my previous way of life in Judaism, how intensely I persecuted the church of God and tried to destroy it. I was advancing in Judaism beyond many Jews of my own age and was extremely zealous for the traditions of my fathers.” Were these Jewish-Christian saints? This little tidbit doesn’t seem to fit the story; however, it does make for dramatic contrast in the epic Romanized tale of his life and ministry.

Paul asserted that he received the Gospel by the revelation of Jesus Christ. [*Galatians* 1:11–12] He claimed almost total independence from the Jerusalem community, and yet appeared eager to bring material support to Jerusalem from the various budding Gentile churches that he planted. In his writings, Paul often mentioned the persecutions he claimed to have endured, physical and verbal assaults, to claim connection with Jesus and his teachings.

In *2 Corinthians 11:25,* he speaks of some of the dangers he had already faced, “I have been in danger from rivers, in danger from bandits, in danger from my fellow Jews, in danger from Gentiles.” In mentioning his “fellow Jews”, Paul is saying that he was Jewish. Paul also claimed to be not only a Christian, but a Roman citizen, which would indicate that he was a Gentile. This has caused a quandary for many scholars – how could he be both? At this time in Christian history, when Jesus’ followers were Jewish converts, how did this “Roman citizen” become one of the greatest leaders of Christianity?

Acts (26:10) also implies that Paul was a voting member of the Sanhedrin. An added wrinkle to Paul’s story is that he claimed to be a Roman citizen. In *Acts* 22, when Paul’s preaching to the Jews incited them to violence, which threatened to create an uprising, the Roman guard had Paul taken into “the castle” in order to scourge, or flog, him to discover his story and why the people were so inflamed with anger. “And as they bound him with thongs, Paul said unto the centurion that stood by, Is it lawful for you to scourge a man that is a Roman, and uncondemned? When the centurion heard that, he went and told the chief captain, saying, Take heed what thou doest: for this man is a Roman. Then the chief captain came, and said unto him, Tell me, art thou a Roman? He said, Yea.”

Acts goes on, “Then the chief captain came, and said unto him, Tell me, art thou a Roman? He said, Yea. And the chief captain answered, With a great sum obtained I this freedom. And Paul said, But I was free born. Then straightway they departed from him which should have examined him: and the chief captain also was afraid, after he knew that he was a Roman, and because he had bound him." (*Acts* 22:22-29)

Some images of Paul depict him in decidedly soldierly garb. Was he a Roman soldier? Did he gain his citizenship by serving in the Roman army?

Some historians have suggested that Paul may have gained his citizenship by serving in the Roman army. There was, however, another way that a Jewish person could claim status as a Roman citizen, which is that of belonging to the royal household of Herod. This possibility aligns well with Paul's statement in Romans 16:11, where he says, "Salute Herodian, my kinsman." These details uniquely identify Saul/Paul as a member of the Herodian royals. The unexplained name change may well signify the shift from a Jewish to a Gentile audience as the focus of teachings of this apostle. It is also possible that this important Christian figure was the Gentile representation (or composite, considering the secrets and pseudonyms within Christianity) of an earlier well-known figure whose name could no longer be spoken.

Professor Robert Eisenman of California State University, suggests that Paul was, indeed, related to Herod the Great. He proposes that the man that Josephus calls "Saulus," a "kinsman of Agrippa," was none other than Paul. There seems to be a confirmation of the relationship in *Romans* 16:11, where Paul writes, "Greet Herodion, my kinsman." This would seem to give Paul some connection to the royal lineage of the Herodian dynasty. This could explain his claim that he was a Roman citizen, as Herod had been appointed regent by the Romans, and the royal house of Herod could claim the benefit of Roman citizenship, since that standing was bestowed on his father, Antipater, and his descendants, by Julius Caesar. In this way, Paul could claim to be both Jewish and a Roman citizen.

Later in *Acts*, the Roman governor, Felix, repeatedly pressures Paul for bribes to release him from prison, presumably, because Paul had great wealth and influence. Though he may have had the means, he did not try to buy his own release.

General scholarly consensus is that *Acts* was composed by a (Koine) Greek-speaking Gentile, for an audience of Gentile Christians. The *Gospel of Luke* and *Acts of the Apostles* are generally thought to have been written by Luke, who was believed to be a follower of Paul. Since Paul preached to the Gentiles, after being spurned by the Jews, it would make sense that these writings would have a Roman/Gentile slant.

The historical reliability of the *Acts of the Apostles*, the principal historical source for the Apostolic Age, has long been argued, the debate becoming quite vehement between 1895 and 1915. Most of these arguments centered on discrepancies between Luke's depiction of Paul, and Paul's own descriptions of his life in his Epistles. German theologian, Adolf von Harnack, was an ardent critic of the accuracy of *Acts*, though his opponents describe his citing of inaccuracies as "exaggerated hypercriticism".

In *Acts*, Luke writes of Paul's epic journey, like the fabulous journeys of Greco-Roman heroes, in the Odyssey, and the Iliad – including travels to far-off lands, shipwrecks, strange creatures. A new element crept into the faith – the "Hellenizing" effect of Roman belief and influence on the stories and teachings. Where Jesus performed miracles in the other Gospels, the fabulous nature of Luke's story gives pause.

Paul was not alone in his revolutionary ideas about spiritual/religious concepts.

Jesus had proposed an end to certain Jewish practices such as animal sacrifice. With the New Covenant such traditions were no longer supported. While the teachings of Jesus, at that time, were still considered a part of the Jewish community, there were ongoing conflicts between opposing ideas. Paul had confrontations with the Jerusalem Church, led by James, the "brother of the Lord", over making changes to Jewish traditions, as did Jesus. He argued with both Peter and James over the question of whether or not circumcision and other Jewish practices should be required of Gentiles who became followers of Jesus' teachings. Eventually, Paul convinced James of his position that such traditions were no longer required.

The "Incident at Antioch" involved a conflict between Paul and Peter, essentially highlighting the deepening division between Jewish Christians who believed in following Mosaic Law, and a Christianity that proposed no need to follow those restrictions. The Council of Jerusalem (or Apostolic Conference), an Early Christian council held in Jerusalem in about 50 CE, was considered by Catholics and Orthodox to be a prototype for later Ecumenical Councils and a key part of the development of Christian doctrines. It was decided at this council that Gentile converts to Christianity were not obligated to follow certain aspects of the Mosaic law, including the rules concerning circumcision of males. The Council did retain prohibitions on eating blood, meat containing blood, and meat of animals not properly slain, and on fornication and idolatry.

In the "Incident at Antioch", Paul accused Peter of being hypocritical, strongly

chastising him on the error of his ways. In Galatians 2:11-14, Paul states, "But when Peter was come to Antioch, I withstood him to the face, because he was to be blamed. For before that certain came from James, he did eat with the Gentiles: but when they were come, he withdrew and separated himself, fearing them which were of the circumcision...But when I saw that they walked not uprightly according to the truth of the gospel, I said unto Peter before them all, If thou, being a Jew, livest after the manner of Gentiles, and not as do the Jews, why compellest thou the Gentiles to live as do the Jews?"

These statements prove that there were divisions between Paul and Peter from the earliest times of Christianity. There were also factions that continued to follow John's teachings, those who revered James (even after his death), and even those who saw Mary Magdalene as the leader of the post-Jesus Church.

We know that Paul was beheaded (as was John the Baptist) – this occurring near Rome, at *Tre Fontane* on the *via Aquas Salvias* (meaning "Healing Waters") where a church was built in the 5th century in honor of the saint's martyrdom. There was a much grander church built by Emperor Constantine in the 4th century on the Ostian Way in Rome, which was built over Paul's sarcophagus. It is one of four major, papal basilicas in Rome, and was called the "Papal Basilica of Saint Paul Outside the Walls." It was expanded by Emperor Theodosius I in the 5th century
and was then bigger than St. Peter's Basilica.

Romans did not allow the women in their communities to have leadership roles. If
Paul were an alter-ego/pseudonym, or a composite of earlier Christian figures, who would he/they be?

THE APOSTLE TO THE GENTILES

In his book, *Follow Jesus or Follow Paul*, Dr. Roshen Enam states that, "Paul abolished the Law, which was followed and preached by Jesus, and corrupted the whole religion, giving it a new form. The main ambition behind all this, in Enam's words, was "to win a larger number" of followers; the followers of a new religion "the Pauline Christianity".

Thomas Jefferson wrote that Paul was the "the first corrupter of the doctrines of Jesus." But did Paul corrupt the teachings or were they corrupted by the Gentile writer of the New Testament texts about Paul? We must understand that, over centuries, such influences came in from many sources involved in the evolution of doctrines and beliefs. When Jesus gave his "Great Commission" to his disciples to go out and spread his gospel of the

Lord to all the nations, he must have known that each nation would have its own influence on the teachings. In his lifetime, these were oral teachings, and not written texts. Oral traditions have a tendency to morph and evolve, which, perhaps, was his intention.

Jefferson considered Jesus the teacher of a sublime and flawless ethic. Writing in 1803 to the Universalist physician Benjamin Rush, Jefferson wrote, "To the corruptions of Christianity, I am indeed opposed; but not to the genuine precepts of Jesus himself. I am a Christian, in the only sense in which he wished any one to be; sincerely attached to his doctrines, in preference to all others; ascribing to himself every human excellence, and believing he never claimed any other." He didn't believe that Jesus ever claimed a divine nature, or to be the "Son of God."

Jefferson was raised as an Anglican, but was greatly influenced by the views of the English Unitarian minister and scientist, Joseph Priestley, whose views included a withering scorn for Platonic and Neoplatonic metaphysics; a fierce loathing of all "priestcraft" which he viewed as being focused on maintaining power over the people; and a Unitarian view of Jesus, wholly compatible with natural law. Priestley suggested that the teachings of Jesus, and his human character were obscured early on, in the Hellenization of Christianity.[56]

While there is undeniable evidence that there was discord and disagreement between Paul and the earliest followers of Jesus, and that Paul wished to relax the strict requirements of the faith for Gentile converts, it might also be argued that Jesus "bent the rules" and taught new ways and new ideas, in the giving of a "New Covenant."

Paul came onto the scene as Christianity was beginning to attract a Gentile following. Both the *Gospel of Luke* and the *Acts of the Apostles* were geared towards a Gentile audience. In essence, one might even consider that the writings about Paul were a product of the Gentile perspective.

Professor F. C. Baur, founder of the Tübingen School of theology in the mid-19th century, was the first modern scholar to critically examine *Acts* and the *Pauline Epistles*. He proposed that Paul was in violent opposition to the 12 Apostles. He judged the *Acts of the Apostles* to be late and unreliable, using the *Clementine Homilies* and other early texts to support his theories of an early division within the church between Petrine and Pauline factions.[57]

Baur posits that the Pauline teachings, after the time of Christ, which insisted that Jesus must be accepted as the "Messiah" of Jewish prophecy, began to create a schism between Christianity and Judaism. While it used to be assumed that the complete division of the two faiths came about shortly after Christianity began – perhaps even in Paul's time, recent scholarship proposes that the schism may have come about much later. It is quite possible that the Bar Kochba Revolt of the 2nd century was the final demarcation point for the separation of Christianity from Judaism. The relationship of Judaism and Christianity at the time of the Revolt is difficult to determine because of the lack (or loss) of documentation in this period. It is known that when this rebellion was suppressed, the Temple and much of Jerusalem was destroyed, and the Jewish community of Jerusalem was soon scattered to the far reaches of the region.

Acts tells us that Paul became the "Apostle to the Gentiles" after his message to the Jews was violently repudiated in Psidian Antioch. Multitudes of non-Jews had gathered to hear the message of Paul and Barnabas, which the narrative says filled the Jews with "envy" and caused them to speak "against those things which were spoken by Paul, contradicting and blaspheming." (*Acts* 13:46) Paul and Barnabas boldly reprimand the Jewish protesters. "It was necessary that the word of God should first have been spoken to you: but seeing ye put it from you, and judge yourselves unworthy of everlasting life, lo, we turn to the Gentiles. For so hath the Lord commanded us, *saying*, I have set thee to be a light of the Gentiles, that thou shouldest be for salvation unto the ends of the earth." (*Acts* 13:47) This is a harsh statement for an Apostle of Christ to make. Did he, or were these words put into his mouth by an early Roman/Pauline follower, such as Marcion or Polycarp? Would Jesus have wanted to exclude Jewish followers, when his first followers, and he himself, were Jews?

When scholars speak of the "lost century", it is not hyperbole. For nearly a hundred years Christian history goes off the map and into a murky time of turmoil and turbulence that makes it hard to know with certainty what actually happened. The Gospels end with Mary Magdalene seeing the resurrected Christ. Then *Acts*, written sometime later, begins with Paul as the Jewish-turned-Gentile leader (Saul/Paul) of the Church. Paul, who, it would seem, never met Jesus, and whose connection to Jesus came through a vision, attends to the Gentile Christians, while James attends to the Jewish Christians, and Peter is somewhere between the two.

In the next chapter of *Acts*, a pretty good reason is found for Paul turning his ministry from the Jews to the Gentiles: Paul, stoned by the Jews and, presumed to be dead, was taken outside the city. However, when the disciples gathered round him, he rose up and returned to the city. He and Barnabus left for Derbe the next day. (*Acts* 14:19-20). From here on, Paul's mission and ministry are strictly for the Gentiles and not the Jews.

Unlike the Four Gospels, and in expected Roman fashion, Paul makes reference to none of the women when speaking of the resurrection of Jesus.

He is understood to mention only Peter and James by name. Where Mary Magdalene was cited as the first to see the risen Christ in all the Gospels of the New Testament (including *Luke*), in *Acts*, it was Cephas who first witnessed the risen Christ. This apparent reference to Peter is an exceedingly important shift in the narrative. None of the other gospels make Peter the first to witness the resurrection of the Lord.

It is even more odd, when we consider that Luke is thought to be the author of *Acts*. Do we simply assume that this is where the Gentile perspective, completely avoiding mention of Mary Magdalene, takes over? Was it now unlawful to mention her name? Or, is there a cryptic, coded message here? Is it possible that *Cephas*, in this passage, is meant to be a hidden reference to *la Petra* – and a confirmation that *she* was the true Foundation Stone of the faith?

Paul says that Christ died for our sins, was buried, and rose again on the third day. "... he was seen of Cephas, then of the twelve: After that, he was seen of above five hundred brethren at once; of whom the greater part remain unto this present, but some are fallen asleep. After that, he was seen of James; then of all the apostles." (1 Cor. 15:3-8, KJV)

One thing that, at first glance, Paul seems to have had in common with Peter, was his less than supportive views on women. In writings attributed to Paul, his view of woman's place within the church clearly indicates a position that is subordinate to that of men – a place of subservience and submission to masculine superiority. This view fits in well with the Greco-Roman norms about woman's place in society, relative to man's.

However, there are numerous scholars who believe that the misogynistic slant of Paul's Epistles was effected through later alterations/additions to the texts. There is great debate about portions of Paul's letters, particularly the *Pastoral Epistles*: *Timothy* 1 and 2, and *Titus*. In *Corinthians*, there is an unmistakable misogynistic slant in Paul's exhortations on the proper behavior of women in the church: "As in all the congregations of the saints, women should remain silent in the churches. They are not allowed to speak, but must be in submission, as the Law says. If they want to inquire about something, they should ask their own husbands at home; for it is disgraceful for a woman to speak in the church." (1 Cor. 14:33)

Bart Ehrman, and other scholars, such as Fuller Seminary theologian J. R. Daniel Kirk, propose that the passage ordering women to "be silent" during worship was not part of Paul's original letter, but was later added to the work.[58] In considering this stance, one must wonder: would there have been mention of the subject of women speaking in church, if they were not already doing so? To repeat the essential line, "...it is disgraceful for a woman to speak in the church." It seems that the statement addresses what is seen to be a problem area, that is, that women were speaking in churches, necessitating intervention to get them back in line. Again, this likely involved alterations to the original text, since women were active in the church in Paul's day.

Did women prophesy or preach in the times leading up to this writing? Two lines before this he also said, "For ye may all prophesy one by one, that all may learn, and all may be comforted." "All" would seem to include women, which leaves the question, is his reprimand to women a gloss, added later to the text?

Paul said that women "are not allowed to speak, but must be in submission, as the Law says." What law is this? Certainly, there doesn't seem to be any record of a Christian law, aside from Paul's statement, that forbids women from speaking in church. This law is not Mosaic law, or Jewish-Christian law, but Roman law, the law of the Gentiles. Women were precluded from public office, or even speaking in public in an official capacity. (*Pandects of Justinian*, vol. i. p. 13.) Paul's followers were now predominantly Roman citizens and so the text must align with Roman precepts (even if the slant was added after the fact). Some of the earliest writings from Christian scripture are Paul's letters to the Gentiles. Interestingly, in his Epistles, Paul does praise the work of the deaconess, Phoebe, and of Junia who he described as "a female Apostle." "Apostle" means messenger; presumably a messenger of the faith would give messages, and one would think, give them in the Church. One must assume that redactors and revisers simply failed to take these women out.

In *Acts*, Peter quotes the prophet Joel, "And it shall come to pass in the last days, saith God, I will pour out of my Spirit upon all flesh: and your sons and your daughters shall prophesy, and your young men shall see visions, and your old men shall dream dreams." This vision of Joel's states that *both* men and women will prophesy. It is not seen as being purely the domain of men. There were, in fact, seven prophetesses mentioned in the Judaic Old Testament text, *2 Kings 22*: Huldah, Sarah, Miriam, Deborah, Hannah, Abigail, and Esther. Even the New Testament mentions "Anna the prophetess," who, along with Simeon, witnessed Mary's presentation of Jesus at the Temple. (*Luke* 2:36–38) In Jewish practice, women were prophesying in the Temple in the time of Jesus.

On the surface, it would appear that some Gnostic sects were much more egalitarian, and accepting of women in leadership roles, but what if women also had a prominent role in the earliest sects of Christianity – before the repression and oppression of women had become entrenched as the norm of the extremely patriarchal culture of later Gentile Christianity?

While Paul seems to have admonished women for speaking in church, he says in 1 *Corinthians* 11:5 that a woman should keep her head covered "while praying or prophesying," which acknowledges that women, in that time period were, indeed, "prophesying". The prohibition against speaking in church is a prohibition later given by the North African writer, Tertullian. In fact, if one were to look for a source for such a stance, Tertullian, or a North African writer with similar ideas, certainly seems a good match.

Peter traveled to North Africa in the first century to preach the Gospel. It is hard to know whether his beliefs about women influenced these later teachings. Tertullian's writings were popular after the eventual failure of the Bar Kochba Revolt, overturning of the Jewish Independence, the destruction of the Temple, and dispersing of the Jews.

Tertullian insists on the need for women to keep their heads covered while prophesying. He adds that it should not be by a crown. Is this an admonition to the Imperials, who included great pomp and circumstance in their devotions to Mary? Or might it be an admonition to the crown and robes in which the Byzantines dressed Mary's relics and image?

In February of 2007, Pope Benedict XVI addressed the subject, "The Apostle accepts as normal the fact that a woman can "prophesy" in the Christian community (I Cor 11: 5), that is, speak openly under the influence of the Spirit, as long as it is for the edification of the community and done in a dignified manner. Thus, he says, the well-known exhortation: "Women should keep silence in the Churches" (I *Cor* 14: 34) is instead to be considered relative. Let us leave to the exegetes the consequent, much-discussed problem of the relationship between the first phrase – women can prophesy in Churches - and the other - they are not permitted to speak; that is, the relationship between these two apparently contradictory instructions. This is not for discussion here."[59] *This* discussion is integral to Christian belief.

There is great irony in these words about women not speaking in the church being attributed to Paul, if we can only see it. The admonition does beg the question – had someone been prophesying with her head uncovered? It is notable that images of The Virgin Mary always show her with her head covered, whereas Mary Magdalene is depicted with her head bare, her long tresses flowing. But then we get into the question of who is the Beloved Disciple, John or Mary (John-Mary) and it isn't so clear whether the head should be covered or not.

In *Colossians*, Christ is described as being the head of the Church, "And he is the head (*kephalé*) of the body, the church: who is the beginning, the firstborn from the dead; that in all things he might have the pre-eminence."

(*Col* 1:18) And again, "For in him dwelleth all the fullness of the Godhead bodily. And ye are complete in him, which is the head of all principality and power..." (*Col* 2:9-10)

Paul explains the need for women to cover their heads when prophesying, while men should not do so. "But I would have you know, that the head of every man is Christ; and the head of the woman is the man; and the head of Christ is God. Every man praying or prophesying, having his head covered, dishonoureth his head. But every woman that prayeth or prophesieth with her head uncovered dishonoureth her head: for that is even all one as if she were shaven. For if the woman be not covered, let her also be shorn: but if it be a shame for a woman to be shorn or shaven, let her be covered." The "shorn" head indicates the Nazirite practice of shaving the head as an act of devotion to the Temple priesthood, thus we might consider that women were allowed to prophesy if their heads were shaven, which would lead to the conclusion that women were also allowed into the "priesthood"!

In what is perhaps a later gloss, Paul further delineates a Greco-Roman "natural order" of things, "For a man indeed ought not to cover his head, forasmuch as he is the image and glory of God: but the woman is the glory of the man. For the man is not of the woman; but the woman of the man. Neither was the man created for the woman; but the woman for the man." The next line is much debated, "For this cause ought the woman to have power on her head because of the angels." In *every* instance where the Greek word *exousia* is used in the New Testament, there is no doubt that it refers to that person's own right to exercise his or her power or authority. Egalitarians interpret *exousia* in just such a way.

Exousia always signifies sovereignty except, according to some scholars, in this instance, where they somehow interpret the opposite meaning! Complementarians see a need for women to prophesy only under the authority of husband and Church: women may pray and prophesy (there is debate over what prophesying is), but they require a spiritual or symbolic covering over their head (man's authority) when they do these spiritual activities. In other words, in this case alone, the word *exousia* is given a connotation of subjection, rather than authority. Men have the accountability as head. The head is responsible for what the woman does under his authority. Everything she does should bring him, and Christ, glory – then God will be glorified through the proper, respective order.

William Ramsay scorned the idea that the term can indicate women's subjection, proclaiming this a preposterous idea, which *a Greek scholar would laugh at anywhere except in the New Testament* (cited in Robertson and Plummer). He steadfastly maintains that *exousia* means "authority" not "subjection" to the authority of someone else.

M.D. Hooker takes it a step further, insisting that, "Far from being a symbol of the woman's subjection to man, therefore, her head covering is what Paul calls it – authority: in prayer and prophecy she, like the man, is under the authority of God."

It is helpful to consider which writings are commonly found questionable by biblical scholars, because then we have a better chance of defining what Paul's true stance in early Christianity might actually have been. It is generally accepted that Paul wrote at least seven of the thirteen letters attributed to him in the Western New Testament canon (with the possibility of some alterations). There is general consensus among biblical scholars that Paul was the author of: *Romans, First Corinthians, Second Corinthians, Galatians, Philippians, First Thessalonians,* and *Philemon.*

In antiquity, *Hebrews* was ascribed to him (no relation to the *Gospel according to the Hebrews*), but the attribution was questioned even then. In modern times most experts do not consider it to have been written by Paul and consider it to be *Antilegomena.* The authorship of the remaining six Pauline epistles is disputed to varying degrees.

If some of the Pauline writings were pseudepigraphy and not really authored by him, then what did he really believe? And if some of his writings were altered, how do we decide what to accept as the true teachings of Paul?

Who was Paul? He is an enigma. There is some mysterious quality in the details of his life story. There are questions that come up. His importance in the early Church makes little sense. Jesus taught the 12 disciples directly, and then Paul somehow became the utmost authority on Jesus' teachings through a vision of the Lord. Paul becomes accepted by James and Peter and the Jerusalem Church. Then the Jewish-oriented teachings became Gentile-oriented. What is missing in this chronology?

Elaine Pagels, Princeton University professor of religion, and authority on Gnosticism, has given the opinion that Paul was a Gnostic. She considers the *Pastoral Epistles* to be "pseudo-Pauline" forgeries written by the anti-Gnostic camp to correct his "errant beliefs", which would account for the difference in tone and content.[60] However, not all Gnostic texts were against feminine leadership.

The *Letter to Timothy*, traditionally attributed to Paul, is often cited as the main biblical directive for prohibiting women from becoming ordained clergy. "Let the woman learn in silence with all subjection. But I suffer not a woman to teach, nor to usurp authority over the man, but to be in silence. For Adam was first formed, then Eve. And Adam was not deceived, but the woman being deceived was in the transgression." 1 *Timothy* 2:11-14, KJV

Again, this particular teaching aligns with that of early Christian apologist, Tertullian, who, in the 2nd century, stated that women were, "the devil's gateway!" It would seem that many of the misogynistic statements about women originated in the mid-to-late 2nd century, that is, after the devastating ruination of Jerusalem at the end of the Bar Kochba Revolt. The importance of this outcome, and it's bearing on 2nd century writings and alterations of original text can't be over-emphasized.

The *Epistle to Timothy* is often quoted to support the existence of an early tradition that women should be barred from any priestly role within the church; that also denied women a part in most of the duties and privileges of church leadership – in essence, from having any meaningful power in the hierarchy of the church. However, Paul's authorship of this letter is greatly contested.

British Jewish scholar, Hyam Maccoby, has noted discrepancies within the writings attributed to Paul. He contends that the writings about Paul in *Acts* and the view of Paul drawn from Paul's own writings describe two very different people. According to Maccoby, Paul, in *Acts,* speaks little of theology. He makes no mention of the importance of faith, or of the "Spirit". Maccoby also points out the absence of references to John the Baptist in the *Pauline Epistles*, although he is mentioned several times in *Acts*.[61] This is an important point to note.

If one were to consider the possibility of alter egos, or composite figures, in the sudden appearance of Paul in Christian history, then it would make sense: an author would not mention one's alter ego in one's history. One possible conjecture is that Paul is just such a disguised or composite figure, much like Mary/John, the beloved disciple. But we must dig deeper.

Maccoby proposed that Paul's theology combined aspects of Judaism, Gnosticism, and mysticism to create the "cosmic savior" theology of Christianity.

In *Matthew* 23:13, Jesus says, "Woe to you, teachers of the law and Pharisees, you hypocrites! You shut the kingdom of heaven in men's faces. You yourselves do not enter, nor will you let those enter who are trying to." Pharisee beliefs were very much based in adherence to Mosaic Law. According to Maccoby, Paul was not a Pharisee, as he claimed, but was instead, most probably, a Sadducee. Maccoby attributes the origins of Christian anti-Semitism to Paul. He also claims that the misogynistic aspects of Paul's writings reflect his Gnostic beliefs, though misogyny and anti-Semitism may have come about through later alterations to the texts.

Also, since much of what we believe about Gnosticism comes from the opposition, it is hard to ascertain that Gnosticism was, generally, misogynistic. Rather than paint all Gnostics as "anti-women," it must be said that Gnosticism, like Christianity, included a broad spectrum of beliefs. Many Gnostic sects were quite egalitarian, giving women prominent leadership roles in their faith. Many of the texts labeled as "Gnostic" demonstrate a high regard for women within Gnostic communities. In the *Gospel of Mary,* the *Gospel of Thomas,* the *Pistis Sophia,* and numerous other documents, Mary Magdalene is depicted as having a strong leadership role during Jesus' life and in the *Gospel of Mary*, seemingly after his death. (Many see Mary's vision of Jesus as post-resurrection). Even Paul's own letters describe some women in leadership roles.

According to authors James McConkey Robinson, and Richard Smith "The confrontation of Mary with Peter, a scenario also found in *The Gospel of Thomas, Pistis Sophia*, and *The Gospel of the Egyptians,* reflects some of the tensions in second-century Christianity. Peter and Andrew represent orthodox positions that deny the validity of esoteric revelation and reject the authority of women to teach."[62] This attitude is prominently displayed in the writings of North African apologist, Tertullian. We should remember that this is the place that Peter went to preach the gospel to the people. They go on to say, "*The Gospel of Mary* attacks both of these positions head-on through its portrayal of Mary Magdalene. She is the Savior's beloved, possessed of knowledge and teaching superior to that of the public apostolic tradition. Her superiority is based on vision and private revelation and is demonstrated in her capacity to strengthen the wavering disciples and turn them toward the Good."[63]

Theologian Karen King considers the Gospel of Mary to provide "... an intriguing glimpse into a kind of Christianity lost for almost fifteen hundred years," opining that it "...presents a radical interpretation of Jesus' teachings as a path to inner spiritual knowledge; it rejects his suffering and death as the path to eternal life; it exposes the erroneous view that Mary of Magdala was a prostitute for what it is—a piece of theological fiction; it presents the most straightforward and convincing argument in any early Christian writing for the legitimacy of women's leadership; it offers a sharp critique of illegitimate power and a utopian vision of spiritual perfection; it challenges our rather romantic views about the harmony and unanimity of the first Christians; and it asks us to rethink the basis for church authority."[64]

King concludes that "both the content and the text's structure lead the reader inward toward the identity, power and freedom of the true self, the soul set free from the Powers of Matter and the fear of death." She states, "The Gospel of Mary is about inter-Christian controversies, the reliability of the disciples' witness, the validity of teachings given to the disciples through post-resurrection revelation and vision, and the leadership of women"[65]

One Pauline quote indicates that women had no place within the hierarchy of the Church, another states that women had such roles in his time, and were praised by him for fulfilling those roles. So, which perspective was truly the perspective of Paul? Also, why did he leave Mary Magdalene out of the picture? Certainly, Paul speaks of certain women who were active in the early church, and even a "Mary" in Rome, but he does not ever refer to the Magdalene.

Acts mentions Mary, the mother of Jesus, as being present in the Cenacle (the Upper Room) at Pentecost, as well as the presence of other women, with no reference to Mary Magdalene. In Paul's *Galatians* 4:4, there is an indirect reference to Mary, the Mother of Jesus: "But when the fulness of time was come, God sent his Son, made of a woman, made under the law." He does not name her. Some Greek and Latin manuscripts, read as *gennomenon ek gynaikos* instead of *genomenon ek gynaikos*, "born of a woman" instead of "made of a woman." In this case, since *gennomenon* is the present participle, it should be rendered in present tense, "being born of a woman." The phrase then becomes, "But when the fulness of time was come, God sent his Son, being born of a woman, made under the law."

Though the phrase is interpreted in different ways, Tertullian points out that the word "made" implies more than the word "born". This is a significant distinction. Tertullian states that it calls to mind the "Word made flesh", establishing the reality of the "flesh made of the Virgin." The concept of a man made of a woman alone suggests the virginal conception of the Son of God, but this too can be interpreted in different ways. Paul's interpretation of the "Incarnation of the Word" supports both the Divinity and the real humanity of Jesus Christ.

In *Romans* 1:3, which refers to the same subject as *Galatians* 4:4, Paul writes *genomenos ek stermatos Daveid kata sarka*, which means, "...made of the seed of David, according to the flesh". This is related to the Jewish prophecy that the messiah would be of the lineage of King David. But here, the unnamed woman is taken out of the picture completely – no woman is mentioned at all, but only "the seed of David." This may reflect the author's opinion on the place of women in society and in Christianity, as secondary to the role of men, but it could also be that certain names were not to be mentioned.

The origin of the theology of atonement can be found in Paul's writings. Jesus' death, according to Paul, was the atonement for, and the expiation of, humanity' s sins, through the crucifixion, death, and resurrection of Jesus. By this sacrifice, God and man are reconciled. This theology is proposed by the Apostle, Paul – or at least, the writings attributed to him. Paul taught that Christians are not only redeemed from sin, but also from "The Law" by Jesus' death and resurrection.

The concept of no longer having to follow the old Mosaic law was known as "Supersessionism" (the idea that the new superseded/replaced the old). This theology contrasts sharply with Dual-covenant theology, which contended that the New Covenant was made in conjunction with the covenants of Mosaic Law. But why would Jesus make a "New Covenant" if people must still follow the Old one? Paul taught that, through baptism, a Christian receives the status of sonship, at which time, the Mosaic Covenant is replaced by the "New Covenant of Christendom." This also goes hand-in-hand with the idea of Adoptionism, where Jesus was seen to become the "son of God" at his baptism.

Paul coined the phrase "freedom in Christ," which he used in *Galatians* 2:4. In *Acts* 13:39 he states: "And by him all that believe are justified from all things, from which ye could not be justified by the Law of Moses." Understandably, mainstream Jews, who viewed the Law as the fundamental basis of Judaism, saw this teaching as equating with lawlessness (i.e., not obeying Mosaic Law).

Paul's ideas about freedom from Mosaic Law is particularly strident in regards to circumcision. He states that being circumcised meant being in bondage to a false ideal, and exhorts the followers of Jesus to "be not entangled again with the yoke of bondage." In other words, he equates circumcision with bondage. He states that, "...if ye be circumcised, Christ shall profit you nothing. For I testify again to every man that is circumcised, that he is a debtor to do the whole law." He further states, "Christ is become of no effect unto you, whosoever of you are justified by the law; ye are fallen from grace. For we through the Spirit wait for the hope of righteousness by faith." He seems to be saying that those who follow circumcision stray from Christianity. He goes on, "For in Jesus Christ neither circumcision availeth any thing, nor uncircumcision; but faith which worketh by love."

When Paul speaks of the issue in regard to the Incident at Antioch, he chastises Peter for his hypocrisy and for fearing those "of the circumcision". (*Galatians* 2:11-12) In this context, it seems that he is referring to the "Jewish Christians" under James, "the brother of our Lord," whom many scholars see as the leader of the Church after the time of Jesus. James believed that Christians should follow Mosaic Law. Initially, James was not pleased that Paul taught that the Law need not be adhered to by Gentile converts, though he eventually accepted Paul's teachings to the Gentile converts to

Christianity.

Paul clearly indicates that Peter accepted that the rebuke was justified. Paul also mentions that even Barnabas, his traveling companion and fellow apostle, sided with Peter. Eventually, Paul and Barnabas parted ways. Paul went on with Silas to Tarsus (Paul's birthplace), Derbe and Lystra. In Lystra, they met Timothy, who would become a devoted follower of Paul's teachings.

Could the statement of Peter living "like a Gentile" while trying to force Gentiles to follow Jewish customs apply not only to customs of eating separately, but other customs as well? We know that Paul's "companion", Luke, was reportedly uncircumcised. Was Peter also? He was a Jew who lived like a Gentile. Was he also of the Herodian lineage or household, with perhaps, Roman as well as Jewish connections and customs? (Certainly, Herod Antipas ruled over Galilee, where Peter came from.)

As Paul expresses so vehemently, if a man is circumcised then he must abide by the whole of Mosaic Law, but he does not say that Peter must abide by such laws, only that he shouldn't put laws upon the Gentiles that he doesn't abide by himself. Since he chides Peter for separating from the Gentiles for appearances sake, it would seem that he is saying that Peter was "of the uncircumcised", just as Luke was. Is it possible that Peter's Gentile leanings indicate that he was, indeed, not a Jew, but a Gentile? Was Peter Roman, or was he simply a Jew who followed Roman customs? Was he perhaps, like Paul, to be considered a Roman citizen due to connections to the Herodian lineage?

Paul never addresses his own status in regard to being "of the circumsized, or of the uncircumsized." Or of having to fulfill all of Mosaic Law, himself. Would this indicate that, as a Herodian, Paul also lived like a Gentile. Or is there some other reason that circumcision would, for Paul, be a moot point?

Many scholars suggest that Paul's theological interpretation of Christian beliefs served to widen the division between Christians and Jews. Paul wrote that faith in and acceptance of Christ as the Savior was the determining factor in salvation for both Jews and Gentiles. Some scholars propose that Paul's focus on Jesus as the redeemer eventually would make the schism between the followers of Christ and mainstream Jews decisive and permanent, and, in fact, probably accelerated the separation of the messianic Christian sect from Judaism.

The Bible gives little about Paul's family. There is mention of Paul's "sister's son" in *Acts* 23:16. He refers to his father as "a Pharisee, the son of a Pharisee" in *Acts* 23:6, and he refers to his mother in Romans 16:13 as among those at Rome. *Acts* identifies Paul as from the city of Tarsus (in present-day south-central Turkey), well known for its intellectual environment [*Acts* 21:39]. In fact, it was the location of one of the greatest universities at the time.

Historian Howard Clark Key states that, "Strabo, the historical geographer of the period, ranked Tarsus even above Athens and Alexandria as a center of intellectual life." Kee finds ideals of Stoicism in the *Epistles of Paul*, and proposes that Paul was undeniably influenced by the teachers of Stoicism in Tarsus at that time. Such a "center of intellectual life" would be the ideal place for a revised, Hellenized story of Christianity to arise.

There is a detailed history of Paul's life, much of which comes from his own writings, which would have a great influence on later important theologians in the Church. Augustine, who was a follower of the dualistic teachings of Manichaeism, before becoming a Christian, seems to owe a great deal to the theological ideas of Paul. Augustine's foundational work on grace, predestination, and original sin all align with writings attributed to Paul, particularly *Romans*. In the Reformation, Martin Luther based his ideas about faith on Paul's teachings.

We are told that Paul, also known as the 13th apostle, was originally named "Saul," known to be a Jewish name. I would propose that the name, Paul, is a Romanized version of – or perhaps a composite of more than one – powerful figure of early Christianity. Paul's teachings may have included the general format that has come down to us in modern times, however, with the likelihood of later additions to his actual text.

We assume that Paul cannot be James or Peter, since Paul had a confrontation with them both over allowing Gentiles to relax the standards of the requirements set by Mosaic Law.". We also assume that Paul cannot be Stephen, since it is said that Stephen's attackers cast their clothing at the feet of the young Saul. Stephen, like James, was stoned by the Jews for calling Jesus the "gate" and the Son of God.

It is possible to make deductions about true identities, but care must be taken in making assumptions in ruling out identities; one must stay open to the idea that, in the Gospel narratives, alter egos were presented, in order to tell a difficult-to-tell story, and multiple identities were often used to represent the same person, while at other times, names may have been conflated to confuse the issue. This seems to be exactly what happened, which makes it quite a challenging process to decipher the "Gospel Truth." The puzzle often ends up with holes, where information is missing, or with overlapping pieces that confuse the issue.

THE CONVERSION OF PAUL

In *Acts*, when Paul had the vision that led to his conversion on the Road to Damascus, the Lord called out to him, saying, "Saul, Saul", in the Hebrew tongue, and later, in a vision to Ananias of Damascus, "the Lord" referred to him as "Saul, of Tarsus". The Hebrew name Saul (or Saulus as he was called by Josephus) is said by some to be the equivalent of the Herodian name of "Phasael".

Paul claimed to be "of the stock of Israel, of the tribe of Benjamin, an Hebrew of the Hebrews; as touching the law, a Pharisee," (*Romans* 11:1 KJV). According to Jerome, Paul's family was not originally from Tarsus, but moved there from Galilee. Paul was named for the most prominent member of the tribe of Benjamin – King Saul.

Interestingly, where Jesus is said to have given Simon the name Peter, Saul uses the name "Paul" after his conversion to Christianity. In *Acts* 13:9, the name-change is indicated, without any explanation: " ... Saul, (who also is called Paul,) ... " Some scholars say that this is an indication of his transformation due to his vision of the Lord. He is called Paul in all other Bible books where he is mentioned. And yet, the change from a Hebrew to a Gentile name may have come after he started preaching to the Gentiles, which came much later.

Until he was about 30 years old, Saul was said to be an outspoken critic of the new cult of unconventional Jews following the teachings of Jesus. As he describes it, he was converted to Christianity when, on the road to Damascus, he experienced a mystical vision of the Lord. The *Acts of the Apostles* states that he lost his sight for three days, and when, with the reluctant help of Ananias of Damascus (who is said to be other than Ananias of Jerusalem), he recovered and became a zealous teacher of the faith. Though it seems that he was not one of Jesus' disciples, his claim to the title of apostle is: "Have I not seen Jesus Christ our Lord?" (I *Corinthians* 9:1).

In this life-changing event on the road to Damascus, which caused Paul to convert to Christianity, he heard a voice saying, "I am Jesus, whom you persecute, arise and go into the city." (*Acts,* Chapter 9) It goes on: "Saul, Saul, why dost thou persecute me? And they that were with me saw indeed the light, and were afraid, but they heard not the voice ... " (*Acts* 22:6-11).

In an interesting correlation to the Old Testament story of King Saul(1 *Samuel* 28), which may have some bearing on the story of Saul/Paul's conversion, King Saul seeks out the Witch of Endor, a woman described as a "ventriloquist." The witch claims to have seen something, but Saul only heard a disembodied voice. In the Jewish texts called the *Yalkut Shim'oni* it suggests that "necromancers" can see the spirits of the dead but are unable to hear their speech, while the person for whom the spirit was summoned hears the voice but fails to see anything.[66] Was the story of Paul's conversion a reference to the story of King Saul? King Saul was the righteous and obedient king; who became disobedient and fell from God's favor. The ghost of Samuel gives Saul no counsel, but only predicts his doom.

In the story of Saul/Paul's conversion, Jesus told Saul, blinded by the vision, to go into the city and wait. Jesus later spoke to Ananias in a vision, and told him to go to the "street which is called Straight", and ask "in the house of Judas for one called Saul, of Tarsus". (*Acts* 9:11) This also is said to be other than Judas Iscariot – but why the coincidence with names from the Jerusalem community?

Ananias objected to helping Saul, complaining to the Lord that Saul had been persecuting "thy saints"; but the Lord told him that Saul was "a chosen vessel unto me, to bear my name before the Gentiles, and kings, and the children of Israel". (*Acts* 9:15) What does this mean – that Saul was a vessel to bear the Lord's name? Ananias complied by laying his hands on Saul. The "scales" of dead tissue on the surface of Saul's eyes fell off, and his sight was restored. After additional instruction, Saul was baptized. (*Acts* 9:18; 22:16) Much later, he is indicated by Luke as "Saul, who is called Paul," and thereafter, the name Paul is used.

Also interesting is that Ananias, the name of the one in Damascus who restored Paul's eyesight, though he is said to be a separate person, is the same name as that of the powerful high priest of Jerusalem, who brought Jesus before the Sanhedrin before turning him over to the Romans, and who also tried Paul.

Paul describes himself as being "extremely zealous" in persecuting Christians, before his conversion. Peter seems to show the propensity for zealotry of a political nature. John's intensity on repentance and judgment prepared the way for Jesus' teaching of a merciful and loving God, but he also had a zealous nature. In *Acts* 8:3, it states that Saul "made havoc of the church, entering into every house, and haling men and women, committed them to prison." It was written that he participated in the stoning of Christianity's first martyr, St. Stephen (from the Greek, "Stephanos," meaning "crown, garland.") Though Stephen is known as the Protomartyr, the most commonly known stoning of a Christian was that of James, the "brother of Jesus".

Hans-Joachim Schoeps has proposed that the stoning of James at the command of Ananus (the younger), also referred to in *The Recognitions* as an assault on James by Saul on the temple steps, was supplanted by the story of the stoning of Stephen. He proposes that the name, Stephen, was borrowed from a Roman official beaten by Jewish insurgents whom Josephus depicts ambushing outside the city walls.[67]

The name, "Stephen," meaning "crown" suggests both the "crown" of long hair worn by the Nazirite (which James was, according to early church writers) and the crown of martyrdom. James' declaration of the Son of Man at the right hand of God in heaven, as well as his "Christ-like" prayer for his persecutors were also attributed to Stephen. *Acts* 7:52 states, "Which of the prophets have not your fathers persecuted? and they have slain them which shewed before of the coming of the Just One; of whom ye have been now the betrayers and murderers!" The Just One is often seen to mean James, but it is hard to tell if Stephen speaks in reference to his own impending death, or if this line is meant to indicate that James was already dead when "Stephen" was stoned.

As soon as Paul's sight was regained *Acts* tells us that "He straightway preached Christ in the synagogues, that he is the Son of God. But all that heard him were amazed, and said; Is not this he that destroyed them which called on this name in Jerusalem, and came hither for that intent, that he might bring them bound unto the chief priests? But Saul increased the more in strength, and confounded the Jews which dwelt at Damascus, proving that this is the very Christ." Though it doesn't give the reason, it says, "And after that many days were fulfilled, the Jews took counsel to kill him: But their laying await was known of Saul. And they watched the gates day and night to kill him. Then the disciples took him by night, and let him down by the wall in a basket."

It states in *2 Corinthians 11:32* that, "in Damascus the governor (ethnarch) under Aretas the king kept the city of the Damascenes with a garrison, desirous to apprehend me; and through a window in a basket was I let down by the wall, and escaped his hands." The ethnarch did it to please the Jews, who (*Acts* 9:24) "watched the gates day and night to kill" Paul.

Saul fled to Jerusalem, where, " ... he assayed to join himself to the disciples: but they were all afraid of him, and believed not that he was a disciple. But Barnabas took him, and brought him to the apostles, and declared unto them how he had seen the Lord in the way, and that he had spoken to him, and how he had preached boldly at Damascus in the name of Jesus. And he was with them coming in and going out at Jerusalem. And he spake boldly in the name of the Lord Jesus, and disputed against the Grecians: but they went about to slay him. Which when the brethren knew, they brought him down to Caesarea, and sent him forth to Tarsus." Things finally settled down at this point, "Then had the churches rest throughout all Judaea and Galilee and Samaria, and were edified; and walking in the fear of the Lord, and in the comfort of the Holy Ghost, were multiplied."

During his time in Damascus, Paul writes of an affliction that he terms "a thorn in his flesh." In 2 *Corinthians* he states, "And lest I should be exalted above measure through the abundance of the revelations, there was given to me a thorn in the flesh, the messenger of Satan to buffet me, lest I should be exalted above measure. For this thing I besought the Lord thrice, that it might depart from me. And he said unto me, My grace is sufficient for thee: for my strength is made perfect in weakness." This is variously interpreted to be some kind of illness, a physical or mental infirmity such as Mary Magdalene's seven demons, or a spiritual challenge as when Jesus was tested by Satan.

He states, "Most gladly therefore will I rather glory in my infirmities, that the power of Christ may rest upon me. Therefore I take pleasure in infirmities, in reproaches, in necessities, in persecutions, in distresses for Christ's sake: for when I am weak, then am I strong." This is seen to be an early endorsement of the path of suffering as a necessary part of Christian worship.

There is an interesting footnote to this chapter of *Acts*, having to do with Peter's healing abilities, "And it came to pass, as Peter passed throughout all quarters, he came down also to the saints which dwelt at Lydda. And there he found a certain man named Aeneas, which had kept his bed eight years, and was sick of the palsy. And Peter said unto him, Aeneas, Jesus Christ maketh thee whole: arise, and make thy bed. And he arose immediately. And all that dwelt at Lydda and Saron saw him, and turned to the Lord." The name Aeneas is said to be the original name of King Aretas, whose daughter was forsaken by Herod Antipas in favor of his brother's wife. This was the situation that John the Baptist complained about – it is said that John was beheaded because of his adamant opposition to Herod's actions. The daughter of Aretas fled to her father in Damascus, sometime after 34 CE.

Paul's conversion, "On the Road to Damascus," is, generally, said to have occurred around 34 CE. After 3 years in the wilderness in Arabia, he is said to have fled from the governor of Damascus in 37, then continued to travel the region, preaching to the Gentiles, before being taken to Rome, where he was beheaded for his teachings.

It is quite possible that there are many truths hidden in the narratives of Paul's life. However, it seems that many of the puzzle pieces of early Christianity have been altered to such an extent that it is nearly impossible to put together a coherent picture of the truth.

PAUL'S MINISTRY

The historical reliability of the *Acts of the Apostles*, has been greatly debated by biblical scholars and historians of Early Christianity. German theologian Adolf von Harnack in particular was very critical of the accuracy of *Acts*, though according to modern scholarship, his allegations of its inaccuracies have been described as greatly exaggerated.[68]
A key topic of debate is the historicity of Luke's depiction of Paul. There are early writings that mention Jesus and the origins of Christianity such as the *Antiquities of the Jews* by the Roman-Jewish historian Josephus, and the *Church History* of Eusebius of the 4th century.

According to the majority viewpoint, *Acts* describes Paul differently from how Paul describes himself, both factually and theologically. *Acts* differs with Paul's letters on important issues, such as the Law, Paul's apostleship, and relationship to the Jerusalem church. Scholars generally prefer Paul's account over that in *Acts,* but the conservative view is that the *Acts* is accurate.

Theologian, Holland Lee Hendrix believes that the author of *Luke/ Acts* was a disciplined historian, who was writing for a wealthy benefactor. His perspective proposes that the stories of Paul's life were "embellished" with novelistic tendencies and poetic license, in the manner of the epic poems and prose of ancient Greece. In *Luke/Acts* these stories had become "thoroughly Romanized." He writes, "In fact, it's such a good story that many scholars have compared it to the novelistic literature of the time, and have interpreted *Luke/Acts* as really an early Christian romance, with all the ingredients of romance, down to shipwrecks and exotic animals and exotic vegetation, cannibalistic natives – all kinds of embellishments that one finds in the romance literature of the time." [69]

We know that, in the early centuries, there were attempts to "harmonize" the Gospels, that is, to mingle the differing stories into one story, as in the *Diatessaron,* compiled by Tatian in the 2nd century. Was Paul, in a similar manner, a composite figure, meant to embody important early Christian figures in one, literally, "Romanized" personage?

Acts states that after his conversion, he stayed on in Damascus. "But Saul kept increasing in strength and confounding the Jews who lived at Damascus by proving that this Jesus is the Christ." Legend has it that John the Baptist's head was venerated in Damascus, but it isn't clear at what point the relic was translated to Damascus. By the 4th century CE, the temple of Jupiter in Damascus was the largest temple in Roman Syria, meant to rival the Jewish Temple. In 391, it was converted by the Christian emperor

Theodosius I, into a Christian basilica, which became. in the 6th century, the Cathedral of Saint John. In the 7th century, when Damascus fell into the hands of the Arabs, the cathedral was renovated into the Ummayad Mosque, which became the fourth holiest site in Islam. John the Baptist was an honored prophet of Islam, and his relics (his head) are still venerated there.

Paul preached in Thessalonica where, "many were saved," but he was driven out of town. In Lystra, Paul was stoned for his teachings, and left for dead, though he managed to survive. (*Acts* 14:19) Paul, it seems, was in good company – he is not the only one to give a new teaching that went against Mosaic Law, or to suffer stoning for his teachings. In *John* 10:30, when Jesus went into Solomon's Porch at the Temple, on the "Feast of Dedication," the Jews surrounded and questioned him. He told them that he was the "Good Shepherd." Jesus said, "My sheep hear my voice, and I know them, and they follow me: And I give unto them eternal life; and they shall never perish, neither shall any man pluck them out of my hand. My Father, which gave them me, is greater than all; and no man is able to pluck them out of my Father's hand." He ended by saying, "I and my father are one. Then the Jews took up stones again to stone him."

Solomon's Porch or Portico (*John* 10:23; *Acts* 3:11; 5:12), was a colonnade, or cloister, located on the eastern side of the Temple's Outer Court (Women's Court) in Jerusalem, named after Solomon, King of Israel, and not to be confused with the Royal Stoa, which was on the southern end of the Temple Mount platform.

The author of *Acts* describes Paul's travels as three separate journeys. The first, led initially by Barnabas, takes Paul from Antioch to Cyprus, to southern Asia Minor (Anatolia), and back to Antioch. In Cyprus, Paul rebukes and blinds Elymas the magician who criticized their teachings. After which, Paul is described as the leader of the group. In Pamphylia, where the Jewish contingent reacted to his preaching by rioting in the streets, Paul announced a change in his mission, which from then on, would focus on the Gentiles. [*Acts* 13:13-48]

This might be seen as the initial break between Judaism and the "Jewish sect" of Christianity. However, we must keep in mind that this change in direction, away from Mosaic Law, was actually set in motion by Jesus: in the earliest writings, it is recorded that Jesus brought a "New Covenant" to the Jewish people, and that Jesus was also attacked and decried by the Orthodox Jews for breaking with the old traditions. It is, in fact, said to be one reason for his trial and crucifixion.

When a famine occurred in Judea, Paul and Barnabas journeyed to Jerusalem somewhere between 45 to 46 CE, to deliver financial support from the thriving Christian community at Antioch. The earliest dispersion of the followers of Jesus was to Pella, but, according to *Acts*, Antioch had a large population of early adherents of the faith. It became an alternative community of the faith, after Stephen's death by stoning, and it was here that the followers of Jesus were first called "Christians."

Most scholars agree that there was an important meeting between Paul and the Jerusalem church sometime between 48 to 50 CE. It is described in *Acts* 15:2 and is usually seen as the same event mentioned by Paul in *Galatians* 2:1. The key question raised was whether or not Gentile converts needed to be circumcised. Paul claims in his letter to the *Galatians* that Peter (called "Cephas"), James, and John accepted his mission to the Gentiles: "And when James, Cephas, and John, who seemed to be pillars, perceived the grace that was given unto me, they gave to me and Barnabas the right hands of fellowship; that we should go unto the heathen (that is, the Gentiles), and they unto the circumcision (meaning the Jews)."

Antioch was a major focus for Paul's evangelizing. Paul stood firm that Gentile converts did not need to become Jews to follow Christ: that they did not need to get circumcised, or follow Jewish dietary restrictions. However unorthodox Paul's teachings were, in *Romans*, he also saw the value of the Law as a moral guide.

There is an interesting account in *Acts of the Apostles*: "In the time of Felix it was said to Paul by the centurion in Jerusalem, when the multitude of the Jews raised a disturbance against the apostle, 'Art not thou he who before these days made an uproar, and led out into the wilderness four thousand men that were murderers?' " It is hard to determine what reference is being made in this comment.

Josephus gave an unflattering account of Judas and the Zealot Movement in *Antiquities*. Though Josephus was a general in Galilee during the Jewish war, he surrendered to Roman troops (some saw him as a traitor). His books were written under the patronage of the Roman emperor, and in many instances, reflected an undeniably Roman attitude. Whenever Josephus uses the word "robbers" (*lestai* in Greek), he is speaking of "revolutionaries against Rome." This word is used in the *Gospel of Mark* to describe those who were crucified alongside of Jesus, which makes them not common thieves, as we might think, but rather assigns them the same crime with which the Sanhedrin had accused Jesus. Perhaps they not thieves, but rather revolutionaries, as Jesus was seen to be – three revolutionaries?

Early church scholar and theologian, Eusebius. recounts a story from Josephus that may be related, "While Claudius was still emperor, it happened that so great a tumult and disturbance took place in Jerusalem at the feast of the Passover, that thirty thousand of those Jews alone who were forcibly crowded together at the gate of the temple perished, being trampled underfoot by one another. Thus, the festival became a season of mourning, for all the nation, and there was weeping in every house. These things are related literally by Josephus." Since Josephus states that this disturbance took place in 48 CE, while Cumanus was procurator of Judea, and Paul's journey to Jerusalem is given as somewhere between 48 and 50, it is possible that he had some connection to the mentioned events.

Cumanus brought extra troops to Jerusalem to prevent unruliness among the great mass of people, which Josephus diplomatically explains, was the custom at the time of the Passover feast. One of the soldiers, intending to insult the Jews, conducted himself indecently, which caused such an uproar that the procurator felt it best to collect his troops upon the temple hill. Here, again, Josephus has given the Romans an innocent role in events. They were not threatening the people – it was the crowd's own fear that caused the problem. Seeing the soldiers amassed on the hill, so greatly alarmed the huge crowds assembled there that they fled in all directions, trampling each other to death in their efforts to escape. (Josephus, *War of the Jews*, 2.227) Josephus' account would appear to be a kind of white-washing of events.

Josephus, in his *Jewish War*, gives the number of the slain as ten thousand, in his later account in *Antiquities*, as twenty thousand (a considerable jump, to be sure). Since Josephus had a habit of exaggerating numbers, it is hard to say which number is closer to the truth. If it were only ten thousand, that would be a horrifying number of people who died of trampling.

Eusebius follows these accounts with an estimate of thirty thousand; in any case, it was a very large number. To further muddy the picture, Valesius writes that this disturbance took place under Quadratus in 52 CE, while Eusebius, in his Chronicle, gives the eighth year of Claudius (48 CE), and Orosius, VII, gives the seventh year.

Acts states that around 50–52 CE, Paul spent 18 months in Corinth, where Aquila and Priscilla became faithful followers, helping Paul in his missionary journeys. The couple followed Paul and his companions to Ephesus (in modern-day Turkey), starting up one of the strongest and most faithful churches of that time.

In 52, the missionaries sailed to Caesarea, and then traveled north to Antioch. They stayed for about a year before leaving on their third missionary journey. In this journey, Paul traveled through Galatia and Phrygia, and then back to Ephesus, which had, by then, become an important center for early Christianity, and where he stayed for almost 3 years.

There is an early tradition that Mary, Mother of Jesus, traveled to Ephesus, after the time of Jesus. In present-day Ephesus, there is a house that has, since the 19th century, been venerated as the "House of the Virgin Mary." The site is visited by many pilgrims who consider it the place where Mary lived until her assumption. The *Gospel of John* states that Mary went to live with the Disciple whom Jesus loved, whom many identify as John the Evangelist. Both Irenaeus and Eusebius of Caesarea wrote in their histories that John later went to Ephesus, which provides a basis for the early belief that Mary went to Ephesus with John, and lived there until her death. Other traditions propose that she died in Jerusalem, from where she was assumed into heaven.

In *Acts* 19, in Ephesus, Paul is said to have performed numerous miracles, healings and exorcisms. From there, he spread missionary activity into more distant regions. While living in Ephesus, Paul wrote 4 letters to the church in Corinth, admonishing them for their pagan behavior. Paul left Ephesus after an attack from a local silversmith resulted in a pro-Artemis riot involving most of the city. Here, there is mention of an artefact which fell from the heavens: "And when the townclerk had appeased the people, he said, Ye men of Ephesus, what man is there that knoweth not how that the city of the Ephesians is a worshipper of the great goddess Diana, and of the image which fell down from Jupiter?" (*Acts* 19:35)

Paul next traveled through Macedonia into Achaea, and, as he was getting ready to leave for Syria, the threat of Jews who were plotting against him, forced him to go back through Macedonia. It is believed that he visited Corinth again, for three months around 56–57 CE. On the way back to Jerusalem, Paul and his companions also went to: Philippi, Troas, Miletus, Rhodes, and Tyre. Paul stayed for a time in Caesarea, where he and his companions joined Philip the Evangelist, before eventually returning to Jerusalem. Paul arrived in Jerusalem in 57 with a second collection of money for the community there. Eusebius, in *Historia Ecclesiae* states that, "Paul also makes mention of the same James the Just, where he writes, '...Other of the apostles saw I none, save James the Lord's brother.'"

Acts reports that he was warmly received, but it goes on to recount how he was interrogated by James for his teachings. In 18:12-16, Paul is accused of "persuading...people to worship God in ways contrary to the law." Paul underwent a purification ritual in order to give the Jews no grounds to bring accusations against him for not following their law. However, he continued to preach that circumcision, Jewish dietary restrictions, and other requirements of the Torah were not requirements of salvation. Instead, he insisted that belief in Jesus as the Savior was the requirement for salvation – which many see as the cause of a rift with the Jews.

Paul's appearance at the Temple, in Jerusalem, nearly incited a riot, and he narrowly escaped being killed by the crowd by being taken into custody. He was a prisoner in Caesarea for almost two years, until 59 CE, at which time a new governor reopened his case. Accused of treason, he appealed to Caesar, claiming his right as a citizen of Rome to appear before a proper court and to defend himself against the charges.

If Paul were a Jewish citizen, he would not have had the right to a court appearance. Paul says he was Roman citizen "by birth". (*Acts* 22.27-8) *Acts* makes a clear reference to the connection, "Now there were in the church that was at Antioch certain prophets and teachers ... which had been brought up with Herod the tetrarch *and Saul.* (*Acts* 13.1) This also confirms Paul's Herodian connection.

A centurion told the colonel of Paul's Roman citizenship, and he went to great lengths to provide a suitable escort for his safety, "Get ready a detachment of two hundred soldiers, seventy horsemen and two hundred spearmen to go to Caesarea at nine tonight. Provide horses for Paul so that he may be taken safely to Governor Felix." (*Acts* 23:24)

On the way to Rome, Paul and his companions, were, temporarily, shipwrecked on Malta, and finally, around 60 CE, were brought, by sea, to Rome, where Paul would stand trial for his alleged crimes. On the foundering ship that carried Paul to Italy for his trial before Caesar, some of the men wanted to kill the prisoners, rather than take a chance on their escape during the shipwreck, but there was a centurion that "wanted to spare Paul's life and kept them from carrying out their plan."

So, we see in this narrative that, aside from Festus, who sided with the Jews, it was the Jews who wished to kill Paul, and the Romans who took great care to see that Paul was treated fairly. It is significant that it was a Roman soldier who protects Paul on the voyage to Rome.

In Chapter 24 of *Acts* it speaks of Paul's later trial before Festus, after being incarcerated under Felix for two years in Rome. "And Festus said, King Agrippa, and all men which are here present with us, ye see this man, about whom all the multitude of the Jews have dealt with me, both at Jerusalem, and also here, crying that he ought not to live any longer. But when I found that he had committed nothing worthy of death, and that he himself hath appealed to Augustus, I have determined to send him. Of whom I have no certain thing to write unto my lord. Wherefore I have brought him forth before you, and specially before thee, O king Agrippa, that, after examination had, I might have somewhat to write. For it seemeth to me unreasonable to send a prisoner, and not withal to signify the crimes laid against him."

In like manner, Jesus, in his trial before Pilate, is found innocent by Pilate, and it is the Jewish mobs that insist on his execution. Pilate, literally, "washes his hands" of the situation, and leaves the responsibility for Jesus death to the Jewish people.

Acts states that Paul, while under house arrest and awaiting trial, preached in Rome for two years. Since it is not clearly documented what happened after this time, some speculate that Paul was freed by Nero and continued to preach in Rome. Others propose that Paul traveled to other countries, including Spain and Britain, before his martyrdom. Altogether, Paul spent about 5½ to 6 years of his life in imprisonment

His trial is assumed to have ended in his acquittal sometime around 65 after being held for several years, at which point it seems he went to Macedonia. Upon his return to Rome, he was arrested once again and imprisoned. Because he was a Roman citizen, he received a different punishment than non-Roman citizens who were usually crucified, and, it is said, was beheaded between 66-68 CE, at *Aqua Salviae.*

Eusebius of Caesarea, in the 4th century, gives an account of Paul's death by beheading, in the reign of the Roman Emperor Nero. (*Ecclesiastical History,* 2, 25, 5) This event has been dated either to the year 64, when Rome was devastated by a fire, or a few years later, to 67. The *San Paolo alle Tre Fontane church* (Three Fountains Abbey) was built on the location where the execution was believed to have taken place. Legend says that his head bounced three times, and a fountain sprung up at each stop – hence the name Tre Fontane, or Three Fountains. His body was taken about two miles away to be buried in land owned by a friend, where the Basilica of St. Paul Outside the Walls was later built.

The testimony of ecclesiastical antiquity is that Paul's death by beheading at Rome happened about the same time that St. Peter was crucified there. Dionysius, bishop of Corinth, 170 CE, says that Peter and Paul went to Italy and taught there together, and suffered martyrdom about the same time.

The earliest allusion to the death of St. Paul comes in a letter written by Clement of Rome, around 90 CE. It states: "By reason of jealousy and strife, Paul, by his example, pointed out the prize of patient endurance. After that he had been seven times in bonds, had been driven into exile, had been stoned, had preached in the East and in the West, he won the noble renown which was the reward of his faith, having taught righteousness unto the whole world and having reached the farthest bounds of the West; and when he had borne his testimony before the rulers, so he departed from the world and went unto the holy place, having been found a notable pattern of patient endurance."

It must be noted that Paul was accused of treason, tried in a court of Rome and then beheaded. It does not say that Paul was found guilty of treason, but events indicate that this was the outcome of the trial. Treason would have been seen as the highest possible crime against the Roman Empire. It seems that being found guilty of treason would have meant the most heinous treatment and the most reviled historical references, at least in Rome. In fact, one might be declared *damnatio memoriae* – one's name might be wiped from the records. There is no history of such recriminations, beyond the fact that Paul was tried and beheaded.

It is interesting that later writers like Jerome spoke only of the brotherhood between Peter and Paul as leaders of the Church, and not of their disagreements. Jerome's commentary indicates that Peter was crucified upside down to avoid being crucified in the manner of Jesus, which is seen as confirmation that Jesus was crucified. Regarding Paul's death, Jerome states, "He then in the fourteenth year of Nero on the same day with Peter was beheaded at Rome for Christ's sake and was buried in the Ostian way." (*De Viris Illustribus (On Illustrious Men),* Chapter 5)

This comment is unique to Jerome, and seems to be an embellishment to the story of the great Apostles' deaths. This story validates the succession of the Church of Rome from its two most famous founders, but perhaps more importantly, it reinforces, by association, that, though Paul was buried in the Ostian Way, and Peter in the Triumphal Way (with all its connotations), Paul is, in fact, on a par with Peter – he is his equal, and his apostleship is as valid as Peter's.

JOHN AND MARY

The phrase, "the disciple whom Jesus loved" is used six times in the *Gospel of John* but not at all in the other Gospels of the New Testament. John 21:24 states that the *Gospel of John* is based on the written testimony of this disciple, named John. Since the 1st century, John the Evangelist, one of the disciples of Jesus, has been associated with the "Beloved Disciple" in the *Gospel of John*. Some scholars propose that this disciple was Mary Magdalene, and that alterations were made to the story in the 2nd century to make Mary a separate figure from the Beloved Disciple. It could, reasonably, be an alteration to the text that puts both Mary Magdalene and the Beloved Disciple at the tomb at the same time. The narrative in *John* 20 is certainly awkward. Why is the "other disciple" not named? In the unsanctioned (apocryphal) text of the *Gospel of Mary*, Mary (assumed by most to be Mary Magdalene) is often noted as being loved "more than the other disciples."

The apocryphal *Gospel of Phillip*, speaks of "Magdalene, the one who was called his companion." (In Islam, the Prophet's closest followers are called not disciples, but companions.) In this gospel, also, it is mentioned that Jesus kisses Mary often on her [...missing text] translated as "on her lips" or "on her mouth." This is a metaphor often used to describe the transference of wisdom teachings from one to another. *The Song of Songs*, which is considered to be an allegorical text, described so in the Jewish *Mishnah* of around 200 CE, has a similar line, "Let him kiss me with the kisses of his mouth: for thy love is better than wine."

In one place in the narrative, of the *Gospel of Phillip* the other disciples question, "Why do you love her more than all of us?" Jesus responds, "When a blind man and one who sees are both together in the darkness, they are no different from one another. When the light comes, then he who sees will see the light, and he who is blind will remain in darkness". This is high praise of Mary Magdalene's dedication and wisdom. The other disciples, including Peter, are "the blind", and Mary Magdalene is the one "who sees." In the *Gospel of Mary*, she is the "woman who knew the all".

The *Pistis Sophia* states: "In the place where I shall be, there will be also my twelve ministers, but Mary Magdalene and *John the virgin* shall be higher than all the disciples." John the virgin – an interesting moniker to use for him. John and Mary are notable in the New Testament Gospels. Of course, we must question identities: John the disciple, John the Evangelist, John the Virgin, John the Baptist – all separate identities? Then we have the Marys: the Virgin Mary, Mother Mary, Mary of Bethany, Mary Magdalene. A confusing array of Johns and Marys indeed!

The lives of John the Baptist, and the Virgin Mary are woven together in the early *Gospels of Matthew* and *Mark*, the narratives moving back and forth between their lives, and their activities.

In *Luke*, we are given two prayers that relate to these two saints: the *Benedictus* – the "Canticle of Zacharias", and the *Magnificat* – the "Canticle of Mary." The *Magnificat*, the prayer from Luke's Gospel (1:46-55), is the Blessed Virgin's hymn of praise to the Lord: "My soul doth magnify the Lord, and my spirit hath rejoiced in God my Savior; Because He hath regarded the lowliness of His handmaid. For behold, henceforth all generations shall call me blessed; Because He who is mighty hath done great things for me...Even as he spoke to our fathers, to Abraham and to his posterity forever..." In the Magnificat, she doesn't mention the miraculous birth, but says that the great things that God did for her are similar to what he did with previous prophets.

It is clear from his actions in the *Gospels of Matthew* and *Luke*, that Zacharias was a priest of the Jewish Temple. However, his name does not appear on lists of the high priests from that era. It would seem that the name is a pseudonym for a high priest in the time period of John the Baptist's youth. Yet the *Protoevangelium of James, an apocryphal text from around 145 CE,* claims that Zacharias was the high priest, a position whose duties would be performed in the Holy of Holies. The text also conflates him with an earlier high priest, Zechariah, who was killed between the altar and the Temple.

The name Zacharias means, "God remembers." But the term, *zakah,* which means "offerings" may give a hint for this name. There was grumbling, found in various writings regarding the time period of Ananias", about how the high priests were taking the money donated to the Temple (the *zakah*) for their own use. It is possible that the name Zacharias references him as one of these high priests. The *Benedictus* was the prayer spoken by Zacharias upon the birth of his child, John the Baptist – extolling the arrival of the "prophet of the Lord," and the fulfillment of the prophecies of Abraham: "[The Lord] has raised up for us a mighty savior [horn of salvation], born of the house of his servant David...You, my child, shall be called the prophet of the Most High; for you will go before the Lord to prepare his way, to give his people knowledge of salvation by the forgiveness of their sins."

Luke records the furor raised by the people when Zacharias' wife, Elizabeth, named the child, "John": "And it came to pass, that on the eighth day they came to circumcise the child [in some versions it says 'what the Law of Moses commands']; and they called him Zacharias, after the name of his father. And his mother answered and said, Not so; but he shall be called John. And they said unto her, There is none of thy kindred that is called by this name." Zacharias had been struck dumb by the Angel Gabriel, because he doubted, when Gabriel told him so, that his wife could still conceive: "And they made signs to his father, how he would have him called. And he asked for a writing table, and wrote, saying, His name is John. And they marveled all...And fear came on all that dwelt round about them: and all these sayings were noised abroad throughout all the hill country of Judaea. And all they that heard them laid them up in their hearts, saying, What manner of child shall this be! And the hand of the Lord was with him."

What was so different about this child or this name that news of the birth, and his name should spread like wildfire throughout the countryside? If the unveiled secrets of the Da Vinci Code are to be believed – that John and Mary were one and the same, then Elizabeth naming the child "John" would, understandably, have been seen as quite unusual. If, as Dan Brown has suggested, it is true that Mary and John are one, then the two sets of parents must be integrated. According to the *Protoevangelium of James*, Zacharius, father of John, raised Mary in the Temple, from the age of three.

THE WEDDING AT CANA

The story of the wedding at Cana. in the New Testament – is noted for being the occasion of Jesus' first miracle – the changing of water into wine. Certain important details of the wedding are left very vague, such as, the identity of the groom and bride. Since the disciples attended, along with Jesus, and a woman (some say, his mother) who said to him, "They have no wine," and Jesus replied, "Oh Woman, what has this to do with me? My hour has not yet come." Still, he performed the miracle according to her wishes.

The identity of the bride and groom has been debated since early times. It had to be a couple that was involved with Jesus and his mission. Many believe that the "woman" was Mary, Mother of Jesus, making her the overseer of the wedding, and that it was, therefore, Jesus' wedding, presuming Mary Magdalene to be the bride. This version supports traditions of the *desposyni*, the descendants of Jesus, the supposed children of the Lord.

It does not appear that Jesus and Mary were married in the traditional sense, though there may have been an underlying metaphor in such a narrative. In this first miracle, the first outward display of the Jesus/Mary mission, one might say that they were "in union" with each other, but this Mary was the Magdalene, "companion" of the Lord.

There are other interpretations of the story. Simon the Zealot, born in Cana of Galilee, is often suggested for the role of bridegroom, because of his birthplace. Some scholars believe this to be the same Simon whom Jesus called "Peter", which seems quite plausible, while others do not. Some equate Simon Iscariot with Simon Peter, while others do not. The Sicarii, from which Iscariot may well derive, were extreme zealots, which would make the first pope much more political than would, perhaps, be seemly.

One folk tradition states that Jesus, his mother and disciples, came to Simon's wedding feast. When the wine ran out, Simon witnessed the miracle of the Lord changing water into wine, and was so profoundly affected that he left his bride in order to follow Christ. Many scholars say that this could not be Simon Peter, though it is clear that he was married at some point, as the *Gospel of Luke* describes the healing, by Jesus, of Peter's "mother-in-law".

Many artists through the centuries seem to make Peter the groom. In fact, in the guidelines for the *Manual of Greek Art* by Didron, the bridegroom is, by tradition, to have grey hair, and a round beard – the standard depiction of Peter in artworks in general. Giotto's painting of the *Wedding at Cana* demonstrates this standard, with a haloed Jesus at the head of the table, next to the young bride, and the haloed, grey-haired and bearded saint sitting next to her. A haloed woman is seated in the center of the table, facing the viewer, said to be Mary, Mother of Jesus.

There is an old Greek tradition that the marriage at Cana was that of John the Evangelist and Mary Magdalene. Anna Brownell attests to this tale from the 13th century when the passionate enthusiasm for Mary Magdalene was at its height. In this tradition, immediately after the wedding feast, much like two of the earliest monastics, Benedict (meaning "Blessed") and his twin-sister, Scholastica (meaning "scholar, rhetorician, orator"). St. John and Mary, "devoted themselves to an austere and chaste religious life, following Christ and ministered to him."

* * *

CHAPTER III. THE LIFE OF JESUS

JESUS THE CHRIST

In *Luke*, Jesus makes a rather sardonic comment, "John the Baptist came neither eating bread nor drinking wine; and you say: He hath a devil. The Son of man comes eating and drinking: and you say: Behold a man that is a glutton and a drinker of wine, a friend of publicans and sinners. And wisdom is justified by all her children" (*Luke* 7:33-35).

John was the last of the Jewish Prophets, an extreme ascetic, who chastised and castigated sinners, and Jesus was the new, more moderate one who proposed forgiveness of sins – but more than that, in Christian teachings Jesus was the *Messiah*. the "anointed", kingly one, the "Son of God", who fulfilled the prophecies of the Old Testament. Though John and Jesus were different in many ways, both were judged by non-believers. Jesus pointed out the judgmental attitudes toward both himself and his forerunner.

We don't hear much of John's youth in the Bible, but the idea of "the word of the Lord" coming to him in the desert is striking. The Quran says of John, "...and We gave him Wisdom even as a youth, And piety (for all creatures) as from Us, and purity: He was devout, And kind to his parents, and he was not overbearing or rebellious." (*Surah Maryam*, 12 -14)

In the same way, little is given of Jesus' early childhood. In the Aramaic bible, there are references to Mary's thoughts during Jesus' childhood. In *Luke* 2:19, when the shepherds were amazed by the things the Magi had to say about the baby, Jesus: "Mary kept all these words, pondering them in her heart." Jesus is mentioned in his presentation to Simeon in the temple, when Simeon tells Mary "Behold this child is set for the fall, and for the resurrection of many in Israel, and for a sign which shall be contradicted. And thy own soul a sword shall pierce, that, out of many hearts, thoughts may be revealed" (*Luke* 2:34-35). This passage is often interpreted as foreshadowing the sorrow of Mary at seeing her son crucified.

In Orthodox tradition, the Presentation of Christ is called, "The Meeting of Our Lord and God and Savior, Jesus Christ". The devout prophetess, Anna, also present at this occasion, gave thanks to the Lord, and spoke of him to all who sought redemption in Jerusalem.

Jesus is next mentioned at age 12, when his parents retrieved him from the Temple. According to the narrative, he had been, inadvertently, left behind by their caravan, and when, after a couple of days travel, he was discovered to be missing, they came back for him. The *Gospel of Luke* states: "Then, after three days they found Him in the temple, sitting in the midst of the teachers, both listening to them and asking them questions. And all who heard Him were amazed at His understanding and His answers. When they saw Him, they were astonished; and His mother said to Him, "Son, why have You treated us this way? Behold, Your father and I have been anxiously looking for You." And He said to them, "Why is it that you were looking for Me? Did you not know that I had to be in My Father's house?" But they did not understand the statement which He had made to them. And He went down with them and came to Nazareth, and He continued in subjection to them; and His mother treasured all these things in her heart." The Aramaic Bible translation is, "and His mother treasured all these words in her heart."

In Slavonic *Josephus*, a youthful John also spent time conversing with the Jewish elders. "And when he had been brought to Archelaus and the doctors of the Law had assembled, they asked him who he is and where he has been until then. John responded: "I am pure; [for] the Spirit of God hath led me on, and [I live on] cane and roots and tree-food. But when they threatened to put him to torture if he would not cease from those words and deeds, he nevertheless said: "It is meet for you [rather] to cease from your heinous works and cleave unto the Lord your God." *Luke* sums up eighteen years of John's life in just a few lines.

Jesus, in his youth, began a life of work and poverty, and he "was subject to them [Mary and Joseph]," and he "advanced in wisdom, and age, and grace with God and men" (*Luke* 2:51-52). There is a gap of nearly two decades before the narrative of Jesus' life continues. We jump from his "retrieval from the temple" at age 12, to the adult Jesus, who first comes into the picture when John speaks of him to his own disciples: "The next day John seeth Jesus coming unto him, and saith, "Behold the Lamb of God, which taketh away the sin of the world. This is he of whom I said, After me cometh a man which is preferred before me: for he was before me. And I knew him not: but that he should be made manifest to Israel, therefore am I come baptizing with water." (*John* 1:29-32)

Regarding the baptism of Jesus, the *Gospel of John* states, "And John bare record, saying, I saw the Spirit descending from heaven like a dove, and it abode upon him. And I knew him not: but he that sent me to baptize with water, the same said unto me, Upon whom thou shalt see the Spirit descending, and remaining on him, the same is he which baptizeth with the Holy Ghost. And I saw, and bare record that this is the Son of God." (John

1:33-34)

Yet again, John describes Jesus as the Lamb of God, "Again the next day after John stood, and two of his disciples; And looking upon Jesus as he walked, he saith, Behold the Lamb of God! And the two disciples heard him speak, and they followed Jesus. Then Jesus turned, and saw them following, and saith unto them, What seek ye? They said unto him, Rabbi, where dwellest thou? He saith unto them, Come and see. They came and saw where he dwelt, and abode with him that day: for it was about the tenth hour. One of the two which heard John speak, and followed him, was Andrew, Simon Peter's brother." (*John* 1:35-40)

This passage indicates that Andrew, a disciple of John, became, at John's prompting, the first follower of Jesus. It was Andrew who brought Peter into the circle of the followers of Jesus: "He first findeth his own brother Simon, and saith unto him, We have found the Messiah, which is, being interpreted, the Christ. And he brought him to Jesus. And when Jesus beheld him, he said, Thou art Simon the son of Jona: thou shalt be called Cephas, which is by interpretation, a stone (rock)." (*John* 1:40-42)

Jesus would also gather into the fold Phillip of Bethsaida, and, through him, Nathanael. Philip went to Nathanael, saying, "We have found him, of whom Moses in the law, and the prophets, did write, Jesus of Nazareth, the son of Joseph." When Jesus related to Nathanael that he knew what had happened prior to their meeting, that he had seen him under the fig tree, and that Phillip had called to him. Nathanael responded, "Rabbi, thou art the Son of God; thou art the King of Israel." (*John* 1:45-49)

Jesus chides Nathanael for believing only because of Jesus' gifts, telling him that he shall see much greater things than these, "Verily, verily, I say unto you, Hereafter ye shall see heaven open, and the angels of God ascending and descending upon the Son of man." (*John* 1:51) This passage seems to refer to the Transfiguration on the Mount.

Early Church Father, Origen, and others propose that this was Mount Tabor, in lower Galilee. However, the wording reminds us of Jacob's ladder, where Jacob laid his head down on a certain stone, "And he dreamed, and behold, there was a ladder set up on the earth, and the top of it reached to heaven; and behold, the angels of God were ascending and descending on it!" His description, referring so clearly to Jacob's experience makes one wonder if the Mount in question was not the Temple Mount, where the Holy of Holies, and perhaps, Jacob's stone resided.

Most scholars agree that John baptized Jesus at "Bethany beyond the Jordan," wading into the water from the eastern bank. The Precursor had been preaching and baptizing for some time, when Jesus came to be baptized by him. Some questioned why He "who did no sin" (1 *Peter* 2:22) should seek John's "baptism of penance for the remission of sins" (*Luke* 3:3). The Fathers of the Church say that this was preordained by the Father as the time when Jesus should become manifest to the world as the Son of God.

In the beliefs of Adoptionism, this moment, when the dove of the Holy Spirit descended upon Jesus, was believed to be the moment that Jesus became the Son of God. In his *Dialogue with Trypho*, in the early 2nd century, Justin Martyr said, "And when Jesus came to the Jordan, and being supposed to be the son of Joseph the carpenter ... the Holy Spirit, and for man's sake, as I said before, fluttered down upon Him, and a voice came at the time out of the heavens ... 'You are My Son, this day I have begotten you'." There were those in the early Church who saw this as the moment that Jesus was "begotten", made manifest, or born, as the Son of God.

By submitting to it, Jesus sanctioned John's baptizing. "But John stayed him, saying: I ought to be baptized by thee, and comest thou to me?" (*Matthew* 3:14). These words, implying that John knew Jesus, conflict with the declaration of John recorded in the Fourth Gospel: "I knew him not" (*John* 1:33). It is clear that John, at this point, at least recognized the holiness of Jesus, but why should he say this? John's mother, Elizabeth, was a cousin of Mary – how is it that John does not know Mary's son? John himself says that his ministry of baptism was in preparation for the coming of the Lamb of God, yet, in mentioning Jesus, he twice repeats that he "knew him not." This seems an odd thing to say, when scripture tells us that Mary visited John's mother, Elizabeth – her kinswoman – before the birth of either John or Jesus. Were they such distant cousins that they never saw each other? And even if this was the first time that John saw Jesus in many years, would it not be mentioned in the gospel that this was his cousin?

Some interpret this to mean that he didn't yet know him as "the Lamb of God," but it is a curious statement. Mary visited her "kinswoman" Elizabeth, but in the sparse details of the youth of Jesus, of John, and of Mary's entire life, there is no mention of any relationship between Elizabeth's son, John, and Jesus, "son of Mary." There is nothing to indicate a relationship between them from the time of birth until the moment of this declaration at Jesus' baptism by John. John only came out of the desert when he began his ministry. Jesus was raised in Nazareth, a small, dry, isolated village near the Sea of Galilee. "And the child grew and became strong, filled with wisdom. And the favor of God was upon him." (*Luke* 2:40) Perhaps there was no opportunity for the two to know each other.

However, we might relate this idea of "knowing," to Jesus' description of the Paraclete, in *John* 1:16, "...Even the Spirit of truth; whom the world cannot receive, because it seeth him not, neither knoweth him: but ye know him; for he dwelleth with you, and shall be in you." In this statement on the Paraclete, to "knoweth him" equates to having him dwell within you. Though Jesus is not said to be the Paraclete, it is an intriguing description.

Jesus is baptized by John: "Suffer it to be so now. For so it becometh us to fulfil all justice. Then he suffered him [allowed him]. And Jesus being baptized, forthwith came out of the water: and lo, the heavens were opened to him ... And, behold, a voice from heaven, saying: This is my beloved Son, in whom I am well pleased" (Matt 3:15-17).

The mission of John the Baptist, the final prophet of Judaism, was to prepare the way of the Lord; the mission of Jesus was to make a course-correction for an entire faith. Judaism taught that the Law was absolute, God was vengeful and punishing, that if you didn't do as God wanted, you would suffer the eternal fires of hell. Jesus taught that God is Merciful and Loving, and that all sins could be forgiven. More than this, all are meant to become "Christ-like." The Catholic Catechism makes a number of statements on this subject:

"The Word became flesh to make us 'partakers of the divine nature'."

"For the Son of God became man so that we might become God."

"The only-begotten Son of God, wanting to make us sharers in his divinity, assumed our nature, so that he, made man, might make men gods."[70]

John's childhood is not detailed in the Canonical Gospels or the Apocryphal texts. Little is said of John's early years beyond the statement in *Luke* that "...the child grew, and was strengthened in spirit; and was in the deserts, until the day of his manifestation to Israel." From there, we jump to his adulthood when "the *word of the Lord* was made unto John, the son of Zacharias, in the desert." This particular phrase brings up questions. In the *Gospel of John* there are many references to Jesus as "the Word." John used the word *Logos* to express a Hebrew concept that was used in the Old Testament. It is necessary to understand the varying meanings of the use of the terminology.

In Judaic theology, God revealed Himself to the prophets *by the Word.* The term is used in the sense of the creative or directive word or speech of God manifesting His power in the world of matter or mind. This term is used especially in the *Targum* as a substitute for "the Lord" when an anthropomorphic expression is to be avoided. The Old Testament used the term *dabir* to mean "the word" as inspired wisdom in spoken (oracular) prophecy or writings. It is an inspired idea or teaching.

The term *Memra,* is an Aramaic term used by the Rabbis to mean "the word" as divine wisdom in action, a form of divinity which was sometimes described as being distinct from God. The *Memra* was the agent of creation and the means of salvation. *Memra* is often substituted for the name of *Jehovah* in the Scriptures.

Some Christians see the term to mean the Second Person of the Trinity, that is, the Holy Spirit, proposing that it was *Memra* who appeared to Abraham at Mamre, to Jacob at Bethel, and to Moses on Mount Sinai. Daniel Boyarin, in his book*, Border Lines: The Partition of Judaeo-Christianity,* writes that within the traditions of the *Targum*, the *Memra* is a *hypostastis*, a person of the Godhead; in the rabbinic midrash, YHWH was the one who spoke and thus created the world. He comments on Nicene beliefs, "Athanasius and his fellows insist that God alone, without a mediator, without an angel, without a Logos, is the creator. Logos theology is, ultimately, as thoroughly rejected within Nicene Christianity as within orthodox rabbinism."[71] That may be so, however, Logos theology eventually became the teaching of mainstream Christianity, creating much upheaval along the way.

In the Old Testament "the Word" was a *theophany,* the means by which God became visible in the world. It is often equated with "the youth" (the Son), rather than "the old man" (the Father). Enoch was seen to be the human form of "the youth" who became Metatron, after his Divine transformation. In the *Gospel of John*, Jesus is equated with the "Creative Word", that is, the *memra* (Divine Wisdom in action) rather than the *dabir*, which is connected to prophecy, and the Holy of Holies in the Temple.

Boyarin suggests that, within Judaic writings, the idea of there being two deities was proposed even by highly respected rabbis, and required subsequent correction. The *Talmud* gives an account of the discrepancy in the teachings within Judaic theology, where David is equated with the Messiah. It relates that Akiva, the highly respected 2nd century rabbi proposed a resolution to the issue, "One passage says: His throne was fiery flames; and another Passage says: Till thrones were places, and One that was ancient of days did sit! — There is no contradiction: one [throne] for Him, and one for David; this is the view of R. Akiba."

However, the *Talmud* gives an opposing opinion as well from R. Jose the Galilean (rabbi Jose may indicate Joseph, "the Galilean". a clue to Joseph's true identity). He asked: "Akiba, how long wilt thou treat the Divine Presence as profane! Rather, [it must mean], one for justice and one for grace. Did he accept [this explanation from him, or did he not accept it? — Come and hear: One for justice and one for grace; this is the view of R. Akiba." (*Talmud - Mas. Chagigah* 14a).

The second argument puts David on an equal par with deity, which, in

Judaism, was in conflict with the theology of the One God. In the same way, this concept was problematic within Christianity, where Jesus is seen as the Messiah and the Son of God – part of the triune Godhead.

In Christianity, this idea of more than one identity within the Godhead was resolved first in the original Nicene Creed, which affirmed the co-essential divinity of the Son, and supported a "belief in the Holy Spirit", ending with anathemas against Arian propositions. Essentially, Arius's teachings opposed the theological views held by *Homoousian* Christians, regarding the nature of the Trinity and the nature of Christ. Arius proposed a belief that the Son of God did not always exist but was begotten within time by God the Father, therefore Jesus was not co-eternal with God the Father.

At the Second Ecumenical Council a later addition was made to the formula of the Nicene Creed, which became known as the doctrine of the Holy Trinity – One God in three equal persons: the Father, Son, and Holy Ghost. We might see this doctrinal stance as an outgrowth of attempts to resolve Old Testament issues, which includes the Old Man (the Father), the Youth (the Son – which is also to say, the *Logos*), and the *Shekinah* (the Holy Spirit). These difficulties were either inherited from Judaic teachings, or ongoing in both traditions when Judaism and Christianity were still one.

THE TRANSFIGURATION ON THE MOUNT

From the time of Origen onward, the location of the "Transfiguration" was often given to be Mount Tabor, 11 miles west of the Sea of Galilee. However, Origen said this in the 3rd century, and the Gospels do not give the name of the mountain.

The more traditional site of the ascension is considered to be the "Mount of Olives". Before the conversion of Constantine in 312 CE, early Christians honored the ascension of Christ in a cave on the Mount, and by 384, the ascension was venerated on the present site, uphill from the cave. In *The Mount of Olives*, Sophronius writes, "How surpassing sweet thou art, lofty Mountain, from which Christ the Lord looked into heaven!" He seems to speak of the Transfiguration on the Mount, when the heavens opened and God praised his "Beloved Son, in whom I am well-pleased".

The Transfiguration was a pivotal event recorded in the New Testament. In *Matthew's* account, Jesus and three of his apostles go to the "Mount of Transfiguration," where Jesus' closest disciples witness him speaking to the prophets, Elijah, and Moses, and becoming radiant with light. It is the same three apostles that go with Jesus to Gethsemane (also on the Mount of Olives) to pray, Peter, James, and John. They witness the heavens open and God speaking, as he also did in the narrative of the Baptism of Jesus. Peter and John briefly confirm the event in their own writings (II *Peter* 1:16-18, *John* 1:14).

In the 2nd century, Theodotus taught that it was at Jesus' baptism in the Jordan, that the Christ came down upon Jesus in the likeness of a dove. Therefore "wonders were not wrought in him" until the Spirit (which Theodotus called Christ) came down and was manifested in Him through baptism by John. Some have said that the Transfiguration on the Mount is the point where human nature united with God, in the full union of body and spirit, the joining of the temporal and the eternal, with Jesus becoming the bridge between heaven and earth.

The Gospels express this phenomenon of the Transfiguration by the word *metemorphothe,* which the Vulgate renders as *transfiguratus est*. The Synoptic Gospels explain that, "His face did shine as the sun and his garments became white as snow." This dazzling brightness emanating from Jesus seems to be attributed to this union of body and spirit: Divinity radiating from the human form.

It also parallels the narrative of Moses, speaking to God on Mt. Sinai, where he was given the Ten Commandments, "And it came to pass, when Moses came down from Mount Sinai with the two tables of testimony in Moses' hand ... that Moses wist not that the skin of his face shone while he talked with him. And when Aaron and all the children of Israel saw Moses, behold, the skin of his face shone; and they were afraid to come nigh him." (*Exodus* 34:29-30)

So, not only was Jesus seen with Moses on the Mount, when he spoke to God and received the New Covenant, but he also became radiant, as Moses did when receiving the Old Covenant. Old Testament scholar, Meredith Kline, proposed that the glory in both instances, although transcendently greater in Jesus' case, was the "reflection of the glory of the *Shekinah*." This aligns with the Jewish concept of the "indwelling presence of God," which, initiated by his baptism by John, was fully achieved by Jesus at the Transfiguration on the Mount.

Upon witnessing Jesus speaking with the prophets, "Then answered Peter, and said unto Jesus, Lord, it is good for us to be here: if thou wilt, let us make here three tabernacles; one for thee, and one for Moses, and one for Elias. While he yet spake, behold, a bright cloud overshadowed them: and behold a voice out of the cloud, which said, This is my beloved Son, in whom I am well pleased; hear ye him. And when the disciples heard it, they fell on their face, and were sore afraid. And Jesus came and touched them, and said,

Arise, and be not afraid. And when they had lifted up their eyes, they saw no man, save Jesus only. And as they came down from the mountain, Jesus charged them, saying, Tell the vision to no man, until the Son of man be risen again from the dead." (*Matthew* 17:1-9, KJV)

The Law, once given through Moses "by the ministry of angels," was now given through Jesus as the more perfect Law: the Law of Christ. In the apocryphal *Gospel of the Holy Twelve*, it states, "And Jesus said unto them, Behold, a new law I give unto you, which is not new but old. Even as Moses gave the Ten Commandments to Israel after the flesh, so also I give unto you the Twelve for the Kingdom of Israel after the Spirit. For who are the Israel of God? Even they of every nation and tribe who work righteousness, love mercy, and keep my commandments, these are the true Israel of God. And standing upon his feet, Jesus spake, saying: Hear O Israel, JOVA [Jehovah], thy God is One; many are My seers, and My prophets. In Me all live and move, and have subsistence."

Jesus goes on to give his New Covenant: "And Jesus said unto them... Lay no other burden on those that enter into the kingdom, but only these necessary things. This is the new Law unto the Israel of God, and the Law is within, for it is the Law of Love, and it is not new but old. Take heed that ye add nothing to this law, neither take anything from it." The Law of Moses was focused on prohibitions, or "thou-shalt-nots." In this apocryphal gospel, the Law of Jesus stated six laws in their negative orientation, and six laws in the positive – what was right and good to do. Certain actions are forbidden, and certain duties endorsed. In general, all are summed up in the greatest commandment of Christ in the Gospels, "Love ye one another." This list of laws does not appear in the Transfiguration narratives of the New Testament Gospels.

For some scholars, the New Covenant laws are demonstrated to supersede the Old ones; they are no longer written on stone, but will be "written in their hearts." (Hebrews 8:10) It goes on to state, "For I will be merciful to their unrighteousness, and their sins and their iniquities will I remember no more." In the making of a New Covenant, "he hath made the first old. Now that which decayeth and waxeth old is ready to vanish away." This idea, called "Supersessionism", or replacement theology, is a Christian doctrine which asserts that the New Covenant through Jesus Christ supersedes the Old Covenant God made with Moses. Many of those who follow this interpretation propose that it was Jesus' intent to abolish animal sacrifices, and other practices of Mosaic Law.

According to theologian, Larry D. Pettegrew, when God tore the veil in the Temple at Jesus' death, He "clearly indicated the [Old Covenant] was no longer in existence".[72] *Hebrews* 8:7-13 supports Pettegrew's position that the Old Covenant was made "obsolete" to make way for the New. This is a huge shift in beliefs, from a focus on Law on a legalistic – and judgmental – priesthood, to a focus on compassion, and the heart. The only way for such a shift to come about was to dissolve the old way, and to wholly replace it with a new one. The New Covenant describes an altogether different relationship between God and the Jewish people; this is no longer the Old Testament God of vengeance and punishment, but the New Testament God of mercy and love, as taught by Jesus. Though there very likely were corruptions in the writings of Paul, perhaps by writers other than Paul, it is rather unfair to say that he is the "first corrupter of the faith." The teachings of Jesus were, undeniably, a sea change from previous Jewish beliefs – in fact, a whole new belief system, based in love and forgiveness, which Paul also taught.

Martin Luther, one of the foremost leaders of the Reformation movement in the 16th century, read certain symbolic meanings into the Transfiguration, with Moses and Elijah representing the Law and the Prophets, proposing that their discourse with Jesus symbolizes that Jesus has fulfilled "the Law and the Prophets."

In Orthodox teachings, the Transfiguration is seen to include the three Persons of the Holy Trinity: God the Father who spoke from heaven, God the Son, who was transfigured, and God the Holy Spirit who appeared in the form of a cloud. In the Eastern Church, the Transfiguration is called the "Small Epiphany" – the "Great Epiphany" being the Baptism of Jesus, when God also spoke from heaven, and the Holy Spirit appeared in the form of a dove.

It is possible that these two events, the Baptism of Jesus and the Transfiguration on the Mount are the beginning and ending of the Ebionite Gospel, which Epiphanius claimed was "not wholly complete, but falsified and mutilated". Perhaps the missing parts of the gospel of this early Judeo-Christian sect was the first gospel and the other sections were added to the beginning and end of its text. It would make for a very neat and concise framework. Then Jesus' life would be book-ended with God's own statement of love for his Son: "This is my son, in whom I am well pleased." But it would also support the Adoptionist premise that Jesus became the "Son of God" with these events.

The Transfiguration narrative appears in the *Gospels of Mark, Matthew,* and *Luke*, but is not mentioned in *John*. However, in *John*, some scholars interpret the baptism of Jesus as his Transfiguration; throughout that gospel, one might say that Jesus is shown to be the "Living Word" and the embodiment of the Lord. According to Fr. Patrick Reardon, "In every scene of this gospel, then, from the Lord's appearance at John's baptismal site all the way through the Lord's death and Resurrection (*John* 7:39; 12:16,23,28), the divine light appears among men."

If, as many claim, the crucifixion did not happen, then the Transfiguration would be the point where Jesus left the earth plane for the realms of heaven. In other words, the Transfiguration on the Mount was the moment when Jesus ascended. However, in the New Testament this was a brief journey, from which he returned. This concept would align fairly well with the narrative of Muhammad's ascension. It is clear in scriptures that after each of these events, the respective prophets returned from the heavenly realms to the earth-plane.

The Ebionite Gospel is said to have made no mention of the genealogy of Jesus, or of the Nativity. It does not support the idea that Jesus' death was for the atonement of sin.

Plate 3 - The Transfiguration - Raphael

Paintings of the Transfiguration on the Mount often present a night-time landscape, with the light of the Transfigured Christ radiating out into the darkness.

In the painting of The Transfiguration by Raphael, in around 1516 to 1520, he has Jesus rising up into the heavenly realms, where he meets with the prophets of Judaism. Peter and John are seen on the height of the mountain below him. In the foreground can be seen a crowd of people, with one woman directly aligned below with Jesus above.

Across from her is an older man who resembles Peter. Did the master painter give us two sets of the two disciples? The arm position of Jesus resembles that in paintings of Simon Magus, who claimed he could levitate, and did so, until being brought down by the prayers of Peter and Paul. Cyril of Alexandria, in the sixth of his Catechetical Lectures, wrote that Magus "was actually careening through the air in a chariot drawn by demons," when the apostle's prayers "brought him to earth a mangled corpse."

Plate 4 - The Transfiguration - Ludovico Carraci

In the painting of the Transfiguration by Lodovico Carracci, in 1594, Jesus rises into the heavens, while Peter and John, fall back in astonishment. Here, John is aligned below with Jesus above. Jesus is looking down at Peter with one finger raised, in the manner of John the Baptist in some paintings by Da Vinci. Who is the figure on their knees on the right, in garments of gold? It is hard to tell if there is a beard or not.

Epiphanius, quoting the Old Testament, wrote of the Transfiguration: "Know ye not that ye are the temple of God, and *that* the Spirit of God dwelleth in you? 'It is manifest that the flesh which was of Mary and came of our race was also transformed into glory [in the Transfiguration], having acquired, in addition, the glory of the Godhead, heavenly honor and perfection and glory, which the flesh did not have from the beginning, but received there in the union with God the Word.', " Epiphanius, in *Panarion* 69, as quoted in *Concordia Triglotta*, p. 1115) This seems to be a reference to Mary, the "Temple of the Lord."

This commentary bears reflection. "...the flesh which was of Mary... was also transformed into glory [in the Transfiguration]." One might read this as meaning that the flesh which was birthed of Mary (which it does not say) was transformed into glory. It says that the flesh did not have the glory of the Godhead from the beginning. This the flesh "received there in the union with God the Word."

THE LAST SUPPER

The Last Supper was the meal of Passover (in Hebrew, *Pesach*), one of the most widely observed Jewish holidays. It commemorates the Exodus, when the ancient Israelites were freed from slavery in Egypt. It begins on the 15th day of the month of Nisan (April), and goes for seven or eight days. In Christianity, it is called *Pascha*, otherwise known as Easter, which is the celebration of the resurrection of Jesus, which goes hand in hand with the idea of being freed from the weight of sin. It is the root word of the "Paschal Lamb."

The fifth chapter in the Quran, *Al-Ma'ida* - (The Table) contains a reference to the Last Supper, describing a miraculous table sent down from God to Jesus and the apostles, which may incorporate Gospel narratives of the Last Supper with stories of the Israelites, under Moses, receiving sustenance through "manna from heaven" or apocryphal tales of Mary miraculously being fed by the angels: "Said Jesus the son of Mary: "O Allah our Lord! Send us from heaven a table set (with viands)...for thou art the best Sustainer (of our needs)." Allah said: "I will send it down unto you: But if any of you after that resisteth faith, I will punish him with a penalty such as I have not inflicted on any one among all the peoples." Quran 5:112–115. There is no such miraculous nature of the meal in the Gospel narratives.

In *John* 11:45-46, it states that after the raising of Lazarus from the dead, "Then many of the Jews which came to Mary, and had seen the things which Jesus did, believed on him. But some of them went their ways to the Pharisees, and told them what things Jesus had done." The chief priests and the Pharisees convened a council, and were saying, "What are we doing? For this man is performing many signs. If we let Him go on like this, all men will believe in Him, and the Romans will come and take away both our place and our nation." (*John* 11:48)

In *Mark* 6:4, Jesus sadly and prophetically reflected, "A prophet is never without honor except in his own country, among his own kin and in his own house."

After deliberation, the High Priest, Caiaphas gives his decision – that it is best to sacrifice one life, for the sake of the nation. The *Gospel of John* also states that Caiaphas, "prophesied that Jesus was going to die for the nation, and not for the nation only, but in order that He might also gather together into one the children of God who are scattered abroad. So, from that day on they planned together to kill Him. Therefore, Jesus no longer continued to walk publicly among the Jews, but went away from there to the country near the wilderness, into a city called Ephraim; and there He stayed with the disciples." Ephraim may be a city near Bethel, however, it was also the name of a large area north of Jerusalem, in what is now considered to be the northern West Bank (Cisjordan), which had great stretches of desert.

It goes on, "Now the Passover of the Jews was near, and many went up to Jerusalem out of the country before the Passover to purify themselves. So they were seeking for Jesus, and were saying to one another as they stood in the temple, 'What do you think; that He will not come to the feast at all?' Now the chief priests and the Pharisees had given orders that if anyone knew where He was, he was to report it, so that they might seize Him."

In the *Gospel of John*, despite the danger, Jesus returned to Bethany to visit Mary, Martha, and Lazarus: "Jesus, therefore, six days before the Passover, came to Bethany where Lazarus was, whom Jesus had raised from the dead. So they made Him a supper there, and Martha was serving; but Lazarus was one of those reclining at the table with Him. Mary then took a pound of very costly perfume of pure nard, and anointed the feet of Jesus and wiped His feet with her hair; and the house was filled with the fragrance of the perfume." Because of this act, the symbol for Mary Magdalene is the alabaster jar, or box, which contained the expensive perfume.

The narrative continues, "But Judas Iscariot, one of His disciples, who was intending to betray Him, said, 'Why was this perfume not sold for three hundred *denarii* and given to poor people?' Now he said this, not because he was concerned about the poor, but because he was a thief, and as he had the money box, he used to pilfer what was put into it. Therefore Jesus said, 'Let her alone, so that she may keep it for the day of My burial. For you always have the poor with you, but you do not always have Me.' "

In *John* 7: 37-40 it states that Jesus showed himself in the crowds, and was not accosted. "In the last day, that great day of the feast, Jesus stood and cried, saying, If any man thirst, let him come unto me, and drink. He that believeth on me, as the scripture hath said, out of his belly shall flow rivers of living water. (But this spake he of the Spirit, which they that believe on him should receive: for the Holy Ghost was not yet given; because that Jesus was not yet glorified.) Many of the people therefore, when they heard this saying, said, Of a truth this is the Prophet."

In *John* 13:10-11, Jesus washes the feet of his disciples, and Peter resists, asking in surprise, "Lord, dost thou wash my feet?" and, "Thou shalt never wash my feet." But Jesus answers, "If I wash thee not, thou hast no part with me." Peter responds in a zealous manner, "Lord, not my feet only, but also *my* hands and *my* head." Jesus goes on, "He that is washed needeth not save to wash *his* feet, but is clean every whit: and ye are clean, but not all. For he knew who should betray him; therefore said he, Ye are not all clean." He said this while speaking to Peter.

In John's narrative of the Last Supper, Jesus states that what follows will be a fulfillment of scripture, "He that eateth bread with me hath lifted up his heel against me." After saying this, he was troubled in spirit. He said, "Verily, verily, I say unto you that one of you shall betray me." The disciples show confusion and concern about Jesus' meaning, as depicted in Da Vinci's painting of that moment.

There was "leaning on Jesus' bosom, one of his disciples, whom Jesus loved." Peter asks this one to ask Jesus about the betrayer's identity. The Beloved Disciple, who in the Gospels is traditionally recognized as the disciple, John, in Gnostic texts, is said to be Mary. Since the writing of the book, The Da Vinci Code, it is commonly assumed that the disciple John is Mary, as in Mary Magdalene.

"The one lying on Jesus' breast saith unto him, Lord, who is it? Jesus answered, He it is, to whom I shall give a sop, when I have dipped it. And when He had dipped the sop, he gave it to Judas Iscariot, the son of Simon." Jesus' betrayal came at the hand of the son of Simon Iscariot, whom some insist is not Simon Peter.

It is not surprising that Peter would want to know who Jesus would indicate as his betrayer. The question that arises is this – Peter was sitting at table with the Lord, why does Peter ask the Beloved Disciple to ask the important question of Jesus? Why doesn't Peter ask the Lord himself, but rather use Mary as the go-between?

THE BETRAYAL OF CHRIST

In *Luke* 3:1, it states, "In the fifteenth year of the reign of Tiberius Caesar – when Pontius Pilate was governor of Judea, Herod tetrarch of Galilee, his brother Philip tetrarch of Iturea and Traconitis, and Lysanias tetrarch of Abilene – during the high priesthood of Annas and Caiaphas, the word of God came to John son of Zechariah in the desert."

"The word of God came to John." In the Gospels, the "word of God" is seen to represent Jesus, but, since we know that John was a Prophet, the "word of God" might also be seen to represent the gift of prophesying, or even the "indwelling presence of the Shekinah."

In *John* 11:5, it says, "Now Jesus loved Martha, and her sister, and Lazarus." Mary is the sister, whom, along with her siblings, was beloved by Jesus. Martha and Lazarus were not described as disciples. Some scholars say that Mary of Bethany is not Mary Magdalene, or that Mary Magdalene was not a disciple, but there is evidence to the contrary in Gnostic texts, where Mary Magdalene's leadership role is quite evident. By the Middle Ages, the Magdalene was known as the "Apostle to the Apostles." The sticking point, for some, is the separation of the identities of Mary Magdalene and Mary of Bethany.

Certainly, some of the apocryphal Gospels show Peter in a less than flattering light. Even in the New Testament Gospels, many of Jesus' harshest chastisements are directed towards Peter. In two chapters, Jesus mentions Simon Peter and Satan in the same breath. In *Matthew* 16, in response to Peter's lack of understanding about the necessary fulfillment of prophecy, Jesus says to Peter, "Get thee behind me, Satan". In *Luke* Chapter 22, it states that the Lord said, "Simon, Simon, behold, Satan hath desired to have you, that he may sift you as wheat..."

Then Peter said, "Lord, I am ready to go with thee, both into prison, and to death." And Jesus responds to the contrary, "I tell thee, Peter, the cock shall not crow this day, before that thou shalt thrice deny that thou knowest me." After the meal, three of the disciples go with Jesus to the Garden of Gethsemane; he asks them to stay awake and pray with him. The three are said to be Peter, John, and James.

Jesus goes a short distance from them to pray alone, kneeling on "the Rock." There is a tradition, demonstrated in Fra Angelico's painting of the *Agony in the Garden*, relating that, while the men fell asleep, the women, who waited outside the gates of the garden, stayed awake and prayed.

His anguish in *Luke* 23:43-46 is clear: "And there appeared an angel unto him from heaven, strengthening him. And being in an agony he prayed more earnestly: and his sweat was as it were great drops of blood falling down to the ground. And when he rose up from prayer, and was come to his disciples, he found them sleeping for sorrow, And said unto them, Why sleep ye? rise and pray, lest ye enter into temptation."

Jesus' Agony in the Garden is a very deep and personal anguish, for he knows the hearts of those around him, and knows the depth of the coming betrayal, which is not fully revealed in the narratives of the Gospels. He prays, "Father, if thou be willing, remove this cup from me: nevertheless not my will, but thine, be done." He exhorts his disciples three times to stay awake and pray, hoping that, somehow, there will be a change of heart, a change of outcomes, and three times he returns to find them sleeping. Again, on the third occasion, he says "Are you still sleeping and resting? Look, the hour is near, and the Son of Man is betrayed into the hands of sinners. Rise, let us go! Here comes my betrayer!" The betrayer is Judas Iscariot, the son of Simon Iscariot/Simon Peter. It is a personal agony, and a betrayal on a scale that we have not heretofore understood. Being who he was, Jesus could have created a miracle, but, though he encouraged his disciples to "awaken," and pray, he left the outcome to the will of God, or even, we might say, to the free will of his companions.

Through the night, Peter does, indeed, deny the Lord three times. At the moment when Peter denied him for the third time, "The Lord turned and looked straight at Peter. And Peter remembered the word of the Lord, how he had said unto him, Before the cock crow, thou shalt deny me thrice. And Peter went out, and wept bitterly."

There are many paintings of the emotional moment of Peter's realization of his betrayal of the Lord, what we might call the "apophatic moment", artworks which are often entitled, "Peter's Denial." There is an interesting contrast in examining the juxtaposition of two paintings of this moment – especially in conjunction with the above narrative. One painting is from the 19th century, painted by Carl Henrich Block, and one is by Rembrandt, from the 17th century. Rembrandt's painting gives one artist's point of view; though other renderings are quite different, we can make some assumptions by comparing his work with the standard representations. Close examination is needed.

Rembrandt's painting depicts Peter in the foreground with the servant woman. While Peter denies that he is a follower of Jesus, we see, in the background, the Centurion, escorting a cloaked figure who turns and looks directly at Peter, as the passage from *Luke* 22:61 states.

In the painting of Peter's Denial by Carl Heinrich Bloch, from the 19th century, one sees a standard depiction of Jesus, standing between two pillars, hands bound behind his back, with the centurion and a group of others. As he is being taken away, he turns his head to look at a very regretful Peter.

In another, painted in 1660 by Rembrandt, Peter is talking to the woman in the courtyard. A figure can be seen in the doorway, standing next to the centurion. The figure's head is turned to look directly at Peter, however, the cloaked figure is not the standard depiction of Jesus. Most copies of the painting on the web are so dark and dim that one barely notices the figures in the upper right corner, particularly the decidedly feminine cloaked figure being escorted by the Roman soldier.

In the same way that various narratives make the connection of two identities by intertwining their stories, Judas Iscariot and Simon (Iscariot) are connected within the *Gospel of Luke.* "Then entered Satan into Judas surnamed Iscariot, being of the number of the twelve. And he went his way, and communed with the chief priests and captains, how he might betray him unto them." (*Luke* 22:3-4)

Several lines later, "And the Lord said, Simon, Simon, behold, Satan hath desired *to have* you, that he may sift *you* as wheat: But I have prayed for thee, that thy faith fail not: and when thou art converted, strengthen thy brethren." (*Luke* 22:31-32)

In the painting of the scene by Caravaggio, The Taking of Christ, Caravaggio, 1602, it is often noted that the head of Jesus and the head of John (far left, arms raised in shock and fear), seem to be united. The shining black armor of the soldier is also mentioned as a strange and glaring focus of the painting. But the alignment of the arm of the solder and the arm of Judas is odd. It is not generally mentioned that, with the lighting and alignment, the two arms also seem to be joined as one. John's head connects with Jesus' head, and the arm of the Roman soldier connects with the body of Judas. What is the wily Caravaggio saying here?

As with the third arm in Da Vinci's "Last Supper," this painting was done by a master, who thoughtfully laid out his arrangement ahead of time, quite likely, with numerous practice sketches to get it right. This arrangement is not accidental, but what is the artist trying to say?

Why did it require Judas' kiss of betrayal to point out the one that was Jesus? Didn't the people know who Jesus was? In the *Gospel of John*, the reaction of the group of men and officers in response to Judas' identifying kiss is quite telling. "Jesus therefore, knowing all things that should come upon him, went forth, and said unto them, Whom seek ye? They answered him, Jesus of Nazareth. Jesus saith unto them, I am *he*...As soon then as he had said unto them, I am *he*, they went backward, and fell to the ground." (*John* 18:4-6)

Why did the group of men that came with Judas fall back at Jesus' acknowledgment that "I am *he*"? (The italics are included in the Gospel text.) Although the text doesn't explain their reaction, it clearly denotes the standard depiction of astonishment – they were staggered by the news, stunned and bewildered (perhaps, even afraid). They fell backwards at the identification! Why so? Obviously, they recognized this one, who was a highly visible and highly honored figure within the priestly court. They were shocked and couldn't believe that this was Jesus the Christ, the prophesied Messiah!

THE HOUSE OF ANANIAH

Josephus writes, in *Antiquities of the Jews*, of the priestly dynasty of Ananus (also given as Annas, Ananias, or Ananiah): "Now the report goes, that this elder Ananus proved a most fortunate man; for he had five sons, who had all performed the office of a high priest to God, and he had himself enjoyed that dignity a long time formerly, which had never happened to any other of our high priests."

Caiaphas was, technically, the longest ruling high priest, however, it is said that he was but a puppet of Ananias, just like Ananias' sons. Caiaphas is often depicted wearing a turban, as a sign of distinction and wealth, much like Joseph of Arimathea. Ananias and Caiaphas are both painted as quite wealthy and tied to power and earthly treasures. There is a remarkable comment in *Luke* 3:2, "Now in the fifteenth year of the reign of Tiberius Caesar...*Annas and Caiaphas being the high priests,* the word of God came unto John the son of Zacharias in the wilderness." Luke speaks as if there was a joint priesthood, however it is generally proposed that Caiaphas was the actual priest at this time, with Ananias, by virtue of influence, and force of character, being the real power behind the priesthood.

Josephus was correct in stating that Ananias ruled for a long time. Ananias was the head of a powerful sacerdotal (priestly) family, and even after his own deposition, he was, essentially, the power behind the office throughout the reign of his sons and son-in-law, whose names, and periods of leadership, follow:

Annas the elder –also given as Ananias,
Ananus, Ananiah, Hananiah (6–15)
Eleazar (Elazar) ben Ananus (16–17)
Joseph ben Caiaphas (18–36/37), son-in-law,
married to the daughter of Annas
Jonathan ben Ananus (36–37)
Theophilus ben Ananus (37–41)
Matthias ben Ananus (43)
Ananus ben Ananus (63)

In his text, *The Wars of the Jews* or *History of the Destruction of Jerusalem,* Josephus speaks of a Jesus ben Ananias, who he described as a madman who wandered the streets of Jerusalem predicting its downfall, crying "Woe to Jerusalem". It would seem that Annas (Ananias, Ananus) the elder had no son named Jesus, however, Annas did have a son named Jonathan. Why would Josephus give us this name, Jesus ben Ananias and not give the relationship of this one to the most powerful priestly family of the time period? Most likely, because the people of the time well understood of whom Josephus spoke!

While Josephus certainly had loyalty to Ananias the elder, there was a different perspective given in the Talmud about the priestly family, where the "Woe" was seen to be sent in a different direction:

"Woe to the house of Annas!
Woe to their serpent's hiss!
They are high priests; their sons are
keepers of the treasury, their sons-in-law
are guardians of the temple,
and their servants beat people with staves."
(*Pesahim* 57a)

Many references are made to the greed of these high priests, who took the *zakah* – the charitable contributions to the poor – for their own use. Here it is not only the sons of Annas, but the son-in-law (Caiaphas) as well.

Many meanings have been given for the name of the town, Bethany, which was a couple of miles from Jerusalem, on the other side of the Mount of Olives. including "house of dates", "house of figs" or even "house of misery". It is now known by the Arabic name, *al-Azariyah* (or *al-Eizariya*) from *el-'Azir*, the Arabic form of Lazarus of Bethany (note the similarity to Eleazar/Elazar of the priestly family). However, William F. Albright's identification is that "Bethany" came from the Hebrew, *Beth Ananyah*, meaning "house of Ananiah."[73] E. Nestle gives the same etymology, suggesting that Bethany is derived from the personal name Anaiah, a shortened version of Ananiah, therefore becoming Beit Anya (Beit Ania)[74],a village near Bethel mentioned in the *Book of Nehemiah* (11:32).

The Jewish Virtual Library describes Bet Hananyah as the town where Mary, Martha, and Lazarus resided. A modern tourism site, custodia.org, run by Franciscan monks, in 2020, gives a similar description, "Along the road from Jerusalem down toward Jericho, behind the Mount of Olives is the Arab village of *al-Azarìya*, the Bethany mentioned in the Gospel (from the Hebrew word *Bet 'Ananya*, which means the house of Ananìa). In Jesus' time, much like today, Bethany was a suburb of Jerusalem, a small town just on the edge of the Judean desert, where some of his closest friends lived, such as Martha and Mary with their brother Lazarus."

It goes on to state, "In Biblical times, Bethany was among the villages rebuilt by members of the tribe of Benjamin after returning from exile in Babylon (*Nehemiah* 11:32). The ancient name Bethany can be interpreted as a simplification of *Bet Hananya*, or the home of an unspecified Ananias. It was during the Byzantine period that the original name of the town was replaced with that of the village of Lazarus, resulting in the current Arabic name *al-Azariya*." This is modern documentation of the relationship of the town, Bethany (*Beit Aniah*) to the house of *Ananiah* (however unspecified they might say it is).

It was said that the family of Annas had gained much of their wealth from the four "booths of the sons of Annas", which were said to be market stalls located on the Mount of Olives. Were these, in fact the tombs of the King's Valley across the Cedron Valley from the Temple Mount? *Jehoshaphat* was the name of the Cedron Valley at one point, and was the name given to the Church of Our Lady of Jehoshapat.

The tombs still standing intact are, from north to south, the so-called "Tomb of Absalom", which rises in front of the second tomb, the "Cave" or "Tomb of Jehoshaphat", the third being the "Tomb of Benei Hezir" (Hebrew for "sons of Hezir", the Hezir priestly family) built c. 2 BCE. which was previously called "The Tomb of St. James", and the fourth called the "Tomb of Zechariah", which could well be the *nefesh* of the Tomb of Benei Hezir, the patriarch of the Hezir family.

An inscription on the tomb of Benei Hezir states, "This is the grave and the Nefesh (burial monument) of Eliezer Hania Yoazar Yehuda Shimon Yochanan Benei (sons of) Yosef Ben (son of) Oved Yosef and Elazar Benei (sons of) Hania, Kohanim of the Hezir family. This would have been a wealthy family, able to afford a burial cave in the Cedron Valley. In connection to the house of Ananias, several of the names are there: Eleazar, Ananus (Hania) the younger, Jonathan (Yochanan), and Joseph (Yosef). Those missing are Theophilus and Matthias.

Until the 19th – 20th century, including in David Roberts' *The Holy Land, Syria, Idumea, Arabia, Egypt, and Nubia*, it was called the "Tomb of St. James" (brother of the Lord).

Jehosaphat was a king of Judah (c. 873–849 ce). In the 4th century, according to the *Bordeaux itinerary*, the Cedron Valley takes the name of the Valley of Josaphat. Eusebius and St. Jerome corroborate this idea. There was also a Church of St. Mary of the Valley of Josaphat. In Joel 3, in the bible, it says, "I will gather together all nations, and will bring them down into the valley of Josaphat: and I will plead with them there for my people, and for my inheritance Israel, whom they have scattered among the nations". This is seen as a reference to the Day of Judgment, when Divine Judgment will be made upon humanity. The Cedron Valley is said by many to be the place of that judgment.

Did the sons of Ananias set up tables at these holy sites to sell ceremonial items to the pilgrims to the Holy City? The sons of Ananias certainly also had market stalls inside the temple complex, in the Court of the Gentiles, where they had a monopoly on the sale of sacrificial animals, as well as on the exchanging of money into temple coins for the offerings. This enabled them to charge exorbitant prices, effectively gaining their wealth through the exploitation and oppression of the poor. When Jesus entered the temple, and saw the money-lender's, he overturned their tables and drove them out of the temple, saying, "My house shall be called a house of prayer for all nations, but you have made it a den of robbers" (*Mark* 11:17). When the chief priests heard about this, they looked for a way of killing Jesus.

These four tombs may well have been related in some way to the House of Ananiah. Ben Hezir would have been the head of the priestly family, that is, Ananias. St. James for whom the tomb was previously named, would have been one of the sons also (for many reasons, this would seem to equate to the first of these sons listed, which is Eleazar (Lazarus). The tomb of Zechariya may be a blending of the ancient prophet Zechariah and Zacharias, father of John the Baptist.

Absalom, for whom another tomb stood, was the "rebellious son of King David", killed for trying to overthrow his father's kingdom. He was tracked down by his father's armies and died "hanging from a tree" on the Mount of Olives by his long, lush hair. (Who was the "rebellious son" of Jesus' time?).

The Pulpit Commentary speaks of Ananias' presence at Paul's trial also, "He had probably lately returned from Rome, having been confirmed, as it seems, in his office by Claudius, to whom Quadratus, the predecessor of Felix, has sent him as a prisoner, to answer certain charges of sedition against him." Apparently, Ananias was cleared of the charges.

It goes on, "He seems to have been high priest for the unusually long period of over ten years - from 18 CE to about 36-37 CE. (Josephus, '*Ant. Jud.*,' 20. 5:2; 6:2, 3; 8:8) *The Pulpit Commentary* also says, "But, on the other hand, Josephus ('*Ant. Jud.*,' 20. 8:5) speaks of a certain Jonathan being high priest during the government of Felix, and being murdered by the *Sicarii* at his instigation; which looks as if Ananias's high priesthood had been interrupted." Some scholars have indicated that the status of high priest may have been a lifelong title, even if retired from the duties of the office. What is more notable is that a high priest named "Jonathan" was murdered by the Sicarii, the most incendiary branch of the Zealots.

Luke's manner of addressing Theophilus in *Acts*, as "most excellent Theophilus" would suggest that Theophilus was a Roman governor. Though many would not consider this person to be the high priest, Theophilus was the name of one of the priestly sons of Ananias. The high priests may have had exceedingly close connections to the Roman government, and the Herodians had the privilege of Roman citizenship. These two powerful families were, quite possibly, one.

The names of the high priests of the house of Ananias are quite interesting. A certain connection of names jumps out from the list, relating to the narrative of the arrest and subsequent trial of Jesus. Caiaphas was the high priest, who, according to tradition, organized the plot to kill Jesus. He is also said to have been involved in the Sanhedrin trial of Jesus. He was the son-in-law of Ananias, a previous high priest who retained the title and much of the prestige and power of that role. The first name of Ananias' son-in-law was, in fact, Joseph. Joseph Caiaphas - this is the Caiaphas of the Gospel texts; can he also be Joseph, the elder who was betrothed to Mary?

In the Protoevangelium of James, Joseph, the husband of Mary, is said to be James' father, something which is not stated in the canonical Gospels. In rabbinical writings more than two centuries after the death of Jesus, there are references to Jesus as "Messiah ben Joseph" or "Joshua (Jesus) ben Joseph". This would seem to be figurative, since Jesus was not, physically, considered to be the son Joseph.

Flavius Josephus, the historian, writes of the aftermath of the death of Jesus ben Ananias, "The fury of the Idumaeans being still unsatiated, they now turned to the city, looting every house and killing all who fell in their way, But, thinking their energies wasted on the common people, they went in search of the chief priests; it was for them that the main rush was made, and they were soon captured and slain. Then, standing over their dead bodies, they scoffed at Ananus for his patronage of the people and at Jesus for the address which he had delivered from the wall. They actually went so far in their impiety as to cast out the corpses without burial, although the Jews are so careful about funeral rites that even malefactors who have been sentenced to crucifixion are taken down and buried before sunset."

Being a friend of the Romans, Ananias/Ananus (the elder) was murdered by the people at the beginning of the First Jewish-Roman War. His son Eliezar ben Hanania was one of the leaders of the Great Revolt of Judea.

Josephus writes of the failure of the Jewish Revolt of 70 CE, "I should not be wrong in saying that the capture of the city began with the death of Ananus; and that the overthrow of the walls and the downfall of the Jewish state dated from the day on which the Jews beheld their high priest, the captain of their salvation, butchered in the heart of Jerusalem." Josephus seems to have allegiance to Ananias. But where is Joseph Caiaphas in this account?

Josephus holds Ananias/Ananus in highest regard, describing him as "A man on every ground revered and of the highest integrity, Ananus, with all the distinction of his birth, his rank and the honors to which he had attained, yet delighted to treat the very humblest as his equals. Unique in his love of liberty and an enthusiast for democracy, he on all occasions put the public welfare above his private interests. To maintain peace was his supreme object. He knew that the Roman power was irresistible, but, when driven to provide for a state of war, he endeavored to secure that, if the Jews would not come to terms, the struggle should at least be skilfully conducted. In a word, had Ananus lived, they would undoubtedly have arranged terms – for he was an effective speaker, whose words carried weight with the people......" Ananias and Caiaphas were close, so it isn't surprising that Josephus speaks so highly of Ananias.

"They who but lately had worn the sacred vestments, led those ceremonies of world-wide significance and been reverenced by visitors to the city from every quarter if the earth, were now seen cast out naked, to be devoured by dogs and beasts of prey." (*Jewish War* 4, 314-325)

Josephus, clearly, had a sense of loyalty to the elder Ananias/Ananus, but not so to Ananus the younger: "The younger Ananus, who had been appointed to the high priesthood ...was rash in his temper and unusually daring. He followed the school of the Sadducees, who are indeed more heartless than any of the other Jews...when they sit in judgement....King

Agrippa (II), because of Ananus' action, deposed him from the high priesthood which he had held for three months" (*Antiquities* 20; 199, 203).

Josephus, the historian, who seems to have first-hand knowledge of this priestly family, and is the first to write of them, says of Ananus the younger, who became the high priest around 63 CE: "And now Caesar, upon hearing of the death of Festus, sent Albinus into Judea as procurator; but the king deprived Joseph of the high priesthood, and bestowed the succession to that dignity on the son of Ananus, who was also himself called Ananus." He is saying that Ananus the younger, basically, stole the priesthood away from Joseph (his brother-in-law). If this was Josephus, then certainly he would write of the heartlessness of this high priest.

The youngest of the five sons was named after his father, though his name is usually spelled "Ananus." Where the elder two acted, perhaps, out of fear and greed, Josephus, understandably, paints the younger Ananus as being callous and cruel. Josephus states, "This younger Ananus, who as we have told you already, took the high priesthood, was a bold man in his temper, and very insolent; he was also of the sect of the Sadducees, who were very rigid in judging offenders, above all the rest of the Jews, as we have already observed ..."

This description resembles that of Paul, who, in his own words, said he had "persecuted the Church of God and laid waste to it" (Galatians 1:13, Philippians 3:6) and been "a blasphemer, a persecutor, and injurious" (1Timothy 1:13). Scholars interpret the phrase, "Church of God" to mean the early Christians, but perhaps it could be defined as the Jerusalem community prior to Jesus' arrival on the scene.

Certainly, John the Baptist, considered to be the last of the Jewish prophets, was a fiery and zealous defender of the Jewish faith before Jesus' time. He often castigated his fellow Jews for the inconstancy of their faith. In *Matthew* 3:7-10, *John* states, "But when he saw many of the Pharisees and Sadducees come to his baptism, he said unto them, O generation of vipers, who hath warned you to flee from the wrath to come? Bring forth therefore fruits meet for repentance: ... And now also the axe is laid unto the root of the trees: therefore every tree which bringeth not forth good fruit is hewn down, and cast into the fire."

Josephus writes, "... when therefore, Ananus was of this disposition, he thought he had now a proper opportunity (to exercise his authority). Festus was now dead, and Albinus was but upon the road; so he assembled the Sanhedrin of the judges, and brought before them the brother of Jesus, who was called the Christ, whose name was James, and some of his companions; and when he had formed an accusation against them as breakers of the law, he delivered them to be stoned; but as for those who seemed the most equitable of the citizens, and such as were the most uneasy at the breach of the laws, they dislike what was done." (*Antiquities of the Jews*, IX, Chapter 1)

Several 19th -century writers such as Johann Nepomuk Sepp and the Abbé Drioux, proposed a concealed reference to Ananias the elder in the parable of the Rich Man and Lazarus, which describes a "rich man" with five sons.[75] In this parable, a beggar named Lazarus, covered in sores is brought to the gate of the "rich man." It doesn't state clearly that the rich man had anything to do with his suffering or his death, only that the beggar hungered for even a crumb from the rich man's table – but the beggar then dies. It states clearly that, in the afterlife, the rich man suffers in the fires of hell, and begs that Lazarus might simply dip the tip of his finger in cool water to wet his tongue, "because I am in agony in this fire." This is seen by Lightfoot and others to be a parody of the beliefs of the Pharisees, regarding the afterlife.[76]

Abraham replies to the rich man, "Son, remember that in your lifetime you received your good things, while Lazarus received bad things, but now he is comforted here and you are in agony. And besides all this, between us and you a great chasm has been set in place, so that those who want to go from here to you cannot, nor can anyone cross over from there to us.'"

"He answered, 'Then I beg you, father, send Lazarus to my family, for I have five brothers. Let him warn them, so that they will not also come to this place of torment. Abraham replied, 'They have Moses and the Prophets; let them listen to them.'...He said to him, 'If they do not listen to Moses and the Prophets, they will not be convinced even if someone rises from the dead.'"

This parable is speaking of those of the Sanhedrin, who, first of all, were not convinced even when Lazarus was raised from the dead, which because of Abraham's statement, also implies that they did not listen to Moses and the Prophets. It also seems to suggest that they will not believe in the death and resurrection of Christ, himself.

In *Matthew*, Chapter 13, Jesus speaks to the people of Nazareth in parables, and his four brothers are mentioned, "And it came to pass, that when Jesus had finished these parables, he departed thence. And when he was come into his own country, he taught them in their synagogue, insomuch that they were astonished, and said, Whence hath this man this wisdom, and these mighty works? Is not this the carpenter's son? is not his mother called Mary? and his brethren, James, and Joses, and Simon, and Judas? And his sisters, are they not all with us? Whence then hath this man all these things? And they were offended in him. But Jesus said unto them, A prophet is not without honor, save in his own country, and in his own house.

And he did not many mighty works there because of their unbelief." It is notable that he includes, "*in his own house*."

In this narrative, there are five brothers, but one of them is Simon.

Is the rich man dressed in purple and fine linen (c f. *Exodus* 28:8) meant to be Annas? Annas seems to be indicated as the "father" in *Luke* 16:27, ("send him to my father's house") and the "five brothers" of *Luke* 16:28 are Ananias' five sons (with Caiaphas as their brother-in-law). The name of Lazarus is an alter ego, and is actually one of the five brothers, who belonged to the priesthood. You might guess that this is Eleazar, but that is not the name that we know him by.

Though the spelling of the two names is quite different, phonetically, the name Caiaphas is very similar to the name *Cephas*, the Aramaic spelling of the name that Jesus was said to have given to Simon Peter. (The Greek word for "rock" was a very different spelling, that is, *Petros*, from which derives the name that is so familiar to us, Simon Peter.)

The connection, in Aramaic is, notably, much clearer: "But Shimeon Kaypha had a sword on him and he drew it and struck the servant of The High Priest and took off his right ear...Yeshua said, "Kaypha (Peter), put the sword in its sheath. The cup that The Father has given me, shall I not drink it?" Then the company and a Captain of a thousand, and guards of the Judeans, seized Yeshua and bound him. And they brought him to the presence of Hannan (Annas) first, because he was Father-in-law of Qaypha (Caiaphas), who was The High Priest that year. But it was Qaypha who counseled the Jews that it was better that one man should die for the sake of the nation." And so we have Cephas/Caiaphas, and Kaypha/Qaypha.

After the third denial of Peter, "Then led they Jesus from Caiaphas unto the hall of judgment: and it was early; and they themselves went not into the judgment hall, lest they should be defiled; but that they might eat the Passover." (*John* 18:28)

In the mid-5th century, a Byzantine shrine dedicated to Peter's repentance was erected on this spot where, according to *Luke* 22:62: " ... Peter went out, and wept bitterly." This shrine was destroyed by Muslims in 1010, and then was rebuilt by the crusaders in 1102 CE and named Church of St. Peter in Gallicantu (a French word meaning "cock's crow"). There may be more than one hidden meaning in the word. *Galli* also is the Latin spelling for Gaul (France), and is the place that the three Mary's are said to have ended up, according to various legends, along with other followers of Jesus. It is also where the wealthy Joseph of Arimathea had tin mines. He was referred to by the Romans as *Nobilis Decurio,* or Minister of Mines to the Roman Government. There were caves and cisterns below *Gallicantu* church, and south of the site, is located the tomb of Ananias, in the valley of Gehenna, which was said to be cursed – here, the legend goes, some of the ancient kings of Judah sacrificed their children by fire.

Shimeon Kaypha is the Aramaic spelling for Simon Peter, Qaypha for Caiaphas. Certainly, others have made the connection between Simon Peter and Joseph Caiaphas, as suggested in the artwork of *The Denial of Saint Peter* by Caravaggio, from 1610 CE. This dramatic work portrays the moment that Peter realizes his betrayal of the Lord. One can see the anguish in Peter's face. The position of his hands suggest distress. The painting of the moment where the woman accuses Peter of being a companion of Jesus, and he denies the Lord for the third time is quite affecting. The woman's intense gaze is focused on the Roman soldier, whose face is nearly invisible in shadow.

In the *Gospel of Matthew*, when Jesus is brought before Caiaphas, this high priest commands: "I adjure thee by the living God, that thou tell us whether thou be the Christ, the Son of God." Jesus responds, "Thou hast said: nevertheless I say unto you, Hereafter shall ye see the Son of man sitting on the right hand of power, and coming in the clouds of heaven." (*Matthew* 26:64)

The narrative goes on, "Then the high priest *rent his clothes*, saying, He hath spoken blasphemy; what further need have we of witnesses? behold, now ye have heard his blasphemy." Caravaggio is no fool – his depiction of Peter's Denial is a deliberate, though veiled, reference to the underlying truth. In Caravaggio's painting, Peter's Denial is also the moment of the high priest rending his clothes, further connecting Peter with Caiaphas.

Other paintings of "Christ before Caiaphas," a popular subject of Christian art, demonstrate a similarity to Caravaggio's *Denial of Peter*. Both Giotto's and Duccio's paintings of *Christ before Caiaphas* show the high priest rending his clothes, just as Peter seems to be doing in Caravaggio's painting.

In the New Testament Gospels, there are places where identities overlap in difficult ways. In the paintings by Giotto and Duccio, Peter is outside in the courtyard, while Caiaphas is inside rending his clothes. There is a thin separation of space between Peter and Caiaphas, deliberate in the gospels, as well as in these paintings. By the time of the writing of *Acts*, identities were overlapping to such a degree that one can no longer sort out who is whom. This would seem to be intentionally so.

* * *

CHAPTER IV. THE CRUCIFIXION AND ITS AFTERMATH

ANANIAS, THE HIGH PRIEST

Ananias was appointed by the Roman legate as the first High Priest of the newly formed Roman province of Judaea in 6 CE (just after the Romans deposed Archelaus, Ethnarch of Judaea). Subsequently, Judaea was brought directly under Roman rule.

Ananias officially served as High Priest for ten years (6–15 CE), when at the age of 36, he was deposed by the procurator, Gratus. Though officially removed from office, Ananias continued to be one of the nation's most influential figures, aided by the familial connection to the office through five sons/his son-in-law as High Priests. His death is unrecorded, but his son Ananus the Younger, also known as Ananus ben Ananus was assassinated in 66 CE for his connections to, and collaborations with Rome.

Ananias appears in the Gospels and Passion plays as the high priest before whom Jesus is brought for judgment, prior to being brought before Pontius Pilate. *Matthew* 26:57 names the location as Caiaphas' house and *John* 18:13 mentions Ananias' residence; some question whether it is the same location or another is intended. Since Caiaphas was Ananias' son-in-law, it is possible that it was the same house. Syrian pilgrim, Theodosius Archidiaconus, in 530 CE, stated that there were 100 paces between the house of Caiaphas and the hall of judgment. (*Nuovo Bull. di Arch. Crist. vi.* 184, Rome, *1900)* Other scholars have claimed that Caiaphas may have lived in the same house as his father-in-law, Ananias.

At Jesus' trial, the high priest asked Jesus of his disciples, and of his doctrine. "Jesus answered him, I spake openly to the world; I ever taught in the synagogue, and in the temple, whither the Jews always resort; and in secret have I said nothing. Why askest thou me? ask them which heard me, what I have said unto them: behold, they know what I said. And when he had thus spoken, one of the officers which stood by struck Jesus with the palm of his hand, saying, Answerest thou the high priest so? Jesus answered him, If I have spoken evil, bear witness of the evil: but if well, why smitest thou me? Now Annas had sent him bound unto Caiaphas the high priest."

In Paul's trial, he also was brought before Ananias, who is shown to be brutal and vindictive. In this narrative, Paul's words in defense of his innocence, likewise, bring a harsh reaction from Ananias, "And Paul earnestly beholding the council, said, Men and brethren, I have lived in all good conscience before God until this day. And the high Priest Ananias commanded them that stood by him, to smite him on the mouth. Then saith Paul unto him, God shall smite thee, thou whited wall: for sittest thou to judge me after the Law, and commandest me to be smitten contrary to the Law?"

This is an odd and extremely bold statement to make in such circumstances! "And they that stood by, said, Revilest thou God's high Priest?" (Compare to Jesus' trial, "Answerest thou the high priest so?")

The meaning of the following lines has long been debated, "Then said Paul, I wist not, brethren, that he was the high Priest: For it is written, Thou shalt not speak evil of the ruler of thy people." The words "I wist not," means, "I did not know." He claims that, even though he was brought to Ananias for judgment, he didn't realize that Ananias was the high priest. It seems a very illogical statement for such an intelligent person to make!

The solution is rather simple, actually. Though Ananias had a great deal of power, he had, actually, been deposed from the priesthood in 15 CE. Paul must surely have known this. Perhaps, even more meaning was contained in Paul's words: "God shall smite thee, thou whited wall…" Paul sees through the whitewash, and daringly speaks a deep truth, essentially: "How dare you judge me!" and "I didn't realize that YOU were the high priest!"

For comparison, Jesus, said, "Woe to you, scribes and Pharisees, hypocrites! For you are like whitewashed tombs, which outwardly appear beautiful, but within are full of dead people's bones and all uncleanness. So you also outwardly appear righteous to others, but within you are full of hypocrisy and lawlessness." (*Matthew* 23:27-28)

Paul's statements bring into focus the question of who was the rightful high priest during his own trial. Caiaphas reigned from 17 – 36 CE. Who was the ruler at this time? *John*, Chapter 11 suggests that Caiaphas was the high priest the year that Jesus was tried and crucified, but again, it is said that Ananias was the true power behind the priesthood at that time. Jesus is said to have been crucified in 33 CE (though the exact timeline has also been a source of great debate). In 36 CE, Jonathan became the high priest.

Paul gives clear evidence of the high priest's identity with his statement: "For it is written, Thou shalt not speak evil of the ruler of thy people." This seems not to be an apology, but, instead, a bold contradiction to Ananias' actions. Though he may be speaking of the priesthood, or of royal leadership, he might be speaking of an other-worldly role and honor. Paul, we are told did not die by crucifixion. After years of house arrest in Rome, he was beheaded.

It was not just the master painters of the Renaissance, but the Gospel-writers themselves who wanted to make a record of the truth – though it might be hidden in symbolic form, in pseudonym, and metaphor. They did so under challenging circumstances, even under threat of death, for that which must not be spoken. They left us narratives which we must look at with open hearts – reading between the lines, as in ParDeS studies, as in Kabbalist practice, as in the mysticism of Judaism, Christianity, and Islam, asking, "What were they really trying to say?"

However, without considering traditions and writings outside of the New Testament, we might never put it all together. There are clues, even in books that are not religious in nature, but what we might term, "pseudo-historical."

THE TRIAL

When Jesus was arrested, John's Gospel says, "Then the detachment of soldiers with its commander and the Jewish officials arrested Jesus. They bound him and brought him first to Annas, who was the father-in-law of Caiaphas, the high priest that year." Caiaphas was the one who had advised the Jewish leaders that it would be best if one man died for the greater good of the people. (*John* 18:12 - 14)

In the narrative of Jesus being taken to "the high priest", there are a number of unclear statements. "Simon Peter was following Jesus, and so was another disciple. Now that disciple was known to the high priest, and entered with Jesus into the court of the high priest, but Peter was standing at the door outside. So the other disciple, who was known to the high priest, went out and spoke to the doorkeeper, and brought Peter in...." (*John* 18:15-16) It seems that, whenever the story gets intensely important and intriguing, the text gets murky. Why not simply say which disciple was present here? Generally, these confusing narratives seem intended to hide the identities of those present. With the sheer number of alter egos involved in any of these narratives, it becomes difficult to write the narrative at all! We must consider that an effort was made to preserve the truth, but in an oblique way that would suffice for the Roman rulers, and would not endanger the life of the author.

The *Gospel of Matthew* 26:3-5, states, "Then the chief priests and the elders of the people were gathered together in the court of the high priest, named Caiaphas; and they plotted together to seize Jesus by stealth and kill Him. But they were saying, 'Not during the festival, otherwise a riot might occur among the people'."

Acts of the Apostles begins after the Lord was "taken up" in ascension to heaven. However, it does speak of Paul, who was taken before the high priest for trial. He spoke of his own zealousness toward God, "And I persecuted this way unto the death, binding and delivering into prisons both men and women." This may be an attempt to show the Gentiles that, though they may have persecuted Christians in the past, they, too, can be converted to the faith. However, the question does arise: what temporal (earthly) power did Paul, the "tentmaker" from Tarsus, have to persecute Christians? It isn't clearly stated what gave Paul the power to do so. Certainly, the power of the Roman government was the highest ruling party of the times, and a lesser power would have been found in the Herodian dynasty, but there was another great power structure within the Holy Land, and that was the hierarchy of the Temple Priests.

There are many correlations between the trials of Jesus and of Paul as noted in the Ignatius Catholic Study Bible.[77] Both Jesus and Paul begin their trials in front of a Jewish court, and end with the Jewish people in an uproar. After their Sanhedrin trials, they each go before a Roman governor – Pilate (perhaps a pseudonym, meaning "javelin") in the case of Jesus, and Felix in the case of Paul. Neither governor finds any guilt in their prisoner. Paul was "found accused about questions of their law, but charged with nothing deserving death or imprisonment" (*Acts* 23:29). This is the equivalent of the statement of Pilate in *Luke*, "Behold I did not find this man guilty of any of your charges against him." (*Luke* 23:15)

Next, both are sent by the Roman governor to Kings with greater jurisdiction. Both of the kings involved, King Herod who judges Christ and King Agrippa who judges St. Paul are family in the same line of kings. Both kings send their prisoners to the Roman governor, finding no crime within them. In *Acts*, it states, regarding Paul, "Then the king rose, and the governor ...; and when they had withdrawn they said to one another, 'This man is doing nothing to deserve imprisonment'" (*Acts* 26:31)

In *Acts*, there was another similar trial by those of the powerful "House of Annas (Ananias, Ananiah)". Here, the priestly dynasty overseen by Annas, were gathered to question not Jesus, nor Paul, but Peter and John. "And it came to pass on the morrow, that their rulers, and elders, and scribes, And Annas the high priest, and Caiaphas, and John, and Alexander, and as many as were of the kindred of the high priest, were gathered together at Jerusalem." Again, those in attendance get a bit confusing. Was John there as high priest or as defendant? Caiaphas makes his final appearance in the New Testament, in *Acts* where he is named second among the Sadducean leaders who assembled to try Peter and John, for their miraculous healing of the lame man. This demonstrates that the author of *Acts* either didn't know of certain hidden identities, or he knew and wanted to, let's say, obfuscate the issue. In this text, Peter and John are shown to be pious and righteous followers of Jesus' teachings.

Peter and John, who, for their healing work, were called before these leaders for judgment, "Being grieved that they taught the people, and preached through Jesus the resurrection from the dead. And they laid hands on them, and put them in hold unto the next day: for it was now eventide. Howbeit many of them which heard the word believed; and the number of the men was about five thousand."

When asked, "by what power" do you do these things, Peter, filled with the Holy Spirit, rather than John, speaks boldly to the Sadduceans, "Be it known unto you all, and to all the people of Israel, that by the name of Jesus Christ of Nazareth, whom ye crucified, whom God raised from the dead, even by him doth this man stand here before you whole." Caiaphas and the other priests, impressed by the words of Peter, realized that the two men had no formal education, yet spoke eloquently about the man they called their Savior.

Acts 4:5-12 gives a very Petrine perspective on their trial before the Sanhedrin, "And it came to pass, on the next day, that their rulers, elders, and scribes, as well as Annas the high priest, Caiaphas, John, and Alexander, and as many as were of the family of the high priest, were gathered together at Jerusalem. And when they had set them in the midst, they asked, "By what power or by what name have you done this?" Then Peter, filled with the Holy Spirit, said to them, "Rulers of the people and elders of Israel: If we this day are judged for a good deed done to a helpless man, by what means he has been made well, let it be known to you all, and to all the people of Israel, that by the name of Jesus Christ of Nazareth, whom you crucified, whom God raised from the dead, by Him this man stands here before you whole."

In *Acts*, which depicts Peter as a righteous man, Caiaphas accuses Peter, who is aligned with the holy miracle-making of John, of healing a crippled man. Peter stood up to his accusers, giving a metaphorical reference to Jesus, "This is the 'stone which was rejected by you builders, which has become the chief cornerstone.' Nor is there salvation in any other, for there is no other name under heaven given among men by which we must be saved." Peter is quite heroic in these scenes, though admittedly under the auspices of the Lord's guidance.

Together the two disciples stand up to Caiaphas' accusations, and Peter's courageous rebuttals are met with – acceptance! In *Acts*, the overall picture of the rulers, and of Peter's role in Christianity becomes twisted, shaped into alignment with Petrine ideals; in opposition to the less than courageous Peter of the Gospels, who misunderstood Jesus' mission, who slept instead of praying as Jesus asked, who denied Jesus three times, is made into the hero! One might consider that each of the Gospels, themselves, were shaped to present the viewpoint of one segment of the followers of Jesus.

In *Acts*, it is a mild, equable and forbearing Caiaphas who sent the apostles away, mildly agreeing with the other priests that the word of the miracle had already been spread too much to attempt to refute it. Caiaphas did them no harm – but only told the priests to warn the apostles not to spread Jesus' name. However, when they gave Peter and John this command, the two adamantly refused, saying "Judge for yourselves whether it is right in God's sight to obey you rather than God. For we cannot help speaking about what we have seen and heard."

An educated guess would be that this was an effort by the followers of Peter to promote Petrine leadership of the Church. This example shows us clearly that many narratives were polemical in nature, and meant to either praise one figure (or faction), and/or vilify another. This is a sanitized version of events, meant to remove blame from Caiaphas, and to make Peter a brave and honorable man equal to John - not surprising when you follow the clues connecting them. Both Peter *and* Caiaphas are found to be blameless in this text, written by a Gentile for the Gentiles.

The differences in the depiction of Paul and his teachings is only a part of the problem. When you begin to see the bigger picture, it becomes clear that *Acts* muddies and confuses the issue of identities by introducing alter egos (alternate identities) within the same scene. This would seem to be a deliberate attempt to hide the truth – within scriptural writings. Why would that be so? We must keep in mind that the winners write the histories, in such a way as to glorify their own "acts", and the losers are, essentially, minimized or even written out.

In the Gospels, Caiaphas accuses Jesus of blasphemy and rebelliousness. He chooses the "sacrifice of one man's life" for the greater good of the Jewish people. Caiaphas and Annas are shown to be brutal and selfish – Caiaphas, in fact, has a temperament much like that of Peter, who is shown in some of the apocryphal texts to be easily roused to anger and loud protestations, and even in the New Testament Gospels, is often chastised by Jesus for his unruly behavior and temper. Peter, whom Jesus has prayed for three times (warning him against falling into temptation) denies Jesus three times, as Jesus had already predicted. While Judas is described in the gospels as the betrayer of Jesus, Peter is also shown to betray him, but, seemingly, by default and omission.

Caiaphas was the son-in-law of Annas/Ananias by marriage to his daughter and, though Ananias was the power behind the priesthood, Caiaphas ruled longer than any other high priest in New Testament times. This would likely be an indication of his having, in some manner, ingratiated his way into the good graces of the Romans.

In the narrative of Jesus being taken to the court of the high priest, why is that priest's name not given? (It is clearly stated that the high priest in Paul's trial was Ananias.) John says that Jesus was taken first to Annas for questioning. Josephus makes mention that during the time of Jesus in first century Jerusalem, the house of Ananias stood near the Palace of the Asmonaeans (Hasmoneans), on the eastern part of the Upper City. It is also clear that the palace of the high priest where Jesus was examined before the Council in Jerusalem, the *Sanhedrin*, was not only mentioned in the Bible as the House of Caiaphas, but also became a site for the Christian church of St. Peter in Gallicantu, on the Hill of the Upper City. Some have claimed that the house of Ananias and the house of Caiaphas were only steps away from each other. But, since they obviously worked closely together, and Caiaphas was the son-in-law of Ananias (married to Ananias' daughter), and Ananias was still the power behind the priesthood, perhaps their living spaces were adjoined in the palace of the high priest at that time.

This court was authorized only to do two things – to administer the "bitter water" to those women caught in adultery, and to sentence members of the priesthood. "It [Great Sanhedrin] sat in judgment on women suspected of adultery, and sentenced them to drink the bitter water." (*Sotah* I.4) Is it possible that the rabbinical commentary on Mary's *sotah* trial related in a most roundabout, tangential way to this detail of the court where Jesus was tried? In other words, not at all based in truth, but only a satirical jest meant to connect Mary and Jesus to the same court?

John 11:47-54 states, "Then the chief priests and the Pharisees gathered a council and said, "What shall we do? For this Man works many signs. If we let Him alone like this, everyone will believe in Him, and the Romans will come and take away both our place and nation." And one of them, Caiaphas, being high priest that year, said to them, 'You know nothing at all, nor do you consider that it is expedient for us that one man should die for the people, and not that the whole nation should perish.' .... Then, from that day on, they plotted to put Him to death."

Matthew 27:1-2 states, "When morning came, all the chief priests and elders of the people plotted against Jesus to put Him to death. And when they had bound Him, they led Him away and delivered Him to Pontius Pilate the governor."

In the Gospel accounts, it was not the healing of a crippled man, but something much more amazing that brought the censure of the Sanhedrin. In *John* 11, the high priests called a gathering of the Sanhedrin in reaction to the miraculous event of Jesus' raising of Lazarus from the dead. The crippled man in *Acts* is a replacement for Lazarus – and a lesser miracle replaces the greater one of raising Lazarus from the dead. However, with the lesser miracle, the two Apostles are spared and allowed to continue healing.

In *John* 12:9-11, Caiaphas and the chief priests extend their accusations to also include Lazarus himself, and begin to plot his death. The *Gospel of John* states that, because of Lazarus many people were "believing in" Jesus; we also know that James confirmed that Jesus was "the way", and "the gate," for which James was stoned to death.

In the *Gospel of Matthew*, after the raising of Lazarus from the dead, Caiaphas considers, with "the Chief Priests and Pharisees", what to do about Jesus, whose fame was growing. They fear that this miracle will make the Romans "come and destroy both our holy place and our nation." *Matthew* proposes that Caiaphas makes a political calculation, to sacrifice one man for the greater good of the nation, however, the other side of the story is that, as a wealthy and leading member of the Sadducees, Caiaphas' policy of accommodation to Rome exacerbated the feeling that the priesthood had become corrupt and no longer represented the interests of the Jewish people. In other words, Caiaphas was more oriented to Roman sentiment and goals, in essence, he was "in cahoots" with the Roman government.

In *Matthew* 26:57-67, Caiaphas, other chief priests, and the Sanhedrin of the time are depicted interrogating Jesus. They are seeking grounds with which to put Jesus on trial, but are having difficulty in doing so.

For Jewish leaders of the time, there were serious concerns about Roman rule and the problems of an insurgent Zealot movement attempting to eject the Romans from Israel. The Romans would not perform execution over violations of Jewish law, and therefore the charge of blasphemy would not have mattered to Pilate. Caiaphas' legal position, therefore, was to establish that Jesus was guilty not only of blasphemy, but also of proclaiming himself the Messiah, which was understood as the return of the Davidic king. While blasphemy was not important to Rome, this claim would have been an act of sedition and prompted Roman execution.

As demonstrated in the *Book of Susanna*, The Law required that two or more witnesses had to give consistent testimony before a fact could be admitted as evidence in a court (Deuteronomy 19:15; 17:6). After much effort, they finally found two people who testified against him.

The *Mishna* describes how two witnesses also must overhear blasphemous statements in order to go forth with stoning. The Palestinian Gemara adds: "Thus; for the enticer two witnesses are placed in concealment in the innermost part of the house; but he is made himself to remain in the exterior part of the house, wherein a lamp is lighted over him, in order that the witnesses may see him and distinguish his voice. Thus, for instance, they managed with Ben Sot'da [a variant of Stada or Satda] at Lud. Against him two disciples of learned men were placed in concealment and he was brought before the court of justice, and stoned."

The two witnesses at Jesus' trial stated that Jesus said, "Destroy the temple and in three days I will build it up". Jesus wasn't speaking of the physical Temple, but of his own body (*John* 2:19-22). The high priest challenged Jesus to defend himself against this charge, but Jesus remained silent. Finally, Caiaphas, attempting to force Jesus to say something that could be used against him, demands that Jesus say whether he is the Christ. Jesus' reply to Caiaphas is, "*You* have said so." *John* 26:64. In anger, Caiaphas then charged him with blasphemy and ordered him beaten.

Now, clearly, in the record of the trial itself, there is no indication that Caiaphas has said this. However, this is a very ingenious "codified" message. Who has stated that Jesus is the Christ – aside from Jesus? In *Matthew* 16:13-16, just before the scene where Jesus gives the keys of the kingdom to Simon Peter, the Lord asks his disciples: "Whom do men say that I the Son of man am?' And they said, 'Some say that thou art John the Baptist: some, Elias; and others, Jeremias, or one of the prophets.' He saith unto them, 'But whom say ye that I am?' And Simon Peter answered and said, 'Thou art the Christ, the Son of the living God.' " Ah, the ingenious intricacies of the Gospels!

The connection of Jesus words at his trial to the words of Peter, earlier in the same gospel, gives a deeper insight into the narration of Jesus in the Garden of Gethsemane, and the depiction of his Agony there. In *Matthew* 26:38, Jesus says, "My soul is overwhelmed with sorrow to the point of death. Stay here and keep watch with me." Later he says "Watch and pray so that you will not fall into temptation. The spirit is willing, but the flesh is weak." He knows that Peter's decision has already been made; Jesus has seen the outcome of the night's events, and prays that it will somehow be changed, if the need for earnest prayer and divine assistance can be impressed upon Peter – but it was not to be. If you look again at Caravaggio's painting of the *Denial of Peter*, you might see that the work is more convoluted than it first appears.

Psalm 69 seems a reference to the agony of Jesus' crucifixion, "I looked for sympathy, but there was none, for comforters, but I found none. They put gall in my food and gave me vinegar for my thirst." It also says, "I am a stranger to my brothers, an alien to my own mother's sons; for zeal for your house consumes me, and the insults of those who insult you fall on me."

As with questions of whether or not Jesus suffered on the cross, one must ask if Jesus suffered in the Garden at Gethsemane, when, the gospel states, that the stress of the situation caused him to "sweat great drops of blood". Was it only the human part that suffered? Was it simply meant to be a record of the true unfolding of events, and who it was that, from the human perspective, betrayed him? You can get into deep existential ponderings of the problematic nature of the story. If Jesus knew that he must be sacrificed in this way – if he called Peter "Satan" for trying to stand in the way of this necessary event, with himself as the "sacrificial lamb" who takes away the sins of the world, then why pray and agonize in hopes that Peter would not betray him?

Was there agony, or was that a human interpolation? What human would not suffer in this situation? On the other hand, the Cathars of the 13th century, reportedly, went to their deaths joyful and singing. Did the Lord do less than this?

We must, of course, understand that there would be innumerable alternate narratives over the centuries. This was a record of events according to each of those ones who wrote the New Testament Gospels. Even these four accounts don't match exactly. However, the different perspectives would multiply very quickly.

THE CRUCIFIXION

The North African Christian apologist, Tertullian, wrote of the female sex, in the 2nd century, "For your deceit, the very son of God had to perish!" What deceit does he refer to? Ostensibly, this was in the context of Eve's sin – but her sin was of disobedience, and not deceit. Or does he speak of a woman other than Eve? In his treatise *On the Apparel of Women* he writes, "Don't you know that you are an Eve?... Don't you know that you are the Devil's Gateway? All too easily you destroyed so easily God's image, man. Because of your deed — namely, death—even the son of God had to die!" That's a pretty harsh sentence on women, in general, and particularly it seems, the woman in question in Tertullian's text. He refers to her sin as being responsible for the need for the crucifixion of Jesus.

After Judas kissed Jesus on the cheek to indicate that he was the one they wanted, Jesus said to the chief priests, the officers of the temple guard, and the elders, who had come for him, "Am I leading a rebellion that you have come with swords and clubs? Every day I was with you in the temple courts, and you did not lay a hand on me. But this is your hour—when darkness reigns." (*Mark* 14:48-49)

We are familiar with the crucifixion story in the four gospels: the Passion of Jesus, the stripping and flogging of Jesus, the soldiers "casting die" for the clothing of Jesus, the "crown of thorns" jammed on his head, the nailing of Jesus to the cross by his hands and feet, the offer of a bitter gall-soaked sponge for his thirst. The thrusting of Longinus' spear in Jesus' side – releasing blood and water. We have record of Jesus being broken down to the point of very humanly crying out, "My God, My God, why have you forsaken me?" We are told that Jesus suffered a long, slow and painful death, finally surrendering to his circumstances, with his last words being, "Father, unto you I commend my Spirit."

With his death came darkness and earthquakes. "And Jesus cried out again with a loud voice, and yielded up His spirit. Then, behold, the veil of the temple was torn in two from top to bottom; and the earth quaked, and the rocks were split." (*Matthew 27:50–51*)

The portrayal of Mary weaving began to occur about the fifth century onwards with basket and bobbin of thread. According to the *Protoevangelion of James*, when Gabriel entered Mary's house to announce the joyous news of the Incarnation of the Logos, she was spinning purple and scarlet thread to make a veil for the temple, in other words, a tent to cover the Holy of Holies. The purple seems to indicate her descent from the royal house of David, the scarlet also a color of royalty, perhaps, to signify that the Savior took flesh and blood from her flesh and blood. In this same text, when Elizabeth hears Mary's knock at her door, she "casts down the scarlet," indicating that she also was involved in spinning or weaving the threads of the veil. The Apostle Paul, interestingly, and, perhaps, sarcastically, was known as the "tentmaker from Tarsus."

The rending of the Temple veil is often interpreted to mean that with Jesus' death, the veil between heaven and earth was opened "top to bottom," clearing the way for humanity to connect directly with heaven once more. One perspective might be that he barrier between the "two waters" was reopened, and it was this very moment that accomplished the salvific mission of Jesus.

It should not surprise us that, in the writings of the victors, the

Romans are found completely guilt-less in the narrative – instead, it is the Jews who wanted Jesus dead. (It must be noted that John the Baptist also was depicted as being killed by the Jews – the royal Jewish court of Herod, though that court had ties to the Romans.) Was the "Crucifixion Story" influenced by the Romans – by Jewish Christian scribes under orders from the Romans? Was the "Roman soldier" of rabbinical satire on the parentage of Jesus, a reference to a Jewish general who surrendered to the Romans, and wrote the history of the Revolt under the patronage of the Emperor?

Josephus was said to be a general in the Jewish army in the Jewish Revolt of 70 CE. He levied an army of 100,000 young men, armed with old arms collected from the populace, and organized and trained them following Roman methods (*The Jewish War* 2.20.7 582) to fight against the Romans. He eventually surrendered to the Roman army, and then wrote histories of the time period that were acceptable to his friend and patron, Vepasian. Because Josephus prophesied that Vespasian would become the emperor, he was not only spared, but embraced and integrated into Roman society.

In *John* 18, Jesus is brought before Annas and Caiaphas and questioned, with intermittent beatings. Afterward, the other priests (without Caiaphas) take Jesus to Pontius Pilate, the Roman governor of Judea, and insist upon Jesus' execution. Pilate tells the priests to judge Jesus themselves; they respond that they lack the authority to do so. Pilate questions Jesus, afterwards stating, "I find no basis for a charge against him." Pilate then offers the gathered crowd the choice of one prisoner to release — a Passover tradition. He left the decision to the Jewish people. Instead of letting Jesus go, they freed the thief, "Barabbas". As many scholars have noted, "bar abbas" means "son of the Father," which leaves a possible loophole in the story.

The Jewish people are clearly made the guilty party in the Gospel narratives. Pilate, though he disagreed with their choice, gave in to the wishes of the Jews, and, literally, "washed his hands" of the issue (pouring water over his hands in the manner of the high priests before doing sacrifice), then turning over the responsibility for Jesus' death to the Jewish people. The name, Pontius Pilate has certain connotations. Pontius may mean "one from Pontus." Pilate means "javelin," and so, one is reminded of the Spear of Longinus, as well as the concept of the *stauros* as a stake, pole, or pale (used for impalement).

Mary Magdalene stayed with Jesus at the cross after all the male disciples except John the Beloved had fled. If you look through the many artworks of the great master painters, you will find many paintings that leave you with questions. There are numerous formats for depictions of the crucifixion. One common depiction has a triangular format, with Jesus above on the cross and John the Beloved and Mary Magdalene below, forming the base of the triangle. Sometimes, Mother Mary is included, but usually outside of the triangle of the other three.

In paintings of the "Descent from the Cross," a different format is used, with Mary Magdalene often depicted kneeling at the foot of the cross, holding the feet of Jesus, while John stands with his head above hers, or sometimes halfway up the ladder, supporting the limp body, as Jesus, above them, is lowered from the cross. So we have Jesus as the highest (heavenly) authority, the prophet John at the next lower level (the level between heavenly and earthly ideals), and Mary at the bottom, at the earthly level. Often in this format, John is wearing red, or red and green, and Mary Magdalene is wearing some shade of gold. Here, her hair is golden, rather than the red hair that she is often depicted as having. Each format makes its statement, but this one, in particular, holds a symbolic truth that is very important.

Two paintings of *Descent from the Cross* by Peter Paul Rubens show a common format for the figures, with a progressive descent of vertical figures and others that are more laterally oriented. If you spend some time looking at the images in the context of what you've read on the subject, it can be very instructive.

In both versions, the figures at the top are called "workers". While it isn't described so in the New Testament, it would seem that Rubens is giving his own take on the story. Are these figures the two brothers, in the first painting, Andrew (left) and Peter, with his white hair and beard (right) leaning over the crossbar? At the next level below them are Joseph of Arimathea, in turban and rich robes (left), and Nicodemus on the right. You might say that these four figures are aligned with the lateral bar of the cross.

Might there, perhaps, be layers of identities and alter egos in this arrangement? Aligning with the central (vertical) post of the cross is, first, Jesus, then John (in red) and then Mary Magdalene at the foot of the cross, with one of the Mary's next to her. Mother Mary is in dark blue robes at the left, reaching up to her son. The cross as a symbol is often described as the Divine (vertical post), crossing down into the material plane (horizontal). There is also a diagonal flow, created by the white of the cloth supporting Jesus' body, from Peter in one corner, to Jesus, to the three Marys in the opposite corner.

Plate 5 - Deposition from the Cross - Peter Paul Rubens

It is interesting that, in another Rubens altarpiece at the Cathedral of Our Lady at Antwerp, Netherlands, many of the same figures can be seen. His, "Elevation of the Cross", shows the raising of the cross with Jesus upon it, before his death: the worker with white hair and beard, the turbaned figure with rich robes, Mother Mary and John standing in the left-hand panel, and three women gathered on the ground below them.

In Rubens' second painting of the *Descent from the Cross*, the same two "workers" are at the top of the painting, though their positions are reversed. Joseph of Arimathea and Nicodemus are, again, below these two (though it is harder to tell which is which, and harder to see the one on the left, receding into the shadows).

Plate 6 - Descent from the Cross - Peter Paul Rubens

The vertical alignment is, again, the body of Jesus, John supporting the weight of Jesus' body, and Mary Magdalene at his feet, with one of the Marys next to her, and Mother Mary to the left - which, in both paintings of the scene, leaves the question of which is Mary of Clopas, and which is Mary Salome? The three Marys who were always with Jesus were identified as Mary, mother of Jesus, her sister, and the companion of Jesus (the

Magdalene). Does this indicate that Mother Mary *was* one of these two Marys?

The *Gospel of John* 19:25 states: "Near the cross of Jesus stood his mother, his mother's sister, Mary the wife of Clopas, and Mary Magdalene." In this case, Mother Mary would seem to be Mary Salome (a form of *shalom*, which means "peace" and is related to Hiero Solyma – Holy Peace, or Jerusalem), which would make the other woman in the scene Mary of Clopas.

The old woman with her headscarf may represent the old prophetess of the Temple, Anna (which is also the name of Mother Mary's mother), and thus, the shadowy head so close above the old woman may be seen to be Simeon. Anna's pose gives a crafty air to this one. It is a painting of various overlapping alter egos, of ones that the artist (privy to many of the secrets of the artist's guilds of Europe) would have placed there, removing Jesus' body from the cross. One might assume that these would be the extended members of the Holy Family.

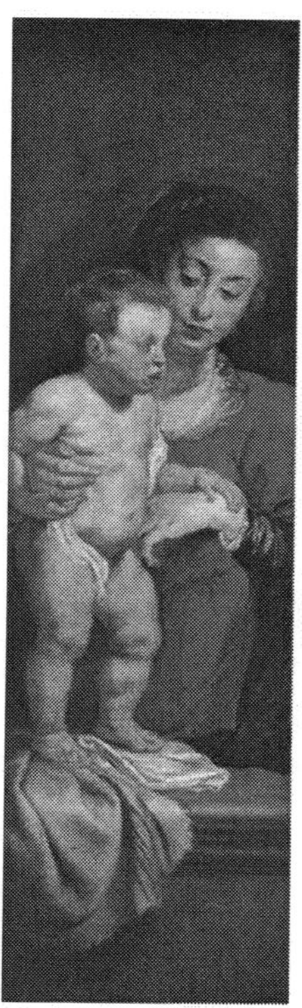

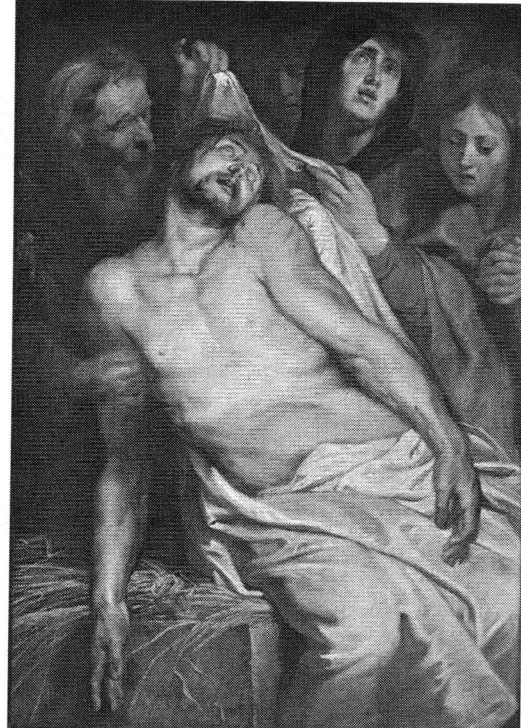

Plate 8 - Lamentation of Christ - Peter Paul Rubens

In the 17th century triptych by Rubens, called *Lamentation*, it would seem to be the Madonna and John in the side panels. However a black veiled Mother Mary is depicted in the central scene, with, it seems, the Magdalene at her side (with the features of the woman in the left panel) and John's face barely visible behind her. Who has Rubens depicted at the left, then? It is not the face of Mother Mary, but of Mary Magdalene from the central panel, with the infant Jesus. The woman above Jesus' head wears the dark veil of the Virgin Mary. The woman holding the infant on the left wears the colors of John (seen on the right). Who is meant to be whom?

The *Deposition* by Jacopo Tintoretto (1518/19 – 1594) brings to mind paintings of Simon Magus falling to earth, but here, the positions are reversed, with the Magdalene (with braided hair) in the "airborne" position, arms outstretched. In this work there is a close mingling of five figures: Jesus' body stretched out across the canvas – the others with their limbs entwined, John supporting his body.

Plate 7 - The Deposition - Tintoretto

The Virgin Mary seems to be fainting in grief – or is it more than that? She mirrors the position of Jesus, and together, they form the X, from the Greek word, Christos, which comes into English as "Christ". Here, again we have three Mary's. Which is Mary of Clopas, and which is Mary Salome?

Medieval tradition saw Clopas as the second husband of Saint Anne and the father of "Mary of Clopas". Catholic and Orthodox traditions believed that Clopas, also known as Cleophas (who saw the risen Christ on the road to Emmaus), is a brother of Saint Joseph. (Eusebius of Caesarea, *Church History*, Book III, ch. 11)

In the name, "Mary of Clopas", the "of" is used to denote her connection to (belonging to) a male figure, in this case, Clopas. However, in this time period, it could denote "married to", or it could denote "daughter of". Many scholars suggest that she was married to Clopas.

The apocryphal *Gospel of Pseudo-Matthew*, which was written in around the 7th century, states that Mary of Clopas was daughter of Clopas and Anna: "Jesus met them, with Mary His mother, along with her sister Mary of Clopas, whom the Lord God had given to her father Clopas and her mother Anna, because they had offered Mary the mother of Jesus to the Lord. And she was called by the same name, Mary, for the consolation of her parents." This would make Mother Mary and Mary of Clopas sisters - but it may simply be an effort to explain why there were two sisters named Mary. There is the possibility, again, of them being alter egos of the same person. It is unnecessarily confusing, and so, might be presumed to be deliberately murky.

There is another explanation for this situation. *Mar* (from Classical Syriac: Mār(y), written with a silent final *yodh*) is a title of respect in Syriac, literally meaning 'my lord'. It is given to all saints and is also used before the Christian name of bishops. The obscure variant *Marya* or Moryo is used in the Syriac *Peshitta* Old Testament to render the Tetragrammaton (God's name/"Our Lord"). How does this relate to the phrase used for Mary, "Our Lady"? The corresponding feminine form given to women saints is Marth. (Mary of Bethany's sister was Martha.) Was Martha one of the "Mary's?

There is a bit of wordplay found in early Syriac lexica, that the letters each have a meaning: ܡ , māruṯā, 'lordship', ܪ , rabbuṯā, 'majesty', and ܝ, iṯyā, 'self-existence'

In Mishnaic Hebrew, the Aramaic word Mar(y) is pronounced *mar*, and it is used as a formal way of addressing or referring to a male person. The Aramaic-speaking Jews shared many cultural attributes with the Syriac Christians. In the Modern Hebrew "Mar" is used without distinction for any male person, like "Mr." in English. However, in Rabbinical circles of Jews from the Middle East, the Aramaic variant form *Maran*, (Aramaic: our lord) is still a title used for highly appreciated Rabbis. One might see the three Mary's as belonging to the nobility, or even, could it be, as part of the priestly caste?

ISLAMIC VIEW ON THE CRUCIFIXION

We know that there are discrepancies among the stories of the crucifixion. The Gnostic texts do not mention the crucifixion of Jesus. The Ebionites, one of the earliest sects of Christianity, though they attested to the crucifixion, did not believe in the concept of it being for the atonement of sin. The Cathars, and the Bogomils (from Bulgaria), as well as the Muslims, specifically state that the crucifixion of Jesus did not happen.

Islamic texts categorically deny the idea of the crucifixion of Jesus. The Quran states that Jesus was not crucified but instead, was raised up by God unto the heavens, through bodily ascension. "...That they said (in boast), 'We killed Christ Jesus the son of Mary, the Messenger of God'; but they killed him not, nor crucified him, but so it was made to appear to them, and those who differ therein are full of doubts, with no (certain) knowledge, but only conjecture to follow, for of a surety they killed him not - Nay, Allah raised him up unto Himself; and God is Exalted in Power, Wise." Quran, *surah* 4 *(An-Nisa), ayat* 156-158

A verse from the Quran explains the anti-Trinity reasoning that Christ cannot equate to God: "In blasphemy indeed are those that say that Allah is Christ the son of Mary. Say: "Who then hath the least power against Allah, if His will were to destroy Christ the son of Mary, his mother, and all every-one that is on the earth? For to Allah belongeth the dominion of the heavens and the earth, and all that is between. He createth what He pleaseth. For Allah hath power over all things."

The crucifixion of Jesus would have gone very much against the theology of the Quran. The Biblical stories recounted in the Quran, (e.g., *Job*, *Moses*, *Joseph* etc.) and the narrative of the beginning of Islam, demonstrate that it is "God's practice" *(sunnat* Allah) for faith to triumph over evil and adversity. For Jesus to die on the cross would have been unthinkable – the Quran asserts that they undoubtedly failed: "Assuredly God will defend those who believe," and, "He confounds the plots of the enemies of Christ."

There is a minority of Muslims who believe that the crucifixion was historically accurate. Mahmoud Ayoub speaks for this small segment of the faith: "The Quran is not here speaking about a man, righteous and wronged though he may be, but about the Word of God who was sent to earth and returned to God. Thus the denial of killing of Jesus is a denial of the power of men to vanquish and destroy the divine Word, which is forever victorious."

Like the Muslims, the Cathars and Bogomils also denied the crucifixion. With so many protests against the validity of the Crucifixion story, what would be the reason for including the story if it were not the truth? Certainly, Eusebius used the symbol of the cross (sort of) to support the idea that Constantine had been given the *Chi Rho* vision as a reinforcement of Christian beliefs. However, it may be that the crucifix as the manner of Jesus' death was meant to reinforce the guilt of the Romans – whatever may have been written of Jewish guilt in the New Testament. Perhaps it is the hidden statement: death by crucifixion was a Roman form of corporal punishment, and not a Jewish one. But the assigning of guilt is complicated.

MIDRASHIC WRITINGS

In the Talmud there are, seemingly, a number of veiled derogatory references to Mary and Jesus, though there has been much debate on the subject. Some rabbis have claimed that Joshua and its derivative names were very common in the time period that they were written, and not necessarily references to Jesus.

Later scholars have a range of opinions on satirical references to Jesus in the *Talmud.* Jacob Z. Lauterbach (1951) recognized only relatively few passages that actually have Jesus in mind, while others concluded that most of the references were related to Jesus, but were non-historical satirical oral traditions which circulated among Jews as more or less folk tales. Schafer (2007) concluded that the passages were, in fact, parodies of parallel stories about Jesus in the New Testament, incorporated into the Talmud in the 3rd to 4th centuries, that illustrate the inter-sect rivalry between Judaism and nascent Christianity.[78] Some editions of the Talmud removed the references around the 13th century. However, most modern editions published since the early 20th century have restored most of the references.

A long tradition of interpreting the name, "Yeshua ben Pantera" as a reference to Jesus exists outside normative Jewish commentary. The early use of the name by Celsus, the pagan philosopher, gave an account of Jesus which he claimed to have obtained from a Jew, who insisted that Jesus was the illegitimate child of Mary and a soldier named Pantera. Other spellings include Pantiri, or Pandera. Also, the first name, "Yeshu," is sometimes used. There is a conversational passage in the Talmud:

> "The master said: Jesus the Nazarene practiced
> magic and deceived and led Israel astray."
> "Jesus son of Stada is Jesus son of Pandira?"
> Rav Hisda said, "The husband was Stada
> and the lover was Pandera."
> "But was not the husband Pappos son of
> Yehuda and the mother Stada?"
> No, his mother was Miriam, who let her
> hair grow long and was called Stada.
> Pumbedita says about her: "She was unfaithful
> to her husband."

In *Jesus in the Talmud* by Peter Schäfer, he writes, "His mother's true name was Miriam, and "Stada" is an epithet which derives from the Hebrew/Aramaic root *sat.ah/sete'* ("to deviate from the right path, to go astray, to be unfaithful"). In other words, his mother Miriam was also called "Stada" because she was a *sotah*, a woman suspected, or rather convicted, of adultery."[79]

While there may be many levels of puns in this passage, some scholars suggest that "*stada*" is a pun on the phrase "*stat da*" meaning that she has "turned away from her husband." The phrase brings to mind the words of Jesus on divorce in *Luke* 16:18: "Whosoever putteth away his wife, and marrieth another, committeth adultery: and whosoever marrieth her that is put away from *her* husband committeth adultery." Jesus, like John the Baptist, might also have had Herod Antipas in mind in this statement, for taking his brother's wife.

There is also a possible connection of *stada* to the Greek word "*stata*," which derives from the same root as the words "*stauros*," and "*stauroo*," (which are, generally, translated as "cross" and "crucifixion") and "*stabat*" (which means "standing"). In paintings of the crucifixion scene, there is a format known as the "*stabat mater*," which translates to the "Standing Mother," and depicts Mary at the foot of the cross. It is possible that the term is a pun on this word, as it was connected in Christianity to Mary.

Another take on the meaning of Pantera/Pandira is that it may be a distorted reference to the story of Mary's conception of Jesus, according to gospel accounts, before she and her husband Joseph had completed the period of their betrothal. In contrast to the doctrine of the Virgin Birth, the old Jewish tale (the non-Talmudic *Toledot Yeshu*) alleges that Mary sinned with a man named Pandera, Pantera, or Panthera. Some scholars say this is a pun on the Greek word, *parthenos*, which means "virgin." Thus we would have a satirical commentary in Jesus ben Pandera, the "Son of a Virgin."

In the Presentation of Jesus at the Temple to the elderly Simeon, a significant figure from the older religion (Judaism) testifies to the new religion. Simeon, in *Luke* 2:25-35, who has been waiting all his long life to see the Messiah, can now die fulfilled. In reaction to such Christian propositions, the Jews composed polemical writings, like the *Toledoth Yeshu* which gives a sharply satirical version of the life of Jesus. (Much as Josephus does with his story of Jesus ben Ananias.) This Jewish "History of Jesus" is an anti-Christian polemic and a refutation of the idea of Jesus as the Messiah of Jewish prophecy. Some scholars conclude that the *Toledot Yeshu* is an elaboration on anti-Christian themes in the Talmud. Robert Van Voorst calls the *Toledot* a record of popular polemic "run wild".[80] (Brings to mind some modern-day political diatribes.)

Though the satirical stories claim that Jesus was an illegitimate child, who practiced magic (a common polemical accusation), and heresy, seduced women, and died a shameful death, they also display a paradoxical respect. As Joseph Dan notes in the *Encyclopedia Judaica,* "The narrative in all versions treats Jesus as an exceptional person who from his youth demonstrated unusual wit and wisdom, but disrespect toward his elders and the sages of his age."[81] However, it was not Jesus' mission to continue in the paths of certain Judaic teachings - blood sacrifices, legalism, and exclusionism - but to bring a New Covenant that would lift people onto a higher path.

The opinion of Father Edward H. Flannery is representative: “This scurrilous fable of the life of Jesus is a medieval work, probably written down in the tenth century.” He goes on to say, “Though its contents enjoyed a certain currency in the oral traditions of the Jewish masses, it was almost totally ignored by official or scholarly Judaism. Anti-Semites have not failed to employ it as an illustration of the blasphemous character of the Synagogue."[82] But Christians did much the same with slurs on the character of the Jews and the Muslims.

The Wagenseil version of the narrative tells of a great misfortune which struck Israel in the year c. 90 BCE.[83] In this story a man of the tribe of Judah, Joseph Pandera, lived near a widow who had a daughter called Miriam, a virgin was betrothed to Yohanan, a Torah-learned and God-fearing man of the house of David (perhaps the source of the story of John and Mary marrying at Cana). Before the end of a certain Sabbath, Joseph, lusting after Miriam, knocked on her door and pretended to be her husband, but she only submitted against her will. When Yohanan came later to see her, she noted his strange behavior. Thus they both knew of Pandera's crime and Miriam's fault. Without witnesses to punish Pandera, Yohanan left for Babylonia.

Then Miriam gave birth to Yeshua, whose name in this tale was later depreciated to Yeshu. When old enough, she took him to study the Jewish tradition. One day he walked with his head uncovered, showing disrespect, in front of the sages. This betrayed his illegitimacy and Miriam admitted him as Pandera's son. Scandalized, he fled to Upper Galilee.

The sages tried to hang Yeshu on a tree, but the trees kept breaking, so they finally hung him on a cabbage stalk. Later his body was missing from his tomb, but they found a gardener had taken the body, which they recovered, tied to a horse's tail and dragged to Queen Helene. She praised them for revealing him as a false prophet.[84]

This particular story was set about a hundred years before the time of Jesus. Another similar version was set about a hundred years after the time of Jesus, but many scholars find both stories to be rabbinical satire about Jesus and Mary.

Fearing that the oral traditions might be forgotten, Judah HaNasi undertook the mission of consolidating the various opinions into one body of law which became known as the *Mishnah*, and was published in about 200 CE. (Codex Judaica Cantor, NY, 2006) At the time when the Talmud was still in a state of formation, negative commentaries on Jesus and Mary were common. Even after the time of the completion of the Talmud, which occurred in the 2nd to 4th centuries CE (after the Bar Kochba Revolt), the Rabbinical Jesus-tradition continued to be expressed in the *Gemara* (commentary on the *Mishnah*), and the *Midrashim* (homiletic literature), especially the *Midrash Kohelet* or *Midrash on Ecclesiastes*.

There are some references in Christian texts to the ideas expressed regarding Mary in the Jewish Midrash. In the *Gospel of Matthew,* Joseph, apparently not comprehending the nature of Mary's divine conception of Jesus, didn't want to expose Mary to public shame, so he considered divorcing her (undoing their betrothal) quietly. An angel appeared to him in a dream and said, "Joseph, son of David, do not fear to take Mary as your wife, for what is conceived in her is through holy spirit. And she will give birth to a son, and you shall call his name Jesus, for he will save his people from their sins." (*Matthew* 1:19-21) The *sotah* Trial of the Bitter Waters is not mentioned in the canonical gospels, but the *Gospel of Matthew* tells of Joseph's concern upon learning of Mary's conception of the Lord. For Joseph, it was a serious dilemma. All of the Christian narratives describe a miraculous conception and birth – not the usual human birth at all.

The apocryphal *Gospel of Pseudo-Matthew*, from the early 7th century, claims that the Virgin Mary underwent the process of *sotah*, when Joseph discovered that she was with child – after their betrothal, but before they became husband and wife. This story would seem to be a response to satirical references to her pregnancy, and Virgin motherhood. In this pseudepigraphical story, she was not harmed by the bitter waters (it was not your typical pregnancy, after all). She was finally believed; she had truly been overshadowed by the Holy Spirit and "had not known man", and the marriage went forward.

In Jewish tradition, a woman accused of adultery underwent the humiliating process of *Sotah*, the "ordeal of the bitter waters" described in the Priestly Code in the *Book of Numbers*. This trial by ordeal was administered to a wife whose husband suspected her of adultery, but who had no witnesses to make a formal case.

The priest states that if the woman is innocent, the "water of bitterness" will not harm her, but, he says, "...if thou be defiled, and some man have lain with thee besides thy husband--then the priest shall cause the woman to swear with the oath of cursing, and the priest shall say unto the woman--the LORD make thee a curse and an oath among thy people, when the LORD doth make thy thigh to fall away, and thy belly to swell; and this water that causeth the curse shall go into thy bowels, and make thy belly to swell, and thy thigh to fall away ..."

Some scholars interpret this to be, more or less a way of shaming the woman into confession. Others claim that it was, in fact, a process of giving the woman a drug or chemical that would cause a miscarriage, if indeed, there was an unborn child – thereby making sure that she would have no child that did not belong to her husband. Women were the property of their husbands – this was the law. There was no corresponding law regarding an adulterous husband.

According to *Mishnah, Sotah,* 9:9 the practice was abolished sometime during the first century CE under the leadership of Yohanan ben Zakkai. (Yohanan is Jonathan.) Rabbinical commentary indicates that, even if it had not been abolished, the rite would have ended with the fall of the Temple (in approximately 70 CE), because, according to the Law, the ceremony could not be performed elsewhere. Also, Yohanan Ben Zakkai stated: "When adulterers became many, the ordeal of the bitter water stopped, for the ordeal of bitter water is performed only in a case of doubt. But now there are many who see their lovers in public". It is also said that under Yochanan's influence, animal sacrifices were abandoned in favor of prayer as the primary means of atonement between man and God. Could this Jewish sage, Yohanan Ben Zakkai, have been another identity for John son of Zacharias, who was beheaded for castigating Herod Antipas for taking his brother's wife in adultery?

In the "Ordeal of the Bitter Water", the woman was humiliated by having her breasts bared, furthermore, the priests unbound the woman's hair, things which were not done in public. It was meant to be humiliating – this was meant to be a deterrent to women even considering being unfaithful!

Details of the trial of the Bitter Waters is documented in *Numbers* 5:11-31, as well as in *Nashim* ("Women or Wives"), in the *Talmud*. There may be some reference to the teachings in *Chassidut*, where the higher water is water of joy, the experience of being close to God, while the lower water is water of bitterness, being separate or far from God, requiring penance in order to bring one back to unity with God.

In later Jewish writings, Jesus and Mary are framed within often satirical references to the upstart sect that was once part of Judaism. Jesus may have been considered a rebel to the established traditions of Judaism, but the devastating aftermath of the 2nd century Bar Kochba Revolt is the source of the real rancor, stemming from Jews blaming Christians for the ruination of the city – and, it would seem, of Judaism itself – thus their understandably scurrilous slurs on the characters of Jesus and Mary.

The Hebrew name "Yeshu" instead of "Yeshua," is said to be satirical wordplay, an acrostic representing a polemical statement. The three consonants j, s, and v, with which the name Jeshu was written, represent the first letters of the three words: j = *jinimach,* sh = *sh'mo,* v = *v'zichro,* which mean, "may be blotted out his name and his memory"![85] This brings to mind the use of *damnatio memoriae* by the Romans, who often erased a traitorous name from monuments and tombstones, as well as from any historical reference.

"Spin-doctoring" was not exclusive to the Christian faith. It was practiced by various theologians of any and all of the major religions. However, perhaps because of the in-depth study of the Torah practiced by rabbis, and the Jewish faithful, in general, it was so well-developed in rabbinical writings against Christianity as to be considered an artform, which is why we must carefully consider the use of double meanings in any rabbinical text. The negating of Jesus' Messianic role by Orthodox Jews created an ongoing tension between the faiths.

These polemical traditions were developed and expanded, and reached their full expression in the Middle Ages. The *Toledot Yeshu* literature originated in the Middle Ages and still continues. In these writings, a detailed picture of the life of Jesus was put forth, of which the authors of the Jewish Talmud had no anticipation. The satires include a mean fanaticism, malicious delight in defamation, and vulgar imagination which is generally seen as outrageous in lack of respect. We must remember that this can be seen in Christian satires which claimed that the Jews were anything from low-mannered , to over-sexed, to baby-killers.

R. Shimeaon ben 'Azzai said: "I found a genealogical roll in Jerusalem wherein was recorded, 'Such-an-one is a bastard of an adulteress.'" McDowell and Wilson state, on the authority of Joseph Klausner, that the phrase *such-an-one* "is used for Jesus in the *Ammoraic* period (i.e., fifth century period)." The Ammorim were Jewish scholars who "said" or "told over" the teachings of the Oral Torah, from about 200 to 500 CE in Babylonia and Israel. (This was after the time not only of Jesus, but of the Bar Kochba Revolt.) Their legal discussions and debates were eventually codified in the *Gemara*. It is hard to know how much these polemical writings influenced, through corrections, or additions to the text, the previous writings of Judaism.

Another passage from *Sanhedrin* 106b includes details that some apologists connect to Jesus of Nazareth:

"Balaam also the son of Beor, the soothsayer, [did the children of Israel slay with the sword]. A soothsayer? But he was a prophet! R. Johanan said: At first he was a prophet, but subsequently a soothsayer. R. Papa observed: This is what men say, 'She who was the descendant of princes and governors, played the harlot with carpenters....!" R. Hanina claims that Balaam was thirty-three or thirty-four years old; the text goes on to say, "Thou has said correctly; I personally have seen Balaam's chronicle, in which it is stated, 'Balaam the lame was thirty years old when Phinehas the Robber killed him."

There are stories about the Perpetual Priesthood of Phinehas, who earned this for his lineage because of some reconciliatory act. While he is mentioned in Ps 106, it isn't clear what he did wrong that required reconciliation. Marko Martilla writes, "In the beginning of the 2nd century B. C. E., Ben Sira highlights Phinehas in his lengthy work, "The Praise of the Ancestors" (Sir. 44–50). Just as in Ps 106, Ben Sira also leaves out the violent details of Phinehas' intervention. For Ben Sira, Phinehas is a significant figure because Ben Sira favored the hereditary, Aaronite priesthood. Ben Sira makes a remarkable addition to his sources by claiming that Phinehas' descendants would be granted an everlasting high priesthood. A statement like this links priestly and royal aspects tightly together."[86]

A footnote in the Jewish Encyclopedia explains: "Balaam is frequently used in the Talmud as a type for Jesus ... all the Balaam passages are anti-Christian in tendency. Balaam being used as an alias for Jesus, Phineas the Robber is thus taken to represent Pontius Pilate, and the *Chronicle of Balaam* probably to denote a Gospel." (Is Phinehas Pontius Pilate, or is he a high priest? Or is Pontius Pilate a high priest?) It states, "in the case of the wicked Balaam [Jesus]: whatever you find written about him, lecture upon it to his disadvantage."

This is a very important acknowledgment of rabbinical attitudes towards Jesus after the Diaspora – that any mention of Balaam (code for Jesus) should be unflattering. In common polemical fashion, Christian churches were described as tents for Baal prostitution, with young women inside hoping to get customers drunk and disrobe and worship the "IDOL," Jesus, through prostitution.

The passage in *Sanhedrin* 106b includes the statement, "They subjected him to four deaths, stoning, burning, decapitation and strangulation." Since one cannot be killed in all these manners, this bit of rabbinical satire would seem to imply that the manner of death may have been given differently in different texts. Notably, we do not see crucifixion.

Interestingly enough, these Jewish legends also show a conflation of Mary, mother of Jesus, with Mary Magdalene. The Hebrew for "Miriam, the women's hairdresser" is *Miriam megadla nashaia* (translated as Mary M'gaddla, the hairdresser). One might see this as a deliberate garbling of Gospel references to Mary Magdalene and Jesus' mother Mary. However, it must, again, be noted that Islam makes reference to only one Mary (Maryam). Why would a Jewish satire of Mary and Jesus, conflate Jesus' mother with Mary Magdalene?

According to Origen, the pagan philosopher, Celsus, authored an anti-Christian work titled *The True Word*, which calls into question the truth of Jesus, who is called "The Word" in the Gospels. This work, itself, is said to have been lost, excerpts preserved only through Origen's refutation of the text, which was interspersed with his own replies. Was there an actual work by the title *The True Word*? There is a common rhetoricist's device of debating an issue by first giving the opposition's perspective (real or imagined) and then refuting it.

The meaning of the name, Celsus, is: lofty, high, and tall, but also, haughty, arrogant, and proud. Perhaps such a polemical text never existed, or such an author as Celsus. Perhaps many refutations of accusations towards Christianity were simply exercises in rhetorical expression.

The Greek term, *Progymnasmata*, which means "before" and "exercises," describes a system of rhetorical exercises, meant to delineate basic rhetorical concepts and strategies. Some of the exercises in the handbook written by 4th century rhetorician, Aphtonius of Antioch include the use of: fable, narrative, anecdote (*chreia*), proverb (*maxim*), refutation, blame (*invective*), tribute (*encomium*), comparison (*syncrisis*), characterization (impersonation or *ethopoeia*), description (*ekphrasis*), thesis (theme), and deliberation –defending/attacking a law.

These exercises were used to help a student learn by practicing and increasing rhetorical skills. George A. Kennedy writes, " ... a major feature of the exercises was stress on learning refutation or rebuttal: how to take a traditional tale, narrative, or thesis and argue against it."[87] Evans (1977: 81), who wrote about the standards of philosophical argument, mentions that "Aristotle requires of the serious dialectician ... fidelity [according with the real or expressed views of the other party] in representing the views of others ..."[88] However, Aristotle indicates in several places (Topics 105 b 6; *On Sophistical Refutations* 174 b 21) how this principle of fidelity for genuine refutation could be exploited in sophistical refutation, by only giving the appearance of the real view of the other party as the basis for one's refutation.

This is a clear indication that refutations in general, such as Origen's *Contra Celsus*, may, in fact, have been rhetorical works that first proposed the opposition's viewpoint, and then gave rebuttal of each point mentioned. The lack of corroborating evidence suggests that Origen was using the rhetorical device of a false opponent, attributing a variety of statements to him, for the purposes of dialectical argument. It is quite possible that Celsus was not a real person, and that his antagonistic "claims" were simply put forth by Origen, himself, as a kind of "straw man" strategy, and as a foil for Origen's own position.

The True Word, which was "only preserved in the writings of Origen," addressed many foundational teachings of Christianity by refuting its philosophical and theological claims, by marking it as being related to the uneducated and lower class, and by branding it as dangerous to the Roman Empire. According to Origen, Celsus mounted a broad, as well as a personal, campaign against Jesus. As with any smear campaign, everything was fair game: Origen claims that Celsus discounted and disparaged Jesus' ancestry, conception, birth, legitimacy, childhood, ministry, death, resurrection, and ongoing influence in the region.

The work by Celsus was said to have been written in the late 2nd century CE, before the final redaction of the *Talmud* and *Tosefta*, but after the first account of the story appeared, during the time of Eliezer ben Hyrcanus (that is, after suppression of the Bar Kochba Revolt, and Hadrian's destruction of the Jewish Temple). Origen has Celsus equating Yeshu to Jesus and Pandera to the name Panthera, as well as drawing from the story of the heretic, ben-Stada.

In both the *Talmud* and the *Mishna*, the term *minuth*, meaning "heresy" was applied by Jews to Christians. In rabbinical writings, not only Jesus, but all Christians were heretics. In the eyes of the Jewish rabbis, Christians were "heretical Jews."[89] In rabbinical satire, Ben Stada, is said to be the illegitimate son of Miriam the braider, and a man named Pandera. Though no connection is made in the *Talmud* or *Tosefta* between this Pandera and Yeshu ben Pandera, Celsus connects them. He also connects "Miriam the braider" to Mary. The mention of the lover-soldier is a detail drawn from yet another story – that of Miriam, the daughter of Bilgah, who in the *Talmud*, is not connected to Miriam the braider, or to Mary.

The *Talmud Sukkah* (56b) states: "Our Rabbis taught, It happened that Miriam the daughter of Bilga apostatized and married an officer of the Greek government. When the Greeks entered the Sanctuary, she kicked with her shoe upon the altar, crying out, 'Lukos! Lukos![Wolf! Wolf!]. Until when will you consume Israel's money, and not stand by them in the time of oppression?' When the Sages heard of the incident, they fastened down her ring and closed up her cabinet..." The ring was used to tie the sacrificial animal, the cabinet held utensils used in the act of sacrifice. This is said to have happened before 63 BCE, and not in the same century as Mary and Jesus, but it seems to have been conflated with other stories to indicate Jewish slurs against Mary as a disobedient daughter of the faith.

The Talmud places Yeshu ben Pandera in the mid-2nd century CE. Perhaps there is some relationship to the story of the messianic Bar Kochba, who was said to have led the Jewish revolt in the mid-2nd century and created a free nation of Israel that lasted for more than 2 ½ years. Bar Kochba means "Son of a Star." For the time period that his revolution was successful, he was seen, perhaps by both Christians and Jews, as the star of the campaign for independence from Rome. When Hadrian crushed the revolt and destroyed Jerusalem, Bar Kochba became known by the orthodox Jews as Bar Kosiba, the "Son of a Liar."

So, we have the references in Islam to one Mary, we have the satirical conflation of Marys made by the pagan writer, Celsus, and we also have a co-mingling of the two Mary's in certain Jewish records. It seems that these conflations were a way of speaking on the subject in a cryptic way, so as to make a point, but not in an open manner. Perhaps it was necessary to speak cryptically on the subject – one could so easily be killed for one's opinions in certain times.

Jews maintained the tradition in the 5th century that Mary was a hairdresser, but M'gaddla seems to refer to Mary Magdalene, not the Mary traditionally called the mother of Jesus. At the 1240 Disputation of Paris, Donin presented the allegation that the *Talmud* was blasphemous towards Mary, the mother of Jesus (Miriam in Hebrew). The texts cited by critics include *Sanhedrin* 67a, *Sanhedrin* 106a, and *Shabbath* 104b. However, the references are not specific, and some insisted that they do not refer to Jesus' mother, or even proposed that they refer instead to Mary Magdalene.[90]

According to *Chiltons*, the Rabbis of this era considered hairdressing to be "one step away from prostitution." In general, *Midrash* writings tended to marginalize the beliefs of other religions by the use of allegory, and puns; thus, the play-on-words of the names, Mary M'gaddla, and Yeshua ben Pantera, instead of Mary Magdalene and Yeshua ben Joseph. Perhaps these writings influenced Pope Gregory I's idea that Mary Magdalene was a reformed prostitute.

It was not unusual for rabbis to use puns for their cryptic as well as their satirical value. (Our stand-up comedians of today had nothing on the rabbis of the 1st and 2nd Centuries!) However, even in its polemical statements about Jesus and Mary, the Midrashic commentary is confirmation of their factual existence, and of their influence in the region in that time period. Also, because the early followers of Jesus were considered to be a radical sect, outside the accepted norms of Judaism, and perhaps, even the cause for the failure of the Bar Kochba Revolt, Jesus and Mary would, understandably, be the target of Jewish Rabbis who wished to discredit them, and Christianity, in general.

On the other hand, Islam, whose Quranic *surahs,* generally mirror Christian narratives, portrays Miriam and Isa in a very positive light. Islam does not regard Jesus as the "Son of God," but honors him as a great prophet who came before Muhammad. Judaism, understandably, portrays them much less favorably.

The Quran includes a narrative of the virgin birth of Jesus. It states that, Mary was in the midst of the desert in *Bayt Lahm* (Bethlehem), when the pains of childbirth came upon her. Mary cried in pain and held onto a palm tree, whereupon, a voice came from "beneath her." The narrative of the infant speaking is seen to refer to Jesus, speaking from within her (her womb). The voice said "Be not grieved; God has provided a rivulet under thee; and shake the trunk of the palm and it shall let ripe dates fall upon thee, ready gathered. And eat and drink and calm thy mind". Jesus was born of Mary, while she was in the desert.

Forty days later she carried him back to her people. The Quran goes onto say that Mary vowed not to speak to any man on that day, as God was to make Jesus perform his first miracle. In *Surah Maryam*, it states that Mary brought Jesus to the Temple, where she was taunted by all the men, except Zachariah, who believed in the virgin birth. Having been commanded by Gabriel to a vow of silence (in the Quran narrative, at least), she simply points to the infant Jesus who, miraculously, speaks: "Indeed, I am the servant of Allah. He has given me the Scripture and made me a prophet. And He has made me blessed wherever I am and has enjoined upon me prayer and *zakah* as long as I remain alive And [made me] dutiful to my mother, and He has not made me a wretched tyrant. And peace is on me the day I was born and the day I will die and the day I am raised alive.' That is Jesus, the son of Mary - the word of truth about which they are in dispute." Jesus is the "word of truth."

In the Quran, after hearing Jesus speak, the people say to her: "O Maryam! Truly, an amazing thing have you brought! O sister of Aaron! Your father was not an adulterous man, and your mother was not an immoral woman!" (*Surah Maryam* 19:28) Why this particular exclamation? There were already satirical stories at this time that such was true. But we must also consider - who is the adulterous man in the New Testament?

In the rabbinical stories of Jesus the illegitimate son of a Roman soldier, it would seem blatantly obvious that the Jewish rabbis were criticizing Christianity. It appears to be in opposition to belief in the Virgin birth, and Jesus as "the Messiah". The question remains: why a Roman soldier? It seems to be an intentional jab, but towards whom?

THE SPEAR OF LONGINUS, THE CENTURION

It is clear that Christianity was taken over by those who originally oppressed and persecuted the early Christians. When people think of the Christian teachings of the Roman Catholic Church, they would do well to consider that, well before Constantine, in all his imperial benevolence, took it upon himself to "catholicize", or universalize, this contagiously spreading belief system, the Romans had been slaughtering Christians by the thousands, and entertaining themselves in the Colosseum with the wildly popular sport of throwing early Christians to the lions. The "Diocletian persecution," a period of extreme brutality towards Christians, happened just prior to Rome's acceptance and legalization of Christianity under Constantine.

The legalization of Christianity was a sea change, a huge shift in societal norms. Massive numbers of Gentiles were being converted to Christianity during this time period, and the faith was taking on a life of its own. Eventually, after many clashes and uprisings, and the most brutal repression, the Roman conquerors gave in to the irresistible tide, while also syncretizing many belief systems into one. In striving to create a peaceful empire, Constantine's efforts may have created a distortion of the original teachings. Could this be part of the accusation in rabbinical commentary suggesting that Jesus was the son of Mary and a Roman soldier? If the Jewish community wanted to make a scathing statement about the Roman elite, who is the Roman soldier that they would most likely be referring to?

There was a lance that was honored as the holy relic that was used by a centurion to pierce Jesus' side at the crucifixion. But was the lance already a holy relic, long before the time of the crucifixion? Might we transpose the spear or lance as being the "rod," such as the rod of Aaron, the high priest, or the staff of Moses. Did each of these brothers have a rod of the high priesthood? If, indeed, it was not a lance, but a rod of the high priesthood, then its holiness would have been related to its use by the Jewish high priests, which would have implications regarding the Roman soldier. The name of the centurion, was Longinus (from *longche,* which means "lance").

The earliest image of the crucifixion in an illuminated manuscript, is found on the cover of the Rabbula Gospel, from the 6th century. It shows a man to the left of Jesus and one to the right, each holding a long pole. The first is said to be Longinus, with his spear, and the second is said to be Stephaton with a pole on which rests a gall-soaked sponge, which, in mockery, was offered to Jesus to drink.

While the word, LOGINOS on the Rabbulas manuscript, is often said to be an early reference to the Centurion, Longinus, there is a more likely interpretation. Notably, the original spelling as LOGINOS, with the first "n" missing, does not seem to be a reference to a lance, but rather the diminutive form of LOGOS, meaning, "The Word". And so, it might be interpreted as, "the little Word." The name could be seen as being above the head of the soldier holding a spear, written in horizontal Greek letters, LOGINOS. But it could more likely be said to be written beside the figure of Christ on the cross. The change to the name Longinus seems to be a later addition to the story, to connect it to *longche*. It makes an inventive pun on both words, and takes away focus from Jesus as "the little Word." Thus, Longinus "of the lance" may have other connotations.

The name, Longinus is said to be Latinized from the Greek *longche*, the word used for the lance mentioned in *John* 19:34, which would indicate that it was, very likely, not the actual name of the centurion, but rather a codified pseudonym for one who carried the lance. We must keep in mind that the stories are, many times, coded references, carrying hidden truths. Pilate (meaning "javelin") "washed his hands" of the fate of Jesus, allowing the people to have their way. The high priests of the Temple were known to ritually "wash their hands" before any sacred act, particularly sacrifices. Is this phrase meant to connect to Pilate's role in the death of Jesus as being the decision of a high priest?

The *Midrash Yelamdenu* (*Yalḳ*. on Ps. ex. § 869) states that "the staff with which Jacob crossed the Jordan is identical with that which Judah gave to his daughter-in-law, Tamar. It is likewise the holy rod with which Moses worked, with which Aaron performed wonders before Pharaoh, and with which, finally, David slew the giant Goliath. David left it to his descendants, and the Davidic kings used it as a scepter until the destruction of the Temple, when it miraculously disappeared." This would be a Holy artefact, long before the time of Jesus.

However, the Old Testament depicts each of the two brothers, Moses and Aaron of the high priesthood, with their own rods. Moses' rod, cited in *Exodus* 4:2 first signified his work as a shepherd, tending his sheep. In Exodus 4:20, it becomes a symbol of his authority over the Israelites (*Psalm* 2:9, *Psalm* 89:32, *Isaiah* 10:24 and 11:4, *Ezekiel* 20:37). The rods of Moses and Aaron were endowed with miraculous power, demonstrated during the Plagues of Egypt (*Exodus* 7:17, 8:5, 8:16-17, 9:23, and 10:13). When the Israelites came to the Red Sea in their flight from the Egyptians, God commanded Moses to raise his rod and the waters were parted (*Exodus* 14:16). Moses strikes his rod against a stone, bringing forth water. (*Exodus* 17:2-6).

One of the first dependable historical reference to the Holy Lance, as a post-resurrection relic, was made by the pilgrim, Antoninus of Piacenza, in 570 CE, which is a rather late "proof" of its authenticity. In his descriptions of the holy places of Jerusalem Antoninus wrote that he saw in the Basilica of Mount Zion "the crown of thorns with which Our Lord was crowned and the lance with which He was struck in the side". Presumably, this refers to the Byzantine basilica Hagia Sion that was built under John II, Bishop of Jerusalem in the early 5th century. The lance is also mentioned as a relic in the *Brevarius* at the Church of the Holy Sepulchre, which was consecrated in the 4th century, but in both of these cases, the name of Longinus, the Centurion, is not mentioned.

Arculf states that the lance was in Jerusalem when he was there in 670 CE. Bede simply repeats the words of Arculf. Willibald's failure to mention the spear, in 723 CE, though he mentions other holy relics in the city, seems to confirm that it was not in Jerusalem at that time.

John 19:34 states that, "One of the soldiers pierced his side with a lance and immediately there came out blood and water." The crucifixion narrative states that "blood and water" flowed from the wound – something which Origen considered as one of the holy mysteries. Scientific explanation finds this quite compatible with death by crucifixion. The symbolism of the blood and water flowing from the body of Christ, affords allegorical interpretation: it represents one of the key mystery teachings of the Church, and one of the main themes of the *Gospel of Matthew*, which is the *homoousian* interpretation adopted by the First Council of Nicaea, that "Jesus Christ was both true God and true man." The blood symbolizes his humanity, the water his divinity.

A ceremonial remembrance of this is done when a Catholic priest says Mass: The priest pours a small amount of water into the wine before the consecration, an act which acknowledges Christ's humanity and divinity and is said to represent the issuance of blood and water from Christ's side on the cross.

Many paintings of the crucifixion contain references to the spear of Longinus. One might see this as a sincere effort to accurately depict the crucifixion scene. It was reproduced by many artists in that light. Such a tangible relic, in itself, was seen to provide "proof", and reinforcement of the crucifixion story.

According to legend, Longinus, thrust the spear in Jesus' side, some traditions say, as a mercy, to speed his death, and end his suffering, while others say it was to make sure that he was dead. An early tradition, found in the pseudepigraphical "Letter of Herod to Pilate", said to date from the 4th-century, claims that Longinus suffered terribly for having pierced Jesus. In this narrative, he was condemned to a cave where a lion mauled him every night until dawn, after which his body healed again, in a pattern that would repeat till the end of time. Other legends of the Lance of Longinus followed, giving the lance supernatural powers for various military operations. One legend contends that this lance, made holy by the blood of Christ, was carried by Constantine into battle, bringing him glorious success in his military operations.

The centurion who witnessed the crucifixion is unnamed in the Gospels, and so he would seem to have little significance to the crucifixion story. He is first named in the pseudepigraphical *Gospel of Nicodemus,* also known as *The Acts of Pilate,* circa the 4th century, a late addition which gives us reason to question the historicity of the name. This gospel was appended to the apocryphal *Acts of Pilate.*

Later traditions turned Longinus into a Christian convert, and even a saint, but Sabine Baring-Gould observed: "The name of Longinus was not known to the Greeks [Eastern Christianity] previous to the patriarch Germanus, in 715. It was introduced amongst the Westerns from the Apocryphal *Gospel of Nicodemus.* There is no reliable authority for the *Acts* and martyrdom of this saint."[91] How might we interpret the story of one who attended the crucifixion, with spear (rod) in hand, which was used to pierce Jesus' side, who later was considered to be a saint?

Contradicting the portrait of Longinus as a sinner is another work which claims to be a letter from Pilate to Herod. Here Procla (Pilate's wife) and Longinus are both converted after personally meeting Jesus after the Resurrection. (Pilate also becomes a Christian in this work.) In this letter, Longinus is identified with the centurion.

Pilate lamented his own actions, writing to Herod that, "Persuaded by you, I did a terrible thing on that day the Jews brought to me Jesus, the one who is called the Christ. They, along with the centurion, reported to me how he was crucified and arose from the dead on the third day. But I myself was persuaded to send messengers to Galilee. They saw him in the same flesh and in the same appearance; and he revealed himself in the same voice and with the same teaching to more than five hundred godly people, who as witnesses brought forth their testimony about this, expressing no doubts in the matter but preaching extensively the resurrection and declaring the eternal kingdom—so that the heavens and the earth appeared to rejoice at his holy teachings."

It goes on, "When he said these things, my wife, Procla, heard them, along with the centurion, Longinus, who had been entrusted to watch over the suffering of Jesus, and the soldiers who accompanied them. They all came, weeping and grieving, to proclaim these things to me."

Outside of Christianity, the name, Longinus, appears in the assassination of Julius Caesar. Brutus is the assassin of Julius Caesar (*Et tu Brute*!). However, Brutus had a co-conspirator, who was commonly known as Cassius. His full name was Gaius Cassius Longinus. If there was, indeed, a Roman soldier who pierced Jesus' side with a spear at the crucifixion, the later traditions made political use of the story. This name of a famous traitor in the crucifixion story, could well be a reference to Longinus as one of the betrayers of Jesus. In Dante's "Inferno," three people are portrayed as sinful enough to be chewed in one of the three mouths of Satan, in the center of Hell, for all eternity, as a punishment for their crimes (similar to the story of Longinus being eternally mauled by a lion). They are Cassius (Longinus), Brutus, and Judas Iscariot, the betrayer of Jesus.

The image of Jesus on the cross, with the wound in his side, echoes the story of Adam, with a wound in his side, where the rib was taken to form Eve. The two examples are very much alike. Is this coincidental or deliberate? In Adam's case, it is said to represent the closeness of the woman, created from his side so as not to be above him or below him, but to walk at his side. Is there an intended connection of this story with Mary, who often stands beside Jesus at the crucifixion? How might Longinus be connected to this Jewish narrative of Eve created from the side/rib of her husband?

The "Spear of Longinus" may have to do with the reference to Jesus being hung upon a "stauros," which is interpreted to actually mean a "pale" or pole, and not a cross. Certainly, the Talmud gives the account that Jesus was stoned, and then, perhaps, his remains impaled, or hung on a tree, as a deterrent to others. There are many possible connotations to consider in the development of this particular facet of the Crucifixion Story.

The Talmud describes the death of Jesus as first by stoning, and then hanging. (It doesn't mention a crucifix), "And it is tradition: On the eve of Passover they hung Jeshu [the Nazarene]. And the crier went forth before him forty days (saying), [Jeshu the Nazarene] goeth forth to be stoned, because he hath practiced magic and deceived and led Israel astray. Anyone who knoweth aught in his favor, let him come and declare concerning him. And they found naught in his favor. And they hung him on the eve of the Passover."

It goes on, "Ulla said, 'Would it be supposed that [Jeshu the Nazarene] a revolutionary, had aught in his favor?' He was a deceiver and the Merciful (i.e. God) hath said (*Deut.* xiii 8), 'Thou shalt not spare, neither shalt thou conceal him.' But it was different with [Jeshu the Nazarene] for he was near the kingdom."' (*Sanhedrin* 43a) It isn't clear what was different for Jesus, but the phrase, "near the kingdom," would seem to refer to a connection to the royals of Judea.

There is an interesting detail regarding Clopas (Clophas or Cleophas). Hegesippus, wrote, around 180 CE, that he had learned from the grandsons of Jude the Apostle that Clopas was the brother of Joseph, husband of the Virgin Mary: "After the martyrdom of James, it was unanimously decided that Simeon, son of Clopas, was worthy to occupy the see of Jerusalem. He was, it is said, a cousin of the Savior."[92] Epiphanius says not only that Joseph and Cleopas were brothers, he adds that they were sons of "Jacob, surnamed Panther."[93] Here, along with the satirical Wagenseil version of the *Toledot Yeshu*, which told of Joseph Pandera, who took advantage of the young woman, Miriam, we have the connection: Panther, Pantera, Pandira, through the lineage of Joseph.

THE SON OF GOD

The *Gospel of Matthew* details the terrifying and awe-inspiring events at the moment of Jesus' death: "Jesus, when he had cried again with a loud voice, yielded up the ghost. And, behold, the veil of the temple was rent in twain from the top to the bottom; and the earth did quake, and the rocks rent; And the graves were opened; and many bodies of the saints which slept arose, And came out of the graves after his resurrection, and went into the holy city, and appeared unto many."

The *Gospel of Matthew* 27:54 gives the reaction of the centurion and the other witnesses to these events, "Now when the centurion, and they that were with him watching Jesus, saw the earthquake, and those things that were done, they feared greatly, saying, Truly this was the Son of God."

The famous sculptor, Bernini, carved a very affecting statue of

Longinus in the early 17th century, depicted in the moment of his apophatic realization that, truly, this was the Son of God. His arms are flung outward in shock, the spear in his right hand, his face with the undefined white eyes, suggesting blindness, or perhaps, amazement.

Located in an alcove of St. Peter's Basilica (take note) Bernini's *Longinus* seems to stare up at the top of the *ciborium* – the massive bronze covering with four Solomonic columns, standing over the altar (and tomb of St. Peter). The top of the structure holds a sphere of the earth, topped by a cross. Not coincidentally, this entire structure was also created by Bernini, and so, the positioning of this sculpture seems quite deliberate.

Plate 9 - Longinus - Bernini

"This was the Son of God" - where was this comment made before? It is the third time these words are spoken in this gospel. As already noted, several chapters earlier, when Jesus asks Peter, "Who do you think that I am?" he responds, "Thou art the Christ, the Son of the living God." (*Matthew* 16:16) In this same gospel, the only gospel used by the early sect of the Ebionites, a gospel written in times when the truth could not be spoken, not only does Peter state that Jesus is the Son of God, but later, Jesus responds to Caiaphas' accusation of blasphemy on this point by saying, "*you* have said so", when, in fact, only Peter has said so at this point in this gospel.

After the trial and the crucifixion, Longinus is the third person to make this statement. It is not coincidence. The narrative is a codified confirmation of the identity of the Roman Soldier, first connecting Peter to Caiaphas, and then to Longinus. The text clearly indicates that the centurion was one of the three who made this statement. In his astonished experience of the death of Jesus – in his apophatic moment of realization captured in Bernini's theatrical statue at the Basilica of St. Peter – Longinus, the Roman Soldier, exclaimed, "Truly this was the Son of God." (*Matthew* 27:54, *Mark* 15:39)

JOSEPHUS AND THE JEWISH WAR

Titus Flavius Josephus, was born in Jerusalem (then part of Roman Judea), as Yosef ben Matityahu, to a father of priestly descent and a mother who claimed royal ancestry. He was a first-century Romano-Jewish historian, who describes himself as the author of a treatise called *The Wars of the Jews,* "Joseph, the son of Matthias, by birth a Hebrew, a priest also, and one who at first fought against the Romans myself, and was forced to be present at what was done afterwards, [am the author of this work]". (*Jewish Wars* Book 1, Preface, Paragraph 1, 1:3)

Josephus initially fought against the Romans as an important leader of the Jewish armies during the First Jewish–Roman War. He was head of Jewish forces in Galilee, (the town that Peter and his brother, Andrew, came from) until surrendering in 67 CE to Roman forces, led by Vespasian, after the six-week siege of Jotapata. Josephus not only opted out of a suicide pact with his fellow soldiers upon their capture (for which he was vilified by many of his countrymen), but he also saved his own neck in the long-term by prophesying that Vespasian would become Emperor of Rome. Vespasian, in response, kept Josephus as a slave and interpreter. After Vespasian became Emperor in 69 CE, he granted Josephus his freedom, and Josephus assumed the emperor's family name of Flavius. One wonders if, perhaps, Josephus had connections to the Romans long before he became a historian of Jewish history for a Roman audience.

During the First Jewish-Roman War, there was another writer, Justus, a Jewish leader in Galilee, who ran into conflict with Josephus,. When the Romans had reconquered Galilee, Justus sought sanctuary with the Tetrarch Agrippa. Vespasian, who led the Roman troops, demanded that Justus be put to death, but Agrippa spared him and merely imprisoned him. The tetrarch even appointed Justus as his secretary, but later dismissed him as unreliable.

Interestingly, Justus wrote a history of the war in which he blamed

Josephus for the troubles of Galilee. Justus portrayed his former master, in an unfavorable light, but did not publish the work until after Agrippa's death. Justus also wrote a chronicle of the Jewish people from Moses to Agrippa II, which might be seen as an opposing work to Josephus' *Antiquities.* Both of Justus' works survive only in fragments.

Flavius Josephus, Justus' rival, criticized the Tiberian's account of the war and defended his own conduct in the *Autobiography*, from whose polemical passages we derive most of what we know about Justus' life. If Justus was a pseudonym for a writer (or a perspective) of an important figure of the times, we might consider the possibility of this being the view of James the Just or his followers.

Considered a traitor by many of his Jewish compatriots, Josephus fully defected to the Roman side, surrendering in 67 AD to Roman forces led by Vespasian after the six-week siege of Yodfat. He was granted Roman citizenship, and became an advisor and friend of Vespasian's son Titus, serving as his translator when Titus led the Siege of Jerusalem in 70 CE. Since the siege proved ineffective at stopping the Jewish revolt, the city was destroyed by the Romans, and the looting and destruction of Herod's Temple (Second Temple) soon followed.

Josephus recorded Jewish history, particularly focusing on the 1st century CE and the First Jewish–Roman War (66–70 CE), including the Siege of Masada. His best-known works are: *The Jewish War* (c. 75) and *Antiquities of the Jews* (c. 94). *The Jewish War* recounts the Jewish revolt against Roman occupation. *Antiquities of the Jews* chronicled the history of the world from a Jewish perspective, but for an ostensibly Greek and Roman audience. These works are often cited as valuable texts that provide rare insight into 1st century Judaism and, though not directly addressed by Josephus, the development of Early Christianity.

In *Antiquities*, Josephus writes of the Christians being forewarned to leave Jerusalem through terrible visions of chariots and troops in the clouds, earthquakes and "a great noise," and "a sound as of a great multitude, saying, 'Let us remove hence'." He follows this by making the very interesting statement about one called "Jesus, the son of Ananus." In some texts, his name is given as Jesus ben Ananias, or in some Hebrew texts, as Jesus ben Hananiah.

In *Antiquities*, Josephus wrote, "But, what is still more terrible, there was one Jesus, the son of Ananus, a plebeian and a husbandman, who, four years before the war began, and at a time when the city was in very great peace and prosperity, came to that feast whereon it is our custom for every one to make tabernacles to God in the temple..." . This Jesus continued his prophecy for more than seven years until he was, reportedly, killed by a stone from a catapult during the Roman siege of Jerusalem during the war.

Many scholars want to separate this Jesus from the Jesus of the bible, and make him some unknown crazy man. The name ben Ananus is intriguing as well. Ananus/Ananias was the high priest in the time of Jesus, who had five sons in the priesthood. Josephus says that the Romans flogged Jesus ben Ananus.

To say that Josephus, the Jewish soldier-turned-Roman-historian, was influential is a great understatement. Much of our understanding of the history of the time came from his texts. It would appear that his influence may be much more than most have recognized.

He states that this particular Jesus, "...began on a sudden to cry aloud, 'A voice from the east, a voice from the west, a voice from the four winds, a voice against Jerusalem and the holy house, a voice against the bridegrooms and the brides, and a voice against this whole people!' This was his cry, as he went about by day and by night, in all the lanes of the city." (Josephus, *Antiquities*, Book VI, Chapter V)

The Jesus in Josephus' story is prophesying doom upon the city of Jerusalem. It is important to keep in mind that this story is told by Josephus, whom many of the Jews saw as a traitor for surrendering, and becoming a "whitewashing" historian for the Romans.

Josephus makes Jesus ben Ananus out to be, not only crazy, but a lowly plebeian – a commoner, a "husbandman", a "farmer." In other words he was not patrician, but was, rather, a poor, crude, and coarse person; essentially, in Josephus' estimation, a person of no consequence. More than that, Josephus makes this Jesus a threat to the people. Scholars generally claim that this is not Jesus, son of Mary, but that would be too coincidental. Why would he make another Jesus out to be such an important figure, and include him in his history of biblical times. However "Romanized" his version was, he was simply using the device of a pseudonym – and a very telling one at that.

Jospehus continues, "However, certain of the most eminent among the populace had great indignation at this dire cry of his, and took up the man, and gave him a great number of severe stripes; yet did not he either say any thing for himself, or any thing peculiar to those that chastised him, but still went on with the same words which he cried before. Hereupon our rulers, supposing, as the case proved to be, that this was a sort of divine fury in the man, brought him to the Roman procurator, where he was whipped till his bones were laid bare; yet he did not make any supplication for himself, nor shed any tears, but turning his voice to the most lamentable tone possible, at every stroke of the whip his answer was, 'Woe, woe to

Jerusalem!'"

This seems to be a derisive paraphrasing of *Matthew* 24:2 where Jesus responds to the remark of one of the disciples on the great buildings on the Temple Mount. Jesus gives prophecy of complete destruction of the Temple, "Seest thou these great buildings? there shall not be left one stone upon another, that shall not be thrown down." The statement also appears in *Luke* 21:6, and *Mark* 13:1. This prophecy came true in the destruction of Herod's Temple (the Second Temple) in 70 CE, by Titus and his Roman troops.

Josephus depicts this Jesus as crazy, though we might note that he was flogged, as Jesus ben Joseph (son of Mary) was, and maintains his silence, just as Jesus did in his trial. Josephus writes, "And when Albinus (for he was then our procurator) asked him, Who he was? and whence he came? and why he uttered such words? he made no manner of reply to what he said, but still did not leave off his melancholy ditty, till Albinus took him to be a madman, and dismissed him. Now, during all the time that passed before the war began, this man did not go near any of the citizens, nor was seen by them while he said so; but he every day uttered these lamentable words, as if it were his premeditated vow, 'Woe, woe to Jerusalem!'"

According to Josephus, Jesus ben Ananus lived until the time of the siege in 70 CE, "Nor did he give ill words to any of those that beat him every day, nor good words to those that gave him food; but this was his reply to all men, and indeed no other than a melancholy presage of what was to come. This cry of his was the loudest at the festivals; and he continued this ditty for seven years and five months, without growing hoarse, or being tired therewith, until the very time that he saw his presage in earnest fulfilled in our siege, when it ceased; for as he was going round upon the wall, he cried out with his utmost force, 'Woe, woe to the city again, and to the people, and to the holy house!' And just as he added at the last, 'Woe, woe to myself also!' there came a stone out of one of the engines, and smote him, and killed him immediately; and as he was uttering the very same presages he gave up the ghost." Josephus' account does not say that this Jesus was crucified.

In biblical accounts, Jesus the Christ was a great leader, teacher, and miracle-worker, born of the lineage of David – he was no less than the Son of God. In Josephus' account, Jesus, son of Ananus, was not a wise man, or a master teacher, who had a huge following in the region, but was just some babbling crazy person speaking curses on the city. There is no record of "Forgive them, Father, for they know not what they do." Instead of dying with the words of submission, "Father, into Thy hands I commend my spirit," Josephus has this Jesus submit to his fate with, "Woe, woe to myself also!" The Jesus ben Ananus of Josephus' "history" brought it all upon himself.

Herod the Great bequeathed to his youngest son, Herod Antipas, nothing but the tetrarchy of Galilee and Perea, While Antipas went to Rome to fight for more of his father's territory, Augustus ratified the terms of the last will. Josephus, who, in the first part of the "History of the Jewish War," speaks of him as Herod in relating the division of Judea; adding, "he who was called Antipas" ("B. J." ii. 9, § 1).

While it is possible that rabbinical satire about the Roman Soldier fathering the child of Mary M'gaddla had to do with Imperial intrusion into and appropriation of the Christian faith, it is likely that the Roman soldier comes closer to home than any of the Roman Emperors. Was this man a Jewish leader, who worked in tandem with the Roman government to suppress the early Christian movement – someone who served as translator for Titus during the siege on Jerusalem - someone like Josephus, the traitor-historian, who seems to have white-washed any Roman fault in the execution of Jesus.

By whose authority did Josephus create his "Romanized" version of the story of Jesus? By the authority of the Roman Emperor-soldier, Titus, whom he worked for. What term could be more derogatory than calling Josephus a "Roman Soldier" - an indictment of the betrayal by the Jewish soldier, Josephus, in collaborating with the Romans?

It states in the *Infancy Gospel (the Arabic Gospel of the Infancy of the Savior),* regarding the birth narrative of Jesus: "We find what follows in the book of Joseph the high priest, who lived in the time of Christ. Some say that he is Caiaphas." Indeed, we know that Joseph Caiaphas was married to the daughter of Ananias. But what book was written by Joseph the high priest? Josephus admits that he, himself, was a high priest. It was said later in the Syrian Church that Caiaphas had been converted to Christianity, and was identical with the historian, Josephus!

Simon Peter, Joseph Caiaphas, Josephus – it makes the head spin. And let's not forget Joseph of Arimathea, who offered a burial site of his own family for the burial of Jesus. This Joseph was a rich man as in the allegory in Jesus' teachings: "sooner can a camel go through the eye of a needle than a rich man go to heaven". Joseph of Arimathea is often depicted as richly dressed, with white hair and turbaned head, much like Tertullian. He is depicted thus in paintings of the "Deposition" or "Descent from the cross". Josephus also is depicted in this manner.

And lastly, the Joseph that we learn so little about...Joseph, the earthly "father" of Jesus. Why do we not know more about him? Because his identity was hidden in the form of many alter-egos, surely, recognized in early

Christianity, but not so much in modern times.

PENTECOST: THE COMFORTER COMES

In *Matthew* 3:11, John the Baptist states, "I indeed baptize you with water unto repentance: but he that cometh after me is mightier than I, whose shoes I am not worthy to bear: he shall baptize you with the Holy Ghost, and with fire".

Acts of the Apostles 2:1-4 gives a narrative of the miraculous occurrence at the *Cenacle* (the Upper Room) on Mt. Zion, on Pentecost, where 120 followers of Jesus were gathered, "And when the day of Pentecost was fully come, they were all with one accord in one place. And suddenly there came a sound from heaven as of a rushing mighty wind, and it filled all the house where they were sitting. And there appeared unto them cloven tongues like as of fire, and it sat upon each of them." In Judaic teachings, the *Shekinah* is often described as a flame or fire.

There are echoes of this event in the *Gospel of John*, when Jesus makes a post-resurrection appearance to the disciples in a room that was locked for fear of the Jews. It isn't clear that this was the Upper Room of the account in *Acts*. "Jesus said to them again, 'Peace be with you. As the Father has sent me, so I send you.' When he had said this, he breathed on them and said to them, 'Receive the Holy Spirit. If you forgive the sins of any, they are forgiven them; if you retain the sins of any, they are retained.'"(*John* 20:19)

In her book, *Holy Misogyny: Why the Sex and Gender Conflicts in the Early Church Still Matter,* April D. DeConick states that the Holy Spirit was considered to be the breath of life. In accordance with the Jewish term *ruah*, the Holy Spirit (or "breath"), when given a gender, was seen as feminine – the power of God that instructs and saves, that purges, and judges, and purifies, "washing away the sins of Israel, and cleansing the stains of impiety." DeConick writes, "Even more startling, the Spirit is said to be God's covenant with Israel. She is his sacred Law. As such, the Law is a spirit that rests in his people. The priests taught that the Jewish Law and other teachings of the Lord (the Jewish God, *Yahweh*) were carried by his Spirit and given to the prophets, who, in turn, delivered them to the people of Israel."[94]

In the Jewish Temple, the *Shekinah* came to rest upon the Mercy Seat atop the Ark of the Covenant, in the *Debir*, the Holy of Holies. For this reason, the high priest was the only one allowed into this inner sanctuary, only once a year, and had to be purified in order to sustain the high level of purity required to be able to witness the "presence of God," without being harmed. Mary, was, of course, called the Ark of the New Covenant, in reference to her status as the "bearer of God." In Jewish terms, the breath of God, the *Shekinah*, had come to rest within her, and become the "indwelling presence". The name, Jesus, in Aramaic form, is Yeshua, from *yesh*, meaning "being." The Greek spelling of his name, *Iesous,* incorporates the root word *ousia*, which means, "being, essence, presence", and has a second meaning of *hypostasis*, which would relate to the *hypostatic* union – that is, the union of divine and human natures in the single person of Christ.

DeConick goes on to say, "The story of Balaam particularly caught the attention of later Jewish interpreters since the great Angel of the Lord, the angel who is Yahweh's earthly manifestation, bids Balaam to go out and not worry about his speech. The Angel of the Lord tells Balaam that he will only be able to say the words that the Angel will inspire him to speak. But later in the narrative, when Balaam speaks on behalf of God, it is the Spirit of God who comes upon him and delivers the discourse. On this account, Philo of Alexandria, a Jew writing at the turn of the Common Era, understood that the "Angel of the Lord" and the "Spirit" were the same entity. Josephus, a Jewish historian in the late first century CE, understands them to be synonymous too. Might we then say that the Angel of the Lord that came to Mary at the Annunciation was one and the same with the *Shekinah* of Judaism?

The Holy of Holies was called the *debir* in Hebrew, from the root word, *dibbur*, meaning "speech", but often with connotations of Divine Speech, or revelation, which connects the Holy of Holies to prophecy. In the *Gospel of John*, Jesus is introduced with the phrase, "In the beginning was the Word, and the Word was with God, and the Word was God."

In the Old Testament the "word" of God is often personified as an instrument for the execution of God's will (*Psalm* 33:6; 107:20; 119:89; 147:15-18). By making the connection of Jesus to the "Word," *John* is in a sense pointing back to the Old Testament where the "Word" of God is associated with the personification of God's revelation, the *Shekinah* expressed through Jesus. In Greek philosophy, the term *Logos*, meaning "Word," was used to describe the intermediate agency by which God created material things and communicated with them. In the Greek worldview, the *Logos* was the bridge between the transcendent God and the material universe. Therefore, for his Greek readers, John's use of the term *Logos* signified a mediating principle, or messenger, between God and the world.

In regards to the coming of the Paraclete, Jesus stated: "But the Counsellor, the Holy Spirit, whom the Father will send in my name, he will teach you all things, and bring to your remembrance all that I have said to you." (*John* 14:26) And later Jesus also states, "Nevertheless I tell you the truth; it is expedient for you that I go away: for if I go not away, the Comforter (the *Paraclete*) will not come unto you; but if I depart, I will send him unto you". (*John* 16:7) This indicates that Jesus departed in order to make space for the *Paraclete*. In Christianity, this is seen to be the Holy Spirit.

Christians, generally, believe that the Paraclete came to the Upper Room where the disciples were gathered, in the form of the Holy Spirit at Pentecost. Though it is not mentioned as such in the Gospels, *Acts* 2 gives an account of the events of Pentecost, where the disciples were gathered in the Upper Room. "These all with one mind were continually devoting themselves to prayer, along with the women, and Mary the mother of Jesus, and with His brothers."

In Pope John Paul II's *Redemptoris Mater*, in 1987, he states that in the Upper Room, "We see Mary prayerfully imploring the gift of the Spirit, who had already overshadowed her in the Annunciation." This pope, who was devoted to Mary, connects the "overshadowing" of Mary by the Holy Spirit with the descent of the Holy Spirit on those gathered in the Upper Room at Pentecost. In other words, the gifts of the Holy Spirit were accessible to all who followed the teachings of Jesus.

In *Acts* 2, Peter takes the floor, exhorting and inspiring those gathered to also accept the gifts of the Holy Spirit. His long monologue ends with, "Then Peter said unto them, Repent, and be baptized every one of you in the name of Jesus Christ for the remission of sins, and ye shall receive the gift of the Holy Ghost. For the promise is unto you, and to your children, and to all that are afar off, *even* as many as the Lord our God shall call. And with many other words did he testify and exhort, saying, Save yourselves from this untoward generation. Then they that gladly received his word were baptized: and the same day there were added *unto them* about three thousand souls." (*Acts* 2, 38:41) *Acts* says that, because of Peter's exhortations and wise words, three thousand souls were converted. In this scene, Mary speaks not at all, and disappears from *Acts* altogether at this point. Soon after, the "Apostle to the Gentiles," Paul, makes his first appearance.

In *Acts* it states that when those in the Upper Room began speaking in tongues: "And there were dwelling at Jerusalem, Jews, devout men, out of every nation under heaven. Now when this was noised abroad, the multitude came together, and were confounded, because that every man heard them speak in his own language." In some sense, this reflects the opposite of the Tower of Babel, where "speech was confounded" and the people could no longer understand each other.

There are Christian paintings of this event, depicting a group of haloed figures with "tongues of flames" above their heads – the fire of the Holy Spirit having descended upon them. One might also see a reflection of this in the Persian paintings of Muhammad (and his companions) with head and sometimes, bodies surrounded by flames of holiness.

Acts goes on, "While the disciples spoke in tongues, Peter stood up with the eleven and proclaimed to the crowd that this event was the fulfillment of prophecy." In *Acts* 2:17, it says: 'And in the last days,' God says, 'I will pour out my spirit upon every sort of flesh, and your sons and your *daughters will prophesy* and your young men will see visions and your old men will dream dreams." Peter proclaimed this to be the beginning of a continual outpouring that would be available to all believers from that point on, Jews and Gentiles alike – an indication that Peter also endorsed the mission to the Gentiles (not to mention endorsing female prophets here).

Acts gives that, after returning from Mount Olivet, the 12 Disciples along with about 108 others, received the Baptism of the Holy Spirit in the Upper Room. *Acts* 2:41 then states: "Then they that gladly *received His word* were baptized: and the same day there were added unto them about three thousand souls." This verse states that those baptized "received His word" (like Mary, who submitted to His word at the Annunciation). This statement reflects the idea of Adoptionism, where the descent of the Holy Spirit at Jesus' baptism made him the Son of God. In essence, at Pentecost, they were all made Sons, and since women were present, Daughters of God, also.

It is interesting to note, in *Acts* 1:26, that Mary is the only one to be mentioned by name other than the eleven apostles. After this point, she disappears from biblical accounts, although it is held by Catholics that in Revelation, she is the woman "clothed with the sun."

THE ASSUMPTION OF MARY

Psalms 132:8 Says, "Arise, O Lord, into thy resting place: thou and the ark, which thou hast sanctified". Christian tradition tells us that while Jesus "ascended" into heaven, Mary, at her death was "assumed" into heaven. What is the significance and the distinctions between these two terminologies and concepts? The doctrine of the Assumption of Mary developed over centuries, likely beginning in 451 CE, with the story told to Emperor Marcion when he requested the relics of Mary to be delivered to Constantinople. The Patriarch of Jerusalem explained to the emperor that there were no relics of Mary in Jerusalem, that "Mary had died in the presence of the apostles; but her tomb, when opened later ... was found empty and so the apostles concluded that the body was taken up into heaven."

Methodius wrote of the Presentation at the Temple that Mary, the Ark of God, had received the Lord into her pure bosom and "she presented Him there to God the Father-the Son joint-partner of His throne, and inseparable from Him – together with that pure and undefiled flesh which He had from her assumed ..." [95]

Methodius states that, "We adore God — *who assumed flesh from the Virgin*, and therefore is God according to the Spirit; man according to the flesh." He goes farther than most to emphasize Mary's role as Mediatrix and Co-Redemptrix – it is Mary who makes the Incarnation possible. He quotes Habakkuk, "'For then shall You be shown forth,' He says, 'as upon a kingly charger, by Your pure and chaste mother, in the temple, and that in the grace and beauty of the flesh assumed by You.' All these things the prophet, summing up for the sake of greater clearness, exclaims in brief: 'The Lord is in His holy temple'."[96] (*Habakkuk* 2:20)

Eutyches admitted that there was a union of two natures, the divine and the human, but he denied that they remained as two natures after the incarnation, asserting that the two natures had become united into one nature. St. Cyril stated, "Mother of God, who contained the infinite God under your heart, whom no space can contain: through you the most Holy Trinity is revealed, adored, and glorified..." He goes on, "demons are vanquished, Satan cast down from heaven into hell and our fallen nature again assumed into heaven."

Pope John Paul II spoke on the dogma of the Assumption of Mary, in a General Audience of 1997, "These descriptions of Mary's relationship to Jesus give an indication of why, at her death, she was assumed into heaven at her 'Assumption'. Although the New Testament does not explicitly affirm Mary's Assumption, it offers a basis for it because it strongly emphasized the Blessed Virgin's perfect union with Jesus' destiny. This union, which is manifested, from the time of the Savior's miraculous conception, in the Mother's participation in her Son's mission and especially in her association with his redemptive sacrifice, cannot fail to require a continuation after death. Perfectly united with the life and saving work of Jesus, Mary shares his heavenly destiny in body and soul." [97] This is about the most concise and powerful explanation for Mary's Assumption into Heaven that this pope could give.

In the somewhat different teachings regarding the Dormition

narrative (the "Falling Asleep of Mary) in the Orthodox Liturgy/eastern Christianity, an angel meets Mary on the Mount of Olives, and brings to her a palm branch from the tree of life in paradise and announces to her that her time of death has come. The apostles gather round her, as Mary prepares for her death. When the moment comes, the crowds are put to sleep, all except the apostles and three virgins, who see Jesus and a host of angels appear. She makes her goodbyes to the Apostles, with the words, "Rejoice! I am with you all the days of your lives." This is very similar to Jesus' words at the end of the Great Commission, "Lo, I am with you always."

At the beginning of the 5th century, a pilgrim from Armenia visited "the tomb of the Virgin in the valley of Josaphat", and about 431 CE, the *Breviarius de Hierusalem* notes in that valley "the basilica of Holy Mary, which contains her sepulchre. Thenceforth pilgrims of various rites repaired thither to venerate the empty tomb of Mary." This would have been the Church of the Sepulchre of St. Mary - the great Temple-like *Nea Ekklesia* was not built until around 527–565 CE.

Epiphanius wrote, c. 390, before the dogma of Mary's assumption was set, "Say she died a natural death. In that case she fell asleep in glory, and departed in purity and received the crown of her virginity. Or say she was slain with the sword according to Simeon's prophecy. There her glory is with the martyrs, and *she through whom the divine light shone upon the world* is in the place of bliss with her sacred body. Or say she left this world without dying for God can do what He wills. Then she was simply transferred to eternal glory." (*Haer.* lxxix, 11).

At the Council of Chalcedon (451), St. Juvenal, Bishop of Jerusalem, made known to the Emperor Marcian and Pulcheria, who wished to claim the body of the Mother of God, that Mary died in the presence of all the Apostles, but that her tomb, when opened upon the request of St. Thomas, was found empty; whence the Apostles concluded that the body was taken up to heaven.

The Assumption of Mary is mentioned in the East, in the sermons of St. Andrew of Crete, St. John of Damascus (the Damascene), St. Modestus of Jerusalem and others. In the West, St. Gregory of Tours (*De gloria mart.*, I, iv) mentions it first. John of Damascus, wrote three homilies on the Assumption of Mary in the 8th century. His work was fundamental to the formulation of Church dogma on the subject.

On Mary's Assumption, John Damascene asserted: "He who had been pleased to become incarnate (of) her...was pleased...to honor her immaculate and undefiled body with incorruption...prior to the common and universal resurrection." He goes on, "And just as the all holy body of

God's Son, *which was taken from her*, rose from the dead on the third day, it followed that she should be snatched from the tomb, that *the mother should be united to her Son;* and as He had come down to her, so she should be raised up to Him, into the more perfect dwelling-place, heaven itself. It was meet that she, who had sheltered God the Word in her own womb, should inhabit the tabernacles of her Son." He also said of Mary, "From her we have harvested the grape of life; from her we have cultivated the seed of immortality. For our sake she became Mediatrix of all blessings; in her God became man, and man became God."

Hippolytus gives a very interesting and convoluted description of the Ark and its relationship not only to Mary but to Jesus, as well. "At that time, the Savior coming from the Virgin, the Ark, brought forth His own Body into the world from that Ark, which was gilded with pure gold within by the Word, and without by the Holy Ghost; so that the truth was shown forth, and the Ark was manifested...And the Savior came into the world bearing the incorruptible Ark, that is to say His own body." [98] Now that's an interesting statement!

Along with Mary, the Apostles visit heaven; they are returned to earth, while Mary remains in heaven. There are many other icons that make the image much clearer.

In many depictions of Mary's Dormition, her body rests on a kind of platform or bed, perhaps made of rock, or stone, much like a sarcophagus, or even a stone manger. In some depictions of the Dormition, such as El Greco's 16th century *Icon of the Dormition*, Jesus takes Mary's soul, in the form of an infant in swaddling clothes (now there's a connection that should be explored), which he is carrying to heaven. This symbolism was common in the artwork of Eastern Christianity.

* * *

CHAPTER V: JEWISH WAR AND INDEPENDENCE

THE KITOS WAR

The First Jewish-Roman War was just a precursor to other violence that was to follow. Sixty years after the First Jewish War, from 115 to 117 CE, came the rebellions of the Kitos (or Quitos) War, a name related to the Roman general Lusius Quietus, whose troops eventually crushed the rebellions.

After the First Jewish Revolt in 70 CE, the Romans installed a *praetor* as a governor and stationed an entire legion, the X Fretensis in Judea.

Paulus Orosios, Christian orthodox priest and theologian, and author of the first world history by a Christian, wrote of the Kitos rebellions, "The Jews ...waged war on the inhabitants throughout Libya in the most savage fashion, and to such an extent was the country wasted that, its cultivators having been slain, its land would have remained utterly depopulated, had not the Emperor Hadrian gathered settlers from other places and sent them thither, for the inhabitants had been wiped out." [99]

Where Jewish writings often trashed the Romans as barbaric and inhumane, the writings of the Spanish-Christian historian, Paulus Orosius, whose own life history is sketchy, at best, makes the Jews the barbaric ones.

From the Roman perspective, Trajan, who ruled from 98 CE to 117CE, was held to be a great soldier-emperor, who presided over the greatest military expansion in Roman history, leading the empire to attain its maximum territorial extent by the time of his death. He was known for his philanthropic rule, overseeing extensive public building programs and implementing social welfare policies, which earned him an enduring reputation as the second of the "Five Good Emperors" who presided over an era of peace and prosperity in the Mediterranean world.

During seven years of peace, he built many roads, monuments, and buildings, and provided welfare assistance to widows and orphans. He was also famous for some less-than-humane activities, hosting a gladiatorial festival in the great Coliseum in Rome, which provided chariot racing, beast-fighting and gladiator-style battle. This gory spectacle reputedly left 11,000 dead (mostly slaves and criminals, not to mention the thousands of ferocious beasts killed alongside them) and attracted a total of five million spectators over the course of the festival.

Despite his many benevolent works. Trajan's reign also saw many uprisings and much violence. The Kitos War, also known as the *Tumultu Iudaico* (Tumult of the Jews) was a major rebellion of the Jews in multiple regions of the Roman Empire. When the inhabitants of Babylonia revolted, they were suppressed by Quietus, who was rewarded by being appointed governor of Judaea.

Also known as the "Revolt against Trajan", the revolt was initiated in large Jewish communities of the region, such as: Cyprus, Cyrene (modern Libya), Aegipta (modern Egypt) and Mesopotamia (modern Syria and Iraq). It led to mutual killing of hundreds of thousands of Jews, Greeks and Romans, ending with a total defeat of Jewish rebels and the merciless and complete genocide of the Jews in Cyprus and Cyrene by the newly installed Emperor Hadrian.

According to Eusebius of Caesarea, in Cyrene, the rebels were led by a Lukuas or Andreas, who called himself "king". Like the Christian historian and theologian, Paulus Orosius, the Roman historian Lucius Cassius Dio blamed Jewish violence for the depopulation of Libya, and gave ghoulish details of the atrocities committed by the Jewish insurgents. The Jewish Encyclopedia, though it does question the accounts of sources opposed to the Jewish uprising as "embellished" also confirms, "By this outbreak Libya was depopulated to such an extent that a few years later new colonies had to be established there." (Eusebius, *Chronicle* from the Armenian, fourteenth year of Hadrian). Bishop Synesius, a native of Cyrene in the beginning of the 5th century, also speaks of the devastation wrought by the Jews.

In Cyprus, a band of Jewish rebels took control of the island, killing tens of thousands of civilians. According to Cassius Dio, the Cypriot Jews reportedly massacred 240,000 Greeks in total, though this number may be exaggerated. (*Dio's Rome,* Volume V) A small Roman army was dispatched to the island, soon reconquering the capital. After the revolt was put down, laws were created forbidding Jews to live on the island.

After years of constant campaigning, Trajan suffered heatstroke. He began the long journey back to Rome in order to recover, but his health deteriorated rapidly. He was taken ashore at Selinus in Cilicia, where he died.

Lusius Quietus, the conqueror of the Jews of Mesopotamia, also led the Roman army in Judaea. He laid siege to Lydda, where the rebel Jews had gathered under Julian and Pappus. Lydda was taken and many of these Jewish soldiers were executed; the "slain of Lydda" are often mentioned reverently in the Talmud. Rebel Jewish leaders Pappus and Julian were among those executed by the Romans in the same year. [100]

Trajan's cousin and successor, Hadrian, assumed the reins of government in 118. As emperor, he took the unpopular, but far-sighted, decision to end the war, abandoning much of Trajan's eastern conquests, including the province of Mesopotamia, and stabilizing the eastern borders. The situation in Judaea remained tense for the Romans. As with the aftermath of the Jewish Revolt of 70 CE., strong measures were taken to control the population. Hadrian, made a permanent installation of Roman troops of the *Legio VI Ferrata* in Caesarea Maritima in Judaea. The Roman occupation of Judaea brought 14 years of uneasy relations with the Jews, before the, perhaps unavoidable beginnings of the Bar Kochba Revolt.

THE KING MESSIAH

Akiva (Akiba/Yacoub/Jacob/James),
the greatest of the four sages, the *Tana'im*
that entered Pardes from the Holy Place.
Akiva, who said of the Son of a Star,
"Indeed, *this* was the King *Messiah*."
Mystery of mysteries!
In what century did they actually live?
The Independence won in his name,
when the Jews and the Christians were still one.
Bar Kochba, an alter ego? For whom?
For one whose name could not be spoken?
Akiva, and his "King Messiah",
both a century too late.

But history succumbs to the vagaries of time,
veiled truths, and the chaos of the "Lost Century".
The truth remains, but cryptically,
in stories, legends, hidden messages,
though slightly skewed.
Even the revered rabbi's statement of Kingship
could not convince, after the diaspora,
and the desolation, when the "Son of a Star"
became the "Son of Lies".

THE JEWISH INDEPENDENCE

Bar Kochba's initially successful fight against the Romans brought three years of Jewish Independence from Roman interference – hard-fought and hard-won. In the years of the Independence, it is said that Rabbi Akiva called Bar Kochba the "son of a star". The woman and child in the catacombs of Rome, the star above their heads is reference to *Numbers* 24:17 which prophesized: "There shall come a star out of Jacob". Is it even possible that another *Messianic* figure would have existed in this time period without the kind of documentation and reference that had been made to Jesus?

The Book of Enoch was considered as scripture in the *Epistle of Barnabas* (16:4) and by many of the early Church Fathers, such as Athenagoras, Clement of Alexandria, Irenaeus and Tertullian. 1 *Enoch* is the first text to contain the idea of a preexistent heavenly *messiah*, called the "Son of Man". Both 1 *Enoch*, and 4 *Ezra*, promote the expectation of the kingly *messiah* of *Daniel* 7, expanding him into "an exalted, heavenly *messiah* whose role would be to execute judgment and to inaugurate a new age of peace and rejoicing."

However, Tertullian wrote c. 200 that the *Book of Enoch* had been rejected by the Jews around that time period because it contained prophecies pertaining to Christ. Of course, this was after the crushing of the Jewish Revolt, and the dispersion of the Jews. This would be the time of the most intense rejection of such teachings - for the Jews to reject what had perhaps been accepted as sacred teachings prior to the Bar Kochba Revolt.

One must seriously consider that the name "David" was used in early writings to represent the true *messiah*. For it was not David who was thought to be the messiah, but rather one of the lineage of David, the "Davidic king." In Jewish rabbinical debate on the Divine Nature of the messiah, Akiva's position was quoted as, "There is no contradiction: one [throne] for Him, and one for David; this is the view of R. Akiba." In the same way, Akiva, who was said to have named Bar Kochba as the "King Messiah", we must consider the possibility that this name was a disguised reference to the "Davidic King," who lived and died a century earlier.

THE BAR KOCHBA REVOLT

The presence of Roman soldiers in Judea, and the ongoing tensions of the earlier conflicts fostered the background dissatisfaction of the Jews in the region, leading up to the Bar Kochba Revolt (also spelled Kokhba). This general discord had been intensified by Hadrian's construction of a new city, Aelia Capitolina, over the ruins of Jerusalem and, particularly, the erection of a temple to Jupiter on the Temple Mount directly over the place where the Jewish Temple had stood. The Church Fathers and rabbinic literature emphasized the role of Rufus, governor of Judea, in provoking the revolt.

There is little commentary from historians on the relationship between Christianity and the Jewish revolt. Up until Hadrian's suppression of the Revolt, Christian holy sites were being honored in Jerusalem. During the time of Jewish Independence, hard-won by Jewish rebels in the region in 132 CE, Simon Bar Kochba was seen as the greatest Jewish hero. Not only that, but Bar Kochba was claimed, by the great Rabbi Akiva, to be the Messiah!

Because of the early success of the guerrilla warfare of Jewish rebels in the Bar Kochba uprising, and the great losses incurred upon the Roman army, the response of the Roman legions became quite merciless. After three years of independence, the Revolt was put down. According to Cassius Dio, 580,000 Jews perished in the war and many more died of hunger and disease. In addition, many Judean war captives were sold into slavery. Some scholars describe the Roman's brutal aggression toward the Jewish people as a genocide.

One result of the devastation of the Jewish people was that the idea of Jewish *messianism*, which had been thriving in Jerusalem, was now abstracted and often vilified. There was a significant backlash to messianic beliefs after the failure of the revolt, which spotlighted Jesus as a false prophet. Rabbinical thought became deeply cautious and conservative, and rabbinical commentary became very satirical, and polemical towards both Roman and Christian ideals, and was even, sometimes, dystopian.

Confidence in new Prophetic revelation shut down after the Biblical return from Babylon in Second Temple Judaism, shifting to canonization and exegesis of Scripture after Ezra the Scribe. Lesser level prophecy of *Ruach Hakodesh* remained, with angelic revelations, esoteric heavenly secrets, and eschatological deliverance from Greek and Roman oppression of Apocalyptic literature among early Jewish proto-mystical circles.

If Jerusalem was a holy site of Christianity immediately after the death and resurrection of Jesus, and Jesus' tomb was a holy site before Hadrian's destruction of the city, then why isn't Christianity more prominent in the records of the Bar Kochba Revolt? The general silence on the subject is rather remarkable. Most sources do not mention Christianity in connection with the Revolt, though Jerusalem would have been important to Christians, as well as to Jews, which may be the greatest evidence that the two faiths were still united at the time. It is said in some accounts that the Christians left the city before the revolt began, having been forewarned by prophecy of the impending devastation.

Robert Goldenberg asserts that it is increasingly accepted among scholars that "at the end of the 1st century CE there were not yet two separate religions called 'Judaism' and 'Christianity'".[101] Daniel Boyarin proposes a revised understanding of the interactions between nascent Christianity and Judaism in late antiquity, viewing the two religions as intensely and complexly intertwined throughout this period. Boyarin writes: "for at least the first three centuries of their common lives, Judaism in all of its forms and Christianity in all of its forms were part of one complex religious family, twins in a womb, contending with each other for identity and precedence, but sharing with each other the same spiritual food".[102]

He goes on to say, "Without the power of the orthodox Church and the Rabbis to declare people heretics and outside the system it remained impossible to declare phenomenologically who was a Jew and who was a Christian. At least as interesting and significant, it seems more and more clear that it is frequently impossible to tell a Jewish text from a Christian text. The borders are fuzzy, and this has consequences. Religious ideas and innovations can cross borders in both directions." He is saying that Jewish texts may well have been influenced by Christian ones, too.

Perhaps, until this time, the Jewish community believed in a Messianic leader, but, something that is not widely considered is this - it didn't necessarily have to be a present-tense Messiah! The holy sites of Christianity were within the city of Jerusalem. However, the horrifying repercussions of the Revolt left Jerusalem in ruins, and, presumably, both Jews and Christians in exile. It would seem that the devastating consequences of the failed Bar Kochba Revolt brought the crisis which definitively divided the two camps.

It is possible that post-war blame and vilification of Christianity by Jewish leaders may well have wiped out any positive accounts of the relationship between Judaism and Christianity up until this time. In *Jews, God and History*, Max I. Dimont states that, with the brutal suppression of the Bar Kochba Revolt, "The alienation process was completed. Judaism and Christianity became strangers to each other … A wall of misunderstanding and hate was erected by the narrow zealotries of the two faiths."[103] Historical accounts focus on Hadrian's efforts to eradicate Judaism, but the question that arises is this: was it not Jewish, but Christian teachings that were more successfully obliterated, or sent underground, by Hadrian's decrees? Again, it may well have meant a death sentence to speak certain names or teachings in that time period.

Eusebius claims, in his *Life of Constantine*, that the site of Hadrian's temple had originally been a Christian place of veneration, but that Hadrian had deliberately covered these Christian sites with earth, and built his own temple on top, due to his hatred for Christianity. It seems that this was the tomb of Jesus, a site now called the Church of the Holy Sepulchre, which is in the Christian quarter of the walled Old City of Jerusalem. By the early 2nd century, Hadrian had turned the site into a temple of Aphrodite; several ancient writers described it as a temple to Venus (the Roman equivalent to Aphrodite). There are indications that the Sepulchre, itself, was simply buried in rubble, and was excavated in the renovations of the city in the 4th century.

The site of this Temple is historically understood to be the location of the tomb of Jesus in the Christian section of Jerusalem. However, the tombs of the Kings were located across the Cedron Valley from the Temple Mount, with the tomb and grotto of Mary in that area also, near Gethsemane. Is it possible that the Holy Sepulchre, the tomb of Jesus, was located at or beneath the surface of the Temple Mount at this time – or across the Cedron Valley from the Temple? Some have claimed that the Cedron Valley was filled in and built over by the Romans, as well as the edifices beneath the Temple Mount. The rock-cut tomb (aedicule) of Jesus might well have been cut away from its original location and moved to the Gentile area of Jerusalem sometime after the revolt.

The destroyed Temple of Solomon and other sites were rebuilt by Hadrian and renamed in honor of Roman Gods and Goddesses. The holy sites of early Christianity were not reopened as Christian sites until the time of Constantine, when he and his mother, Helena, spent a great deal of money to dig out, rebuild, and renew the honoring of these sites as the focus of the newly legalized religion.

The construction of the Western Wall (also called the Wailing Wall), where Jews were allowed to come once a year to mourn their losses, is a curious thing. The long, doorless, windowless, structure is odd. The Wall appears to be an effort to close off some part of the old Temple, perhaps to seal off the caves and tunnels that ran beneath the Temple during the Bar Kochba Revolt. Or was it to keep the Jews – and Christians – from their holiest site?

In the third year of the Independence, Hadrian's brutal suppression of the revolt brought death, destruction, diaspora. To the devastated Jewish people, the great hero, Bar Kochba, the "Son of a Star", became Bar Kosiva, the "Son of Lies." From hero to villain, in one fell swoop – one of the great reversals of fortune, and of history. The Jewish tolerance, and even support, fell away – who can blame them? Untold suffering and pain, starvation, devastation – someone was to blame. The Holy Places gone. No Holy of Holies! Even Jacob's pillow – the stone of Beth El – was it gone, too? The relics lost, or hidden. The people, devastated, the city destroyed. *This* was the break, the disowning and disinheriting by Judaism of *Messianism* and of its own offspring, Christianity.

* * *

CHAPTER VI. ROME

THE TROPHIES AT ROME

After the martyrdom of Peter and Paul, Rome displayed the "trophies" of the two saints – that is to say their relics (bones), which were considered by their Christian followers to be sacred. Divisions were to be found in the community at Rome, even before the legalization of Christianity, riots occurring in the streets over Church leadership. Later, riots occurred in Alexandria, and even in the Holy City of Jerusalem.

Who was the first "pope" – the first Bishop of the Church – when there was not yet a papacy? Peter? Paul isn't mentioned in this regard – though he is credited, along with Peter for the founding of the Church in Rome. The earliest sources do not agree with one another regarding the order of the early Roman bishops. Some sources place Linus immediately after Peter, while others place Clement of Rome before him, and still others hold that Linus was actually the first bishop of Rome, being appointed by Saint Paul to that office before Peter came to Rome. But, in that case, wouldn't Paul be considered the first leader of the Church in Rome?

According to the earliest succession lists of bishops of Rome, passed down by Irenaeus and Hegesippus and attested by the historian Eusebius, one named Linus was entrusted with his office by the apostles Peter and Paul after they had established the Christian church in Rome. This would seem, to some, to make Linus the first pope, but from the late 2nd or early 3rd century somehow the convention began of regarding Peter as first pope.

The *Liber Pontificalis* also names Linus as the second Bishop of Rome after Peter. It states that Peter consecrated 2 bishops, Linus and Cletus/ Anacletus for the priestly service of the community, while devoting himself instead to prayer and preaching. It also states that Clement, whose name means "Mercy" was the one that he appointed as his successor. Jerome described Linus as "the first after Peter to be in charge of the Roman Church". John Chrysostom wrote that "Linus, some say, was second Bishop of the Church of Rome after Peter", and the *Liberian Catalogue* described Peter as the first bishop of Rome and Linus as his successor.

There is an honorary marble tile with the name of Linus, who is now deemed to be the second leader of the Church. But was it a partial tile – with the full name being Paulinus? Could it be that Paul was the first pope, before the order was changed to place Peter in the role? Clement, is often given as the pope after Peter (as in Tertullian's take on it).

There is also some confusion on the popes Cletus and Anacletus – or were these tongue-in-cheek alter-egos of the first two saints? Why should there be confusion about this simple question? Why is it not clear who led the Church in this period of time? Was it further muddied by the fact that the real names could not be spoken?

Under the persecution by Emperor Maximinus Thrax, there was a schism, with followers supporting two papacies, that of Hippolytus and of Pope Pontian, with Hippolytus later considered to be the first antipope.

The name "Pontian" could represent, "one from Pontus." Pontus was one of the communities that Peter addressed in 1 *Peter*, after the death of Jesus. The name, "Hippolytus," brings to mind the Greek myth of Hippolytus – with the schismatic Christian saint likewise dragged to death by wild horses, in this case, at Ostia in Rome. Prudentius described the subterranean tomb of the saint and states that he, himself, saw there a picture representing St. Hippolytus' execution.

In 1551, a mutilated marble statue of a seated figure (originally female) was found in the cemetery of the *Via Tiburtina* in Rome, by Pirro Ligorio (1500-1583), who reconstructed it as the Statue of St. Hippolytus. It is suggested that the statue personified one of the sciences, but there are certainly other possibilities. Interestingly, perhaps as ironic commentary, the statue was restored, but in the form of a man.[104] "A cemetery on the *Via Tiburtina*", where the statue was found, is also the location where Hippolytus' remains were, reportedly, interred. Carved on the sides of the seat of this statue was a paschal cycle, and on the back, the titles of numerous writings by Hippolytus, along with titles of other works by Eusebius of Caesarea and Jerome. Why were these works grouped together on an ancient statue of a woman (inscribed with the paschal cycle honoring Easter), that was re-carved into the form of a man?[105]

Were Pontus and Hippolytus alternate names for the "Trophies" of Christianity's earliest saints? Whether these were two living people vying for the papacy, or two factions arguing over the question of the first pope of the Church is debatable. Hippolytus and Pope Pontian (or their relics) were said to be exiled, in 235 CE, to Sardinia, Italy, where they died, working in the tin mines. According to legend, Joseph of Arimathea made his fortune from the tin mines of Britain.

In Baur's historical theory, Catholicism resulted from the eventual accommodation necessitated between the Petrine and Pauline factions of the Church, beginning in the late 2nd century. The tradition that Peter and

Paul co-founded Rome's Church in the mid-1st century and were martyred together, is generally regarded as a fiction, though some still believe it to be so.

THE MAGNA MATER – ROMAN GODDESS, CYBELE

From the period of Republican to Imperial Rome (510 BC – AD 476), a number of temples to the Roman goddess, Cybele, existed in Rome. Originally an Anatolian mother goddess, the cult of Cybele was formally brought to Rome from Phyrgia during the Second Punic War in the 2nd century BCE. After a consultation with the prophetic Sibylline Books, this guidance was given as a way to ward off invasion by Germanic tribes (Goths and others).

The worship of Cybele spread through the empire, as far as Mauretania, where the ceremonial "tree-bearers" and the *religiosi* restored the temple of Cybele and Attis after a devastating fire in 288 C.E. A group of the faithful provided renovations, including a silver statue of Cybele. The chariot that carried her in procession received a new canopy, with tassels in the form of fir cones. Some scholars believe that the popularity of the Cybele cult in Rome and throughout the empire may have inspired the author of *Book of Revelation* to describe her as the "mother of harlots" who rides the Beast.

In 203 or 205 BCE., Pessinos's meteoric cult object that embodied the Great Mother was ceremonially removed to Rome, marking the official beginning of her cult there. Thus, by 203 B.C.E., Rome, had adopted her cult as well. Publius Cornelius Scipio Nasica went to the port of Ostia, accompanied by the matrons, to meet the goddess. He was to receive her as she left the vessel, and he was to place her in the hands of the matrons who would then bear her to the "Temple of Victory", a temple on the Palatine Hill, dedicated to the Goddess, Cybele. The day on which this event took place, April 12, was observed afterwards as a festival, the *Megalesia.*[106]

Around 43 CE, Roman Emperor Claudius I, also known as the Pontifex Maximus, had claimed the status of High priest over all cults, including the cult of Cybele, which centered around the "Temple of Victory" on the Palatine Hill. Its devotees engaged in rites that included music and ecstatic dancing which sometimes ended in frenzied self-castration of the men, who became its eunuch priests, and were called *Galli.*

At the transept end of the temple stood a massive *ciborium* or *baldachin* (a covering with four posts or pillars) over a sacred statue to Cybele, behind which a reinforced structure held in place the massive Simulacrum (black meteorite) of Cybele. Some sources say that the meteoric stone may have been kept on a pedestal within the temple cella; or incorporated into the face of a statue and set on a pediment. However, it is possible that a much smaller meteoric stone, was eventually placed in her statue, as her face. Five hundred years after the institution of the *Megalesia to celebrate the Magna Mater (Great Mother,) Cybele,* Arnobius described the stone of Cybele as being tawny and black, and irregular in shape. He describes it as "a kind of stone, not a large one, one that can be carried in a man's hand."[107]

It is unclear where the large, several hundred-ton stone went, but it disappeared from historical mention. One explanation is that, in 1730 CE, it was excavated from its chapel, only to be discarded for lack of recognition. However, it is possible that it was incorporated into some part of the current edifice where it is no longer visible.

There was great Roman devotion to Cybele, before the beginnings of Christianity in Rome. She became known in Rome as the *Magna Mater*, which means "the Great Mother", or *Magna Mater deorum Idaea* ("great Idaean mother of the gods").

Macrobius wrote, "In like fashion the Phrygians, who have kept unchanged the performance of their rites and the tales attached to them, allow us to understand the Mother of the Gods and Attis along the same lines. For surely no one doubts that the Mother of the Gods is thought to be the earth: the goddess is carried along by lions, animals whose powerful, hot-blooded attacks capture the nature of heaven, whose sphere embraces the air that carries the earth." (*Macrobius* vol. I 281).

It makes sense that, in syncretization with Christian beliefs, a Christian Basilica was built over one of the sites of a temple to Cybele, the Great Mother, on the Esquiline Hill. It was dedicated as the Basilica di Santa Maria Maggiore (St. Mary Major). This basilica was later called "St. Mary of the Manger" and was also referred to as "the Bethlehem of the West." Precious relics – pieces of Christ's crib were sent from Bethlehem to Pope Theodore I in the 7th century by St. Sophronius, then the patriarch of Jerusalem.[108]

One of her temples stood on the right bank of the River Tiber, near the racecourse of Caligula (Gaianum), known from several inscriptions on fragmentary marble altars, dating from 305 to 390 CE, found under the façade of S. Peter's in 1609. (Severano, *Sette Chiese*, 95) This is thought to be the *Phrygianum* of the Not. (*Reg. XIV*) In modern times, a *tholos* (circle of columns with a rounded roof), adorned with frescoes, stands at the top of the *Via Sacra*, where the Clivus Palatinus branched off to the south, to the immediate left of the arch of Titus. At the top of a flight of 13 steps is a statue of the *Magna Mater* seated under an arch. A passage in Cassius Dio is seen to refer to a temple here. (*Dio*, Lucius Cassius, *XLVI.33.3)*

A coin of Faustina the Elder depicts the same temple, with curved roof and a flight of steps, at the top of which is a statue of Cybele enthroned. This is consistent with a colossal, fragmentary statue of the goddess, found within the temple precincts. [109]

The temple remained in use until the late 4th century. It was destroyed in 394 CE, on the orders of Emperor Theodosius I during the Persecution of pagans in the late Roman Empire, when Christianity became the official religion of the Roman Empire.

THE PAPAL BASILICAS OF ROME

There are four grand basilicas that were built in Rome, soon after the legalization of Christianity: St. John's Lateran, Santa Maria Maggiore, the Church of St. Paul Outside the Walls, and St. Peter's Basilica. These four Roman patriarchal basilicas are under the special patronage of the popes.

St. John's Lateran was the first large Church in Rome, consecrated in 324 AD – with the unique title of "archbasilica". There is a plaque on the facade of the church, which reads, "Most Holy Lateran Church, mother and head of all the churches in the city and the world". In the 12th century the canons of the Lateran claimed that the high altar housed the Ark of the Covenant and several holy objects from Jerusalem. The basilica was thus presented as the Temple of the New Covenant.

It was originally dedicated to Christ the Savior and, centuries later, co-dedicated to both John the Baptist and John the Evangelist. The archbasilica and Lateran Palace were re-dedicated twice. Pope Sergius III dedicated them to Saint John the Baptist in the 10th century in honor of the newly consecrated baptistry. Pope Lucius II dedicated them to John the Evangelist in the 12th century. Thus, while the primary Patron is still Christ the Savior, Saint John the Baptist and Saint John the Evangelist became co-patrons of the archbasilica, and the official name became rather a mouthful, "the Archbasilica of the Most Holy Savior and Saints John the Baptist and John the Evangelist at the Lateran". For simplicity, it is often called "St. John's Lateran".

It is still called the ecumenical "Mother Church" of the Catholic faithful. Despite the building of Vatican City and St. Peter's Basilica with its dramatic Bernini sculpture of the *Cathedra Petri* (the chair of St. Peter) – this early church is still the official seat of the Bishop of Rome – the Pope. We are very familiar with one of the St. John's in this church name, and one, not as much – the John who went out and evangelized, like the evangelizer, Paul – converting people to the faith.

In Italian the two Johns become, *Santi Giovanni Battista ed Evangelista* or St. John the Baptist *and* Evangelist. This terminology seems to make the two as one. And with the Most Holy Savior, they were three of the most important Christian figures from the time that the earliest church in Rome was built, until the 12th century.

The basilica of Santa Maria Maggiore. translated as "Saint Mary Major," might also be translated as "highest" or "greatest." One of the first churches in Rome in honor of the Virgin Mary, it was built immediately after the Council of Ephesus of 431, when the church declared Mary to be the "Holy Theotokos," the God-bearer. The Roman Breviary states, "After the Council of Ephesus (431) in which the Mother of Jesus was acclaimed as Mother of God, Pope Sixtus III erected at Rome on the Esquiline Hill, a basilica dedicated to the honor of the Holy Mother of God. It was afterward called Saint Mary Major and it is the oldest church in the West dedicated to the honor of the Blessed Virgin Mary."

The Roman Pontifical adds that "...Pope Liberius selected a venerated picture that hung in the pontifical oratory. It had allegedly been brought to Rome by St. Helena." This icon has long resided in a chapel at the Papal Basilica of Santa Maria Maggiore, in Rome. It is one of many images attributed to St. Luke. According to legend, after the Crucifixion, when Mary moved to the home of St. John, she took with her a few personal belongings--among these a table reputedly built by the Redeemer in the workshop of St. Joseph.

It is said that, when pious virgins of Jerusalem beseeched Luke to paint a portrait of the Mother of God, he used the top of this table to reproduce her image. Tradition states that St. Luke painted, while Mary recounted the life of her son (which Luke later recorded in his gospel). Legend also holds that the painting remained in and around Jerusalem until it was discovered by St. Helena in the 4th century. Joan Carroll Cruz states that, together with other sacred relics, the painting was transported to Constantinople where Helena's son, Emperor Constantine, "erected a church for its enthronement." This means that, if these paintings were one and the same, it was first displayed in Constantinople in the late 4th century, before being housed in the basilica in Rome.

This important painting is done in an icon style known as the *Hodegetria*. Eventually, it became known as *Salus Populi Romani* ("Salvation of the Roman people"), after this title was sanctioned at the Edict of Milan, in 313 CE as a Marian title. To be very clear, it was meant as a title for the Blessed Virgin Mary.

Significantly, at the dedication of the basilica, in the 5th century, the painting was placed above the door to the basilica's baptistery. Later it was moved to the nave, and from the 13th century, it was preserved in a marble tabernacle. Miraculous properties have been attributed to the icon, which was carried around Rome many times. In 593 CE, Pope Gregory had it carried through Rome, praying for an end to the Black Plague.

The *Salus Populi Romani* has been a favorite icon of many Popes and has been seen as an important Roman Catholic Mariological symbol, especially in Rome. Since 1613, this icon has been located in the altar tabernacle of the *Cappella Paolina*, the Pauline Chapel, built specifically to house it. We should keep in mind that, under the reign of Antonius Pius (138-161) and at the height of the popularity of Gnostic Valentinius, the Emperor ordered the Catacomb temples of Rome, which were then being used for Christian worship, to be sealed shut.

In 193 CE, Emperor Septimus Severus, was the first Emperor to lift the ban on "Paulinity", that is to say, the following of Pauline teachings, as a Capital Crime.

Saul-Paul was, in Latin, Saulus-Paulus. The name "Paul" means "small and humble," and is sometimes given as meaning "Little One," which can be looked at in different ways. Some scholars say it reflects his conversion by Christ and that he would now see himself as small in comparison to the greatness of Jesus. In any case, in the diminutive form of "Paolina," it becomes a double diminutive, "Little, Small One," or "Very Little One," which, again, may be a form sincerely reflecting his humility. "Paolina" is not only the diminutive form of the name, but is also the feminine form (rather than the masculine, Paolo, or Paolino in the diminutive), presumably, in order to adjoin to the feminine form of the noun "cappella". The *Cappela Paolina* is also referred to as the "Lady Chapel" for the image of the Madonna. Does Paul, the small, humble one, relate to the "little holy saint" Agnes (meaning "pure, holy one"), whose image in the catacombs is one of the first Christian "mother and child" images?

The French etymology gives that the word "chapel" is derived from the word "cape." It makes reference to the story of a relic of Saint Martin of Tours. Tradition has it that, when he was still a soldier, Martin cut his military cloak in half to give part to a beggar, while he wore the other half over his shoulders as a "small cape" (Latin: *capella*). The beggar, the stories claim, was Christ in disguise, and Martin experienced a conversion of heart, becoming first a monk, then abbot, then bishop. This narrative resembles that of the cape of St. Paul of Thebes, the first "desert father" whose honored cloak was cut in two and given to Athanasius and his disciple, Serapion.

In a document from 1240 CE, the *Salus Populi Romanus* painting was referred to as *Regina Coeli* ("Queen of Heaven"). It was repainted in the 13th century (visible in the facial features), but other layers suggest it is a much earlier piece. In the 14th century, when the popes returned to Rome after the period of the Avignon papacy, the buildings of Santa Maria Maggiore (St. Mary Major) became a temporary "Palace of the Popes," due to the deteriorated state of the Lateran Palace. The papal residence was later moved to the Palace of the Vatican in what is now Vatican City.

In 1953, the icon was again carried through Rome to initiate the first Marian year in Church history. In 1954, the icon was crowned by Pope Pius XII as he introduced a new Marian feast known as the "Queenship of Mary." Pope Paul VI, Pope John Paul II and Pope Benedict XVI all honored the *Salus Populi Romani* with personal visits and liturgical celebrations.

The mosaics of Santa Maria Maggiore, beautiful works of Late Antique art, are also some of the earliest representations of the Virgin Mary in Christian Late Antiquity. The mosaics of the triumphal arch and the nave of the church, glorify the Virgin Mary as the Theotokos, and provide insight into artistic, religious, and socio-political movements of the time. Old and New Testament events depicted in the mosaics of the triumphal arch and the nave emphasize the Hebrew bible as precursor to Christian theology. In the mosaic of the "Coronation of Mary," she is seated next to Jesus, who places the crown on her head. In later images, she would receive her crown from both Jesus and the Father God. This coronation theme is related to Roman traditions of the coronation of Emperors and Empresses, and was not part of the early traditions of Christianity. It crept in after the legalization of Christianity, and the official beginnings of the Roman Catholic Church.

In the late 13th century Arnolfo di Cambio, sculpted at least six nativity statues for the underground "Chapel of the Nativity" in the Basilica of St. Mary Major. Again, another name used for the basilica was "St. Mary of the Manger". Thus, these figurines, were fittingly commissioned in 1292 by Pope Nicholas IV, the first Franciscan pope, who was inspired by St. Francis of Assisi, creator of the first living nativity in Greccio, Italy, in 1223.

There is another papal basilica called the Church of St. Paul Outside the Walls, which stands over an earlier church, which was built in about 390 CE. It was founded by the Roman Emperor Constantine I, reputedly, over the burial place of St. Paul. Unlike St. Peter who was buried in the "Triumphal Way," Paul was said to have been buried in the "Ostian Way." After the Apostle's execution, his followers erected a memorial, called a *cella memoriae*. This first edifice was expanded under Valentinian I in the 370s. In 386, Emperor Theodosius I began erecting a much larger and more beautiful basilica with a nave and four aisles with a transept; the work, including the mosaics, was not completed until Leo I's pontificate (440–461).

In the 5th century, St. Paul's was larger than the original St. Peter's Basilica. The Christian poet Prudentius, who saw it at the time of emperor Honorius (395–423), described the splendors of the monument in a few expressive lines. As it was dedicated also to Saints Taurinus and Herculanus, martyrs of Ostia in the 5th century, it was called, interestingly enough, the *Basilica Trium Dominorum* ("Basilica of Three Lords").

Of the ancient basilica only the interior portion of the apse with the triumphal arch and the mosaics of the latter remain in modern times; the mosaics of the apse and the tabernacle of the confession of Arnolfo del Cambio belong to the 13th century. In the old basilica each pope had his portrait in a frieze extending above the columns separating the four aisles and naves. In 1823 a fire, which was started through the negligence of a workman who was repairing the lead of the roof, resulted in the destruction of the basilica. Alone of all the churches of Rome, it had preserved its primitive character for one thousand four hundred and thirty-five years.

Many countries contributed to its restoration. The Khedive of Egypt sent pillars of alabaster, the Emperor of Russia the precious malachite and lapis lazuli of the tabernacle. The work on the principal façade, looking toward the Tiber, was completed by the Italian Government, which declared the church a national monument. The interior of the walls of the nave are adorned with scenes from the life of St. Paul in two series of mosaics.

There are a number of traditions about the relics of St. Paul. Some traditions state that Paul, along with Peter, was buried in a catacomb on the *Via Appia*, one of the Roman roads which leads out of the city, the relics later being moved to a basilica which was erected in his honor. During the 4th century, Paul's remains, excluding the head, were moved into a sarcophagus. (According to church tradition the head rests at the Lateran.) Paul's tomb is under a marble tombstone in the Basilica's crypt, below the altar. The tombstone bears a Latin inscription "to Paul the apostle and martyr".

The epigraph of Pope Damasus (366-384) at the *Memoria Apostolorum ad catacumbas* on the Appian Way (today the Basilica of Saint Sebastian), says: "Whoever you are who seeks the conjoint names of Peter and of Paul, know that these saints rested (*habitasse*) here a time. The East sent the disciples – they affirm it gladly – and they, thanks to the blood of martyrdom and to the sublime following of Christ, reached the celestial regions and the kingdom of the just. Rome, instead, has deserved to claim them as citizens. This Damasus sings in your praise, O new luminaries". On the basis of this text, and of the presence in the catacomb of numerous inscriptions invoking Peter and Paul jointly, the conjectural hypothesis of a temporary translation of the relics of the two founders of the Church of Rome to this location, in the period of the persecution by the emperor Valerian (258) has been proposed.

A medieval tradition holds that the heads of Paul and Peter were preserved since the 8th century in the *Sancta Sanctorum* and from there transferred by Pope Urban V, on 16 April 1369, in the two silver reliquary busts to the ciborium of the Lateran Basilica. An investigation was made on 23 July 1823 by Cardinal Antonelli; while scientific investigations that ended in uncertainty were conducted some decades ago in researches on Peter.

In regard to the tradition that Paul's remains were buried beneath St. Paul's main altar, and covered with a slab of marble, credible evidence has recently been found. In 2006, Vatican archeologists discovered a white marble sarcophagus hidden beneath the floor of the basilica. It took three years for archeologists to subject the remains to the first ever scientific tests and establish that they belonged to Paul, a Jewish Roman citizen from Tarsus. It is certainly notable that the remains were housed in a "box" of white marble.

Pope Benedict XVI announced the findings during a service at the basilica, as Rome prepared to celebrate the Feasts of St. Peter and St. Paul. "This seems to confirm the unanimous and undisputed tradition that these are the mortal remains of the Apostle Paul," he said.[110]

In the 5th century, Pope Gregory the Great (who first proposed that Mary Magdalene was a reformed prostitute), made renovations at the church. Did this pope discover something that caused him to undermine Mary Magdalene's role in Jesus' mission? The main altar (built over Saint Paul's sarcophagus) and presbytery were extensively modified. The pavement in the transept was raised and a new altar placed above the earlier altar erected by Leo I.

In the 9th century, Pope Leo IV attempted to counter the Saracen threat with a new line of walls encompassing the suburb on the right bank of the Tiber, a district that is still known as the Leonine City. He repaired St. Peter's Basilica, restoring the altar's gold covering (the original was stolen), which weighed 206 lb. and was studded with precious gems, then he appealed to the Christian kingdoms to confront the Arab raiders. Leo also began to restore and embellish the damaged Church of St. Paul Outside the Walls.

In the time period following Leo's restorations, rumors began to circulate about a female pope named John/Joan, whose femininity was revealed by her having her illegitimate baby on the street on the way to her coronation as pope. This is said to be the reason that popes now turn away from the street, called the *Via Sacra*. which became known as the "shunned street" - where the unfortunate incident took place "between the Colosseum and St. Clement's church." Could this have been a reference to the colossal statue of Cybele, which resided at the northern end of the Via Sacra – or was there another statue, a Marian *cella memoriae* along this route? A "mother and child" cella that lost popularity for some unknown reason?

In the 5th century, a church was built called the *Santa Maria Antiqua* (Ancient Church of Saint Mary) in the Forum Romanum. A Roman Catholic Marian church, located at the foot of the Palatine Hill, Santa Maria Antiqua (since renamed as Santa Francesca Romana) is the oldest Christian monument in the Roman Forum. Was there, perhaps, a notable Christian shrine to "Mother and Child" connected to this church, along the route of the Via Sacra? Did it fall out of favor in the 8th to 9th century, with the renovations of St. John's Lateran and the Lateran Palace, or of St. Paul Outside the Walls? Was John once again taking priority over Mary? Or were discoveries made which negated certain "truths" of Christian history?

The Ancient Church of St. Mary contains the earliest Roman depiction of "Santa Maria Regina", the Virgin Mary as Queen (crowned like the Roman Imperials), from the 6th century. She is the crowned figure that sits on the left side of the painting, with Jesus on her lap, in the format of the Madonna Enthroned. Is it this Roman evolution of Marian worship that ignited the satirical stories of the pregnancy of the female pope? Was there backlash to the idea of a "Queen of Heaven", a "Mother of God"?

One does wonder if the restorations of the Church of St. Paul, which was damaged by the Saracens in the late 9th century, may have once again brought attention to some interesting artifacts, leading to the rumors of a female pope.

In 896 CE, fifty years after Pope Leo's death, there was an exceedingly strange trial, called the *Cadaver Synod*, of Pope Formosus (meaning "beautiful or handsome"), who, reportedly, died of natural causes in that year, after a pontificate of four and a half years. Allegedly, nine months after being buried, the pope's remains were exhumed and dressed in papal vestments in the remarkable spectacle of a trial in which the defendant, charged with unlawful usurpation of the papal throne, was a decaying corpse. (Or might we say, relics?) Was there some relationship to the rumors of a female pope, which came up in that time period?

The reign of Formosus as Pope was a disruptive period, marked by power struggles over control of the region by the Franks, Constantinople, and Rome. Formosus traveled to Bulgaria to assist in converting the people to Catholicism, was sent with two other bishops to convey his invitation to Charles the Bald, King of France, to come to Rome and receive the imperial crown from the hands of the pope. When he was recalled to Rome by John VIII, he refused, and was excommunicated in 872 CE. He was reinstated in 876, after promising never to return to Rome or to act in a priestly role. And in 891, he was elected Pope. His troubled papacy lasted 4 1/2 years.

Was the convoluted story of Pope Formosus true? Was he a real person that was sent around the region to secure power for various factions in the Church? Could there be more to the story, regarding his status as Pope?

At the *Cadaver Synod*, Formosus was found guilty of usurping the papal throne by Stephen VI, and his papacy was retroactively declared null.

However, it did not end there - Pope Stephen VI, who carried out the trial, would later be declared insane, and thrown in prison, where it is said that he died. Efforts were made to erase all record of the trial as well as any record on the subject of a female pope. This idea would die down, until it was "resurrected" again during the Protestant Reformation. Though it may have been the most outrageously circus-like trial of its type, it was not, however, the only time that some faction of the Church would put a "leadership figure" on trial posthumously, both before and after this synod.

ST. PETER'S BASILICA AND THE VATICAN

Old St. Peter's Basilica was the building that stood, from the 4th to 16th centuries, where the new St. Peter's Basilica stands today in Vatican City. The *Liber Pontificalis* states that a private race course, a small Necropolis and a grand Basilica were built by Emperor Constantine I as a "gift" to the people of Rome (326 to 356 CE). Construction of the basilica, over the historical site of the Circus of Nero, began during the reign of Constantine. The name "old St. Peter's Basilica" is used to distinguish it from the new basilica, dedicated in 1626 CE. Some theorize that St. Peter's Basilica, and Vatican City itself, was built upon the site of an ancient Phyrgianum, or "oracle temple" of the Goddess, Cybele.

A shrine was located on the right bank of the River Tiber, near the racecourse of Caligula (Gaianum), known from several inscriptions on fragmentary marble altars, dating from 305 to 390 CE, found under the façade of S. Peter's in 1609.[111] This shrine is probably the "Phrygianum of the Not". (*Notitia*, Reg. XIV).

The term, "Vatican", is said to be borrowed from the Latin (mons) Vāticānus, which is a hill on the west bank of the Tiber, said to be of Etruscan derivation. This hill was the traditional site of the apostle Peter's tomb, on which the basilica was built in the 4th century. There is a Latin word claimed by many to be a "false cognate" (a completely unrelated term) to the word "Vatican". That word, *vaticinor,* is derived from *vatis,* or *vatic,* a feminine noun, meaning, "poet, teacher, oracle, prophesier, augur, diviner, seer, soothsayer, the mouthpiece of deity." Many Christian churches were built upon the holy sites of older sites, including those of Goddess-oracle religions.

It is quite likely that at some point the connection, which is strongly supported, was suppressed. The reasons are fairly obvious, since such terms eventually were vilified by the Church and became equated with witchcraft over time – an odd turn of events. Christianity is based on the prophecies of Judaism, and Jesus himself prophesied. It was common in early Christianity to attempt to demonize the traditions of the ancient Goddess religions.

The term, "oracle," is not just grammatically feminine – in some dictionaries, the definition itself is explicitly feminine: "poetess, prophetess, or sibyl." (Sibyl/Cybele.) An oracle is sometimes given to be a priest or priestess, but Cambridge Dictionary defines the term as meaning "a female priest who gave people wise but often mysterious advice from a god."

A number of myths abounded concerning the origins of Old St. Peter's Basilica and Vatican Hill. One is that Emperor Nero (54-68) built a private race track over, or near the most sacred graves of nobles on top of Vatican Hill. The second, considered a fiction by many, is that Simon bar Jonah (St. Peter) and St. Paul were executed at the site of this private track and buried nearby on the hill.

There is also the story of Simon Magus, practicing magic in the Forum, and attempting to fly with the help of demons; he was allegedly brought crashing to the earth in the presence of Nero, by St. Peter and St. Paul. Could this originally have referred to an object of prophecy (read "magic") that fell from the heavens? Did it relate to the Church of Santa Maria Antiqua, which stood within the forum precincts?

Old St. Peter's Basilica was, reportedly, built on the site of Saint Peter's grave, which influenced the layout of the building. The Vatican Hill, on the west bank of the Tiber River, was leveled. Notably, since the site was outside the boundaries of the ancient city, the apse with the altar was located in the west so that the basilica's façade could be approached from Rome itself to the east. The exterior however, unlike pagan temples, was not lavishly decorated.

The church was able to house 3,000 to 4,000 worshipers. It had five aisles, a wide central nave and two smaller aisles to each side, each divided by 21 marble columns, taken from earlier pagan buildings.[112] The Encyclopedia Brittanica states that it was over 350 feet (110 m) long, built in the shape of a Latin cross, and had a gabled roof which was timbered on the interior and which stood at over 100 feet (30 m) at the center. An atrium, known as the "Garden of Paradise", stood at the entrance and had five doors which led to the body of the church; this was a sixth-century addition.

Many of these details, including the orientation of the entrance to the east, and the altar to the west, as well as the Garden of Paradise atrium, are details that seem to follow the design of the Temple of Solomon. A very blatant connection is found in the use of several Solomonic columns around the altar of Old St. Peter's Basilica. According to tradition, Constantine took these columns from the Temple of Solomon and gave them to the church; however, some historians propose that the columns were probably from an Eastern church. When Bernini built his *baldacchin* to cover the new St. Peter's altar, he drew from the twisted design of the old columns. Eight of the original columns were moved to the piers of the new St. Peter's.

The church gradually gained importance over the next twelve centuries, eventually becoming a major place of pilgrimage. Papal coronations were held at the basilica. Charlemagne was crowned emperor of the Holy Roman Empire there in 800 CE. In 846, Saracens sacked and damaged the church. Some basilicas, such as St. Peter's, were outside the Aurelian walls, and thus easy targets for marauders. They were filled with rich liturgical vessels and jeweled reliquaries housing the relics of the saints. The Saracens pillaged St. Peter's and other churches in Rome for these great treasures.[113] Pope Leo IV built the Leonine wall for protection, and rebuilt the parts of St. Peter's that had been damaged.

By the 15th century the church was once again falling into ruin. At first Pope Julius II had the intention of preserving the old building. In 1505, he ordered the demolition of the Old St. Peter's Basilica, to make way for the expansion of the new St. Peters Basilica. Many people of the time were shocked by the proposal, as the building represented papal continuity going back to Peter. The original altar was to be preserved in the new structure that housed it.

The new basilica, which is one of the foremost examples of Renaissance architecture and in its present form, is the largest church in Rome. A number of great Renaissance artists were involved in creating the statuary, and artworks of the great edifice. Over the altar in the present-day St. Peter's Basilica looms a massive bronze *baldacchino,* designed by Gian Lorenzo Bernini in 1623. The original wooden altar can still be seen beneath the triumphal arch in the middle of the transept. It is said that Peter celebrated mass at this very altar.

In a Latin cross church, the high altar is usually placed in the chancel at the end of the longitudinal axis. In St. Peter's it was located in the center of the crossing. Bernini sought a solution where the placement of the high altar above the tomb of the first pope could be reconciled with the height of the basilica's ceiling. The first concern was to bring the altar into scale with the great expanse of space around it. Thus, the enormous structure of Bernini's *baldachin* was built to balance out the distance to the ceiling.

Secondly, Bernini accomplished a resolution to the altar at the crossing – the congregation had a view of the altar, framed by the *baldachin*, balancing the distance between the crossing and the Chair of Saint Peter at the end of the chancel.

In the apse, beyond the altar is the Chair of Saint Peter, enclosed in a sculpted gilt bronze casing that was designed by Bernini and executed between 1647 and 1653 CE. The name derives from the Latin *cathedra* meaning "chair or throne", which is used to denote the chair or seat of a bishop. The term "cathedral" relates to the idea of the seat of bishops. Inside the Chair is a wooden throne, which, according to tradition, was used by Saint Peter. It was, however, actually a gift from Charles the Bald to Pope John VIII in 875.

The *cathedra* appears to be effortlessly supported by four larger than life-size bronze figures, much like the papal traditions of the *sedia gestatoria*, an opulent sedan chair that was supported by poles on the shoulders of several bearer-footmen, who carried the pope through the streets until 1978, when the "pope-mobile" came into use. In this case, the chair is empty – and though it is titled as the Chair of St. Peter, the whole vignette is dominated by the light of the oval window above containing the White Dove, perhaps Bernini's commentary on the utmost importance of Divine Wisdom, and the "overshadowing by the Holy Spirit", in the Church.

The "Doctors of the Church" sculptures include the Western doctors St. Ambrose and St. Augustine of Hippo on the outside, wearing miters, and Eastern doctors St. John Chrysostom and St. Athanasius on the inside, both bare-headed. Rather than being lifted by the heavy bronze figures, the *cathedra* appears to float, almost being prevented from flying off by the "doctors" restraining hands. It hovers over the altar in the basilica's apse, light streaming through the window, illuminating the glory of sunrays and sculpted clouds that surround it. It is a fine example of Baroque art, highlighted by the powerful effects of light.

The feasts of the *Cathedra Petri* brought about the general understanding of the "Chair of Peter" as the episcopal office of the Pope as Bishop of Rome, an office considered to have been first held by Saint Peter, and thus extended to the diocese, the See of Rome.

SIMON MAGUS

There is an intriguing character in the bible, known for his confrontation with Peter in *Acts* 8:9-24. The legendary Simon Magus was called a charlatan and a liar by many of the early church fathers and other writers of Christianity. The non-canonical Apostolic Constitutions also accuse him of lawlessness. In *Acts of the Apostles*, Simon Magus is accused of paying for position and influence in the church, which later became known as the sin of "simony."

The name "Simon" is interesting in its relationship to Simon Peter. Though many scholars propose that the story of Simon Magus is an allegory representing opposition to Peter, the fact that the name, Simon, is used makes one wonder why the originators of this story would have chosen it. Who was in opposition to Peter? Certainly, Paul comes to mind – he is cited by numerous scholars as the likeliest identity of Simon Magus. In the *Gospel of Mary*, there also seems to be great strife between Peter and Mary Magdalene. And, in the New Testament Gospels, the greatest critic of Peter's behavior is none other than Jesus!

The earliest reference to Simon Magus is in the canonical *Acts of the Apostles,* written in about 70 CE, which is the only reference that appears in the New Testament. In *Acts*, Magus is described as a Samaritan who converted to Christianity. The link to Samaritans was emphasized in many Magus narratives. The burial-place of John the Baptist, was in Sebastia/Samaria, and so, has some connection to the Samaritans as well.

Acts 1:1 gives the impression that its contents were written as an account of Jesus' life and actions. In fact, Jesus has very little part in the Gospel. After the first page, it moves into the acts of Peter's ministry, then details about St. Stephen and his death by stoning. Very soon it turns to the life and ministry of the Apostle Paul.

Jerome, who is credited with translating the Bible into the Vulgate version in the 4th century, writes in *Virus Illustribus* (Lives of Illustrious Men): "Simon Peter the son of John from the village of Bethsaida in the province of Galilee, brother of Andrew the Apostle, and himself chief of the Apostles, after having been bishop of the church of Antioch and having preached to the Dispersion the believers in circumcision, in Pontus, Galatia, Cappadocia, Asia and Bithynia, pushed on to Rome in the second year of Claudius to overthrow Simon Magus, and held the sacerdotal chair there for twenty-five years until the last, that is the fourteenth, year of Nero."

At Nero's order, Peter "received the crown of martyrdom being nailed to the cross with his head towards the ground and his feet raised on high, asserting that he was unworthy to be crucified in the same manner as his Lord...Buried at Rome in the Vatican near the Triumphal Way he is venerated by the whole world."

Here, Simon Magus is clearly not Simon Peter. An alternate rabbinical version of this story claims that Hadrian was planning on rebuilding the Temple, but a "malevolent Samaritan" convinced him not to. Some scholars see this as Simon Magus, the Samaritan.

Who was Simon Magus? The question is quite intriguing. The Ebionites, as well as many other sects, spoke against him. Each faction had a slightly different story to tell. In *Acts* 8:9-24, Magus was said to have been baptized by Philip, and later had a confrontation with Peter. Biblical scholar, Ferdinand Christian Baur, proposed that the Clementine references to the notorious Samaritan sorcerer Simon Magus (*Acts* 8:9-24) were actually covert polemics against Paul. Certainly, Paul had confrontations with Peter, including in the "Incident at Antioch."

Two paintings of The Transfiguration, one by Raphael (Plate 3) and one by Carracci (Plate 4), from Chapter III, might be seen to give us two options for the one who, in the Simon Magus satires, fell back to earth and is left behind. John is this one in the painting by Carracci, and Mary Magdalene is the one in the painting by Raphael. In Raphael's work, Jesus is even shown in the arms-flung-wide pose of Magus - a bit of tongue in cheek humor by the master painter?

There is a story in *Sanhedrin* 43a that may be related to the origins of the legends of Simon Magus. It tells the story of "Yeshu the sorcerer," recounting the trial and execution of Yeshu, a sorcerer who, with his five disciples, has enticed other Jews to apostasy. Yeshu, which is used instead of Yeshua, or Jesus, is said to be an acrostic for "may be blotted out his name and his memory."

In this antagonistic account, a herald is sent to call for witnesses in his favor for forty days before his execution, but no one comes forward. In the end he is stoned and hanged on the Eve of Passover. (There is an addition made to *Sanhedrin* 43a in the Florence manuscript of the *Talmud*, in 1177 CE , saying that Yeshu was hanged on the eve of the Sabbath.)

His five disciples, named Matai, Nekai, Netzer, Buni, and Todah are then tried. Much like the puns in the story of Susanna, word play is made on each of their names, along with the manner of their execution. Interestingly, it is mentioned that leniency could not be applied because of Yeshu's influence with the royal government.

In Origen's quoting of Celsus, there are claims that Jesus' miracles were the work of a skilled magician. Origen does not mention Simon Magus – however, in his treatise, *Contra Celsus*, he comments on an interesting parallel to the Simon Magus accounts. Celsus, according to Origen, describes Jesus as a small, homely man, who worked his miracles by sorcery. He stated that this Rabbi, Jesus, kept all Jewish customs, including sacrifice at the Temple in Jerusalem. He had only a few followers and taught them his worst habits, including begging for money. His disciples, amounting to "ten boatmen and a couple of tax collectors"(12 disciples) were not respectable. The reports of Jesus' resurrection Celsus attributed to "a hysterical female". Celsus said such beliefs came from Jesus' sorcery and the crazed thinking of his followers, all to impress others and give the opportunity for others to become beggars.

Celsus is seen to be a Greek philosopher, but his viewpoint includes commentary that was commonly being used in Jewish satire of the time period. In Celsus' story, Jesus' miracles are related to the sorcery of Simon Magus. The "hysterical female", called "Helen" in the text – is, perhaps, a "hellenized" or "Romanized" version of Mary Magdalene. This would be a satirical slant related to accounts in the *Gospel of Mary* of her vision of Christ, generally considered to be a post-resurrection experience.

Philip Francis Esler writes in *The Early Christian World,* "To disprove the deity of Christ required an explanation of his miracles which were recorded in scripture. Celsus does not deny the fact of Jesus' miracles, but rather concentrates on the means by which they were performed. Perhaps influenced by rabbinical sources, Celsus attributes Jesus' miracles to his great skills as a magician."[114] In other words, Celsus' commentary (via Origen's writings) would seem to represent a Jewish satire of Jesus' messianic mission, and of the Christian faith.

There has been much controversy and scholarly debate on the meaning, and historical accuracy, of the story of Simon Magus. While some scholars see the story as a reference to Paul, others suggest Marcion, or leaders of other heretical sects, such as Priscillian, who was killed for practicing sorcery.

The many different sources for information on Simon Magus, who is sometimes called "Simon the Magician," or "Simon the Sorcerer," each present quite different pictures of him – so much so that it has been questioned whether these sources can refer to the same person. The name of Simon Magus is, undoubtedly, a euphemism for some figure in the early days of Christianity, but which personage seems to depend on the perspective of the particular faction writing about him.

Irenaeus pointed to Magus as one of the founders of Gnosticism and the sect of the Simonians. Late in the 2nd century, he wrote in *Adversus Haereses,* that, "This man, then, was glorified by many as if he were a god; and he taught that it was himself who appeared among the Jews as the Son, but descended in Samaria as the Father while he came to other nations in the character of the Holy Spirit. He represented himself, in a word, as being the loftiest of all powers, that is, the Being who is the Father over all, and he allowed himself to be called by whatsoever title men were pleased to address him." These statements could have some relation to Christian teachings that Jesus was the Son of God, as well as to his comment that "I and the Father are One." This antagonistic stance could reasonably represent the viewpoint of Jewish opposition to Jesus, or even Jewish-Christian opposition to Gentile ideas that crept into the faith as Paul's teachings spread to the Romans.

Justin Martyr and Irenaeus were two early church writers to refer to the story of Simon and Helen, which was said to be central to Simonian/ Samaritan doctrine. Justin Martyr wrote that nearly all the Samaritans in his time were followers of a certain Simon of Gitta. This was a village not far from Flavia Neapolis, which was a colony of Roman veterans founded by Vespasian after the Second Temple was destroyed, and so, it would seem that Simon of Gitta might have Roman-influenced beliefs. Is he meant to represent a Gentile Christian of the time period?

In apocryphal works including the *Acts of Peter, Pseudo-Clementines*, and the *Epistle of the Apostles*, Simon is not only powerful as a leader, but, in some of these works, he is also a formidable sorcerer with the ability to levitate, and fly. This might well be a satirical reference to the Christian teaching of Jesus' ascension into heaven.

The Clementine literature polemicizes against the notorious Samaritan sorcerer Simon Magus (*Acts* 8:9-24). Some scholars propose that Luke, the author of *Acts*, took the story of Simon Magus from the *Clementines*. Historian, Adolf Hilgenfeld, eventually proposed that Simon Magus was a real person, insisting as many scholars do, that in the Clementine literature he represents Paul. However, in *Pseudo-Clementines*, it is Saul-Paul who condemns Simon as a sorcerer (Ps. *Clem*. Rec. 1.70.2), which would indicate that this author did not see Paul as Simon Magus. These are two different groups, each polemicizing against the leader of the opposing group and/or promoting their own leader.

According to the early church heresiologists, Simon is supposed to have written several lost treatises, two of which were *The Four Quarters of the World* and *The Sermons of the Refuter.* These works may have shed some light on the identity of Simon Magus, but they are no longer extant. Since there is no surviving copy or even a small segment of the works, but only references to them by other authors, it may be that, as in other cases, there never were actual texts by him. The titles may only be meant to represent a certain point of view. Heretical texts undoubtedly were destroyed in the early centuries, but there are too many questionable things about the legends of Simon

Magus for one to take any of it at face value.

There was a neo-Platonic philosopher, Porphyry, the great pagan antagonist of 3rd century Christianity, whose disciple, Iamblichus, in the time of Constantine, was the chief restorer and defender of the old Roman gods. His efforts are seen to have influenced Emperor Julian in his attempt to return paganism to the status of the official religion in 361-362 CE. Thus, some scholars suggest that, in Clementine writings, Simon represents not Paul, but Iamblichus.

Either Iamblichus or one of his disciples is the author of the treatise "De Mysteriis Aegyptiorum" (The Egyptian Mysteries); clearly, the book is a product of his school and proves that he, like Porphyry, emphasized the magic, or theurgic, factor in the Neoplatonic scheme of salvation.[115] The renounced doctrines and practices of Simon Magus include theurgy (supernatural practices/magic), astrology, divinations, miracles, and claims to union with the Divine, which characterized the neo-Platonism of 320–30 CE. This is why sorcery and astrolabes appear as demonic practices in the 4th century exegetics of Christianity. They were seen to be pagan ideals. Thus, Iamblichus makes a good candidate for the hidden identity of Simon Magus.

The Clementine author defends the Old Testament against the school of Porphyry, and when cataloging its errors, he uses Porphyry's own higher criticism. The citing of ancient history, the ridicule of Greek mythology, and the philosophical elaborations might also be seen to be against Porphyry. The refutation of idolatry is against Iamblichus. So, perhaps it is not against Marcion or Paul, but against Iamblichus or Porphyry that Pseudo-Clement speaks.

Cyril of Jerusalem (346 CE), in the sixth of his Catechetical Lectures prefaces his history of the Manichaeans with a brief account of earlier heresies, including that of Simon Magus. His document says that Simon Magus claimed that he was going to be translated to heaven, and was actually careening through the air in a chariot drawn by demons when Peter and Paul knelt down and prayed, and their prayers brought him to earth, a mangled corpse. Being "translated to heaven" by demons, sounds a lot like a satire of ascension, or perhaps, assumption

In two paintings Benozzo Gozzoli did of the *Fall of Simon Magus* from 1461-2, he painted almost mirror-images of the scene – what seems to be a time-lapse of the narrative, with Magus leaping from a wooden tower, and then brought crashing to the ground at the prayers of St. Peter and St. Paul. In this painting, we see two figures in the same robes. But is it meant to be a sort of a time-lapse of the same person in the air and on the ground? Or is it meant to be a satirical commentary on folk tales of one who ascends, and one who is left behind?

Plate 10 - Fall of Simon Magus - Benozzo Gozzoli

In the *Gospel of John*, Jesus says to his disciples, “You are from below, I am from above; you are of this world, I am not of this world.” (*John* 8:23) This describes Jesus' nature as a transcendent nature, different from the human form of his disciples. This statement presages the centuries of debate on the relationship of Jesus’ divine nature to the human form. Perhaps the story of Simon Magus and his mistress, Helen, is simply a satirical twisting of the story of the mission of Jesus and Mary.

Epiphanius, in *Panarion*, refers to a rather explicit sexual episode said to come from the no longer extant *Greater Questions of Mary* (perhaps not an actual text, but simply a satirical reference to the *Gospel of Mary*, where Peter complains that Mary asks too many questions, and wants her to leave.) It seems to be a very *risqué* version of the Simon Magus narrative. Hereticist Epiphanius says, "they [certain heretics] assert that he [Jesus] gave her a revelation, taking her aside to the mountain and praying; and he brought forth from his side a woman...[like Eve taken from the side of Adam] and began to [sexually] unite with her, and so, forsooth, taking his effluent [the outflowing of his seed], he showed that 'we must so do, that we may live'; and how when Mary fell to the ground abashed, he raised her up again and said to her: 'Why didst thou doubt, O thou of little faith?'"

The satirical text reflects pro-Peter, anti-Mary leanings. This passage seems to be a chastisement of Mary, from the Petrine stance, countering the narrative of both Mary's vision of the Lord, and of Jesus walking on the water, where Jesus chides Peter for doubting and being unable to walk on the water with him, whereupon Jesus says to Peter, "O, ye of little faith." We might also see in these writings a satirical slant on the type of union of Jesus and Mary, and on the Ascension of Jesus, with the human form, in a sense, dropped back to earth, while the divine returned to the Father. The sexual aspect of the story is meant to dishonor them both, in denial of and in mockery of the *hypostatic* union and all that it implies.

And so, we have many options as to the identity of Simon Magus. Metaphor, allegory, and euphemisms were the method of the debate, each version followed by rebuttal, charge by counter-charge, until facts became obscured by the chaotic exhortations of differing beliefs systems. Who was Simon Magus? Simon Magus was "the fall guy" (pun!). According to one faction, it may have been the Emperor or one of his underlings, in other accounts, it seems to have been Paul, and in other versions, oddly enough, it would seem to be Jesus, depending on what faction was giving the perspective. It may be that the earliest mention of Simon Magus was a reference to the meteoric stone which fell from the heavens, and served as a tool of prophecy.

Augustine's work on Grace and Original Sin brought a closer examination of the ideas of Origen, who was a long-revered theologian of the Church. Elizabeth A. Clark proposes that Augustine's theory of Original Sin was an effort to reconstruct what he saw as the faulty Origenist explanation of the soul's pre-existence and its "fall" into the body.[116] There was an Origenist crisis in Augustine's time as well as a later one in the 6th century, when his writings were banned in the west.

Undoubtedly, Augustine's writings influenced a renewed interest in the story of Simon Magus. A theology, long accepted as orthodox within the Church now became problematic. Augustine's ideas brought into question the relationship of Jesus to God the Father, and to the Holy Spirit, and even to Mary. It would seem that euphemisms were the easiest way to discuss problems within the formulas of the Church. You couldn't be called a heretic for speaking ill of Simon the magician.

There is another magician mentioned in *Acts*. Elymas bar Jesus is given as the name of a magician and "false Hebrew prophet."(*Acts* 13:6-8). While at Paphos on Cyprus, Paul and Barnabas are summoned by proconsul Paulus Sergius, whose guest, Elymas bar Jesus, gives them a hard time.

In *Acts* 13:6-9, it states, "When they had gone through the whole island as far as Paphos, they came upon a certain magician, a Jewish false prophet, named Bar-Jesus. He was with the proconsul, Sergius Paulus, a man of intelligence, who summoned Barnabas and Saul and sought to hear the word of God. But Elymas the magician (for that is the meaning of his name) withstood them, seeking to turn away the proconsul from the faith. But Saul, who is also called Paul, filled with The Holy Spirit, looked intently at him and said, "You son of the devil, you enemy of all righteousness, full of all deceit and villainy, will you not stop making crooked the straight paths of the Lord?" This brings to mind two incidents – Jesus telling Peter, "Get thee behind me, Satan!" And the Denial of Peter, when upon Peter's third betrayal, Jesus turns and looks at him directly. It also brings to mind the Incident at Antioch where Paul confronts Peter for his hypocrisy.

According to Paul, Elymas bar Jesus is made temporarily blind by God (in the story of Saul's conversion, he, Saul/Paul is blinded by God's light). It is clear from the passage that Bar-Jesus had the ear of the proconsul and was well known throughout the region. The name is not explained, and there is great scholarly debate over the meaning of the name. *El* usually means *Elohim* or God. The "y" or epsilon, could represent a Hellenized form, which might indicate that Elymas was seen to be a Greco-Roman personage. Several possibilities are given for "mas". The verb *ma'as,* means to reject or despise. That would give the name Elymas the meaning of "God Despises" or "God Rejects", and "bar Jesus" means "son of Jesus", certainly an intriguing name.

How do we make sense of the disagreement and discord among so many factions throughout history? Each faction has created its own version of truth, with its own particular vantage point, its own filters, pseudonyms and euphemisms, and its own tangled web of truth and half-truth, as well as accusations and outright misrepresentations.

So many clues have been lost, whether accidentally or deliberately. And many things that might have been obvious in ancient times are obscured by the passage of time, by the loss of context. In modern times, there are symbols, allegories, and metaphors that most educated people would understand. However, much of what we have left of ancient discourses from various authors contains metaphors that are no longer meaningful, referring to texts that were once common knowledge and have now been lost to the fires of Alexandria or the sands of time – if they ever existed at all.

Those texts that were deemed "apocryphal" or even "heretical" give us an overview of what various factions of the church believed and practiced after the time of Jesus. It is true that the contradictions are profuse, but there are clues to follow if you are willing to step outside the rigid beliefs of human doctrine and dogma, and open yourself to the possibility of finding a greater truth – to soften your focus and allow yourself to "have the eyes to see."

EARLY CHURCH FATHERS

Jesse Lyman Hurlbut, in his book, *The Story of the Christian Church*, (1967) writes, "For fifty years after St. Paul's life, a curtain hangs over the Church, through which we strive vainly to look; and when at last it rises, about 120 A.D., with the writings of the earliest church-father, we find a church in many aspects very different from that in the days of St. Peter and St. Paul."[117]

The period from 70 to 170 C.E., in scholarly circles, has often been referred to as "The Lost Century." It is evident that this hundred-year period was exceedingly turbulent. The lack of documentation of this period of Christian history attests to a time of chaos and strife. Undoubtedly, much changed from the time of Jesus and the Apostolic mission of the 1st century, to the chaotic events of the 2nd century.

In the 2nd century, there was certainly antagonism and persecution of the faith from the Roman rulers. It is hard to say what the relationship between Jews and Christians was at this time, but it is likely that it was quite close, up until the failure of the "Bar Kochba Revolt" and loss of Jewish Independence, which ended in 135 CE. The failed revolt caused a sea change in rabbinical support for the idea of a messianic leader.

There are apocryphal texts from this tumultuous century, with a wide variety of stories on the lives of the apostles, each in their assigned region of ministry, and each with its own slant on the teachings of Christianity. Many of these stories were criticized as "heretical" (or contrary to the mainstream Christian faith), in this time period or later. "Historical references" to Christianity, in great part, come from the polemical writing of texts whose intent was to refute what were deemed to be "heresies." Some truths can be gleaned from commentary by the opposing camp, but, in general, this does not give a full or clear picture of the truth, since such writings were often meant to be polemical and even incendiary.

As Christianity spread, many scholarly converts from the literate circles of the Hellenistic world were drawn to the faith. Some of these converts became bishops and other clergy, who brought Hellenistic influences to their writings and teachings. These men authored many early apologetic works – works that were written to defend and explain the faith, through the methods of Greek philosophy – using reason to refute arguments against the tenets of the faith. The authors of such early texts are known as the Church Fathers, and the study of their writings is called "*patristics*" (a reference to the word "father").

The writings of the Church Fathers have been used as reference and authority for church traditions and questions of doctrinal significance throughout the history of the Church.

While the study of the writings of the Early Church Fathers would be enough to fill many books, some notable, and accepted, Early Church Fathers include Hippolytus, Origen of Alexandria, Clement of Alexandria, Ignatius of Antioch, Polycarp, Justin Martyr, Irenaeus of Lyons, and Tertullian of Carthage, North Africa. Many notable and honored early writers would later be cast out as "heretics."

* * *

CHAPTER VII: DOCTRINE, DOGMA, AND HERESY

In the unfoldment of Christian "history" and formulation of Christian doctrine and dogma, one must understand that the Roman Emperors, had the highest power and influence in deciding which religions were allowed to be practiced. When problems arose within Christianity, after its legalization, it was the Emperors who convoked the councils that decided the theological underpinnings of the faith. They enforced the restrictions on acceptable belief, and the consequences for what was deemed "heretical" or unacceptable.

The term *heresy* is from the Greek αἵρεσις meaning "choice" or "thing chosen." It was used to mean the "party or school of a man's choice" and then, eventually, to describe those beliefs deemed unacceptable by the Catholic Church. The concept has also been used in Jewish or Islamic contexts for those with unorthodox beliefs within those faiths, and also within Protestant Christian communities against other Christian beliefs. Essentially, it is used by those in power to diminish, control, or cast out anyone who disagrees with them. Those who espouse or commit heresy are called heretics.

The word "heresy" was used early on by Irenaeus in his 2nd century tract *Contra Haereses (Against Heresies)* to discredit his opponents within early Christianity, describing his own beliefs and doctrines as orthodox and the Gnostic "choice" of beliefs as heretical. He reinforced his arguments with the concept of "apostolic succession," the derivation of teachings directly from the apostles, according to his own ideas of the succession of the leadership of the Church from the apostles.

With the *Edict of Milan*, in 313 CE, Constantine the Great and Licinius instituted toleration of Christianity in the Roman Empire. According to Roman law, the Emperor was *Pontifex Maximus*, the high priest of the College of Pontiffs of all recognized religions in ancient Rome. From Constantine's time onward, Emperors were involved in enforcing ecumenical decisions and edicts in Christianity, but often also in many ways, shaping the faith. Constantine convened the first ecumenical council to settle the debate over Arianism (though he followed Arian beliefs himself), and then enforced orthodoxy against Arianism by Imperial authority.

The first known legal usage of the term "heresy" in Christian writings, came several decades later, in 380, with the *Edict of Thessalonica* of Theodosius I, which made Christianity the state church of the Roman Empire. Prior to this, there was no state-sponsored support for any particular legal mechanism to counter "heresy". Where, prior to this time, only Emperors enforced persecutions on the populace, this reinforcement of the Church's authority, which was under Imperial authority, now gave church leaders the power to, in effect, pronounce the death sentence upon those whom the Church considered heretical. In many ways, this paralleled the Judaic laws and customs which supported the use of the death penalty for "blasphemy" or other infractions.

In their *Edict to the People of Constantinople,* 380 CE, Emperors Gratian, Valentinian, and Theodosius Augusti, proclaimed, "According to the apostolic teaching and the doctrine of the Gospel, let us believe in the one deity of the Father, the Son and the Holy Spirit, in equal majesty and in a holy Trinity. We authorize the followers of this law to assume the title of Catholic Christians; but as for the others, since, in our judgment they are foolish madmen, we decree that they shall be branded with the ignominious name of heretics, and shall not presume to give to their conventicles the name of churches." The idea of deciding correct theological doctrines and dogma had become a power game.

EARLY HERETICS

There were many heresies that developed in the early Church, including the controversy of Arianism, which led to Constantine's convening of the First Council of Nicea. Epiphanius identified over 80 heresies within the church in the 4th century . Two important heresies that also developed in Rome were Marcionism and Priscillianism, along with Montanism, Novationism and others.

Marcion in the 2nd century, favored using only Pauline epistolary writings and the *Gospel of Luke*, which is considered to be the gospel that is most harmonious with Paul's teachings. Marcion rejected the *Gospel of Matthew*, which was more closely associated with the Twelve Apostles, and Jewish Christianity. In other words, Marcion favored the Gentile perspective.

However, New Testament scholar, Joseph B. Tyson, in his book, *Marcion and Luke-Acts, A Defining Struggle,* proposes that both *Acts* and the final version of the *Gospel of Luke* "were published at the time when Marcion of Pontus was beginning to proclaim his version of the Christian gospel, in the years 120–125 c.e.", with the final version of *Luke*, and the *Acts of the Apostles* as opposition to the errors of Marcion's teachings. Tyson proposes this conflict as "a defining struggle over the very meaning of the Christian message and the author of *Luke-Acts* as a major participant in that contest." Tyson suggests that these texts were meant to correct the Marcionite understanding of Paul as rejecting both the Torah and the God of Israel, and proposes that the stories that involve Peter and the Jerusalem apostles in *Acts* counteract the Marcionite claim that Paul was the only true apostle.

Marcion believed Jesus was the savior sent by God, and that Paul was his chief apostle. In the synoptic gospels of *Matthew*, *Mark*, and *John*, one might make a case for John (Mary Magdalene) in this role. Marcion rejected the Hebrew Bible and the God of Israel. Much like the later Cathars and other Gnostics, Marcionists believed that the wrathful Hebrew God was a separate and lower entity than the all-forgiving God of the New Testament. Eventually, Marcionism became known as one of the first forms of heretical teachings. Tyson also proposes that the author of *Acts* made use of an earlier version of the *Gospel of Luke* and produced canonical *Luke* by adding, among other things, birth accounts and post-resurrection narratives of Jesus.[118]

Marcion of Pontus' year of death is given as 160 CE. In events that were, perhaps, related to the division between Marcion and the author of *Luke/Acts*, turmoil between the followers of "Pope Pontian" and "Anti-pope, Hippolytus, Bishop of Pontus" roiled up several centuries after Marcion's death.

Pontian's pontificate was initially relatively peaceful under the reign of the tolerant Emperor Severus Alexander. After Epiphanius' attacks against Origen's writings as being heretical, Ponian presided over the Roman synod which approved Origen's expulsion and deposition by Pope Demetrius I of Alexandria in 230 or 231.

Hippolytus, reportedly, provoked a schism in the Christian community at Rome, which lasted for some years. His followers supported him as a rival pope to Pope Pontian, causing much strife in Rome. Pope Pius IV identifies him, in the 16th century, as "Saint Hippolytus, Bishop of Pontus" who was martyred in the reign of Severus Alexander through his inscription on a statue found at the Church of Saint Lawrence in Rome.[119]

In 1551, a marble statue of a seated figure (originally female, perhaps personifying one of the sciences) was, purportedly found in the cemetery of the Via Tiburtina and heavily restored as a male figure - thought to represent Hippolytus. On the sides of the seat was carved a paschal cycle, and on the back the titles of numerous writings by Hippolytus.

According to Eusebius, the next emperor, Maximinus, overturned his predecessor's policy of tolerance towards Christianity. Both Pope Pontian and the Antipope Hippolytus of Rome were arrested and exiled to labor in the mines of Sardinia, generally regarded as a death sentence. In light of his sentence, Pontian resigned, the first pope to do so, so as to allow an orderly transition in the Church of Rome, on 28 September 235. In exile, Hippolytus was said to be reconciled with the Church and died for the faith in 235. Pontian, it is said, was beaten to death with sticks by his captors. Both were claimed to be reconciled to each other before their deaths. Both are seen to be martyrs and saints.

Pope Fabian had their bodies returned to Rome in 236 or 237, with Pontian buried in the papal crypt in the Catacomb of Callixtus on the Appian Way, and Hippolytus in a cemetery on the Via Tiburtina. Were these two saints, in some way, connected to the division between Marcion and the author of *Acts/Luke*?

Regarding Marcion, and his teachings, Robert Price, in his book, *The Evolution of the Pauline Canon*, writes, “But the first collector of the Pauline Epistles had been Marcion. No one else we know of would be a good candidate, certainly not the essentially fictive Luke, Timothy, and Onesimus. And Marcion, as Burkitt and Bauer show, fills the bill perfectly.”[120] According to Price, Marcion's role in the formation and development of Christianity is pivotal. Certainly, his large following seems to have developed into, if not the first large Gentile congregation of Christianity in Rome, then at least a very important one, from which a Pauline following developed.

Price engaged in a national discussion with a colleague at University of North Carolina-Chapel Hill, Bart D. Ehrman, about the question of whether or not Jesus existed. Price, a church-going Episcopalian questioned

Jesus's place in history, while Ehrman, a lapsed Baptist claimed Jesus was real.

In his book, *The Amazing Colossal Apostle: The Search for the Historical Paul*, Price suggests that Paul is a composite of several historical figures, including Marcion of Pontos, Stephen the Martyr, Simon the Sorcerer, and the iconoclastic evangelist, Paul.[121] He states that Paul's letters were actually written and edited by other people, including Marcion and another early Church Father, Polycarp of Smyrna. This would certainly explain the difference in tone and material between the Epistles of Paul and the narrative of his life in *Acts*. According to New Testament scholar Hermann Detering, this view of the editing of Paul's letters "represents a paradigm shift in the field of Pauline research."

According to the *Acts of the Apostles*, Paul entered the scene as a zealous persecutor of early Christians, then transformed the movement Jesus founded from a Jewish sect to congregations of Gentile followers that rejected Jewish law. We might also see some connection to John in his zealousness for the Jewish faith, proclaiming judgment and the need for repentance in preparation for the coming of the Lord.

When Thomas Jefferson called Paul, "the first corrupter of the doctrines of Jesus", he was not seeing that *the teachings* of Paul may have been corrupted, and so, it was perhaps not Paul, but followers of Paul or "Paulinity" (whether Marcionists or his opponents) that were at fault. Indeed, Paul took the message of Christ to the Gentiles, but this is just what Jesus directed in his "Great Commission" – telling the disciples to "make disciples of all nations." Preaching to the Gentiles is just what Jesus ordered.

Many scholars have proposed that *Acts* was a second-century "romance" novel or adventure, based on the writings of ancient authors like Homer, Virgil, Euripides, and Josephus, and not based on a real-life account of an apostle named Paul. Some scholars have even used word-print analysis and other techniques to show that Polycarp was Paul's principal editor and sole author of the epistles to *Timothy* and *Titus*, a finding with which Price agrees.[122]

The story of Paul in the *Acts of the Apostles* is not to be found in Paul's epistles. *Acts* contains fanciful "miracle" motifs, including a resurrected Jesus who walks through walls and people who can make earthquakes happen through prayer. Also, only in the *Acts* do we have twelve apostles. Paul's letters mention more apostles, some of them female. In the early Christian church, there were other sources of information about Paul which were for a time considered canonical, fabulous hagiographies like the *Acts of Paul* and *The Acts of Paul and Thecla* (the latter originally part of the *Acts of*

Paul), which give very different (now apocryphal) perspectives on his life and teachings.

Tertullian found the *Acts of Paul* to be heretical because it encouraged women to preach and baptize. This text was considered orthodox by Hippolytus but was eventually regarded as heretical when it was embraced and adopted by the heretical sect known as the Manichaeans - also known as "Christians of St. John", who practiced ritual ablution or baptizing, and who condemned Pauline teachings as falsehoods.

Price proposes that Marcion, a wealthy merchant whose father was an early Christian, traveled to Rome in 140 CE, and was the first collector (if not writer) of the Pauline Epistles. Marcion, like Paul, traveled throughout Asia Minor, converting people, establishing churches, and writing letters to the various early Church communities. Price proposes that, a decade after Marcion's arrival in Rome, Polycarp collected his writings and edited them for orthodox consumption before his own martyrdom in 156 CE. Thus, Marcion's writings were very likely, through Polycarp, comingled with Paul's.

Paul's writings would become foundational works of the Christian faith, while Marcion, himself, would be named a heretic, his writings condemned. He became one of the first "heresiarchs" for his deviations from what would be decided upon as the orthodox position of the main authorities in the Catholic Church. His theology, which is seen as the catalyst for establishing the accepted Church canon, rejected the God of the Hebrew Scriptures and instead affirmed the Father of Christ as the true God. The Church denounced Marcion for these ideas, whereupon he separated himself from the proto-orthodox church.

Adolf von Harnack, in *Origin of the New Testament* (2005) writes, "We have indeed long known that Marcionite readings found their way into the ecclesiastical text of the Pauline Epistles, but now for seven years we have known that Churches actually accepted the Marcionite prefaces to the Pauline Epistles! De Bruyne has made one of the finest discoveries of later days in proving that those prefaces, which we read first in *Codex Fuldensis* and then in numbers of later manuscripts, are Marcionite, and that the Churches had not noticed the cloven hoof."

According to anti-Marcionite sources, Marcion was a follower of Cerdo. Irenaeus writes that "a certain Cerdo, originating from the Simonians, came to Rome under Hyginus ... and taught that the one who was proclaimed as God by the Law and the Prophets is not the Father of our Lord Jesus Christ." (*Against Heresies* 1, 27, 1)

Hippolytus records that Marcion was the son of the bishop of Sinope, in Pontus. Others described him as a wealthy ship owner. He made a huge donation to the Church in Rome, which was returned to him at his excommunication, after which, he returned to Asia to teach the Christian gospel in its Marcionite version.

In 394, Epiphanius claimed that Marcion began as an ascetic, but seduced a virgin, for which he was excommunicated by his father, prompting him to leave his home town. Many scholars have questioned this account. Bart D. Ehrman suggests that this "seduction of a virgin" was a metaphor for his corrupting of the teachings of the Church. However, this comment could, more directly, be reference to one who was the human "father" of Jesus, the virgin's husband, Peter. Was Marcion simply representing a Pauline viewpoint on an earlier Christian figure, who was supported by a certain contingent of Petrine Christian followers in Rome?

Some early Church Fathers, such as Justin Martyr, never mentioned Paul in their extensive writings, so it is debatable whether Christians in Justin's day had ever heard of him. Tertullian defended the addition of "lost parts" of the epistles he believed Marcion had deleted, acknowledging in an indirect way that the Church Fathers had tampered with Marcion's texts. However, it is equally possible that someone with Tertullian's misogynistic leaning , added certain of his own ideas to Paul's epistles.

Marcion's studies of the Hebrew Scriptures, as well as the writings circulating in the early Church, caused him to find that many of the teachings of Jesus were incompatible with the actions of the God of the Old Testament, Yahweh. In attempting to reconcile contradictions between Old and New Testament theology, Marcion developed the idea, around 144 CE, of two gods - a higher and a lower one, similar to ideas that were later professed by the Gnostics. He essentially made the Jewish God YHWH into a lesser God, who created the world, while the true God was a higher, transcendent one.

Marcion affirmed Jesus to be the Savior sent by the Heavenly Father, and Paul, his chief apostle. However, Marcion declared that Christianity described a complete break with Judaism and was entirely opposed to the Old Testament message. He did not claim that the Jewish Scriptures were false, but proposed that they were to be read in an absolutely literal manner, thereby developing an understanding that YHWH was not the same God professed by Jesus. Certainly, the God of the Old Testament was an often vengeful, brutal being – very unlike the Father God of Jesus' teachings.

In his *Antitheses,* Marcion called the God of the Old Testament, the *Demiurge*, a term used in later Gnostic beliefs. This *Demiurge* was the creator of the material universe and was a jealous tribal deity of the Jews, a legalistic and merciless God who punishes mankind for its sins through suffering and death. In contrast, Jesus professed a universal God of compassion and love who looks upon humanity with benevolence and mercy. Marcion saw Jesus as the son of the Heavenly Father but interpreted the incarnation *docetically*, i.e. that Jesus' body only appeared to be a material body, consequently, denying his physical and bodily birth, death, and resurrection.

Marcion included in his canon of accepted books, the *Apostolikon*, a selection of ten epistles of Paul. He saw Paul as the correct interpreter and transmitter of the teachings of Jesus. The gospel that Marcion used did not contain elements relating to Jesus' birth and childhood, though it did contain some elements of Judaism, and material that opposed his own ditheistic beliefs. Marcionism spread greatly within his lifetime, becoming a rival to orthodox Christianity. Despite opposition, it retained its following for several centuries.

The Cathars in medieval France, who claimed to adhere to the original teachings of the faith, may well have embraced a kind of resurrection of these beliefs. They proposed that there was a true God - the God of light and love, and a lesser or false God - the *Rex Mundi,* the king of the world. The latter description seems to have been directed at the Catholic papacy. They were persecuted by the mainstream Church for their ideas, and basically wiped out through various campaigns and massacres in the 13th century.

Another important heresy of early Christianity was that of Priscillianism. In 386, Roman secular officials found the ascetic Gnostic-Christian orator and teacher, Priscillian, guilty of sorcery, and put him to death. His accusers were excommunicated by Ambrose of Milan and Pope Siricius, who, while opposing Priscillian's heresy, “believed capital punishment to be inappropriate at best and usually unequivocally evil", indicating that the power of the Roman Imperials still superseded that of the papacy in this earliest legal decision on heresy.[123]

Priscillian proposed that apostles, prophets, and "doctors" (Latin for "teachers") are the divinely appointed orders of the Church. Doctors, among whom Priscillian reckoned himself, were considered to be the highest order. In Priscillianism, the "spiritual" comprehend and judge all things, being "children of wisdom and light"; and the distinction between flesh and spirit, darkness and light, the "prince of this world" and Christ, are emphasized.

These are Gnostic concepts, which are similar to the beliefs of the Cathars, which arose several centuries later in France. The name of the Cathars, meant the “Pure Ones,” and the goal of Catharism, like that of Priscillianism, was for its adherents to overcome the darkness, and become a “parfait” or perfected one. The Cathars claimed to have the true teachings of Christ – a concept which may go back to Marcion, Priscillian, or other

Christians who, influenced by dualistic Manichaean beliefs, broke away from the mainstream Church early on.

Priscillian distinguished three degrees, though he did not deny hope of pardon to those who were unable to attain full perfection. The perfect in body, mind, and spirit were celibate, or, if married, continent (a term which could mean anything from self-restraint or moderation, to sexual abstinence). Certain practices of the Priscillianists are revealed in condemnatory canons issued by the 580 synod, such as receiving the Eucharist in the church but eating it at home or in the conventicle, women joining with men during the time of prayer; fasting even on Sunday; meditating at home or in the mountains instead of attending church during Lent.

According to Ana Maria C.M. Jorge, Priscillian "... played the role of a catalyst among Lusitanian Christians and crystallized a variety of ascetic, monastic and intellectual aspirations that were either fairly, or even entirely, incompatible with Christianity as it was lived by the great majority of the bishops of the day."[124]

Specifically, as with the later Cathars, women had much more equal roles within the spiritual practices of the Priscillian movement. Priscillian and 5 of his followers were the first to be legally accused and killed as "heretics".

CONSTANTINE'S COUNCIL

The First Council of Nicaea was the first of seven "ecumenical" (worldwide Christian) councils. It was held in the city of Nicaea in 325 CE – convened not by the church, but by the Roman Emperor, Constantine I. His goal was not to define or establish truths, but rather to attain consensus through an assembly representing all of Christendom. His goal was to define a uniform, "catholic" belief system, which the council attempted to achieve in the "Nicene Creed."

Constantine called the council to in order to resolve the "Arian controversy", in which the presbyter, Arius, disputed the doctrinal precepts of Alexander, Patriarch of Alexandria, over definitions regarding the *Logos*, a Greek term for the "Word", which represented the Son of God. We might say that the "Hellenizing" of the faith brought with it a confusion of philosophical and theological Greek ideas and terminology which needed to be sorted out, clarified and agreed upon by the over 250 attendees.

There were arguments over the definitions of terms such

as "essence" (*ousia*), "substance" (*hypostasis*), "nature" (*physis*), and "person" (*prosopon*), each with a variety of meanings derived from the writings of Greek philosophers, which caused confusion for Christian theologians in the doctrinal formulas of the Church. Among other concerns, the word *homoousia*, which was used to propose that the Son is of the same substance as the Father was considered suspect because of its association with heretical Gnostic theology, which had been condemned at the 264–268 Synods of Antioch.

The dispute with Arius primarily revolved around the definition of "begotten" as it is used in the phrase, "God's only begotten son" as well as, "The Son was begotten not made." This definition was central to many later disputes regarding the theology of the faith. Arius defined the word, "begotten", according to biblical use of the term, to mean that Jesus was "birthed from" or "born of" the Father. He proposed that, as a "begotten" creature, the Son must have a beginning (unlike God the Father, who was eternal), and therefore the Son must be lesser than the Father, though still the very first and the most perfect of God's creatures. It does seem a bit ironic that Arius would claim that the Son "was birthed from the Father God." But, essential, since Christianity claimed no Mother God in the Godhead. Ah, the implications of any attempt to define "Divinity"!

There were some who saw "the Word" as the "Indwelling Presence" of God, but indwelling where? Within the body. This would lend itself more to Arius' position. In this case, the "Son" would be the human component - in which the Presence of God dwelled.

The contra-Arian argument was that the *Logos* was "eternally begotten" of the Father, claiming that the Arian view destroyed the unity of the Godhead, making the Son unequal to the Father. They insisted that this viewpoint went against such Scriptures as "I and the Father are one" (*John* 10:30) and "the Word was God" (*John* 1:1). They were unwilling to find it possible that the Word (the Presence of God) was the eternal nature of God, while the Son was the human vessel (container) of that Presence. Instead, they declared, as did Athanasius, that the Son had no beginning, but had an "eternal derivation" from the Father. Thus, the Father was always a Father, and both Father and Son always existed. Therefore, the Son was "coeternal, consubstantial and coequal" to the Father God.

This is a very important distinction in the development of the doctrines of the Church. This idea actually aligns with the belief in the "one nature" of Jesus, where God and Son become one - an idea which would later be attacked, and replaced by the idea of the "two natures" of Jesus, in hypostatic union. (Splitting hairs? But people were excommunicated over such differences in semantics.)

In Alexander's view, the Son was not "born of" the Father in the usual sense, but was part of and therefore, equal to the Father. This first ecumenical council made clear that the "birth" of the Son, Jesus, was not your usual birth, even before attempting to define Mary's role in the matter.

THE INCARNATION

One must acknowledge that the Christian doctrines on the relationship between Jesus' human nature and divine nature are complicated. Such definitions began with New Testament statements on the subject, from Paul's writings, which included statements such as Paul saying in 2 *Corinthians* 5:19, "God was in Christ reconciling the world to himself," and in 1 *Timothy* 3:16 that "...God was manifest in the flesh, justified in the Spirit, seen of angels, preached unto the Gentiles, believed on in the world, received up into glory."

The *Athanasian Creed,* of the 4th century, recognized and affirmed the importance of the doctrine of the "two natures", stating that "He is God from the essence of the Father, begotten before time; and he is human from the essence of his mother, born in time; completely God, completely human, with a rational soul and human flesh; equal to the Father as regards divinity, less than the Father as regards humanity."

The creed clarifies that the divine nature of Jesus is the eternal essence of God. It goes on, "Although he is God and human, yet Christ is not two, but one. He is one, however, not by his divinity being turned into flesh, but by God's *taking humanity to himself*." (An important distinction.) It goes on, "He is one, certainly not by the blending of his essence, but by the unity of his person. For just as one human is both rational soul and flesh, so too the one Christ is both God and human." (This description seems to state that Jesus' divine/human nature was much like that of any human, encompassing both body and soul.) Such doctrinal definitions, which came after Christianity was made legal, were bound to cause confusion.

The Catholic Catechism states, "For this is why the Word became man, and the Son of God became the Son of man: so that man, *by entering into communion with the Word* and thus receiving divine sonship, might become a son of God."(CCC 460) This seems to support Adoptionism, where Jesus is thought to become the Son of God upon his "communion with the Word". This also seems to say that we – all of humanity – can enter into "communion with the Word", and become sons of God.

So many of the doctrinal statements regarding the human body of the Son are given in the context of the flesh/body of the Virgin. In his treatise, *On the Incarnation*, written around 318 CE, Athanasius of Alexandria stated, "The body of the Word, then, being a real human body, in spite of its having been *uniquely formed from a virgin*, was of itself mortal and, like other bodies, liable to death. But the *indwelling of the Word* loosed it from this natural liability, so that corruption could not touch it." The resemblance of the "indwelling of the Word" to the Judaic concept of the "Indwelling Presence" of the *Shekinah*, should be noted – a state that could be achieved by any dedicated initiate to the Jewish Temple mysteries. Here, the *Word* dwelled within Mary.

Athanasius also supported the idea that was used in the Nicene Creed, "For the right Faith is, that we believe and confess; that our Lord Jesus Christ, the Son of God, is God and Man; God, of the Substance [Essence] of the Father; begotten before the worlds; and Man, of the Substance [Essence] of his Mother, born in the world." This wording is meant to clarify how the Son could be always eternally God, but also be finitely human.

In his *Letter to Epictus*, Athanasius brings up an interesting topic: "Or who devised this abominable impiety, for it to enter even his imagination, and for him to say that to pronounce the Lord's Body to be *of Mary* is to hold a Tetrad instead of a Triad in the Godhead?" This stance would seem to apply to those, such as Gregory of Nyssa, whose position indicated a belief in there being "two Sons", one human and one divine - therefore a Tetrad with the Father and the Holy Spirit. Athanasius also ridicules the idea "that the Body of the Savior which He *put on from Mary*, is of the Essence of the Triad." His position being that the body is separate from the eternal nature, thus not a part of the Triad, also known as the Holy Trinity.

Athanasius goes on, "Or how did men called Christians venture even to doubt whether the Lord, Who *proceeded from Mary*, while Son of God by Essence and Nature, is of the seed of David according to the flesh *Romans* 1:3, and *of the flesh of the Holy Mary*?" The exegesis of this subject always revolves around "the flesh of Mary" and how the Lord "assumed" or took on a body from her but the wording is often convoluted, and the meaning therefore obscured. The phrase "proceeded from Mary" brings to mind definitions of the Holy Spirit who "proceeds" from the Father and the Son. And the Son is the Word. Might we say then that the Lord, proceeding from Mary is the Holy Spirit, the *dibbur*, the Word of God?

In *The Rabbinic Mind*, Max Kadushin describes the gift of prophecy – God's communication to the prophet, His utterance of prophecy, or *Dibbur* – as coming from the *Shekinah*. He writes, "The occasions when God 'speaks with' the prophets, when 'the word of the Lord' came upon them, are then regarded as revelations of *Shekinah*."

Athanasius condemns the idea that the Incarnation of the Word was the same as any other descent of the Spirit on the prophets of the faith, "...how can they wish to be called Christians who say that the Word has descended upon a holy man as upon one of the prophets, and has not Himself become man, *taking the body from Mary*; but that Christ is one person, while the Word of God, Who before Mary and before the ages was Son of the Father, is another? Or how can they be Christians who say that the Son is one, and the Word of God another?"

Which begs the question: were there people saying that "the Word," simply descended upon the human, "as upon one of the prophets", and not as a human infant birthed from a human mother? Why should there even be confusion on the subject?

Nestorius, the Patriarch of Constantinople, who was deposed, and whose teachings were condemned, got into some murky territory on the nature of the Incarnation. But his problems were representative of all attempts to define Divinity. It was a dangerous thing to make such an attempt in many periods of Christian history. Nestorius proposed that the Word, which is eternal, and the flesh, which was not, came together in hypostatic union, all of which was Orthodox teaching, however, he stated that Jesus was of two *ousia* (nature, essence or being) and one *prosopon* (person). Cyril took issue with the language: "of two natures", insisting that Jesus was *from* two natures up until the *hypostatic* union, at which time he became one nature.

Nestorius spoke of the nature of the godhead as being "joined to the temple", proposing, that it was not "the godhead of the Son that was recently killed but the flesh which was joined to the nature of the godhead...The body therefore is the temple of the deity of the Son, a temple which is united to it in a high and divine conjunction, so that the divine nature accepts what belongs to the body as its own. Such a confession is noble and worthy of the gospel traditions." It was Mary's body that early theologians called "the Temple of the Lord".

Nestorius also said, "But to use the expression 'accept as its own' as a way of diminishing the properties of the conjoined flesh, birth, suffering and entombment is a mark of those whose minds are led astray...For it is necessary for such as are attracted by the name 'propriety' to make God the Word share, because of this same propriety, in being fed on milk, in gradual growth, in terror at the time of his passion and in need of angelical assistance. I make no mention of circumcision and sacrifice and sweat and hunger, which all belong to the flesh and are adorable as having taken place for our sake. But it would be false to apply such ideas to the deity and would involve us in just accusation because of our calumny." What exactly is Nestorius saying here, and does that bring clarity on exactly why he was desposed and exiled?

John Paul II, who had a great love for Mary, did not technically go outside the accepted doctrinal formulas, but his description of the title of *Theotokos* did make a certain distinction that is not included in the formulas of earlier church fathers: "In this way the name *"Theotókos"* – Mother of God – became the name proper to the *union with God* granted to the Virgin Mary."

The earliest patristic writings of the Church give us clear indications of the truth of the "virgin birth." Cappadocian Father, Gregory of Nyssa in his 4th century, treatise *On Virginity*, wrote: "What came about in bodily form in Mary, the fullness of the godhead *shining through Christ in the Blessed Virgin*, takes place in a similar way in every soul that has been made pure. The Lord does not come in bodily form, for 'we no longer know Christ according to the flesh,' but *He dwells in us spiritually and the Father takes up His abode with Him*, the Gospel tells us. In this way *the child Jesus is born in each of us.*" If only the doctrinal teachings of Christianity had allowed, aligned with, and kept this simple formula.

ARK OF THE NEW COVENANT

In the 20th century both popes John Paul II and Benedict XVI have emphasized the Marian focus of the Church. John Paul II wrote in his Apostolic Letter *Mulieris Dignitatem* (On the Dignity and Vocation of Women): " ... [The Church] gives thanks for all the fruits of feminine holiness". In *Mulieris Dignitatem* John Paul II said, "The Second Vatican Council, confirming the teaching of the whole of tradition, recalled that in the hierarchy of holiness it is precisely the "woman", Mary of Nazareth, who is the "figure" of the Church. She "precedes" everyone on the path to holiness; in her person "the Church has already reached that perfection whereby she exists without spot or wrinkle (cf. Eph 5:27)".

Cardinal Joseph Ratzinger (later Pope Benedict XVI) wrote: "It is necessary to go back to Mary if we want to return to that "truth about Jesus Christ," "truth about the Church" and "truth about man." He suggested a redirection of the whole Church towards the program of Pope John Paul II in order to ensure an authentic approach to Christology via a return to the "whole truth about Mary". So what is that "whole truth about Mary"? We must go back to the early days of the nascent Church to understand what this means.

The Early Church Fathers saw Jeremiah's prophecy as a presaging of the honoring of Mary, the virgin, "for the LORD hath created a new thing in the earth, A woman shall compass a man." Why is this a new thing? What does the prophecy actually mean?

The Byzantine fathers named Mary the *Theotokos* – translated loosely as "The Godbearer", but could more technically be translated, "The one who bears the one who is God."– present tense. The Byzantine metaphor of *Theotokos*, even more loosely translated as "Mother of God" (which would actually, in Greek, be *Mētēr tou Theou*), became Byzantine dogma. The ascetic monks balked at such use of metaphor – for, in fact, how could any human be the mother of the Eternal God?

Each new doctrine and dogma brought with it new thorny issues to sort out. Augustine's doctrine of Original Sin, required a later dogmatic description of Mary as being "without sin" - the Spotless Virgin. The doctrine of the Immaculate Conception of Mary – not her conception of Jesus, but her own conception. For how could a sinner, according to Augustine's doctrine – even a forgiven one – be the bearer of God? She must, therefore, be the one exception. One step in the formulation of doctrine led to another, in a long and twisting road of acceptable Christian beliefs, according to who had the power, or who won the argument at any given moment.

Mariology became a matter of contention in the 16th century, in the time of the Protestant Reformation. Some early Protestants venerated Mary. Martin Luther wrote that: "Mary is full of grace, proclaimed to be entirely without sin. God's grace fills her with everything good and makes her devoid of all evil."[125] However, as of 1532, Luther stopped celebrating the feast of the Assumption of Mary and also stopped supporting the dogma of the Immaculate Conception.

John Calvin remarked, "It cannot be denied that God in choosing and destining Mary to be the Mother of his Son, granted her the highest honor."[126] However, Calvin firmly rejected the notion that Mary can intercede between Christ and man. Following the Council of Trent in the 16th century, as Marian veneration became associated with Catholics, Protestant interest in Mary decreased, and she has faded from most Protestant churches, though Anglicans and Lutherans still honor her.

In Catholicism, both the Eastern and the Western Church honor Mary above all other saints, specifying that the veneration of Mary stems from the great work that God accomplished through her. An early metaphorical reference for the Virgin Mary was "the Ark of the New Covenant." In a

Kontakion from the Greek Orthodox Church, it says of Mary that, "She is the heavenly tabernacle." In essence, Mary's body becomes the Holy Place. This again is a present-tense, and ongoing description, not past-tense or temporary.

In the Old Testament, the Ark of the Covenant of the Israelites symbolized God's promise to Moses to lead his people out of bondage into the land of milk and honey. The correlation of the two stories alludes to Mary leading the people out of the bondage of sin, through her mission as the mother of the redeemer. But, the Ark of the Covenant, in Judaism, was also seen as a container of powerful Divine energies. In the Holy of Holies, the *Shekinah*, the very "presence of God" in Judaic theology, was known to enter and come to rest upon the Mercy Seat atop the Ark.

In Christianity, Mary became the New Ark, when she was "overshadowed by the Holy Spirit", and the "presence of God" came to rest in her. Soon after the legalization of Christianity, Eastern Christianity began developing the early ideas of "Mariology," – theological ideas and formulas applying to Mary.

In Orthodox Christianity also, the *Theotokos* is seen to be the fulfillment of the archetype represented by the Ark of the Covenant. As "The God-bearer," Mary brought forth the New Covenant of the Christ; therefore, the Orthodox honor her as the Ark that bore the New Covenant – the vessel that held the Son, the Word of God.

In the 3rd century, Hippolytus wrote of Mary as the Ark of the New Covenant: "At that time, the Savior coming from the Virgin, the Ark, brought forth His own Body into the world from that Ark, which was gilded with pure gold within by the Word, and without by the Holy Ghost; so that the truth was shown forth, and the Ark was manifested. And the Savior came into the world bearing the incorruptible Ark, that is to say His own body." Are you confused yet? Or does the circumlocution make it clearer?

In *Peristephanon*, written in the 4th century, by Roman Christian poet, Prudentius, he states, "For the holy Virgin is in truth an ark, wrought with gold both within and without, that has received the whole treasury of the sanctuary."

In the same century, Ambrose wrote, "Now what else should we say the Ark was but holy Mary? The Ark bore within it the tables of the Testament, but Mary bore the Heir of the same Testament itself. The former contained in it the Law, the latter the Gospel. The one had the voice of God, the other His Word. The Ark, indeed, was radiant within and without with the glitter of gold, but holy Mary shone within and without with the splendor of virginity. The one was adorned with earthly gold, the other with heavenly."

Ephraim, the Syrian, wrote an interesting commentary, in the 4th century, on Mary as the Ark, "Joseph rose to minister before His Lord, *who was in Mary.* The priest ministered before Thy Ark by reason of Thy holiness. Moses carried the tables of stone which the Lord wrote, and Joseph *bare about the pure Tablet in whom the Son of the Creator was dwelling.* The tables had ceased, because the world was filled with Thy doctrine." Ephraim states that the tablets – the Ten Commandments – were no longer needed, because the Lord "was in Mary." We also get the inference here of Joseph as ministering priest. *Sirach* 24:12-14 speaks of Wisdom, "Then the creator of all things commanded, and said to me: and he that made me, rested in my tabernacle, ... From the beginning, and before the world, was I created, and unto the world to come I shall not cease to be, and in the holy dwelling place I have ministered before him."

Epiphanius makes Mary the container of the uncontainable: "Mary, the holy Virgin, is truly great before God and men. For how shall we not proclaim her great, who held within her the uncontainable One, whom neither heaven nor earth can contain?" The ever more glorious formulas and descriptions of Mary were becoming a source of consternation for those who saw problems with a literal interpretation of these metaphorical statements. We can see why some had issues with the idea that Mary – a human, and more than that, a woman – contained the uncontainable nature of God.

In the 4th century, Athanasius, bishop of Alexandria, wrote of the connection between the Ark and the Virgin, in a tribute of glowing praise: "O noble Virgin, truly you are greater than any other greatness. For who is your equal in greatness, *O dwelling place of God the Word*? To whom among all creatures shall I compare you, O Virgin? You are greater than them all O (Ark of the) Covenant, clothed with purity instead of gold! You are the Ark in which is found the golden vessel containing the true manna, that is, the flesh in which Divinity resides." These glowing praises, written in the 4th century, are, again, in present tense.

Cyril of Alexandria in the 5th century wrote, "The Ark would be the type and image of Christ: for if we look back to the way of the Incarnation of the Only-begotten, we shall see that it is in the temple of the Virgin, as in an ark that the Word of God took up His abode." We might see this idea that the "Word of God took up his abode" in Mary, in the Byzantine icons of the *Panagia* – with Mary, medallion over her heart, containing the Holy Infant, who held up two fingers in blessing...or was it the Greek pose of the orator – the one speaking, the Word?

St. Proclus, in the 5th century states, "...Eve has been healed... and Mary is venerated (adored), because she has become mother and handmaid, cloud and chamber, and ark of the Lord..."

In a similar manner, the Homily from Theodotus of Ancyra (early 5th century CE) addresses this mystery of the faith - but with an intriguing difference, "Hail, ineffable mother of a mystery beyond understanding... Hail, alabaster jar of sanctifying ointment". This is another comparison of Mary to the Place of the White Marble, the Holy Place, the sanctuary of the Temple. But, wait - the alabaster jar is known to be the symbol of Mary Magdalene. He goes on, "Hail, best trader of the coin of virginity; Hail, creature embracing your Creator; Hail, little container containing the Uncontainable."

In the 9th century, the eastern saint, Methodius, describes the mother-virgin mystery, through Mary's presentation of Jesus at the Temple, "She goes up therefore to the temple, she who was more exalted than the temple, clothed with a double glory—the glory, I mean, of undefiled virginity, and that of ineffable child-bearing, the benediction of the Law, and the sanctification of grace..." The *Benedictus* is Zacharia's prayer of John's birth, the *Magnificat* is Mary's acceptance of her role, and the bestowal of God's grace upon her. Ineffable means "inexpressible" – the child-bearing was beyond expression or definition.

Methodius states, "Hence it was that the Ark of God removed from the stable at Bethlehem...and rested upon the mountains of Zion; and receiving into her pure bosom as upon a lofty throne-such as transcends the nature of man – the Monarch of all, she presented Him there to God the Father-the Son joint-partner of His throne, and inseparable from Him – together with that pure and undefiled flesh which He had from her assumed ..."[127] There is that word again, "assumed." He says that Mary received "into her pure bosom... the Monarch of all." Into her heart, not her womb. She presented Him there - at the Temple - from her heart.

Is it any wonder that the formulas of the "two natures" of Jesus were often bound to the descriptions of "the flesh of Mary"?

Methodius writes of Mary, comparing her glorification to that of the Holy of Holies, "Tremendous, verily, is the mystery connected with thee, O Mother Virgin, thou spiritual throne, glorified and made worthy of God..." He goes on to mention the "veil of the temple overshadowing before the ark of the Covenant which typified thee... For if to the ark, which was the image and type of thy sanctity, such honor was paid by God, that to no one but to the priestly order was the access to it open, or ingress allowed to behold it – the veil separating it off, and keeping the vestibule as that of a queen – how great, and what sort of veneration is due to thee from us, who are of all the least, to thee who art indeed a Queen; to thee who art in truth the *living Ark of God,* the Law-giver; to thee who hast verily become the heaven that contains Him who can be contained of none?"

Mary is not just "the Ark", she is the "living Ark of God." The Ark of the New Covenant – necessary, as the old covenant became obsolete: in Christ's teachings, no more "Eye for an eye", but "Love thy neighbor."

In Methodius' description of Jesus' relationship to God as "inseparable from Him – together with that pure and undefiled flesh which He had from her assumed..." we must wonder at the definition of "assumed". Other teachings tell us that Mary was "assumed into heaven"? Are the two concepts related?

Methodius calls Mary "the spotless robe of Him who clothes Himself with light as with a garment. You have lent to God, who stands in need of nothing, that flesh which He had not, in order that the Omnipotent might become that which it was his good pleasure to be. What is more splendid than this? ... for you have lent to God that flesh which He had not. You have clad the Mighty One with that beauteous panoply of the body by which it has become possible for Him to be seen by my eyes." God must be veiled from the eyes of the people, as when the Shekinah rested on the Mercy Seat in the Temple. This is Mary as the intercessor between Jesus and his salvific mission. Here we find the prophecy fulfilled, "a woman shall compass a man."

Methodius further explains his comparison of Mary's body, which contained the Living God, to the required veiling of the Ark of the Covenant "And the posts of the door, says the prophet, moved at the voice of him that cried, by which is signified the veil of the temple drawn before the Ark of the Covenant, which typified you, that the truth might be laid open to me, and also that I might be taught, by the types and figures which went before, to approach with reverence and trembling to do honor to the sacred mystery which is connected with you; and that by means of this prior shadow-painting of the law I might be restrained from boldly and irreverently contemplating with fixed gaze Him who, in His incomprehensibility, is seated far above all." Methodius seems to be saying that the Lord is made known to the world only through the "veil" or mediation of Mary's human form. She does, after all, have the title of the "Mediatrix of all Graces."

John of Damascus wrote a treatise in the 7th century entitled, "Mary Mediatrix between Heaven and Earth." (He also was known for his three homilies on "The Assumption of Mary".) Whereas Judaic teachings had, before the destruction of the Temple, given the place of the meeting of heaven and Earth as the sacred stone in the Holy of Holies, the Damascene said that this crossing point was within Mary - the place of the hypostasis of Divine and human.

The most popular prayer to Mary, in both Eastern and Western Christianity is the *Ave Maria,* also known as the "Hail Mary", which is based on the narrative of The Annunciation of Gabriel to Mary. It also requests her intercession with the Lord:

"Hail Mary, full of Grace, the Lord is with thee, Blessed art thou among women, and blessed is the fruit of thy womb, Jesus. Holy Mary, Mother of God, pray for us sinners, now and at the hour of our death. Amen."

A truly simple formula, if you can sit with the earliest narrative, without all the ostentation, the Imperial deification, the metaphors and iconography, the doctrines and dogma. A simple concept, buried under our noses within all the unthinking rote rosary recitations: "...the Lord is *with* thee."

Did the formulas of the Early Church, the insistence on "two natures" divide the Divine transcendence from the Divine immanence – the spirit from the body? The human from the "Presence of God" that dwelled within it? The Church Fathers would argue the issue of the "two natures" in council after council, for centuries.

ICONS OF THE THEOTOKOS

In a hymn on the Nativity by the Syrian monk, St. Ephraem, he writes, "Blessed be Mary, who without vows and without prayer in her virginity conceived and brought forth the Lord of all the sons of her companions ... Who else lulled a son in her bosom as Mary did? Who ever dared to call her son, Son of the Maker, Son of the Creator, Son of the Most High?" Again, she lulled a son "in her bosom", not in her womb.

Similarly in Hymns 11 and 12 of the same series, Ephraem represents Mary as soliloquizing thus: "The babe that I carry carries me, and He hath lowered His wings and taken and placed me between His pinions and mounted into the air, and a promise has been given me that height and depth shall be my Son's". This statement also might be seen as a basis for the adversarial satire of Simon Magus, lifted and carried through the air by demons.

The icons of the Theotokos generally include the infant Jesus. The only style that does not is the *Hagiosoritissa*, the Intercessor, which portrays Mary with her empty hands held out towards Jesus, palms upward, depicted as the mediator between Christ and man. In Eastern Christianity, John usually mirrors this position on the opposite side of any *deisis* arrangement, with Jesus in the middle.

There are five main types of icons of the Theotokos in Orthodox iconography, which were often displayed in Eastern churches in a grouping of all five:

1. *Hodegetria* (The Guide, or "She Who Shows the Way") - In this type, the Virgin Mary holds Christ, and points toward Him, as a guide to God and salvation.

2. *Eleusa* (Tender Mercy) - In this type, the Theotokos holds her Son, who presses his cheek against hers and wraps at least one arm around her neck or shoulder. Here, the *Theotokos* represents the Church, signifying the fullness of love between God and man, a love that can only be achieved within the bosom of Mother Church.

3. *Panakranta* (All Merciful) – In this type, Mary is regally enthroned with Baby Jesus on her lap, both facing the viewer. The throne symbolizes her royal glory, she alone is perfect among those born on earth. According to the Fourth Ecumenical Council, she presides with Christ over the destiny of the world.

4. *Orans/Orante* (Praying) - Lady of the Sign – In this type, Mary is shown with arms in *orante* position, arms bent at the elbow and held out to the sides, with palms upward, and with Christ enclosed in a circle or "medallion" over her bosom. "Of the Sign," is a reference to the words of *Isaias* 7:14, "The Lord himself shall give you a sign. Behold a virgin shall conceive, and bear a son, and his name shall be called Emmanuel." In the *Panagia* form (an *orante* form), Mary is shown full-length, standing, with the Holy Infant in a medallion over her heart.

5. *Hagiosoritissa* (Intercessor) – In her role as Mediatrix, the Intercessor between God and man, Mary is shown alone, in profile, with her hands held out in supplication.

Along with the standard iconic forms, there are other less common ones. One of these is the Nursing Virgin. This is believed to be one of the earliest ways of depicting Mary – a motif used by the Coptic Christians in Egypt, who incorporated imagery from the ancient sculptures of the goddess Isis and her son Horus.

Another similar format is that found in the 6th century Byzantine icon of the Mother of God "*Nikopea*," which depicts the Virgin Mary seated upon a throne but with her hands holding an oval shield containing the image of the Christ child.

The early rejection of images, along with the need to hide Christian practice from its persecutors, leaves us little archaeological evidence of the earliest Christian art. In the Eastern Church, however, the sacred art form of Icons became very popular in the 5th century. The earliest depictions of Christ, Mary, and saints are preserved in wall-paintings, mosaics and some carvings. These early images are realistic in appearance, in contrast to the later stylization. They are broadly similar in style to the mummy portraits done in wax (encaustic) and found at Fayyum in Egypt, which may indicate their connection to Alexandrian or other Egyptian Christians.

Some of the earliest Christian icons date back to about 200 CE. Aside from those icons said to be painted by Luke, or others, in the period shortly after Jesus' crucifixion, some of the oldest Christian paintings are said to be the murals painted in the Roman Catacombs, dating from that time. The oldest Christian sculptures are found on *sarcophagi* (stone caskets), dating back to the beginning of the 3rd century. The earliest depictions of Jesus generally represent him with a youthful, beardless face. It was some time before the earliest examples of the long-haired, bearded-face images began to be used. The later form would become the standard, recognized as the image of Jesus, but, even then, there was variation.

Since, in the earliest representations, the manner of depicting Jesus was not yet uniform, there was, of course, controversy over which of the two most common icons was to be favored. The first showed Jesus barefaced, that is, beardless, with short and "frizzy" hair; the second showed Jesus with a beard and hair parted in the middle, similar to the manner in which the god, Zeus, was depicted. Some scholars propose that the original form depicted "Semitic" characteristics, and the later one, which became the generally accepted form, depicted a "Hellenized" Jesus.

In 6th century writings, Theodorus Lector insisted that of the two styles of depiction, the one with short and frizzy hair was "more authentic" (*History of the Church* 1:15). To support this, he related a story (excerpted by John of Damascus) that a pagan artist, commissioned to paint an image of Jesus, used the "Zeus" form instead of the "Semitic" form. As punishment, his hands withered. One might see this as a support for Jewish traditions over Greek or Roman ones, but there might also be another, deeper issue that was addressed in this controversy. The beardless face may be more to the point in Theodorus Lector's commentary.

There is a mosaic of the young Christ from the 6th century in the church of the Latomos monastery in Thessaloniki (now dedicated to Saint David). It was covered by plaster during the Iconoclastic period, when many icons and images were being destroyed. Towards the end of this time, an earthquake brought the plaster down, revealing the image (during the reign of Leo V, 813-20).

However, the greater miracle in the story of its creation is that the mosaic which, prior to being hidden, was being constructed secretly, during the 4th century persecution of Galerius, as an image of the Virgin, was transformed overnight into the present image of Christ!

The story goes that St. Theodora, the daughter of Emperor Maximian (286-305), after being baptized as a Christian, was troubled by her idolatrous parents. She told them that she suffered from illness, and she as a result sought (for health reasons) to build a house and a bathhouse for herself in the north part of the city.

Immediately after the workers finished the buildings, she converted the bathhouse into a church, under the guidance of the Bishop of Thessaloniki, St. Alexander. She ordered an iconographer to create a mosaic in the eastern apse depicting the Most-Holy Theotokos, When he was finishing the icon, he was struck with amazement, for the face of the Theotokos had miraculously transformed into that of the bearded Christ. He was carried on a light-bearing cloud, surrounded by the four symbols of the Evangelists, and the Prophets Ezekiel and Habakuk.

The iconographer shared this miraculous occurrence with Theodora, who wanted to keep it a secret. However, one of her servants informed her mother, who called Theodora to give an explanation for what had taken place, and also to participate in sacrifice to the goddess Artemis for the salvation of her father Maximian, who was away at war with the Sauromaton. Theodora refused to reveal the existence of the icon or to sacrifice to the idols. When her father learned this, he had her locked in prison, where she received a martyr's death. The church that she built was burned, however, the icon remained unharmed, as Theodora had previously had it covered with plaster. What is the significance of this miracle story?

The *Hodegetria* is one of the oldest types of the icons portraying the Theotokos and was said to have been painted by the first iconographer, the Evangelist Luke. The first mention of an image of Mary painted from life appears in the 5th century, though earlier paintings on cave walls bear resemblance to modern icons of Mary. In his 6th century *History of the Church* 1:1, Theodorus Lector stated that the Empress Eudokia sent an image that he called the *Icon of the Hodegetria* from Jerusalem, as a gift to Pulcheria, daughter of the Emperor Arcadius. He described it as an image of "the Mother of God ... painted by the Apostle Luke." (*History of the Church*).

A *Hodegetria*, "She who shows the Way" is an icon of the Theotokos (Virgin Mary) holding the Christ Child beside her, pointing to Him as the source of salvation for mankind. In the West, this type of icon is often called "Our Lady of the Way." The most venerated icon of the *Hodegetria* type, regarded as the original, was displayed in the Monastery of the *Panagia Hodegetria* in Constantinople, which was built specially to contain it.

The *Panagia Blachernae* is a 7th century Byzantine *Hodegetria* type icon from Constantinople which was displayed in the imperial palace of Blachernae. Also referred to as the *Theotokos of Blachernae* or *Blachernitissa* (Our Lady of Blachernae), it is an encaustic icon painted on wood, revetted with gold and silver. The icon of the "Most Holy Theotokos and Ever-Virgin Mary," is now kept in Dormition Cathedral in the Moscow Kremlin. A rare copy is located in Russia at the Tretyakov Gallery.

Unlike most Orthodox icons, the *Blachernitissa* is not flat, but is formed in *bas relief*. According to Sacred Tradition, the icon was made of wax combined with the ashes of Christian martyrs who had been killed in the 6th century. Also, unlike most of the later copies, the *Blachernitissa* showed the *Theotokos* standing full-length. It was said to have been brought back from the Holy Land in the mid-5th century by Empress Eudoxia, the Empress who had problems with John Chrysostom.

The icon was double-sided, with a crucifixion on the other side, and was "perhaps the most prominent cult object in Byzantium".[128] Various traditions claim that it resided in the Church of Blachernae for about five hundred years. It was sent to Russia in 1383, before the fall of Constantinople to the Ottomans in 1453. There are a great number of copies of the image, including many of the most venerated of Russian icons, which have acquired their own status and tradition of copying.

At the Church of Our Lady of Blachernae in Constantinople, it is recorded that, "A procession, originating from the time of the Patriarch Timotheos [511-18] — the "*panhgur j*" — would take place every Friday from Blachernae to the Church of the Chalkoprateia, near Hagia Sophia, at the other end of the city."[129] The procession was noted as a regular occurrence. Though this 6th century processional tradition took place in Constantinople, similar processions took place in other Christian cities at the time. The Church of St. Mary of Blachernae (which hosted the icon) was sited close to the Blachernae imperial palace.

There are a number of artworks depicting the *Hodegetria* in its shrine and in its public display at the Church of Blachernae. In the 13th century, the public display occurred every Tuesday, at the Church of Maria Hodegetria, and was one of the great sights of Constantinople for visitors. From 1204–1261, the icon was moved to the Monastery of the *Pantokrator* (All Powerful) where the Venetian See was located, after the Latin invasion of Constantinople. This began the period of Frankish rule. Since none of the illustrations of the shrine at the Hodegetria monastery predate this period, it would seem that the shrine was created after the icon's return.

There are also accounts of the weekly display of the icon, the most colorful of which was detailed by Spaniards, who made a pilgrimage to Constantinople: "Every Tuesday twenty men come to the church of Maria Hodegetria; they wear long red linen garments, covering up their heads like stalking clothes ... there is a great procession and the men clad in red go one by one up to the icon; the one with whom the icon is pleased is able to take it up as if it weighed almost nothing. He places it on his shoulder and they go chanting out of the church to a great square, where the bearer of the icon walks with it from one side to the other, going fifty times around the square. When he sets it down then others take it up in turn." A wall-painting in a church near Arta in Greece, shows a great crowd watching such a display.

The Hamilton Psalter picture of the shrine in the monastery appears to show the icon behind a golden screen of large mesh, mounted on brackets rising from a four-sided pyramidal base, like many large medieval lecterns. The heads of the red-robed attendants are level with the bottom frame of the icon.[130] It brings to mind a line from one of the stories of Hypatia's death, "having lifted the 'chariot' to their shoulders."

The icon of the *Hodegetria* was carried around the embattlements of the city as protection, and as was customary with the relics of the saints, was carried even into battle, at times, by the Byzantines, though it didn't protect that great city from the Latin crusaders in 1204 CE. What treasures – what Holy Relics did the Latins find, and remove to the western See of Rome?

Although there are earlier records of their use, no panel icons earlier than the few from the 6th century from the Greek Orthodox Monastery of St. Catherine at Sinai survive. Full-length versions from the 12th century, both probably made by Greek artists, appear in mosaic in Torcello Cathedral and the Cappella Palatina, Palermo, the latter with the *Hodegetria* inscription.

Another *Hodegetria* disappeared from the Saint Savior cathedral in Chora, during the Fall of Constantinople in 1453. Some stories say that it was cut into four pieces. Some Russians, however, say that after the fall of Constantinople, the icon surfaced in Russia, and was placed in the Assumption Cathedral in Smolensk. This icon is often referred to as "Our Lady of Smolensk." On several occasions, it was brought with great ceremony to Moscow, where the Novodevichy Convent was built in Mary's honor. It is believed to have been destroyed by fire during the German occupation of Smolensk in 1941.

An Italian tradition relates that the original icon of Mary attributed to Luke, sent from Palestine by Empress Eudoxia to Empress Pulcheria, was a large circular icon only of her head (from a round table-top?). When the icon arrived in Constantinople, it was fitted in as the head in a very large rectangular icon of Mary holding the Christ child. Italian tradition states that this composite icon became the one historically known as the *Hodegetria*. If the circular portion was the first icon attributed to Luke, oddly enough, it did not include the Christ Child, in the usual (later) format of Virgin and Child. Whether or not it truly was painted by Luke, the more notable fact is that this earliest icon was of Mary alone.

Another tradition states that when the last Latin Emperor of Constantinople, Baldwin II, was leaving Constantinople in 1261, he took this original circular portion of the icon with him. It remained in the possession of the Angevins, whose dynasty also had it inserted into a larger image of Mary and the Christ child, which is presently enshrined above the high altar of the Benedictine Abbey church of Montevergine. Unfortunately, over the centuries this icon has been subjected to repeated over-painting, so that it is difficult to determine what the original image of Mary's face would have looked like.

It is said that from the *Hodegetria* developed the *Panagia Eleusa* (Virgin of Tender Mercy), where Mary indicates Christ, but he is nuzzling her cheek, which she slightly inclines towards him; with Christ traditionally on the left in these images. In the Eleusa (Eleousa) style of icon, as with others, the Theotokos is often seen to represent the Church, thereby displaying the fullness of love between God and man, a love that can only be achieved within the bosom of the Church, the Mother. Love bridges heaven and earth, the unity tenderly expressed in the touching of the faces.

The Eleusa form of iconography shows the infant, Jesus, tenderly pressing his cheek against his mother's cheek. This image, particularly, resembles a kiss, though it is not clearly stated as such in descriptions of iconography. The *Gospel of Phillip* states, "It is from being promised to the heavenly place that man receives nourishment [...] him from the mouth. And had the word gone out from that place, it would be nourished from the mouth and it would become perfect. For it is by a kiss that the perfect conceive and give birth."

His statement is based on the words of Zacharias about his son, John the Baptist, "And you, child, will be called the prophet of the Most High; For you will go on before the Lord to prepare his ways; To give to His people the knowledge of salvation, By the forgiveness of their sins, Because of the *tender mercy* of our God, ...It is by a kiss that the perfect conceive and give birth." (*Luke* 1:75-78)

In his interpretation of the *Song of Songs*, 12th century monk, St. Bernard of Clairvaux wrote, "But he, he of whom they speak, let him speak to me. Let him kiss me with the kiss of his mouth. Let him not speak to me in them or through them,...But let him kiss me with the kiss of his mouth, whose gracious presence and eloquence of wonderful teaching causes a 'spring of living Water' to well up in me to eternal life."[131]

Bernard equates "the kisses of his mouth" with the revelation of wisdom. "Shall I not find that a richer grace is poured out upon me from him whom the Father has anointed with the oil of gladness more than all his companions, if he will deign to kiss me with the kiss of his mouth?" (Ps 44:8) He also states that, "His living and effective word (a reference to *Heb* 4: 12) is a kiss; not a meeting of lips, which can sometimes be deceptive about the state of the heart, but a full infusion of joys, a revelation of secrets, a wonderful and inseparable mingling of the light from above and the mind on which it is shed, which, when it is joined with God, is one spirit with him." (A reference to l *Corinthians* 6: I 7).

Bernard proposes that the "kiss of his mouth" is a metaphor for the bestowal of wisdom. According to Bernard's statement, the references in the canonical gospels to the Beloved Disciple, whom Jesus loved, and "kissed often about the mouth," was not a physical kiss, but the bestowal of Divine Wisdom. In the *Gospel of Mary* the Beloved Disciple, whom Jesus "kissed often about the mouth" was Mary Magdalene.

The *Panakranta*, the "All Merciful", is a style of icon that reflects the concept of "Mary enthroned," as describe in the Liturgy of St. Basil, "All of Creation rejoices in thee, O full of grace: the angels in heaven and the race of men, O sanctified temple and noetic paradise, the glory of virgins, of whom God was incarnate and became a child, our God before the ages. He made thy body into a throne, and thy womb more spacious than the heavens. All of creation rejoices in thee, O full of grace: Glory be to thee."

All icons of this type have a common feature: the Mother of God is depicted sitting on a throne. She holds the Christ Child on her lap who blesses and presents a scroll of scripture. The throne symbolizes the royal glory of the Theotokos, who alone is perfect among those born on earth. Jesus has a hand on the scroll containing the Scriptures and blesses with His right hand.

The *Panakranta* demonstrates Mary's position as the "Seat of Wisdom". The Old Testament frequently personifies "Wisdom" as an allegorical female who leads righteous men to God.

Wisdom, in the Hebrew Bible is a feminine emanation of God, known as *Hokmah* or *Chokmah*. In the Orthodox Church and the Roman Catholic Church, the personification of Holy Wisdom (Hagía Sophía), generally seen as a feminine aspect, can refer either to Jesus Christ the Word of God, or to the Holy Spirit. In Gnosticism, Sophia (Wisdom) is a feminine figure, analogous to the soul, but also simultaneously one of the emanations of the Monad. Gnostics held that she was the *syzygy* of Jesus (i.e. the Bride of Christ) and was also the Holy Spirit of the Trinity.

Generally speaking, the icon of "Mary Enthroned" by Bugiardini (1475–1554), represents the profound meaning of theological doctrine. It symbolizes the mystery of the incarnation of Christ made man and the glory of the Mother of God. Thus, the solemn attitudes of the Saints present at the glory of the Mother of God, the awed attention of the angels who behold the mystery of the Incarnation.

In this image Mary is flanked by John the Baptist on the right and Mary Magdalene on the left (or John the Evangelist), wearing red and green robes, while John the Baptist wears his red cloak and desert father garb.

Of the more common forms of icons, the *Orante/Orans* style depicts Mary, sometimes standing, sometimes from the waist up, with her arms open wide, or in an attitude of prayer, with the elbows close to the sides of the body and the hands outstretched sideways, palms up.

The Child Jesus is sometimes portrayed in a *mandorla* (a stylized medallion) within or over the bosom of His Mother. Sometimes, there is no *mandorla* and he is suspended mysteriously before her, seeming to escape the laws of gravity. The depiction of the Virgin Mary with her hands upraised in prayer is of very ancient origin in Christian art. In the mausoleum of St. Agnes in Rome there is a 4th century painting of Mother and Child with her hands raised in prayer and the face of the infant Jesus over her heart. In many icons of the *Orante* and *Panagia* style, the Christ child is depicted with one hand raised in a position that is often described a "gesture of blessing." It is also very similar to the orator's gesture, signifying the speaker or teacher, which has some connection to "The Word" – "and The Word was with them."

Panagia is usually a full-length depiction of the *Theotokos*, where she faces the viewer directly, with her hands in the "*orans*" position (open wide), and with a medallion showing the image of Christ as a child in the center of her chest. We might see the description put forth by Methodius as relating to both this form of icon and that of "Mary enthroned": he describes the Virgin Mother as "receiving into her pure bosom as upon a lofty throne-such as transcends the nature of man-the Monarch of all."

In the Great Panagia from Yaroslavl, c. 13th century, a style also called the *Platytéra*, which literally, in Greek, means "wider or more spacious" – is a reference to the phrase that Mary is "more spacious than the heavens."

Plate 11 - Panagia of Yaroslavl

Panagia (also spelled *Panaghia*) is the feminine form of *panágios*, "*pan*," meaning "all" and "*hágios*," meaning "holy," thus, the All-Holy. It is pronounced "*pah-nah-YEE-ah*", and may be transliterated as *Panayia* or *Panaghia*.

In his *Third Letter to Nestorius*, Cyril wrote, "We do not say that his flesh was turned into the nature of the godhead or that the unspeakable Word of God was changed into the nature of the flesh. For he (the Word) is unalterable and absolutely unchangeable and remains always the same as the scriptures say. For although visible as a child and in swaddling clothes, *even while he was in the bosom of the virgin that bore him,* as God he filled the whole of creation and was fellow ruler with him who begot him." In his arguments against the teachings of Nestorius (who, eventually, was deemed a heretic), Cyril went into technicalities that served to confuse the issues. But he did describe the Word of God as being "in the bosom of the virgin that bore him."

The icon, termed “Our Lady of the Sign” is said to represent the Theotokos during the Annunciation at the moment of her *fiat*, when she submitted to call of the Angel of the Lord, Gabriel, "May it be done to me according to your word." (*Luke* 1:38). The image of the Christ child represents him at the moment of his conception within the Virgin. He is depicted not as a fetus, but a child, vested in divine robes, and often holding a scroll, symbolic of his role as teacher.

The medallion is said to be symbolic of Jesus within the womb of the Virgin Mary at the moment of the Incarnation. Jesus shines out from Mary’s heart. In this depiction, Jesus’ arms extend in such a way as to connect to the arms of Mary. In this image format, the “Sacred heart of Mary” is Jesus. As with most Orthodox icons of Mary, the letters ΜΡ ΘΥ (short for "Mother of God") are placed on the upper left and right of the halo of the Virgin Mary.

In Orthodox churches, such an image is often placed on the inside of the apse, directly over the altar. Unlike standard religious mosaics which usually have gold backgrounds, the *Platytera* is often depicted on a dark blue background, sometimes dotted with gold stars as a representation of the Heavens.

Panagia is also the name of Eastern Orthodox churches dedicated to the Virgin Mary. In the East, she is not called “St. Mary”. When she became designated as the “Theotokos”, the Mother of God, the virgin was thenceforth considered to be the holiest of all human beings, of higher status than the Saints, literally a "Saint in the superlative," thus the term *Panagia*, the All Holy, is used specifically for her.

Interestingly, Panagia is also the term used to refer to a *prosphoron*, the "Bread of the All-Holy") which is solemnly blessed during the Divine Liturgy in eastern Christianity. From this loaf of leavened bread (bread made with yeast), a large triangle in honor of the Theotokos is cut and placed on the *diskos* (*paten*) during the Liturgy of Preparation. A particle is removed from the *prosphoron* in honor of the Theotokos (Virgin Mary), and is called *Panagia*. This *prosphoron* is often stamped with an icon of the Theotokos. Before cutting the *prosphoron*, the priest makes the Sign of the Cross over it three times with the liturgical spear, saying: “In honor and commemoration of our most blessed Lady, the Theotokos and Ever-virgin Mary; through whose intercessions accept, O Lord, this sacrifice upon Thy most heavenly Altar.”

He then removes a large, triangular particle and places it to the side of the Lamb, as he says:" At Thy right hand stood the queen, arrayed in vesture wrought of gold and diverse colours." The remainder of the loaf is blessed over the Holy Table (altar) during the hymn *Axion Estin*. We can see that, in Eastern Christianity, the Virgin Mary holds a high rank even within the mysteries of the eucharistic rites.

The priest makes the Sign of the Cross with the *Panagia* over the Sacred Mysteries (consecrated Body and Blood of Christ) as he says, "Great is the name of the Holy Trinity." The remainder of the prosphora is cut up for the *antidoron*, the blessed bread which is distributed at the end of the Liturgy.

In the Roman Catholic Eucharistic Rites (rites of communion), the unleavened bread, upon which the blessing of the Holy Spirit is invoked, is seen to be the body of Christ. In the Eastern Rites, Mary is also honored as an integral part of the act of "transubstantiation", a term particular to the changing of the bread into the body of Christ.

THE DEISIS

The *Pistis Sophia*, an apocryphal Gnostic text, addresses the importance of John and Mary in relationship to Jesus: "But Mary Magdalene and John, the virgin, will tower over all my disciples and over all the elect who shall receive the mysteries of the ineffable. And they will be on my right and on my left. And I am they, and they are I" (*Pistis Sophia* 2:96). In this Gnostic text, John is called, "The Virgin", and both he and Mary Magdalene are in union with Jesus.

While the earliest *Gospels of Matthew* and *Mark* interweave the lives of the virgin Mary and John, the *Gospel of John* intertwines the lives of three important Christian figures: John, Mary and Jesus. The narrative jumps from one to the next and back again.

Church triptychs and other artworks of the Greek Orthodox Church often depict Jesus, John and Mary together, however, it is specifically the Virgin Mary, and usually, John the Baptist. This format is known as the "Deisis" (or "Deesis"), meaning, "supplication or prayer [to God]". In these works, there is a kind of "trinity" with Jesus in the center, the Virgin Mary (in Greek Orthodox terms, the "Theotokos"), on the left, and the "Prodrome", the forerunner, John the Baptist, on the right, both facing Jesus, with their arms bent at the elbow, palms up, similar to *orante* figures, but in the side-pose, commonly known as "the Intercessor," one who intercedes with God for humanity.

John the Baptist was described in the New Testament as wearing a camel's-hair cloak, tied with a leather girdle. In art, he was often depicted in a sheepskin cloak, or a simple cloth robe. Some legends equated him with the "wild, hairy man" of the wilderness, "Iron John," which also contained references to wilderness, and to rocks and water settings.

This configuration of the images of Mary, Jesus, and John makes up the *Deisis* (or *Deesis*) cycle. The Theotokos and John the Baptist turn to Jesus, the central figure, in prayerful intercession on our behalf. In this type of icon, both Mary and John hold their hands in a pose of the "intercessor", in supplication to the Lord, who often holds his own hand in the pose of the orator, the one who is speaking, or "the Word." It is clear that Jesus is the central figure, the one receiving the humble adoration of the two saints. Just as the lives of these three are so intimately intertwined in the Gospel narratives, their presence, together, is of great import in Eastern iconography.

Mary usually wears the red robe of Lady Wisdom, over a blue tunic (or sometimes wears all blue). John wears a green cloak, sometimes over what is perhaps meant to represent sheepskin, an indication of the "wild man" or "hairy man," or even the "green man" with whom he is often associated. In Slavonic "Josephus" there is reference to "The Wild Man" who, in Greek texts, is given to be John the Baptist: "Now at that time there walked among the Jews a man in wondrous garb, for he had put animals' hair upon his body wherever it was not covered by his (own) hair; and in countenance he was like a savage." There is scholarly debate about whether or not these lines about the Baptist were later interpolations, or integration of clerical notes scribbled in the margins of the text. They seem to interrupt what are, otherwise, cohesive paragraphs on other subjects.

In other formats, John is sometimes shown wearing red robes, but in this format, more often green, the color of Nature and the living earth.

Color plays an important role in the symbolism of icons. Blue is the color of the Kingdom of God, red symbolizes life on earth, purple is the color of royalty, gold is reserved for Jesus Christ - indicating the radiance of Heaven, green is the color of hope and eternal renovation, white is the uncreated essence of God, used to represent the resurrection and transfiguration of Christ. If you look at icons of Jesus and Mary, color demonstrates the mirror of their close bond and mission. Jesus often wears a red undergarment with a blue outer garment, the outer garment of blue, mirroring Mary's blue undergarment with a red overgarment (Divinity within humanity).

The *Deisis* was a much more common configuration in Byzantine era churches from the 9th through the 16th centuries than in more recent church iconography, perhaps indicating that its deeper meaning has been lost or forgotten. Its prominent use in the East in earlier times, indicates that there were many who understood its importance within the mysteries of the Church, and the reference to an early and essential "Holy Three" aside from the Holy Trinity.

The Greek letters, IC XC (*iota sigma and chi and sigma*), representing his name, "Jesus Christ" are often placed above the head of Jesus. The line above them shows that they are abbreviated and part of a larger word, a common icon trait. MP OY above the Theotokos (*mu rho omicron gamma*) are the first letters of Mother and God or 'Mother of God'. W O N in Christ's halo (*omega omicon nu*) means 'He who is' or 'I am' signifying the essence, beingness, presence of God, which, again, reflects the description of the Jewish *Shekinah* the "indwelling presence of God."

If we look again at the *Panagia*, we might see a similar symbolism of "indwelling presence of the Shekinah" in the medallion containing the Christ, placed over the heart of Mary. After all, Christianity sprang from Judaic teachings and theology. In Christianity, however, this is interpreted to be the Holy Spirit, or the "Word of God".

The narratives of these three central figures of early Christianity are intertwined in the *Gospel of John*. Beginning with the Annunciation to Zacharias of his son, John's, conception and divine mission, closely followed by the Annunciation to Mary of Jesus. The ministry of John is intertwined with that of Jesus, and Mary's internal understandings; followed by the tribulations of John, his imprisonment and beheading, and finally, Jesus' ministry, trial, and his death by crucifixion.

John the Evangelist is often included in renderings of Christ's family. In art, John is often depicted as his Beloved follower. He leans his head against Christ's breast at the Last Supper (or is that Mary Magdalene?), accompanies Mother Mary during the "Carrying of the Cross" and stands with her at the Crucifixion, though the other disciples have fled. It is said that he will be with Mary at the Last Judgment, when she intercedes with Christ on behalf of the damned. Though some would say that John the Evangelist, so integral to the narratives of the life of Jesus is a different person from John the Baptist, the art of Eastern Christianity, by making them interchangeable, gives us a different truth – that they are one and the same.

The Deisis composition was popular in the East, but was also sometimes used in the West in a slightly different format. In general, this grouping is used in the West in depictions of the crucifixion. The format is the triangle of Jesus above on the cross, with Mary and John making the base of the triangle at the foot of the cross. In these western traditions, it is usually John the Evangelist in his red robes.

It is interesting that, in paintings of the crucifixion by the master painters of the Renaissance there is often only one cross depicted, though there are these three figures, Jesus, John, and Mary. Often, the three appear in paintings of The Last Judgment, where Mary and John, with their prayers and supplications, are seen to intercede for humanity, invoking the Mercy of God. Mary, on the left, is, notably, at the right hand of Jesus, the place of honoring.

There is a Renaissance painting by Masaccio, unusual in that it is a crucifixion scene, while it is titled, "The Holy Trinity". There is purpose in this. The obvious reference is to the close configuration of the Father, the Holy Spirit (the small white dove that rests over Jesus' head) and Jesus, who is the lowest in the vertical depiction of the Holy Trinity. (The vertical line of the cross represents the divine crossing down into the horizontal bar of matter.) Jesus is the person of the Holy Trinity that is incarnate in a human body.

The second triad is triangular (but more lateral than the first), with Jesus at the top, above the two saints, John in red robes to the right, and Mary to the left of the foot of the cross (the other two figures are patrons of the Church, included for their financial support of the work.) Which triad, which "trinity" is Masaccio referring to? Or is it both?

This depiction of the holy three of the East is only a slight modification of the standard configuration of the Deisis of Eastern Christianity. Mary is even depicted with her hand in the position of the intercessor of Eastern iconography.

In Raphael's *La Disputa* (Disputation of the Holy Sacrament), we, again, have an interesting formation combining two versions of a "Holy Three". In the vertical line, we have the Holy Trinity: the dove is at the bottom in the yellow circle below Jesus, between heaven and earth, with Jesus in the center (in the heavens), and the Father God above all. In this depiction, the Holy Spirit proceeds from the Father and the Son.

The horizontal line is a representation of the Deisis: it also has Jesus in the center, with Mary and John (here, John the Baptist, with his staff) on either side, in a lateral configuration. The configuration, essentially, combines the Nicene Trinity with the Eastern Deisis in the form of a cross. "And they will be on my right and on my left. And I am they, and they are I" (*Pistis Sophia* 2:96) How literal were Jesus words meant to be taken in this text, which was considered heretical by the orthodox Church?

Iconography was touted as a way to educate the common people, who couldn't read the teachings. It also explains iconoclasm, the backlash to iconography. Icons gave the people insights into the greater truth, without ever speaking one heretical word!

THE MADONNA OF THE ROCKS

There are other types of representation of this holy triad in different configurations. Some paintings of these three holy figures, depict the Virgin Mary at the top of the triangle, with John and Jesus as infants, often gathered within or beneath her outstretched arms. In paintings with Mary as the adult, she is, understandably, the central figure.

Leonardo Da Vinci painted two famous paintings of *The Virgin of the Rocks*, more commonly known as *The Madonna of the Rocks*. These two very similar paintings show the Madonna and Child Jesus with the infant John the Baptist, in a rocky setting which gives the paintings their name. *The Madonna of the Rocks* plays a key role in Dan Brown's *The Da Vinci Code,* which brought Mary Magdalene front and center in popular culture of modern times.

We are familiar with the configuration of Mary, John, and Jesus, and here, seemingly an angel on the far right. The two infants are close in age and size. In the first painting, the infant John does not hold his signature staff with the cross at the top. Generally, this would be the key to identifying him. It also isn't clear that the figure on the far right is an angel. Perhaps there is a wing behind the figure's shoulder – or is it a rock formation? This figure wears the red and green of John the Baptist, and looks down at the infant Jesus (who raises his hand in blessing) on the right, but points toward the infant John. The face of this "angel" in both paintings is the face of Mary.

The formal title of the second one is more specific, *'The Virgin with the Infant Saint John the Baptist adoring the Christ Child accompanied by an Angel.* It is spelled out that the figure on the right is an angel, who looks in the direction of the infant, John, who holds his staff. Mary, in both paintings looks at neither infant, but rather downward. Many have noted that Mary seems to be cradling something in her right arm, which isn't an arm at all, but turns out to be a golden sash or fold of her robes, the area above it dark and hidden. It is reminiscent of the "third hand" in the artist's Last Supper. Da Vinci was purposeful in his work – what is he trying to say? What dark object would Mary be holding?

The subject of DaVinci's two paintings of the *Madonna of the Rocks,* is the adoration of the Christ Child by the infant John the Baptist, which became part of the medieval tradition of the Holy Family's journey into Egypt. The *Gospel of Matthew* relates that Joseph, the husband of Mary, was warned in a dream that King Herod would attempt to kill the infant Jesus, and that he was to take the child and his mother and flee to safety. There are a series of non-Biblical narratives that relate to the journey to Egypt. One of these concerns Jesus' cousin, John the Baptist, whose family, like that of Jesus, resided in the town of Bethlehem where the Massacre of the Innocents was to take place. According to legend, John was escorted to Egypt by Archangel Uriel, and met the Holy Family on the road.

The Louvre website refers to the angel in the painting as "Gabriel" (but the description of the painting in the Louvre still refers to Uriel). Gabriel's presence accords with the Apocryphal *Gospel of John the Baptist*, which describes John's removal from Bethlehem by Gabriel rather than Uriel. It does not mention the meeting on the road to Egypt. This miraculous tale may be related to the later story of Muhammad being accompanied on his "Night Journey" to the Temple Mount by the Angel Gabriel.

In the Quran, *Sura*:66:12, it states that "Jesus was born when the spirit of God breathed upon Mary, whose body was chaste. When Jesus was born, Allah kept his birth a secret and hid him: So she [Maryam] conceived him, and she withdrew with him to a remote place."

The story of Mary's conception by her parents, Joachim and Anne, is similar to that of John's parents, Zacharias and Elizabeth. They were old, and Anne, feeling that God had rejected her by keeping her childless prayed passionately for God to bless her with a child. An angel informs Anne of her conception, and tells her to meet her husband at the gate of Jerusalem. According to Benedict Chelidonius, 16th century abbott and writer: "Overjoyed Anne threw herself into the arms of her husband; together they rejoiced about the honour that was to be granted them in the form of a child. For they knew from the heavenly messenger that the child would be a Queen, powerful on heaven and on earth".

In traditional depictions of the occasion, they are shown embracing at the gate to the city. However, in Giotto's painting, they not only embrace, but share a kiss. It is thought to be the first kiss in art history.

Giotto's work is an odd composition, that somehow gives an unsettled feeling - a sense of foreboding. The look that is shared between the two saints, the parents of the Virgin Mary, eyes locked, signifies a kind of message. Who is the figure in the black robe, surrounded by women, who surreptiously and with seeming trepidation peers out at the two? She certainly resembles the Virgin Mary, in dark robes with her head covered. But this is supposed to a celebration of Anne's conception of Mary. The master painter, no doubt, has an intention here. What is he saying? And who might the two haloed figures truly represent?

Plate 12 - Meeting at the Golden Gate - Giotto

The *Gospel of Luke* states that, made aware of Herod's threat, Elizabeth fled into the wilderness and hid in a cave while Zacharias continued to serve in the Temple in Jerusalem. Herod sent soldiers to the Temple to find out the whereabouts of the infant John and his mother. Zacharias said that he did not know, and was killed "between the temple and the altar", which may be a conflation of Zacharias with the much earlier high priest, Zechariah, whose tomb was in the Cedron Valley inJerusalem. Elizabeth is said to have lived in the wilderness with her son until her death. John, protected by an angel, dwelt in the wilderness until he came preaching repentance, and was accounted worthy to baptize the Lord.

In the Old Testament "the Word" was a *theophany,* the means by which God became visible, or known in the world such as in the form of "The Angel of The Lord". Are these paintings of the *Madonna of the Rocks* actually intended to be a representation of The Annunciation (with a Da Vinci spin), when Gabriel announced the immanent "birth" of Jesus? Are Da Vinci's paintings of the *Madonna of the Rocks* a depiction of the setting of the Foundation Stone of the Temple Mount? Is Mary in the Well of Souls within the Foundation Stone?

In the New Testament, at the Annunciation to Mary, the words of the Angel of God were carried to her ear, as she was "overshadowed by the Holy Spirit", bringing about her conception of the Lord, through "the Word of God". (See cover art – *The Annunciation* by Simone Martini and Lippo Memmi.) There is a string of words flowing to Mary's ear, as well as rays of light from the Holy Spirit (within the circle of angels above her head.) *Conceptus ex auditu* was an accepted doctrinal teaching for centuries by Da Vinci's time – that is to say the "conception by hearing" of the Word by Mary.

The words are the same as in the prayer known as the Hail Mary*:* "Ave Maria dominus tecum gratia plena." Hail Mary, full of Grace, the Lord is with thee." Mary responds with her *fiat,* in complete submission to the will of the Lord, "Mary said, "Behold, I am the handmaid of the Lord. May it be done to me according to your word."

She was called the Ark of the New Covenant. The ancient ark was kept in the Holy of Holies that rested upon the Foundation Stone. What is hidden in the golden fold of her sash? And why would both Jesus and John be present at the Annunciation? But it seems that Da Vinci understood, and was cleverly revealing, that John was Mary, so he would have been present, too, in one form or the other.

The subject of the Virgin Mary with the Christ Child being adored by John the Baptist was common in the art of Renaissance Florence, where John the Baptist has long been the patron saint. Those who depicted the subject of the Virgin and Child with St. John include the masters, Leonardo da Vinci, Fra Filippo Lippi, Raphael, and Michelangelo.

In the triad arrangement of *The Holy Family with the infant St. John,* from 1503, by Bernardino Luini, John is the infant on the left, with his child-sized staff with the cross at the top lying beneath his right leg. The two infants look very close in age. Perhaps they are, as the Gospels tell, 6 months apart in age, with John as the elder of the two (metaphorical sense?) – perhaps this is meant to signify his role as the forerunner. The infants seem almost a part of Mary, nestled as they are beneath the protection of her cloak. The three figures, and particularly, Mary's hand position in this painting, bring to mind Leonardo Da Vinci's two paintings of the *Madonna of the Rocks.*

Luini also did a painting of the *Virgin and Child with St. Anne and St. John the Baptist,* from 1500, which is much like the paintings done by Da Vinci. It is hard to tell in Luini's painting whose legs we are seeing – are they Mary's or is she (and the Christ-child) somehow seated on Anne's lap?

What is most interesting about the two Da Vinci paintings of the Madonna and Child with St. Anne, is the way that Da Vinci also intertwines mother and daughter. The torsos seem joined, though in a different way in each painting. In one, Mary is on her mother's lap and their bodies almost merge. Anne, the grandmother of Jesus, has a youthful face that resembles his portraits of the Madonna. Since Da Vinci was such a capable artist, this intermingling would seem to be deliberate, and for an intended purpose.

In the other painting, mother and daughter, sitting side by side, seem to be joined down the middle. Mary may be sitting on her mother's lap – the legs of the two figures are confusing. We cannot take this at face value. There is purpose in the artist's arrangement, but what does it mean? Perhaps the hidden meaning has to do with conflation of identities in Christian history. In the detailed sketch, St. Anne's unfinished hand holds up one finger, in the gesture often depicted in Da Vinci's paintings of John the Baptist. One. What did Da Vinci intend?

We might see some connection of these paintings to the story of Simon Magus, who, in the *Acts of Peter*, fell to earth in a place called the Via Sacra (the Holy Way), breaking his legs "in three parts". The Via Sacra is the street in Rome which became known as "the shunned street" for the infamous occasion of illegitimate childbirth by the *papesse*, the female pope, said to be Pope Joan.

In the *Acts of Peter and Paul*, it is four parts, "And immediately, being let go, he fell into a place called Via Sacra, that is, Holy Way, and was divided into four parts, having perished by an evil fate." What were the four parts that this one was divided into? If the Deisis accounts for three, then who is the fourth?

* * *

CHAPTER VIII. COUNCILS AND CONTROVERSIES

THE ALEXANDRIAN CHURCH

Bishop Theophilus of Alexandria was the leader of the Coptic Orthodox Church in Alexandria, Egypt from 382 – 412 CE, during a time of great turmoil in that city. Though he may not be well-known outside of scholarly circles, he played a very important, sometimes very negative role in a number of controversial incidents over the period of his leadership. He was embroiled in the Origenist Controversy of the late 4th century, he attended the Synod of the Oak, which deposed John Chrysostom, treated the pagan and Jewish communities of Alexandria with contempt and brutality, and ordered the burning of the pagan temple of the Serapeum in Alexandria.

In 391 CE, the political climate of the region shifted from Emperor Julian's pro-Jewish, anti-Christian stance. Roman Emperor Theodosius I had issued a decree of "Death to Manichaeans" in 382 CE, shortly before this, making Christianity the only legitimate religion for the Roman Empire in 391 CE (and shortly before Augustine, very wisely, converted from Manichaeism to Christianity - bringing his dualistic ideals with him). Theodosius banned the practice of other religions, which resulted in the abandonment of many pagan temples throughout the Empire, and converted or replaced these edifices with Christian churches. (*Theodosian Code* 16.10.10)

The library of Alexandria had been damaged a number of times. It was accidentally burned in the time of Julius Caesar in 48 CE. After restoration, in the 270's CE, it was destroyed through a series of rebellions and imperial counter-attacks. The connected library of the Serapeum survived the main Library's destruction, only to be vandalized and demolished in 391 CE under a decree issued by the Alexandrian bishop, Theophilus. It had become a gathering place for Neoplatonist philosophers who followed the teachings of Iamblichus.

This came about about after the first Origenist Crisis in 375 CE, when Epiphanius attacked the writings of Origen, who had long been admired as a Christian author, as being heretical. This issue caused turmoil in Theophilus' role as bishop. Some scholars equate Origen of Alexandria with Origen the Pagan, supported by Eusebius' attestation that Origen the

Christian was celebrated as a great philosopher even by pagans.

Though there are conflicting stories on how and why it happened, the Serapeum was levelled, in some accounts, by Roman soldiers, and a wave of destruction of non-Christian idols spread throughout Egypt in the following weeks. The stones from these temples were used to build Christian churches.

In another incident, Theophilus, in attempting to convert the abandoned pagan temple of Dionysus into a church, profaned its subterranean spaces and mocked its sacred objects by parading the *phalli* of Priapus through the Forum, which incited crowds of non-Christians to seek revenge and attack the Christians. The Christians retaliated, with the pagans retreating into the Serapeum, and barricading themselves inside, taking captured Christians with them. It is hard to discern the truth of these matters, as each side accused the other of dreadful wrong-doing. Christian sources report that the Christian captives were forced to offer sacrifices to the banned deities. Those who refused were tortured (their shins broken) and ultimately cast into caves that had been built for blood sacrifices. In this account, it was the pagans that were reported to have plundered the treasures of the Serapeum.

A letter was sent by Emperor Theodosius to the bishop Theophilus, asking him to grant the pagans pardon, but also calling for the destruction of all pagan images, suggesting that these were the source of the commotion. With the Emperor's consent, the bishop destroyed the renowned pagan temples to the gods Mithra, Dionysius, and Serapis.

An alternate account, from the perspective of the Neoplatonists, is put forth by the pagan historian, Eunapius, who claims that an unprovoked Christian mob successfully used military-like tactics to destroy the Serapeum and it was they who stole anything that survived the attack.

Tensions between the various factions within Alexandria were great. In the time of Jesus, there had been riots over the actions of Flaccus, the Roman governor of Alexandria, who permitted a mob to erect statues of the Emperor Caius Caligula in Jewish synagogues of the city, an unprecedented provocation. Philo, who lived at this time, documented the events. Philo writes that Flaccus "was destroying the synagogues, and not leaving even their name." In response to the resistance of the angry populace, Flaccus "issued a notice in which he called us all foreigners and aliens... allowing any one who was inclined to proceed to exterminate the Jews as prisoners of war."[133] He details a horrendous attack on the Jews in 38 CE, who were rounded up, tortured in the most horrifying ways, with whole families murdered – no mercy even for the infants. It was a city of intense strife and division in the intervening centuries.

Eusebius of Caesarea mentions street-fighting in Alexandria, between Christians and non-Christians, as early as 249 CE. Socrates of Constantinople recorded that non-Christians took part in citywide struggles for and against the Early Church Father, Athanasius (meaning "Immortal") in 341 and 356 CE, and that conflicts had generally gone on since the 1st century CE.

In May of 395, four years after Emperor Theodosius banned paganism, the relics of John the Baptist were laid in the basilica that was newly dedicated to the Forerunner on the former site of the temple of Serapis in Alexandria. This was seen by some to mark the end of pagan influence in the city, and the rise to power of Christianity.[132]

HYPATIA

Hypatia was not a Virgin Saint, nor even a Christian, yet her story comes into play during the turmoil in Alexandria under the bishop Cyril, nephew of Theophilus. She was an Alexandrian pagan polymath (according to the story) – the darling of the Neoplatonists – an astronomer, mathematician and philosopher of the 4th century to the turn of the 5th a time of great upheaval within the formative years of the Christian faith, shortly after it was declared the only legitimate religion of the Roman Empire.

Alexandria, Egypt, in the early 5th century was a melting pot of people of various faiths, including Christian, Jewish, and Pagan. The story of Hypatia may not seem important to Christian history, but the pagan woman is an interesting figure from Alexandria in that time period, who was said to have been executed by a mob of angry Christians for her divisive influence on Alexandrian Christianity.

To give some background to the story of Hypatia of Alexandria, one must consider the often-chaotic events of the city. By the 4th century, there had been numerous tumultuous periods of violence among the many factions that lived in the city. There were large populations of Christians, Jews, and Gentiles. There were also divisions within the Christian community, between those who favored Coptic (ascetic) practices, and those who favored Byzantine ones.

The history of Hypatia gives that she was born in the mid to late 300's, lived her life in Roman Egypt, and that she died in March 415 CE, at the hands of a mob that blamed her for causing religious turmoil. Pause and consider what woman might have influenced Alexandrian Christians at this time in history. Hypatia was lauded by many writers from the 4th

Century onward as an exceedingly accomplished woman – a polymath, like many of her male counterparts, of such proportions as to be considered a genius: a Neoplatonic philosopher, mathematician, and astronomer. Her many accomplishments were all the more amazing for the fact that she was a female in an otherwise male-dominated landscape, and pagan where Christianity was becoming the norm. She was widely beloved by pagans and Christians alike.

She had great influence with the political elite in Alexandria. Although Hypatia was a pagan, she was tolerant of Christians. In fact, many of her students were Christian.[134] Late in her life, she was advisor to Orestes, the Roman prefect of Alexandria, who was in the midst of a political feud with Cyril, the bishop of Alexandria.

Hypatia was one of few women of that time to have been written about in such glowing terms by her contemporaries. There are no surviving original works by this auspicious, highly esteemed woman. She was said to have helped her father to write his books on mathematics and science, but, although she was highly praised by certain Greek philosophers of the 4th and 5th centuries, as one of the most learned, wise, and influential teachers of the age, there are no writings that can be directly attributed to her hand. Some historians insist that she wrote a couple of commentaries on the work of others, and that she edited the work of Ptolemy and Euclid, two of the greatest writers of the time.

The text often attributed to her, *The Astronomical Canon*, is considered by many to be a new edition of Ptolemy's *Handy Tables*. And yet, it is brushed off as a common circumstance, and considered reasonable that, for all her prolific wisdom, none of her own works survived, despite her great intelligence and wisdom, great fame, and purported renown. During the Renaissance, she was one of the only women to be included as a great teacher in the painting by Raphael called "The School of Athens." She stands still in the melee of masculine activity, looking outward at the viewer, in her white orator's cloak. Or is it the white robe of the penitent?

In the early 4th Century, it was dangerous to speak openly about controversial events – there was no free press, no "right to free speech." You took your life into your hands when you spoke openly about your own, or others', beliefs. Perhaps the only way to comment on such incidents, safely, was to hide the truth within symbols. This story requires that you read between the lines, that you listen on a different level to hear the truth. There are hidden clues throughout the story, in symbol and metaphor, but one must have "eyes to see" and "ears to hear."

The name, Hypatia, is Greek for "high, supreme one." She was from Alexandria, Egypt, the daughter of Theon Alexandricus. (Theon is a derivative of Theos, or "God.") What we must understand about her name is that Alexandria had deep connections to Greek society, literature and theology, from its founding by Alexander the Great in the 4th century BCE. The entire story is meant to deride her relationship to the Greeks, through the beliefs of Neoplatonism and, figuratively, as a daughter of a Greek God.

Socrates of Constantinople, a contemporary of Hypatia, spoke highly of her in his *Ecclesiastical History*, "There was a woman at Alexandria named Hypatia, daughter of the philosopher Theon, who made such attainments in literature and science, as to far surpass all the philosophers of her own time. Having succeeded to the school of Plato and Plotinus, she explained the principles of philosophy to her auditors, many of whom came from a distance to receive her instructions. On account of the self-possession and ease of manner which she had acquired in consequence of the cultivation of her mind, she not infrequently appeared in public in the presence of the magistrates. Neither did she feel abashed in going to an assembly of men. For all men on account of her extraordinary dignity and virtue admired her the more."

At Theophilus' unexpected death in 412, a violent power struggle over leadership of the diocese broke out between his nephew, Cyril (whom he had been training), and Cyril's rival, Timothy. When Cyril won, he punished Timothy's supporters, closing the Novatianist churches and confiscating their property. Hypatia's Christian student, Synesius, the prolific writer, only wrote one letter to Cyril, in which he treats the younger bishop as inexperienced and misguided (*Letter 12 – Letter to Cyril*, 413 CE).

In a letter written to Hypatia in 413, Synesius requests her intercession in the ongoing civil strife in Alexandria, writing, "You always have power, and you can bring about good by using that power." He also reminds her of her teaching that a Neoplatonic philosopher must introduce the highest moral standards to political life and act for the benefit of their fellow citizens. In another letter to Hypatia, he enumerates his losses and writes, "The greatest loss of all, however, is the absence of your divine spirit."

According to Socrates Scholasticus, in 414, following an exchange of hostilities and a Jewish-led massacre, Cyril also closed all the synagogues in Alexandria, confiscated all the property belonging to the Jews, and expelled a number of Jews from the city. Scholasticus suggests that all the Jews were expelled, while John of Nikiu notes it was only those involved in the massacre.

Orestes, the Roman prefect of Alexandria, who was a close friend of Hypatia, and a recent convert to Christianity, was outraged at Cyril's actions and sent a scathing report to the emperor. The conflict escalated and a riot broke out in which the *parabalani*, a group of Christian clerics under Cyril's authority, nearly killed Orestes.

As punishment, Orestes had Ammonius, the monk who had started the riot, "publicly tortured to death". This was the same Ammonius who was named as one of the "Four Tall Brothers". Cyril tried to proclaim Ammonius a martyr, but Christians in Alexandria were disgusted, since Ammonius was not killed for his faith, but for inciting a riot and leading an attempt to murder the governor. Prominent Alexandrian Christians intervened and forced Cyril to drop the matter. Nonetheless, Cyril's feud with Orestes continued.

Hypatia was said to be connected to the Serapeum of the Library of Alexandria, one of the greatest libraries in the world. As an institution the Serapeum was, in fact, more of a university than just a common library. Perhaps its purpose was even greater than a university. It is said that, carved into the wall above the shelves, a famous inscription read: “The place of the cure of the soul.”

It must be noted that the relics of John the Baptist were laid in the Christian basilica on the former site of the temple of Serapis (the Serapeum) in Alexandria.

No index of the library survives, and it is not possible to know with certainty how large and how diverse the collection may have been. According to the earliest source of information, the pseudepigraphic *Letter of Aristeas,* composed between 180 and 145 BCE, the library was initially organized by Demetrius of Phaleron, a student of Aristotle, under the reign of Ptolemy I Soter, a couple of centuries earlier. The Library contained a Peripatos walk, gardens, a small dining hall, a reading room, meeting rooms and lecture halls.

By Hypatia's time, the Library would actually have been already destroyed, however, the Serapeum, a great auditorium within the sprawling complex, still, seemingly, housed texts and scrolls. It still held classrooms for the teaching of many sciences. These included the major sciences: arithmetic, astronomy, anatomy, but would also likely have included philosophy, and theology.

The marvelous scientific instrument known as the astrolabe, whose invention was ascribed to her (though it was actually invented a century earlier) was being used by that time to read the heavens, to predict astrological influences, to discern alignment with the sun. This tool would become essential to the Muslim determination of the direction of prayer known as *qiblah*. Perhaps, considering the attribution to her of the astrolabe, studies would also have included numerology, astrology, and divination, which were still highly honored pursuits in Egypt.

The Alexandrian school was renowned at the time for its Neoplatonist philosophy, and Alexandria was regarded as second only to Athens as the philosophical capital of the Greco-Roman world. Hypatia, the great female philosopher, taught here. Her students came from all over the Mediterranean. According to Damascius, she lectured on the writings of Plato and Aristotle. He states that she walked through Alexandria in a *tribon*, a kind of cloak associated with male philosophers, giving impromptu public lectures.

Despite Hypatia's popularity, Cyril and his allies attempted to undermine her reputation and discredit her. Socrates Scholasticus mentions rumors accusing Hypatia of preventing Orestes from reconciling with Cyril. (*Ecclesiastical History*, VII.15)

The rumors about her within the Christian populace of Alexandria may be found in the writings of the 7th -century Egyptian Coptic bishop John of Nikiû, who alleges in his *Chronicle* that Hypatia had intentionally hampered the church's influence over Orestes. He wrote of her in very derogatory terms, "And in those days there appeared in Alexandria a female philosopher, a pagan named Hypatia, and she was devoted at all times to magic, astrolabes and instruments of music..." Had John of Nikiû not read the bible stories of David, whose music "pleased the Lord"? He goes on, "... and she beguiled many people through her Satanic wiles. And the governor of the city honored her exceedingly; for she had beguiled him through her magic. And he ceased attending church as had been his custom... And he not only did this, but he drew many believers to her, and he himself received the unbelievers at his house."[135]

We can see an early bias against the sciences and perhaps an early basis for later witch hunts. He states, "... And thereafter a multitude of believers in God arose under the guidance of Peter the magistrate—now this Peter was a perfect believer in all respects in Jesus Christ—and they proceeded to seek for the pagan woman who had beguiled the people of the city and the prefect through her enchantments." *This* Peter was her opponent – a *true* follower of Christ!

John of Nikiû's 7th century account of Hypatia's death stated that they "found her seated on a (lofty) chair; and having made her descend they dragged her along till they brought her to the great church, named Caesarion....For when Hypatia emerged from her house, in her accustomed manner, a throng of merciless and ferocious men who feared neither divine punishment nor human revenge attacked and cut her down ... ." (*The*

Chronicle, LXXXIV.87-88, 100-103) This was said to have occurred in the holy season of Lent.

Emperor Theodosius I had instituted the Roman practice of processionals in Christian devotions. Tertullian (2nd century) uses the word *processio,* from which "procession" is derived, in the sense of "to go out, to appear in public". The phrase, "in her accustomed manner" brings to mind the customs of Byzantine Christians, who participated in regular (like clock-work) processions and ceremonies related to the holy relics and icons of the faith. The season of Lent was often filled with ceremonial events. What was this "lofty chair"? It brings to mind certain methods of conveyance provided in Christian processions. Was it a sedan chair, carried by footmen, or was it perhaps a *sedia gestatoria* like that of the popes? Could it have been a vehicle for certain holy relics of the time period?

The scholar Mangasar M. Mangasarian describes the gruesome nature of the attack on Hypatia, as recorded by various ancient historians: "The next morning, when Hypatia appeared in her chariot in front of her residence, suddenly five hundred men, all dressed in black and cowled, five hundred half-starved monks from the sands of the Egyptian desert -- five hundred monks, soldiers of the cross -- like a black hurricane, swooped down the street, boarded her chariot, and, pulling her off her seat, dragged her by the hair of her head into a -- how shall I say the word? -- into a church! Some historians intimate that the monks asked her to kiss the cross, to become a Christian and join the nunnery, if she wished her life spared."[136]

And now the truly brutal details, "At any rate, these monks, under the leadership of St. Cyril's right-hand man, Peter the Reader, shamefully stripped her naked, and there, close to the altar and the cross, scraped her quivering flesh from her bones with oyster shells...The mutilated body, upon which the murderers feasted their fanatic hate, was then flung into the flames." It was Peter the Reader, who scraped her flesh from her bones – an interesting name, to be sure. In Athens, Greece, there was a voting process in which potsherds or shells (oysters) were used in deciding a ruling of banishment, that is, "ostracization".

Hypatia's attackers were ascetic monks who did not approve of ostentatious parades of richly ornamented relics. Was this a living person attacked by radical Christian monks, who stripped her of her clothes, scraped her flesh from her bones, and burned her mutilated body, or was this an attack on the "incorruptible flesh" of the relics of a saint of the Church?

In the Middle Ages, Hypatia was promoted as a symbol of Christian virtue, perhaps, somehow related to the development of the legend of Saint Catherine of Alexandria.

During the Age of Enlightenment, she became a Protestant symbol of opposition to Catholicism. The controversial nature of the attack against her, interestingly enough, shows up in the long-winded, 18th century title of an Anti-Catholic (Protestant) tract by John Toland, *"Hypatia: Or the History of a most beautiful, most virtuous, most learned, and every way accomplish'd Lady; who was torn to pieces by the Clergy of Alexandria, to gratify the pride, emulation, and cruelty of their Archbishop, commonly, but undeservedly, stil'd St. Cyril."*

The polemical nature of the story of Hypatia, did not, as we can see, end with her alleged brutal death in the 5th century. She became a focus of debate in the time of Protestant Reform in the Christian faith (as did the subject of Mary). As in the numerous and contradictory references to her life from writings of the 5th century, the 18th Century commentary above was rebutted in its time, by the opposition, with an equally long and outrageous title: *"The History of Hypatia, a most Impudent School-Mistress of Alexandria: Murder'd and torn to Pieces by the Populace, in Defence of Saint Cyril and the Alexandrian Clergy from the Aspersions of Mr. Toland,"* by Thomas Lewis, in 1721. She was either amazingly virtuous, or outrageously impudent, depending on who was telling the story! Sounds familiar.

There is a famous painting by Charles William Mitchell, of Hypatia standing naked before the altar in a church. At first glance, with her long reddish tresses covering the lower half of her body, one is reminded of images of the penitent Magdalene.

THE ORIGENIST CONTROVERSY

Early on, Theophilus had supported John of Jerusalem against the hereticist, Epiphanius, who deemed the writings of Origen to be heretical. Theophilus denounced Epiphanius to Pope Siricius for his Anthropomorphism (giving human attributes to God). Theophilus' close confidante, Isidore of Alexandria, was a confirmed Origenist. "The Four Tall Brothers", the accredited leaders of the Origenist party were, at the time, close friends of Theophilus. The "Four Tall Brothers" are given to be four actual monks, among the Egyptian monks of Nitria in the early 5th century, whose names were Ammonius, Dioscorus, Eusebius, and Euthymius.

Nitria was one of the earliest Christian monastic sites in Egypt, established before the communities in Kellia and Scetis. Anthony the Great, the desert monk whose *vita* was written by Athanasius, retreated to the dry Nitrian desert, where he is said to have lived in austerity for 13 years. (Though he is made out to be the first desert monk, there were many others before him.) Between the 4th and 7th century CE, hundreds of thousands of people from the world over joined the Christian monasteries of the Nitrian Desert, some in cenobitic communities and some as hermits, who lived in harsh circumstances in desert caves. These monks, as well as the ascetic monks of other regions became known as the Desert Fathers.

It is hard to comprehend how Origen – who was long honored as a virtuous and wise teacher, became so vilified in the 4th century. Some scholars have proposed that the Origenist quarrel was not about two theologies, but of "*two spiritualities*"*:* one, the intellectual mysticism of Egyptian monks like Didymus, Isidore, Ammonius, and Evagrius, and the literalism of the "simple monks", who had no use for metaphor and allegory. They essentially followed the *Peshat* (simple or direct) interpretation of scripture as demonstrated in the Jewish practice of PaRDes.

The issue began when Epiphanius, the (ridiculously?) meticulous hereticist, who saw Origen, a major theologian in the Eastern church, as having espoused heretical views. Epiphanius asked John II, the bishop of Jerusalem to condemn Origen as a heretic for his teachings. John refused on the grounds that a person could not be retroactively condemned as a heretic after the person had already died.

In this time period, Theophilus, the Bishop of Alexandria, had a quarrel with Isidore over money involving "the Tall Brothers", who, it seems, accused him of avarice and worldliness. At some point, the issue of Origenism came into the squabble. The bishop was "roughed up" and threatened by the monks of Sceta (not, apparently, the Tall Brothers). These monks, displeased with his paschal letter of 399, forcibly invaded his episcopal residence and threatened him with death if he did not chant the *palinody,* a retraction of belief in Origenism. In response to their violent threats, Theophilus retracted with a vengeance! Under this pressure, he made a sudden "about-face" and vehemently (and violently) attacked Origenism.

He switched from espousing the incorporeal view of God held by Origen (that God is Spirit and has no body) to the anthropomorphic view (giving God human attributes) held by many local monks who were hostile to his paschal letter. He recanted his beliefs and reneged on his old alliances. His effort soon became almost a Crusade to tear down his former friends and destroy them, seemingly in order to maintain power, but perhaps a dramatized over-reaction to the way he'd been treated by the monks of Sceta. With soldiers and armed servants, he marched against the Origenist monks, burned their dwellings, and ill-treated those whom he captured." (*Palladius*, vii ; *Socrates*, op. cit.)

For four years Theophilus took aggressive action: condemning Origen's books at the Council of Alexandria (400 CE), expelling the Origenist monks from Nitria, writing to the bishops of Cyprus and Palestine to win them over to his anti-Origenist crusade, issuing paschal letters in 401, 402, and 404 CE against Origen's doctrine, and sending a missive to Pope Anastasius asking for the condemnation of Origenism, with which he had previously aligned.

He was wildly successful – Theophilus assembled the bishops of Palestine at Jerusalem who condemned the errors pointed out to them, adding that these concepts were not taught by them. Anastasius, declared that Origen was unknown to him, but condemned his ideas. Jerome, who had long considered Origen an eminent and worthy Church Father, also did an about-face. He had expended great effort to translate Origen's work as valuable teachings, but now set about translating into Latin the writings of Theophilus, including a virulent diatribe against John Chrysostom, whose ordination to the bishopric of Constantinople Theophilus had opposed.

The New Advent Encyclopedia states that John Chrysostom is generally considered to be the most prominent doctor of the Greek Church and the greatest preacher ever heard in a Christian pulpit. Interestingly, this encyclopedia states, "John — whose surname "Chrysostom" occurs for the first time in the "Constitution" of Pope Vigilius (cf. P.L., LX, 217) in the year 553". This was some 150 years after his death. Presumably, before this time he was called John of Antioch, where his mother sent him to the best schools, and he learned considerable Greek scholarship and classical culture. He became an anchorite, living in a cave near Antioch for two years. His harsh asceticism, fasting, and vigils left him very weak and ill, and he returned to Antioch to recover his health. Here he became a deacon and then a priest, and his eloquence and literary achievements led to him being pressed (unwillingly, it is said) into serving as Archbishop at Constantinople, the center of Christendom at the time, whence he became embroiled in the conflict with Theophilus.

In Theophilus' persecution of Origenist monks, who had so greatly affronted him, Theophilus commanded troops to destroy their desert monasteries. Suddenly under attack from their former friend, Isidore and "the Tall Brothers" beat a hasty retreat to Constantinople, where the Archbishop John Chrysostom, gave them safe haven. Theophilus was called to Constantinople by John in 402 CE to answer the charges of persecution of the desert monks.

Subsequently, Theophilus, called a synod of 36 bishops (mostly from Egypt) who condemned John Chrysostom on 29 charges (including the false charge of treason). One perspective is that, because of Chrysostom's generosity to "the Tall Brothers," the embittered Patriarch of Alexandria planned to ruin him.[137] However, this is a simplified viewpoint. The scenario must be looked at from a wider perspective. This was not a minor skirmish between personalities – this was part of a great (and ongoing) battle for power in the 4th to 5th century, throughout newly legalized Christendom – a huge power struggle among those espousing greatly differing ideals. The major factions included: the Holy City (represented by John of Jerusalem), the North African faction (represented by Augustine), the Egyptian "Alexandrians" (represented by Theophilus), the Egyptian Nitrian monks (including the "Tall Brothers"), the Byzantines (represented by John Chrysostom, highly honored for his sermons and liturgy), and Damasus of Rome (represented by Jerome and his writings).

Some of the Syrian monks supported John Chrysostom (who was originally from Syria), and others opposed him. The "wild-card" was Epiphanius, who saw heresy around every corner, and who, with his anti-heretical diatribes, had garnered the attention and support of the "powers-that-be" in Rome. The names represented ideals, philosophies, theologies, and political agendas. One *must* consider that, though some of the figures were actual, living people, some were quite possibly figureheads for the ideologies, perhaps even the holy relics of saints, and the writings in their names, almost certainly involving pseudonymical-pseudepigraphy! One can almost picture rooms full of library desks filled with hosts of monks from various factions in earnest activity of "scribing" innumerable texts and treatises in the cryptic names of saints long gone.

THE SYNOD OF THE OAK

The Synod of the Oak, which was held near Constantinople, in July of 403 CE, condemned and deposed John Chrysostom as Patriarch of Constantinople. The name of the synod refers to the suburb of Chalcedon called 'The Oak', where it took place. (This should be kept in mind when considering the unusual events of the Council of Chalcedon, which took place some fifty years later). This trial of Chrysostom is widely seen as a politically motivated conspiracy by his opponents, who included Theophilus, the Empress Eudoxia and the wealthy nobles who weren't happy with Chrysostom's criticism of their extravagant imperial lifestyle. Jennifer Barry writes that some historians have argued that "the surplus of evidence reveals a struggle between Johannite and anti-Johannite camps in Constantinople soon after John's departure and for a few years after his death"[138] This is a very pertinent observation, though Johannine is often the term used to refer to the collection of New Testament works that are traditionally attributed to John the Apostle (the Evangelist). These events absolutely involve the Deity of Jesus, put forth in John's gospel, and other Johannine literature.

The prominent people involved in the Synod of the Oak were involved in the Origen Controversy. One of the 46 charges that were levelled was that John had "wrong ideas", that is to say, Origenist leanings, which had to do with the error of believing in a corporeal God. But, wasn't that the whole premise of The Incarnation? This idea would become formalized after the death of Theophilus, in the proposal by his nephew, Cyril, that, in the Son, the Divine (God) was in *hypostatic* union with the human.

The Oriental Orthodox churches, which developed later, use the term "Miaphysite" (the "one nature" Christology of Cyril of Alexandria articulated in his famous dictum, "one nature of God the Word Incarnate.") to describe the nature of Jesus Christ. These churches consider Theophilus to be a saint. Perhaps sainthood has often been a political, rather than a spiritual designation. The truth is probably somewhere between the two extremes of tyrant and saint.

The original intention for Theophilus' summons to Constantinople by the emperor, was for him to apologize before a synod, over which Chrysostom would preside. Certainly, it would seem that the bishop was deserving of censure. Along with soldiers and armed servants, Theophilus had marched against the desert monks, burned their dwellings, and badly treated those he captured. In the Eastern Orthodox *Synaxarion*, the story is much more accusatory: there is a commemoration for 10,000 monks (probably an exaggeration) slain on the orders of Theophilus in his campaign against perceived Origenism. When the desert monks fled to Constantinople to appeal to Patriarch John Chrysostom, Theophilus wrote to Epiphanius of Salamis (the hereticist who started the whole issue) requesting him to prevail upon Chrysostom to condemn the Origenists.

Epiphanius, long in the anti-Origenist camp, had written of Chrysostom as bordering on heretical. Epiphanius seems to have embodied the epitome of near-sighted focus on the minutiae of acceptable beliefs, and also, oblivious to the wider ramifications of his own efforts. He preceded Theophilus in going to Constantinople. He was chastised by Serapion for his actions against Chrysostom, and was warned of the explosive situation that was brewing in the city, and that Epiphanius "would be regarded as responsible for the outrages that might follow. By these arguments Epiphanius was induced to relinquish his designs." (Sozomen, *Eccl. Hist.* 8:14) Perhaps, at some point, Epiphanius realized that he had been manipulated by Theophilus for political reasons. He is said to have left the capital suddenly and, reportedly, never made it back to Cyprus, dying somewhere on his return journey in 403.

The accounts of the "Four Tall Brothers" coming to Constantinople is intriguing. It is a curious name, said by some to be a literal reference to their height, but by others, said to refer to their great stature in the Church.

In an ancient treatise entitled, *A New History of Ecclesiastical Writers*, Evagrius Ponticus states that there were three "Long-brethren" who were being persecuted by Theophilus. This record states that Theophilus was "no friend to S. Chrysostom, because he was obliged to ordain him against his will; but the hatred he bore to him broke out upon the account of three Egyptian Monks, Dioscorus, Ammonius, and Euthymius, Sir-named (surnamed) the Long-brethren."

In this account, they were not four but three, and they were not "Tall Brothers," but rather, "Long-brethren" – they were "long brethren of the Church." Eusebius, from the other account is missing. But Eusebius, meaning "Pious", had already arrived in Constantinople (or was he already there?). Was John the "pious" one? Were these four, indeed, the earliest brethren of the Church - preserved in the caves of the Nitrian desert, famous for its dry conditions and known for its embalming salts?

Here, Theophilus, reproved by Chrysostom for his behavior to the desert monks, and especially to the "Three Long-brethren," managed to convene the Synod of the Oak in order to condemn the teachings of Chrysostom. In the account in this Ecclesiastical history, Chrysostom was summoned to the synod three times, without appearing in the court, and so, was tried "in *absentia*", according to the law. The history says that he was "cited to the Synod to answer those Accusations, but he sent three Bishops and two Presbyters, who in his behalf declared to Theophilus and his Synod, that he was ready to submit to any that might be his Judges, but not Theophilus, his professed Enemy, nor to the Egyptian Bishops, who could not regularly judge the Bishops of Thrace." These are meant to be reasonable excuses, but why on earth did the eloquent speaker, the "Golden-mouthed" Chrysostom, not speak on his own behalf? It is an exceedingly curious thing!

After the third summons, Chrysostom, with the consent of the emperor, was deposed. In order to avoid useless bloodshed, he reportedly surrendered himself on the third day to the soldiers who awaited him. The story goes that the threats of the excited people, and a fire in the imperial palace, frightened the empress, who, fearing some punishment from God for Chrysostom's exile, immediately ordered his recall. Theophilus and his party were forced to save themselves from the angry mobs by fleeing from Constantinople. Chrysostom's re-entry to the capital was met by the great rejoicing of the people. (Palladius, *Dialogus*, ix)

Though Theophilus was forced to flee the city, his cunning power-play was incredibly successful! John Chrysostom's enemies soon had him deposed and exiled a second time, to Comana, in 407 CE. After the upheaval in Constantinople, and once back in Egypt, Theophilus changed his tune once more, and smoothly returned to an endorsement of the reading of Origen, stating that he could "cull the roses from among the thorns."

Strangely, he was reconciled with "the Tall Brothers" without asking them to retract their position - the personal quarrels ended and the specter of "Origenism" vanished. While these events occurred centuries before the "Cadaver Synod", it is quite possible that the two trials are related. As with the martyrs of early Rome, one wonders if, indeed, it was a living man, or relics that were "exiled" from the capitol city. And that this particular figure could be condemned at a Christian council and exiled from the capitol of Christendom is beyond ironic - much like Peter saying in the Gospel of Mary, "Let Mariham leave us". This decision by the Church demonstrates the ridiculous antics (not to mention, semantics) of certain power-hungry Early Church Fathers.

THE NEA EKKLESIA

From the pro-and-anti-John factions of the 5th century, we move to the pro-Marian factions of the 6th. The *Nea Ekklesia,* the New Church, was the jewel of 6th century Byzantine Jerusalem, a Basilica dedicated by Emperor Justinian to "St. Mary", which is more often used to describe the Magdalene, but here, apparently, used in honor of the Blessed Virgin. For many centuries, known as "The Church of St. Mary the New", it is now referred to as the "Church of St. Mary, the Theotokos," just in case anyone should confuse the issue.

The Byzantine glory of the *Nea*, with its grand scale and opulence, was eloquently praised by Procopius, the emperor's court historian who compared the columns at the western entrance to the monumental columns Jachim and Boaz that flanked the eastern entrance into the Temple of Solomon. Procopius went so far as to use the term *hieron*, or "temple", to describe the *Nea.* Procopius certainly described it as being both enormous and beautiful. It was twice the size of the Jewish Temple, which would indicate that it stretched further to the west (since the Cedron Valley bordered the eastern side).

Mary was, by this time, officially called "the Godbearer" or more loosely, "the Mother of God" and Justinian was determined to create a sacred space dedicated to the Virgin that was meant to appropriate the sacred mythology of Solomon's Temple for Christianity, and confirm the supremacy, not only of Christianity, but also of the Virgin as the Ark of the Covenant, over the old Judaic associations of the Temple Mount. This could not have pleased the Jewish population of the Holy City.

The exact location of the *Nea* has been quite mysteriously hard to pin down, and debated for centuries. The oldest surviving original cartographic depiction of the Holy Land and especially, Jerusalem, is a mosaic known as the Madaba map that was installed in a floor mosaic in the early Byzantine church of Saint George in Madaba, Jordan. It dates to the 6th century CE and is also called the Madaba Mosaic Map.

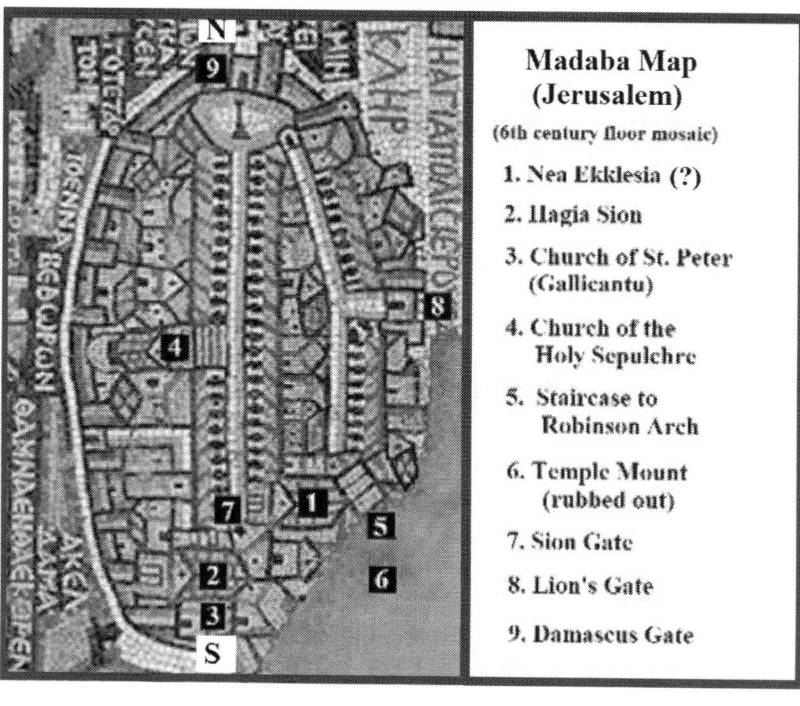

Plate 13 - Madaba Map

Many scholars interpret the Madaba map to place the *Nea Ekklesia* (#1 on the map) close to *Hagia Sion*, an equally large structure in Jerusalem at the time. The *Nea*, traditionally, is shown to be adjacent to the Temple Mount. But the Temple Mount is missing from the Madaba map. (#6 on the map). What details on the Temple Mount were rubbed out, and why? What needed to be erased from history? It is documented that the Christian churches of Jerusalem suffered great damage in the Sassanid (Persian) conquest of the city in 614 CE. which resulted in the deaths of tens of thousands of Christians within the city.

Scholars say that the *Nea* was built on Mt. Sion, but all of Jerusalem was described as Mt. Sion in ancient texts. Hagia Sion, the "mother of all churches" stood on what is now called Mt. Sion, in the southwestern part of Jerusalem – the Jewish Quarter.

The map is usually shown with the city oriented on its side, so that the Greek lettering can be read. However, with the map turned to the usual North-South orientation of the city, the far-right bottom corner shows where much of the map was rubbed out or otherwise destroyed. This is where the Temple Mount and the lower Cedron Valley would have been depicted. While number 1 in the figure is said to be the Nea, it would appear that this was the westernmost part of a huge complex of buildings that stretched onto the Temple Mount, which is missing.

The westernmost courtyard of the *Nea* complex opened onto the *Cardo* – the main roadway, which was extended in Justinian's time to the Sion Gate, beyond which was the Mount of Sion, where Hagia Sion (now called "Church of the Dormition") resides. But the Nea complex was huge. Procopius described porticoes at the southern end of the Nea, like the ancient Royal Stoa of the Temple Mount, with additional columns on the north and the west, and two great columns, which rose up at the western entrance. Perhaps this entrance was reached by the grand staircase of the Robinson Arch. Certainly a large staircase is shown at the eastern edge of the Madaba map, before it comes to the rubbed-out portion. To the west of this, an adjacent hostel, hospital, and monastery are mentioned – where are these on the Madaba map?

Antoninus of Piacenza, in 570, described, next to the *Nea*, a vast complex "with its great congregation of monks, and its guest houses for men and women." For travelers, there was "a vast number of tables, and more than three thousand beds for the sick." A three thousand bed hospital – *this* is the edifice shown on the Madaba map as number 1 (the same general size of Hagia Sion), and claimed by many modern historians to be the *Nea*.

Though modern scholarship and archeology claim that the foundation of the Nea was to the west of the Cardo, the location of the western edifices shown on the Madaba Map make it much more likely that the *Nea* covered the entire southern end of the rubbed-out Temple Mount – standing where the Royal Stoa once stood – where the al-Aqsa Mosque now stands. Why should anyone want to hide this idea?

On the lower level of the Temple Mount, were located "Solomon's Stables", where the Templars are said to have housed their horses in later Crusader times; tongue-in-cheek? The Brazen Sea – the brass ceremonial *mikvah* basin of the Temple, was supported on the backs of nearly life-size brass oxen. The "stables" were connected to the Templar Knights whose patron saint was Mary Magdalene.

Did Emperor Justinian consider the resistance that might arise from his choosing to build a Christian church on the site of the Jewish Temple? The Persian invasion of 614, gladly reinforced by Jewish soldiers, hired by a wealthy Jewish man, Benjamin of Tiberius, and accompanied by Nehemiah ben Hushiel – an enigmatic figure, written of in apocalyptic texts as "Messiah ben Joseph", that is, "Messiah, son of Joseph." A confusing affair, indeed! Certainly, relics were often taken into battle as talisman, as protection. But this would be an odd state of affairs! Would the Jews have found the relics of this figure to be a talisman?

Together with Jewish volunteers and a small Arab contingent, the Persian army brought damage to the *Nea*, (and *Hagia Sion)*, though the *Nea* must have remained somewhat intact, since Sophronius gave his "Nativity" sermon there in 634, only two decades after the Persian conquest of the city – certainly time enough for minor repairs. It was also a couple of years before the conquest of the city by the Saracens. The site of the Jewish Temple was said to be little more than a pile of rubble when Umar first saw it in the 7th century. But the Temple itself was long gone by then – would this have been rubble left by the destruction of a Christian edifice by Jewish soldiers during the Persian conquest - Justinian's "Temple" to Mary?

Certainly, the Jewish contingent that assisted the Persian conquest of the city, were said to have caused destruction to Christian holy sites, including and especially the church which stood on the foundation of their ancient Temple. Would it be surprising if, during that time, those who wanted to erase any memory of the *Nea* would rub out the depiction of it on the Madaba Map as well?

It is said that Umar built a modest wooden prayer-house soon after taking the city. This, Umar's first Holy Place, the al-Aqsa Mosque was built. (This is said to mean "The Farthest Mosque", though it was not farthest until the direction of prayer changed from the Temple Mount to Mecca). The initial structure was built on or at the southern end of the Temple Mount – Umar's shrine to the prophet Muhammad, described as a "small wooden shrine".

There was an earthquake in 658 CE in which Jerusalem was badly damaged, according to the chronicles of Michael the Syrian and Theophanes the Confessor. The structure on the southern end of the Temple Mount, called the al-Aqsa Mosque was rebuilt/expanded by Umayyad caliph Abd al-Malik, and finished by his son, al-Walid, in 705. The first account of the structure is testimony from the pilgrim Arculf, who visited the yet-to-be finished new structure in about 670 CE. Adomnán, who used the details of Arculf's account in his own book, *De Locus Sanctis* (Concerning Holy Places), states that it was an unremarkable rectangular wooden house of prayer large enough to hold some 3,000 people. This is not a "small wooden structure".

Arculf also stated that it was built over some ruins – indeed – what ruins? What structure stood on the southern end of the Temple Mount at the time of the earthquake of 658 – some twenty years after Sophronius gave his Nativity sermon in the *Nea*? By the 630s, Patriarch Sophronius does not even mention the *Nea* in his review of pilgrimage sites of the 630's. Was the *Nea* so profoundly forgotten by the time of Arculf's visit? Was it damaged by earthquake or conquest by then? Was it completely destroyed? Or was it simply considered impolitic to mention? Was it that, after years as an ascetic monk in Egypt, the bishop didn't want to mention or give it his sanction as an important Marian/Theotokos site?

After repairs were made by the Arab caliphs, the large, new structure was completely destroyed by another earthquake in 746, and rebuilt by the Abbasid caliph al-Mansur in 754. It was repaired in 780, and rebuilt again after the earthquake of 1033. Is it surprising that any evidence of the original structure of the Nea might be confused or completely erased by all this destruction and renovation? What would be the repercussion of confirming that the *Nea*, the "Church of St. Mary the New" may have once stood on the very spot where the al-Aqsa Mosque, "the Noble Sanctuary", Umar's sacred shrine built to honor Muhammad, "the Praiseworthy", now stands?

In the Persian invasion and ransacking of the city in 614, those churches and other Christian buildings that survived the onslaught were torn down by the Jews, who fought alongside the Persians against the Byzantine rulers of Palestine. According to Conybeare, the Jews of Jerusalem, "began with their own hands to demolish and burn such of the holy churches as were left standing".[139] This seems to have been the fate of the *Nea*.

In Meir ben Dov's book, *In the Shadow of the Temple* (1985), he writes, "The Jews could not overlook the fact that the stone used to build it had been taken from the Temple Mount, and their anger raged to the point of massacre. This must have been the reason for the enormous effort invested in destroying the *Nea*, which was far more heavily damaged than the Church of the Holy Sepulcher".

He writes that, at the end of the seventh century, when the Moslems began to construct a complex of buildings below the Temple Mount, they used stones "from the ruins of the Nea, which the Christians had not been permitted to restore."[140]

British Orientalist and historian, Guy le Strange, in his book, *Palestine Under the Moslems,* gives a more specific confirmation, which aligns with other scholars opinions, stating that Abd al-Malik used materials from the destroyed "great St. Mary Church of Justinian which must originally have stood on the site, approximately, on which the al-Aksa Mosque was raised."[141] He notes the scant and vague information on the rebuilding of the mosque by 'Abd al Malik as confirmation that some surviving portion of the church was simply incorporated into the structure of the mosque. [142]

A report compiled for Charlemagne in about 808 CE said the *Nea* had been thrown down by an earthquake and engulfed by earth. [143] This would mean that some form of the Nea survived until that time, even if it was, perhaps, called a mosque by then.

Certainly, it is recorded that, in the 12th century, in the second Arab conquest of the city, they cleared out and refurbished the lower levels of the Temple platform, the Stables of Solomon, which indicates that much of the lower structure on the southern end of the Temple Mount remained intact in the 12th century. The area was converted into the al-Marwani Mosque, which is beneath the current al-Aqsa Mosque. Interestingly, also in the lower levels in present day, stand Islamic shrines – called the Mihrab of Maryam and the Nativity of Jesus.

Did Sophronius' sermon cause the shrines to be built there by the Muslims, or were the sanctuaries, perhaps, Christian remnants of the *Nea* also? Is it possible that the upper levels of Justinian's Temple to the All-Praised Theotokos may, likewise, have been transformed, with renovation, and re-building, into the structure of the al-Aksa Mosque, dedicated to the Praiseworthy One of Islam, the Prophet, Muhammad.

SEVEN ECUMENICAL COUNCILS

The Council of Nicaea was convened by Emperor Constantine, to settle the Arian Controversy, the first heretical teaching to be condemned by the Church, and more importantly, perhaps, to define a unified doctrine of the Christian faith. It was the first of seven "ecumenical" or worldwide councils (at least, as far as the Roman Empire stretched). There were many smaller councils over the centuries, but these seven councils were widely accepted by Christianity as a whole. The First Ecumenical Council at Nicea dealt with the formulation of Christian doctrines around the relationship of God the Father and God the Son. The council anathematized the views of Arius, who proposed that the Son was lesser than the Father. These views were deemed to be heretical. In the finalized doctrine of the "Nicene Creed", it was decreed that the Father and Son were: "coequal, coeternal and consubstantial (of the same substance)."

The Second Ecumenical Council, the Council of Constantinople, which was convened in 381 by the Roman Emperor, Theodosius I, took on the question of the relationship of the Holy Spirit to the Father and the Son. Macedonius, in like manner to Arius, was misinterpreting the Church's teaching on the Holy Spirit, saying that the Holy Spirit was not a person ("hypostasis"), but rather a power ("dynamic") of God. Therefore, he believed that the Spirit was lesser than the Father and the Son. This council condemned Macedonius' teaching as heretical and defined the doctrine of the Holy Trinity, decreeing that there was one God in three persons ("hypostases"): Father, Son and Holy Spirit.

This council amended the Nicene Creed to include the Holy Ghost or Holy Spirit as a third and equal part of the Godhead. In lines added to the original Nicene Creed, it states, "And [we believe] in the Holy Ghost, the Lord and Giver-of-Life, who proceedeth from the Father, who with the Father and the Son together is worshipped and glorified, who spake by the prophets." This was an attempt to resolve Old Testament descriptions of the Godhead expressed as the *Shekinah,* as well as New Testament ideas of the Holy Spirit.

In the same century, the *Athanasian Creed* further defined the relationship of the three persons of the Trinity, with a focus on the technicalities of each person's relation to the previous person, "...we worship one God in Trinity, and Trinity in Unity, neither confounding the Persons, nor dividing the Substance...The Father is made of none, neither created, nor begotten. The Son is of the Father alone, not made, nor created, but begotten. The Holy Ghost is of the Father and of the Son, neither made, nor created, nor begotten, but proceeding."

The Third Ecumenical Council, the Council of Ephesus, was held at the Church of Mary in Ephesus, an ancient Greek city which is in modern-day Turkey. It was a council of Christian bishops convened in 431 CE, at the mandate of Roman Emperor Theodosius II. With 250 bishops in attendance, its purpose was, again, to attain consensus in the church through an assembly representing all of Christendom. Through heated confrontations and accusations promoted by Cyril of Alexandria, it confirmed the original *Nicene Creed,* and condemned the teachings of Nestorius, Patriarch of

Constantinople, who held that the Virgin Mary should be called the *Christotokos*, "Bearer of Christ" but not the *Theotokos*, "Bearer of God".

Nestorius insisted that calling Mary the "Mother of God" was improper, since no human can give birth to the eternal God. However, in his writings – deemed heretical, he also states that, "The body therefore is the temple of the deity [the God-nature] of the Son, a temple which is united to it in a high and divine conjunction, so that the divine nature accepts what belongs to the body as its own." He was getting too close to the truth – of course he had to be called a heretic.

Author Jaroslav Pelikan, in his work on the development of Church doctrine, describes the conflicting theologies as being represented by two camps, those who proposed the idea of the "*hypostatic* union" of the human and divine natures, and those who, like Nestorius put forth a belief in the concept of the "indwelling Logos" – the "indwelling Word", a teaching derived from Early Church Father, Origen.[144] The latter would have been the most empowering idea for Christians who wished to become like Jesus, as he had told them they could. Alas, this concept was not the one decided upon.

Cyril who opposed Nestorius, wrote of Mary, "Hail, Mother and Virgin, Eternal Temple of the Godhead, Venerable Treasure of Creation, crown of virginity, support of the true faith, on which the Church is founded throughout the world." Cyril makes her body the "Temple of the Godhead" and eternally so, to boot! (The "Godhead" being a term that equates to the Holy Trinity.) He goes on, "Mother of God, who contained the infinite God under your heart, whom no space can contain: through you the most Holy Trinity is revealed, adored, and glorified ..." He says the infinite God was under her heart, not in her womb. He doesn't explain how the Holy Trinity is revealed through Mary – it would seem that heretical fault can be found in his writings as well.

Nestorius, who had a high standing in the Church in Constantinople, and many supporters, had hoped to prove that his own position was aligned with the Orthodox teachings of the Church, but he was decisively outmaneuvered by Cyril at this Council. Nestorius' teachings were, in the end, anathematized, and he was removed from his See. He retired to a monastery, later recanting his position, however, the judgments resulted in the "Nestorian Schism" – whereby churches supportive of Nestorius, especially in the Persian Empire of the Sassanids, continued to follow his teachings, and were severed from the rest of Christendom. They became known as the Nestorians, or the Church of the East. They are now known as the Assyrian Church of the East, the Chaldean Syrian Church, the Chaldean Catholic Church. and the Ancient Church of the East.

The Council of Chalcedon, the Fourth Ecumenical Council of the Christian Church, took place in the city of Chalcedon near Constantinople in 451 CE, with 630 attendees. It repudiated the Eutychian doctrine of *Monophysitism*, the "one nature" of Jesus Christ, making Eutyches a heretic. It set forth the "Chalcedonian Definition", which describes the "full humanity and full divinity" of Jesus Christ, the Second Person of the Holy Trinity. The importance of this council and its far-reaching repercussions requires a chapter of its own.

The Second Council of Constantinople, which was the Fifth Ecumenical Council, was convoked by the Byzantine Emperor Justinian I in 553 CE. It was an attempt to find commonality and create unity between the Chalcedonian churches (believers in the "two natures") and the non-Chalcedonians (or Monophysites – believers in the "one nature"). Of the 153 attendees, most were Eastern Bishops – only sixteen Western bishops were present.

The council was held to confirm the condemnation issued by edict in 551 by the Emperor Justinian against the "Three Chapters" – the Christological writings and their authors being: treatises written by Theodore of Mopsuestia (died 428), writings against Cyril of Alexandria's *Twelve Anathemas*, written by Theodoret of Cyrrhus (died c. 466), and a letter written against Cyrillianism and the Ephesian Council by Ibas of Edessa (died 457). As early perhaps as 431, Marius Mercator denounced Theodore of Mopsuestia as the real author of the Pelagian heresy, decried as heresy by Augustine, in which Pelagius and his followers emphasized the essential goodness of human nature, and the freedom of the human will. Mercator also prefaced his translation of Theodore's *Ecthesis* with an attack on him as the precursor of Nestorianism. Celestine, one of Pelagius' followers denied Augustine's doctrine of Original Sin, and the requirement of baptism.

At this fifth Ecumenical Council, Nestorianism and *Monophysitism* were again condemned. Specifically, the council once again condemned the teaching that Mary could not be rightly called the Mother of God (*Theotokos*) but in this case, only the mother of the man (*anthropotokos*), a new term for her relationship to Jesus, or the mother of Christ (*Christotokos*) – a continuation of discussions at earlier councils and another confirmation of what was considered to be her rightful and correct title of "Mother of God." One must ask why this debate persisted throughout the centuries? What truths were the numerous fathers of the church wrestling with?

The Third Council of Constantinople, considered to be the Sixth Ecumenical Council by the Eastern Orthodox and Catholic Churches, as well as by certain other Western Churches, met in 680/681 CE. This was another effort to draw together the Chalcedonians and non-Chalcedonians. Emperor Heraclius, under the advice of Patriarch Sergius I of Constantinople, had first proposed that Christ possessed only a divine energy, which was not accepted by the Chalcedonians. Then he proposed that there was no human will but only a divine will. This definition was staunchly opposed by Sophronius when he became Bishop of Jerusalem. The effort to shift the semantics into something acceptable to the Chalcedonians did not work. It was seen as another effort to make Jesus divine only, and not also fully human. The council condemned the concept of the *monoenergism* ("one energy") of Jesus, and *monothelitism* ("one will") of Jesus, as heretical and instead defined Jesus Christ as having two energies and two wills (divine and human).

The Second Council of Nicaea is seen by the Eastern Orthodox Church and the Catholic Church as being the last of the seven ecumenical councils. Protestant opinions on its validity are varied. This council met in 787 CE in Nicaea (site of the First Ecumenical Council) to restore the use and veneration of icons (holy images), which had been suppressed by imperial edict in the Byzantine Empire during the reign of Leo III (717–741).

The veneration of icons had been banned by Leo's son, Byzantine Emperor Constantine V and supported by the Council of Hieria (754 CE), which had described itself as the seventh ecumenical council. However, its decisions were overturned by the Second Council of Nicaea only 33 years later, and were also rejected by Catholic and Orthodox churches, since none of the five major patriarchs were represented.

Constantine V's vigorous enforcement of the ban of icons included persecution of those who venerated icons, which were very popular in Eastern Christianity. Constantine V's iconoclastic tendencies were shared by his son, Leo IV. After the latter's early death, his widow, Irene of Athens, became the first empress regnant of the Byzantine Empire from 797 to 802. Though her husband had held an iconoclastic position, she leaned toward supporting the position of the *iconophiles* (lovers of the icons). As regent for her son, she began efforts to restore the veneration of icons. Since a council, claiming to be ecumenical, had abolished the veneration of icons, another ecumenical council would be required to restore the legality of their veneration. In 786, the council met in the Church of the Holy Apostles in Constantinople. However, soldiers aligned with the opposition disrupted and broke up the assembly.

The council was again summoned to meet, this time in Nicaea, since Constantinople was distrusted. The council reconvened on September 24, 787 at the church of Hagia Sophia. It numbered about 350 members; seven sessions were held. At this council, proof of the lawfulness of the veneration of icons was drawn from several biblical chapters, including: *Exodus* 25:19; *Numbers* 7:89; *Hebrews* 9:5; *Ezekiel* 41:18, and *Genesis* 31:34, but support was also found in the writings of the Church Fathers, whose authority was considered decisive.

The definition of the pseudo-Seventh council (754) was read and condemned and a declaration of faith was issued supporting the veneration of holy images, "For the more they are contemplated, the more they move to fervent memory of their prototypes. Therefore, it is proper to accord to them a fervent and reverent veneration, not, however, the veritable adoration which, according to our faith, belongs to the Divine Being alone – for the honor accorded to the image passes over to its prototype, and whoever venerate the image venerate in it the reality of what is represented."

The iconoclastic debates in the 8th century may well have influenced, initially, the veiled face in depictions of Muhammad, and the eventual ban, in Islam, of any image that depicted him.

THE COUNCIL OF CHALCEDON

The Fourth Ecumenical Council, the Council of Chalcedon, was held in 451 CE, at Chalcedon, a town of Bithynia in Asia Minor, with the goal of creating a consensus on the formula of the nature of Christ. The proceedings were so contentious and divided that it took the miraculous intervention of holy relics to make the final decision.

The council was called to address the issue of Eutyches teachings on the "one nature" of Jesus Christ, known as *Monophysitism*. After much heated argument, the council repudiated the Eutychian doctrine of *Monophysitism*, making Eutyches a heretic. It instead set forth the "Chalcedonian Definition" of the "two natures", confirming the *hypostatic union* – the "full humanity and full divinity" of Jesus Christ, the Second Person of the Holy Trinity.

The Council of Chalcedon was convoked by Emperor Marcian, in 449, in an effort to resolve the ongoing argument, and rancor, resulting from the Second Council of Ephesus, which became known as "The Robber Council". Because of the short notice for the convocation of the Robber Council, Pope Leo sent a letter to Flavian, to be read at the council. It explained Rome's position in the controversy. The letter now known as Leo's Tome, confessed that Christ had two natures, and was not "of" or "from" two natures.

In what appears to be an innate rivalry between the See of Alexandria and that of Constantinople, Pope Dioscorus I, Patriarch of Alexandria, who presided over this council, did not allow Pope Leo's letter to be read. He moved to depose Flavian of Constantinople and Eusebius of Dorylaeum on the grounds that they taught that the Word had been "made flesh" and had not just "assumed flesh" from the Virgin and that Christ had two natures. When Flavian and Hilary objected, Dioscorus called into the church a pro-Monophysite mob, which assaulted Flavian as he clung to the altar. He died three days later from his injuries.

The rancor fomented, with Leo demanding the convocation of a new council and Emperor Theodosius II refusing to budge, and appointing bishops who were aligned with Dioscorus. When Theodosius died, Marcian, an orthodox Christian, was raised to the imperial throne. To resolve the simmering tensions, Emperor Marcian convoked a new council to set aside the 449 Second Council of Ephesus, which then became known as the Robber Council.

Thus, the Council of Chalcedon was called to sort out the mess. This council issued the "Chalcedonian Definition", which declares that Jesus is "perfect both in deity and in humanness; this selfsame one is also actually God and actually man." It should be noted that, had this council not been called, and the Robber Council's definitions not been overturned, then the doctrinal position of the church would have been that of *Monophysitism* or the "one nature" of Christ, rather than the "two natures."

This council's judgments and definitions regarding the divine marked a significant turning point in the Christological debates. The Chalcedonian Definition states that, "Following, then, the holy Fathers, we all unanimously teach that our Lord Jesus Christ is to us One and the same Son, the Self-same Perfect in Godhead, the Self-same Perfect in Manhood; truly God and truly Man; the Self-same of a rational soul and body; co-essential with the Father according to the Godhead, the Self-same co-essential with us according to the Manhood..."

It goes on, "... like us in all things, sin apart; before the ages begotten of the Father as to the Godhead, but in the last days, the Self-same, for us and for our salvation of Mary the Virgin Theotokos as to the Manhood; One and the Same Christ, Son, Lord, Only-begotten; acknowledged in Two Natures unconfusedly, unchangeably, indivisibly, inseparably; the difference of the Natures being in no way removed because of the Union..." Unconfusedly? Ironic, indeed.

It continues, "...but rather the properties of each Nature being preserved, and concurring into One Person and One Hypostasis; not as though He was parted or divided into Two Persons, but One and the Self-same Son and Only-begotten God, Word, Lord, Jesus Christ; even as from the beginning the prophets have taught concerning Him, and as the Lord Jesus

Christ Himself hath taught us, and as the Symbol of the Fathers hath handed down to us."

Oriental Orthodox Churches do not agree with the conduct of the proceedings, or the decisions of the Council of Chalcedon (naming it 'Chalcedon, the Ominous"). After this council, the Oriental Orthodox Churches separated from the rest of Christianity.

What is most unusual about the Chalcedonian Council is the important role of relics in the decision-making. The divisive and even violent confrontations of the council left its representatives at an impasse. It is very telling that they could not find agreement. There was a fairly equal division among those present, who were there to represent all of Christendom.

According to the *Synaxarion of Constantinople*, when no decision could be reached, both parties wrote a confession of their position and they placed them on the breast of the relics of Saint Euphemia within her tomb. Saint Euphemia, known as the All-praised in the Orthodox Church, is a Christian saint, who was said to be martyred for her faith in 303 CE. Chalcedon was directly across the Bosphorus from the city of Constantinople (later called Byzantium, and now, Istanbul), where the relics of important early saints were venerated.

It is interesting that, while the Council of Chalcedon was in session, in 451, Emperor Marcian asked the Patriarch of Jerusalem to bring the relics of Mary to Constantinople to be enshrined in the capitol. The patriarch explained to the emperor, at this time, that there were no relics of Mary in Jerusalem, that Mary's tomb had been "found empty and so the apostles concluded that the body was taken up into heaven." It is ironic that her relics were, quite likely, very close to Constantinople at the time – their presence hidden by a tongue-in-cheek pseudonym. Since no relics could be produced, a new dogmatic/doctrinal formula was required to explain the "assumption" of Mary's body to heaven – a formula that developed from the mid-5th century to the 7th century CE, when it was more fully "fleshed out", so to speak, by John of Damascus.

According to tradition, Euphemia was arrested by the Romans, for refusing to offer sacrifices to the Roman God, Ares. After suffering various tortures, it is said that she died in the arena at Chalcedon from wounds sustained from a lion, much like Agnes of Rome, who was said to have died similarly at the Roman Coliseum - after surviving ordeals with various animals, Agnes was beheaded by a Roman soldier. One of the first images of Virgin and Child is to be found in Agnes' catacomb in Rome – begging the question of whether or not Agnes was a name used for Mary in early Christianity, before the faith was legalized. Her statue is prominently displayed with statues of other important saints on the colonnade in St. Peter's square near the Vatican, in Rome.

It is said that, at the Council of Chalcedon, the tomb of St. Euphemia was sealed up, with the two confessions of faith on her breast. In three days, the tomb was opened (one notes the significance) and the scroll with the Orthodox confession was found to be in the right hand of St Euphemia while the scroll of the Monophysites lay under her feet. Thus, the relics of the euphemistic St. Euphemia, in miraculous manner, decided the outcome of the Council and the resulting "Chalcedonian Definition".

It should also be noted that the 14th century trial of the Templars, whose patron saint was Mary Magdalene, included accusations that they worshiped a jewel-encrusted head, claimed by some to be the head of Baphomet (a cryptic term, whose meaning is much debated), and by others, euphemistically (?) claimed to be the head of St. Euphemia.

* * *

CHAPTER IX. RELICS OF THE SAINTS

THE HOLY BONES

There were Judeo-Christian relics that traveled all of Christendom – first in Rome, as the "trophies" in captivity – two saints who founded the church, as well as the bones of other saints, each with its own faction of followers who were devoted to the honoring and even prominence of their saintly leader. These holy bones were translated from place to place over the centuries – some of which relics, at various times, fell into the hands of the desert monks. Safe-guarded, presented to the faithful as inspiration, as mascot, as talisman, as holy relics, traveling the land, wandering the desert like the ascetic monks who revered them. Hidden, at times, in dry, dark desert caves.

Holy relics, eventually, brought to Eastern Christianity's Marian-devotees, displayed in churches, in opulent array: onyx, gold, and pearls – despite Tertullian's lambaste of the vanity of rich feminine apparel (Perhaps, even, the reason for his verbal assault on women? Was this going on even in his time?) He decried the hubris of such adornments. He protested that, since the man was the head of the woman, women certainly should not wear a crown!

In his particularly misogynistic treatise *On the Apparel of Women* Tertullian writes of woman (seemingly in generic terms), "Because of your deed — namely, death—even the son of God had to die!... And still you have in mind to be adorned (*adornari*) over your tunics of skin?" Nonetheless, her relics were adorned in silks and satins, gold and jewels – in ostentatious Byzantine glory. Likely even carried into battle, for promise of victory. Seemingly, retrieved in the Latin-crusaders' ransacking of Byzantium and returned to the west.

Jacob Baradeus (Jacob-James?), was a desert-traveling monk (perhaps a figurehead), whose followers became the Jacobites. Baradeus, means "saddle-blanket", for he traveled the holy land by horse for many years, as inspiration to the people. Perhaps not as living person, but perhaps the Holy Bones of the Just One, James? – the brother of the Lord, the principal authority of the early Church in Jerusalem, after Peter left – held in high regard by the earliest Jewish-Christians.

Relics were usurped by the conquering Saracens: the head of John the

Baptist, honored in Damascus, Syria, in a Christian basilica that was later converted into a mosque in John's name. Muslims highly honor John as a great and holy man. The Quran states that he is "honorable, chaste, and a prophet from among the righteous." (Chaste – a virgin?) He is called, "Yahya ibn Zakariyya," or "John, son of Zacharias." (Allah said:) "O Zakariyya! Verily, We give you the good news of a son, whose name will be Yahya. We have given that name to none before (him)." *Surah Maryam* 19:7

Sophronius, Orthodox Christian monk, was devoted to St. John Moschus, his constant companion in his year's-long travels of the holy land. Monk and saint, the traveling duo, inspiring allegiance to the Chalcedonian Creed - the Arab-Syriac desert monk, Sophronius, staunch supporter of the Chalcedonian formula, "Two natures in one person"; one person, but separate natures, not combined.

Sophronius honored this St. John, and after years of roaming the countryside together, upon John's "death" – or so they say, he finally escorted John's remains to the monastery at Theodosius. The book describes its author as "a presbyter and monk" who "began his life of renunciation in the monastery of our holy father Theodosius, abbot and archimandrite of all the *cenobia* and monasteries of Jerusalem". When they attempted to go to Mt. Sinai, Moschus wrote that even the Romans were panic-stricken over the occupation by heathens, "whereupon he left Alexandria and took ship for the great city of Rome along with his beloved disciple Sophronius." When Mt. Sinai was found not to be an option, due to Saracen occupation of the area, Sophronius escorted the relics to the monastery in Jerusalem.

It's interesting that St. John Moschus' first story in his treatise, *The Spiritual Meadow* is about an old man named John who wants to travel to Mt. Sinai, but is prevented by illness. He takes refuge in a cave, and stiffens so much that he can't move. A figure appears to him and says, "I am John the Baptist," came the reply, "and I warn you, don't go anywhere, for this narrow cave is greater than Mount Sinai. For the Lord Jesus quite often used to come into this cave when he was visiting me. Promise me that you will stay here and I will restore your health."

His health was restored and he spent the rest of his life in that cave, which later was made into a church where other brothers gathered about him. "The name of that place is Sapsa". Sapsa is located near the Jordan river, where John the Baptist was known to baptize his followers.

Moschus body (relics?), after he had made the circuit of all the important cities of the holy land, were, in the end, returned to the monastery of Theodosius in Jerusalem, where he had begun his travels, and his "spiritual seeking." This monastery is located some 8 kilometers east of

Bethlehem, on the road towards Mar Saba (St Sabbas) Monastery, on the West Bank, Palestine.

It seems quite likely that Sophronius was, in fact, the voice of St. John Moschus, in pseudepigraphical writings meant to show the great honoring of him, albeit in slightly veiled identity. Moschus (St. John) writes of an elder monk (named John), who lives at a cave/church/monastery, where he is visited by the Baptist (St. John), and that is found at the Jordan River, where the Baptist baptized. While Moschus calls Sophronius his own "beloved disciple", perhaps that is simply another hint, from New Testament references, as to Moschus' identity.

It is noted by many scholars that John Moschus does not mention Mary until Book 10, where "there are constant references not just to 'Maria' but to 'Maria sancta Domina nostra Dei genetrix semper virgo', [Our Lady Holy Mary, mother of God ever virgin] every word of which is directed at some particular heresy. She is always thought of as a powerful intercessor in Heaven and she is always 'genetrix', not 'mater' as is usual in later Western thought - 'genetrix Dei' is after all a more accurate translation of the Greek '*theotokos*, god-bearer'."[145] *Genetrix* can be translated as, "originator, creator, foundress", rather than simply as "mother".

In *Anacreontica 19*, a poetic bit of prose by Sophronius, entitled *The Holy City of Jerusalem*, he writes, "Holy City of God, Jerusalem, how I long to stand even now at your gates, and go in, rejoicing! A divine longing for holy Solyma (Hierosolyma/Jerusalem) presses upon me insistently." This would seem to have been written well before he became the Bishop of the Jerusalem See. It is interpreted by many scholars to represent Sophronius' own longing to return to the Holy City. However, it could well have been intended to speak for his holy friend, and constant companion for many years, St. John Moschus, whose remains Sophronius was escorting, and finally returning to the Holy City.

In another text, Sophronius wrote of St. Mary of Egypt, the most pious, saintly woman, who "lived" in a desert cave, like the desert fathers – a true ascetic. Mary of Egypt was said to have lived in the Jordanian desert for more than 40 years. In some versions, she was always honorable, in others, she had "prostituted" herself, for wealth and riches, like the secondary story-line of many other harlot-saints, who "paraded" themselves before the cathedrals – in opulent finery, with retinues (processions?) of devoted and fancy-dressed "acolytes". These saints, like Mary of Egypt, finally repented of their sinful, profane ways, and converted to the faith in the penitent, ascetic ways that redeemed them from sin, according to ascetic clergy.

In Sophronius' hagiography of Mary of Egypt, when Zosimus found this penitent woman, naked – not much more than "skin and bones" from her devoted asceticism and renunciation of the material life, he reverently covered her nakedness with his cloak. Was Zosimus, author of the tale, whose ideology was so similar to that of Sophronius, an alter ego of Sophronius? (Much like Athanasius' hagiography of Anthony, whom that one called the first desert father, was perhaps a thinly veiled reference to himself.) Then, we might say, perhaps, he (Zosimus/Sophronius) lent his *Bishop's* cloak to this holy woman.

In Giotto di Bondone painting of The Hermit Zosimus Giving a Cloak to Magdalene 1320, Mary seems to be enclosed in an anchoritic cave, with only a small window for access to the outer world. But the Magdalene was not an anchorite – what was Giotto's meaning?

Plate 14 - Hermit Zosimus Giving his Cloak to the Magdalene

Metaphors again – relics, hidden away for a time, in a secret place. Like St. Tecla, the "Protomartyr" – first female Christian saint, who escaped her would-be captors when the great holy rock opened and swallowed her whole.

When the tomb of John the Baptist at Sebastia was raided, and the bones burnt, the faithful retrieved them and took them to Athanasius, Patriarch of Alexandria, who "closed them up within a hollowed-out place in the sacristy." The relics of John/Mary were located in Alexandria, Egypt in the 4th century. Is this the origin of the name, St. Mary of Egypt?

Mary's tomb in Jerusalem at the foot of the Mount of Olives, close to Gethsemane, is located in a cave-church, the Church of the Sepulchre of Saint

Mary.

The Syriac Christian *Six Books Apochrypon* account of the "Dormition of Mary" (the eastern equivalent to the Assumption of Mary) contends that the Jews admitted their guilt in the death of Jesus, and states that, after the crucifixion, they buried the cross: "And opposite the top of the *wood of Jesus*, we made a hole in the earth, so that a man's hand might reach the top of *our Lord's wood*; and when an affliction comes upon anyone of us, he that is sick stretches out the tip of his finger, and if it reaches it, he is cured..." Could the "hole in the earth" be the pierced stone of the Temple? Some ancient stories say that the Ark of the Covenant was removed from the Holy of Holies and hidden within a cave beneath the Temple Mount.

It goes on, "...And whosoever was healed, we used to take a fee from him. And it was commanded by us, that whosoever should reveal this secret, should be cast out from among us with his whole family; and that he who revealed it should be slain." That would be a good explanation for how certain truths were kept secret! But "our Lord's wood" is an odd turn of phrase – is it the "True Cross", or might it be a euphemism for "relics"? Truth revealed in satire, folk tale, and hagiography – even in sacred scriptures, for those "with eyes to see". In the Jewish PaRDeS tradition, you are meant to study, to meditate, to question, to ask, to open yourself to revelation of the hidden meanings.

THE TRAVELS OF THE RELICS OF JOHN

Tracking the travels of the relics of John the Baptist is a, seemingly, impossible task. A simplified version of their travels is exemplified in the feasts celebrated in Eastern Christianity: the "First and Second Finding of the Head of John the Forerunner," and "the Third Finding of the head of John the Forerunner."

In Eastern Christianity, the official "first finding of the head of John the Baptist" occurred when the property on the Mount of Olives where the head was buried eventually passed into the possession of a government official-turned-monk named Innocent, who built a church and a monastic cell there. A time period for this discovery is not given. It is not known how long the relics rested there before they were discovered. When Innocent started to dig the foundation, the vessel with the head of John the Baptist was uncovered, but fearful that the relic might be dishonored by unbelievers, he hid it again where it had been found. Upon his death, the church fell into ruin and was destroyed. Might this story have some connection to St. Pelagius, whose body was found in his cave-cell on the Mount of Olives, long after his death?

The "Second Finding" is said to have occurred in the mid-5th century, through a revelation of the holy Forerunner to monks on pilgrimage to the Savior's Tomb in Jerusalem. In the *Scholastic History*, we have one version of the story. (A similar account is to be found in the *Annales* of Marcellinus, who was a chancellor under Justinian.) In 453 CE, Saint John revealed the whereabouts of his head to two monks who had come to Jerusalem:

They hurried to the palace that had been Herod's, and found the head rolled up in haircloth sacks. When they were on their way back to their homeland with the head a poor potter from the city of Emesa joined them on the road. The potter carried the pouch containing the sacred head, which the monks had entrusted to him, but he was admonished by Saint John to get away from them, and he went back to Emesa with the head. As long as he lived, he kept the relic in a cave and venerated it there, and he prospered not a little. When he was dying, he committed the relic to his sister's care, enjoining secrecy upon her, and she passed it on to her successors.

This version makes the potter a heroic figure. The potter may be a reference to the "potter's field" in Jerusalem. The term, "blood money," comes from *Matthew* 27:3-8, in which Jewish priests are given 30 pieces of silver by a remorseful Judas, who cries, "I have sinned in betraying innocent blood." In remorse, he casts down the pieces of silver in the temple, and "hangs himself with a halter". The chief priests took the silver, but decided, "It is not lawful to put them into the *corbona*, because it is the price of blood." They decided to buy the potter's field with the money, to be used as a burial place for the poor. "For this the field was called Haceldama, that is, the field of blood, even to this day." The site is also known as Akeldama, in the valley of Hinnom, where they dug potter's clay.

Or perhaps the term "potter" was simply a hint to the location of the head in a clay pot. We also have a perspective that the monks were careless and the "taking" by the potter was divinely inspired by John himself. Chalcedon, comes to mind not only for the somewhat similar spelling, but moreso, because of its connection to the relics of St. Euphemia, which were housed in that city at some point. The anti-Arian version of the story is that one of the monks took the venerable head of the Baptist in a clay jar to Emesa (now Homs), some 100 or so miles north of Damascus, in Syria. Emesa was a Roman client dynasty of Arab priest-kings.

The Arian *hieromonk*, Eustathius, came into possession of John's head and used it to attract followers to his teaching. He buried the head in a cave, near Emesa. According to this version, he ascribed the miracles wrought through the relic of the Baptist to his own misguided (read Arian) beliefs, he was driven from the cave, abandoning the holy head. Eventually, pious monks settled in the cave and a monastery was built at that place.

In 452, St. John the Baptist appeared to the Archimandrite Marcellus of this monastery in Emesa, and indicated where his head was hidden in a buried clay water jar. Marcellus had a vision while sleeping in the cave, in which a star appeared, leading him to the place where John's head was buried. According to the writings of St. Simeon Metraphrastes (*Menologion*, 10th century), when Marcellus told the bishop of Emesa, Julian, all that had happened, they took up the relic and brought it into the city. A week after its discovery, it was translated to the newly-built church dedicated to St. John. From that time on, the Beheading of Saint John was solemnly celebrated annually there, on the day of the year when the head was found. The timing of the finding in this story seems more than coincidental.

It should be noted that, in 451, one year earlier than the second finding, the Council of Chalcedon issued the 'Chalcedonian Definition,' repudiating the notion of a single nature in Christ, and defining the "two natures in one person and hypostasis" – the ruling that resulted in a major schism between Chalcedonians and Non-Chalcedonians. This ruling caused those Oriental Churches sympathetic with Monophysitism to break away from the orthodox Churches – schisms which have endured to modern times.

Chalcedon was also, at the time of the Council, the location of the tomb of the All-Praised, Great Martyr, "St. Euphemia," whose head was mentioned as a highly revered relic of the Templars in the records of the Templar trials in the 14th century. It was described in numerous different manners. One description gave that it was the "jewel-encrusted skull of St. Euphemia." Perhaps, in the 12th century reconquest of Jerusalem the Templars uncovered, or recovered a "True" relic which they venerated above all others.

The Third Finding of the Head of St. John the Baptist narrates that the head was transferred to Comana of Cappadocia during a period of Muslim raids (about 820), and it was hidden in the ground during a period of iconoclastic persecution, when icons and relics of the saints were threatened with destruction. Pious Christians who left Constantinople, secretly took the head of St. John the Baptist with them, and then hid it in Comana. Comana is the city to which St. John Chrysostom – the great, authoritative Liturgist of the Byzantines, who caused such an uproar with his writings – was carried to, in exile in 407, some 4 centuries earlier. In this same city, the head of John (the Baptist) was recovered in the mid-9th century, and brought back to

Constantinople!

After the Seventh Ecumenical Council (787), which re-established the veneration of icons, the head of St. John the Baptist was returned to the Byzantine capital in around the year 850. When the veneration of icons was restored in 850, Patriarch Ignatius of Constantinople (847-857) saw in a vision (the common method of discovery, apparently) the place where the head of St. John had been hidden. He communicated this to the emperor Michael III, who sent a delegation to Comana, where the head was found. Afterwards, the relic was transferred back to Constantinople, and placed in a church at the court.

So the Eastern narrative purports that the head was (1) in Jerusalem/ Palestine until it was (2) moved to Emesa, Syria, was lost for a time, and then (3) rediscovered in Comana, and later moved to Hebdomon, near Constantinople. However, the "Three Findings" of the head of John the Baptist only give account of the three times that the head was found by the Byzantines. There were, indeed, many other occasions that the head was found and removed by other factions.

If we include the records of the travels of John's relics in Western Christianity, it becomes much more complicated. Many sanctuaries of the Christian world laid claim to some portion of the sacred relics of John at various points in time, making it nearly impossible to determine what really became of the head of John the Baptist. There are many stories about its location, and many churches claiming to possess it at some point including: Amiens, Nemours, and St-Jean D'Angelo, in France, and S. Silvestro in Capite (Rome), not to mention in the Islamic mosque of Yahya ibn Zakariyah (St. John the Baptist) in Damascus, Syria.

Some early writers claim that Herodias had it buried in the fortress of Machaerus. Others insist that the head was kept in Herod's palace at Jerusalem – and that it was found there during the reign of Constantine. From there it was, reportedly, taken secretly to Emesa, in Phoenicia, where it was concealed, the place remaining unknown for years, until it was manifested by revelation in 453. The discrepancies in the various claims render the mystery unsolvable. Tillemont attributes the multiple claims to the honest mistaking of one St. John for another – in any case, there is an unresolved over-abundance of relics of this saint.

Holy Scripture tells us that after St. John the Baptist was beheaded, the impious Herodias forbade the prophet's head to be buried with his body. Instead, she had it buried near her palace. The saint's disciples secretly rescued their teacher's skull and buried it elsewhere. When word reached the royal palace about Jesus' preaching and miracles, Herod went with his wife

Herodias to see if John the Baptist's head was still in the place where they had left it. When they did not find it there, the Gospels state that the royals were afraid that Jesus Christ was John the Baptist resurrected. (*Mt.* 14:2).

Some stories say that John's disciples collected his body, presumably from the castle at Machaerus, and laid it in a tomb. It is not clear whether or not these remains included John's head. There is no mention of John's remains for over 300 years. Then, at the end of the 4th century, the tomb of John the Baptist is recorded alongside that of the biblical prophet Elisha, located in the Palestinian village of Sebastia (also spelled, Sebaste). St. Sebastian, the name of the masculine protomartyr (first martyr) of Christianity certainly may have some relationship to the location of John the Baptist's relics in Sebastia. Sebastia is also the feminine form of the name "Augustus," which means "Majestic, Venerable One."

Around 390, while translating the *Onomasticon* (directory) of the holy places compiled by Eusebius, St. Jerome described Samaria/Sebaste as the place "where the remains of John the Baptist are guarded." A small basilica, founded in the 5th century, was discovered in excavations on the southern slope of the acropolis in Sebastia. The church was believed to be the burial place of the head of John the Baptist. According to another church tradition, after the execution of John the Baptist, his disciples buried his body at Sebastia, Palestine, but Herodius took his severed head and buried it in a dung heap. Later, Saint Joanna, who was married to Herod's steward, secretly took his head and buried it on the Mount of Olives, where it remained hidden for centuries. The tomb of the Virgin Mary is located on the Mount of Olives.

We have the narrative of the desecration of John's tomb and burning of his relics in Sebastia, in Palestine in 362 CE, after which the monks of Philip rescued what was left of his relics and brought them to him for safe-keeping. Phillip, in turn, finding it "beyond him to guard such a treasure," took them to Athanasius, the "Supreme Pontiff" – the Patriarch of Alexandria. (Thus, he is not mentioned in Byzantine records of the First, Second, and Third Findings of the head of St. John the Baptist.) The tomb at Sebastia continued, nevertheless, to be visited by pious pilgrims, and St. Jerome bears witness to miracles being worked there.

Today, the tomb is housed there in the Nabi Yahya Mosque ("John the Baptist Mosque"). In 378 C.E., the Visigoths invaded the Eastern Empire and killed Emperor Valens at the momentous Battle of Adrianople. The division between Valens and his brother, Emperor Valentinius, is often cited as the origin of the separation between the Eastern and Western Church.

Sozomen relates that during Valens' reign, the head of John the

Baptist was discovered by Macedonian monks, who originally dwelt at Constantinople, and were involved in the "Macedonian Heresy." After their practices were deemed heretical, the Macedonian monks went to Cilicia. They guarded the holy relics until the reign of Theodosius, who insisted that the relics be brought to Hebdomon, a suburb to the west of Constantinople.

One story recounts that, when the Imperial Court discovered the Macedonian's possession of the head, and Emperor Valens demanded the relic be moved to the capitol: "Mardonius, the first eunuch of the palace, made known this discovery at court, during the preceding reign; and Valens commanded that the relic should be removed to Constantinople. The officers appointed to convey it thither, placed it in a public chariot, and proceeded with it as far as Pantichium, a district in the territory of Chalcedonia."[146] (That would be Chalcedon, where the All-Praised St. Euphemia's head and relics were known to be later entombed in 451).

Here, the story insists that the mules of the chariot suddenly stopped and would go no further. This was considered a miraculous, God-directed event, which caused Emperor Valens to decide that the holy head should remain there in the Chalcedonian village of Cosilaos, on the other side of the Bosphorus from Constantinople.

Soon after this, Emperor Theodosius came to Cosilaos to reclaim the relic and bring it to Constantinople. "He determined upon removing the remains of the Baptist, and it is said met with no opposition, except from a holy virgin, [*Matrona*] who had been intrusted with the care of the relic. After many entreaties, the woman reluctantly agreed to let him remove the head; for she bore in mind what had occurred at the period when Valens commanded its removal."

The paschal chronicle mentions this translation of the relics from Jerusalem to Hebdomon in 391 CE. Hermias Sozomenus, in the *Ecclesiastical History of Sozomen* writes "The emperor placed it, with the box in which it was encased, in his purple robe, and conveyed it to a place called Hebdoma, in the suburbs of Constantinople, where he erected a spacious and magnificent church," the Church of St. John the Forerunner.[147]

In 395 CE, Theodosius had the relics placed in a new basilica in the saint's name at the site of the old Serapeum at the Library of Alexandria. (Again, this Western Church action is not mentioned in the Byzantine record of the Three Findings.) These relics, reportedly, included his head. Gaudentius, Bishop of Brescia, presented relics of St. John the Baptist at the dedication of his basilica, the *Concilium Sanctorum*, along with relics of other saints, and the bishop of Rouen in northern Gaul also received relics of John the Baptist, Andrew, Luke and Thomas, and of St. Euphemia of Chalcedon.

In the 6th century, two urns covered in gold and silver were, once again, said to be venerated by pilgrims in Sebastia, Palestine. One was said to contain relics of John the Baptist, the other, relics of Elisha. Two churches were built in honor of John during the Byzantine period: a 6th century church on the southern side of the Roman acropolis (on the site that the Orthodox Church believes John was beheaded). The other church, a 5th century cathedral built over the Baptist's reputed tomb, was just east of the old city walls and within the present village of Sebastia. Rebuilt by the Crusaders, it became, at the time, the second biggest church in the Holy Land (after the Church of the Holy Sepulchre in Jerusalem).

Christian sources dating back to the 4th century recorded John the Baptist's burial at Sebastia, along with the remains of the prophets Elisha and Obadiah. While Josephus claimed that the infamous banquet at which John was beheaded was held in Herod's fortress at Machaerus, Jordan (on the eastern side of the Dead Sea), Orthodox Christians maintain that Sebastia, Palestine, was the real venue for the governor's birthday banquet. Was there a reason for the discrepancy? Was the story of John's beheading less than historically accurate? Was it, rather than a factual account, simply a folk-tale meant to indicate the secret location of the holy relics – the head and bones of John the Baptist?

After the Islamic conquest of 1187 the cathedral in Sebastia was turned into a mosque dedicated to the prophet Yahya, the Muslim name for John the Baptist. The mosque, rebuilt in 1892 from the ruins of the cathedral, is still in use. Many Muslims believe it to be the place where Isa (Jesus) will return at the End of Days.

Amiens Cathedral claims that the head of John the Baptist was brought from Constantinople by Wallon de Sarton as he was returning from the Fourth Crusade, and that it now resides at Amiens. John the Baptist's arm and a piece of his skull are also said to be located at the Topkapi Palace in Istanbul, Turkey. The right hand has been claimed as a possession of the Russians, eventually transferred to a monastery in Montenegro in Southeastern Europe. It is also reputed to be kept at the Dionysiou monastery on Mount Athos in Greece.

More recently, in the summer of 2010, an excavation of a 5th – 6th century church in Sozopol, Bulgaria, brought forth the discovery of a reliquary next to an urn inscribed with the name and birth-date of John the Baptist. The bones were carbon-dated to the 1st century C.E., and are believed by many to be those of John the Baptist. The relics, including a skull fragment, part of an arm bone, and a tooth, were found in a small marble sarcophagus like the one described as being moved from Cosilaos to

Constantinople in 391.

On a small island known as 'Sveti Ivan' (Bulgarian for "Saint John") excavations have gone on for a number of years. This island is located in the Black Sea, about a kilometer from the Bulgarian town of Sozopol, one of the oldest on Bulgaria's southern coast. Aerial images reveal that there are at least two prominent sets of monumental archaeological remains on the island. These have been affirmed to be the remains of a church of about the 6th century CE; and a monastery (and church) of around the 13th and 14th centuries CE.

The Umayyad Mosque in Damascus, Syria, known as the Great Mosque of Damascus, formerly the Basilica of Saint John the Baptist, currently lays claim to the head of John the Baptist, honored as a prophet by both Christians and Muslims.

KING ARETAS

In the time of the Apostle Paul, King Aretas, was the Arab king of lands near Judea, from Syria to the rock-cut sandstone city of Petra in southern Jordan. The King's full title, as given in inscriptions, was "Aretas, King of the Nabataeans, Friend of his People." Being the most powerful neighbor of Judea, he was influential in the state matters involving that country and its rulers. Though he was not on the best terms with Rome, he took part in the expedition of Varus against the Jews in 4 BC, putting a considerable army at the disposal of the Roman general.

The first wife of Herod Antipas, Phasaelis, who was King Aretas' daughter, fled to her father, the Nabatean king, when she discovered her husband intended to divorce her in order to take a new wife. This new wife was Herodias, who was already married to his brother, Herod II (also known as Phillip). When Aretas' daughter secretly learned of the plan, she asked for permission to travel to her father's domain. Nabatean forces escorted her to her father – where else but the desert fortress of Machaerus! *Smith's Bible Dictionary* states that Machaerus was a castle of the Herods on the southern border of their Perean domain, nine miles east of the northern end of the Dead Sea. The marriage of Herodias and Antipas, is the one that brought the condemnation of John the Baptist, leading to Antipas' beheading of the saint at Machaerus. Here John was imprisoned, and the feast was held where Salome (sometimes called Herodias, like her mother), asked for the head of John the Baptist, in exchange for dancing for the king.

Some scholars have suggested that the "beheading" was figurative rather than literal, and was simply a matter of taking away John's leadership role, or even his priestly headband. Laurence Gardner states, in *The Magdalene Legacy* that the story of the daughter of Herodias, was misinterpreted". She is unnamed in *Matthew* 14:10, but later connected by Josephus' *Antiquities of the Jews* to a daughter of Herodias named Salome. Elsewhere, she is called "Herodias" like her mother. Though it is not a commonly accepted interpretation, Gardner states that, "Apparently, this daughter requested that John should be stripped of his rank, and that his Zadokite *kephale* (headband) should be given to her. (Because of the poor translation in this respect, this is often presumed to have been the actual head of the Baptist.)"[148]

If Gardner is correct, then does that mean that the daughter, who was given the headband was made a high priest as well? Were women members of the high priesthood? It would seem that John (Mary) was.

Herod Antipas' first wife, the daughter of King Aretas, was named Phasaelis, a feminine form of the name, Phasael, which equates to Saul. Antipas divorced her in order to marry his brother's wife, Herodias, who had one daughter from that first marriage, the infamous Salome.

According to the historian, Josephus, "Herodias took upon her to confound the laws of our country, and divorced herself from her husband while he was alive, and was married to Herod Antipas." This indicates that both Antipas and Herodias divorced their spouses in order to marry each other. One is reminded of the statement in the Quran, regarding Mary's parents, "O Maryam! ...O sister of Aaron! Your father was not an adulterous man, and your mother was not an immoral woman!" (*Surah Maryam* 19:28) Who else do we know was spoken of in such terms at the time?

The tetrarch's divorce added a personal grievance to previous disputes with Phasaelis' father, King Aretas over territory on the border of Perea and Nabatea. In retribution, Aretas, upon receiving news of Antipas divorcing his daughter, invaded his lands, and defeated his armies. This resulted in a Roman counter-offensive being ordered by Tiberius, but in a turn of fortune that benefited Aretas, the plan was abandoned upon the emperor's death in 37 CE.

In 2 *Corinthians* 32-33, Saulus-Paulus speaks of an attempt to capture him, "In Damascus the governor under Aretas the king, kept the city of the Damascenes with a garrison, desirous to apprehend me: And through a window in a basket was I let down by the wall, and escaped his hands." The identity of the "governor" (in some translations, "ethnarch") was not given. This incident seems to have happened in about the time period of Phasaelis' retreat to her father's kingdom, perhaps during the time that Aretas was threatened by Herod Antipas. The narrative in *Acts* 9:23-24 puts it clearly that, "...the Jews took counsel to kill him: But their laying await was known of Saul. And they watched the gates day and night to kill him." It confirms his escape by being let down "by the wall in a basket".

The *Expositor's Greek Testament* states, "The incident took place on St. Paul's return to Damascus from Arabia (*Galatians* 1:17) and is narrated in *Acts* 9:23-25. The date of it is important in the chronology of the Apostle's life. It could not have been before A.D. 34, for coins of Tiberius prove Damascus to have been under direct Roman administration in that year. Tiberius was unlikely to have handed Damascus over to Aretas (fourth of the name), the hereditary chief (2Maccabees 5:8) of the Nabathæan Arabs; for up to the close of the reign of Tiberius – military operations were being carried on against Aretas by the legate of Syria. Hence Damascus was probably not ceded to Aretas until the reign of Caligula, and consequently this episode in St. Paul's life cannot have taken place before the middle of A.D. 37."

Finally, in 39 CE, Antipas was accused by his nephew, Agrippa I, of conspiracy against the new Roman emperor Caligula, who sent him into exile in Lugdunum, Gaul, which is now Lyon, France, some 180 miles inland from the coast of southern France. Josephus states that Antipas died in Spain. Whether the ex-tetrarch removed from Lyons to Spain, cannot be ascertained.

ST. MARTIN OF TOURS

Gaul is the place of St. Maries de la Mer, where the Mary's and other Christian saints reportedly landed on the southern coast of France, after being set adrift in a boat without rudder or sail. Joseph of Arimathea, the rich man who provided the tomb for Jesus' body, also traveled to Gaul, and is credited by some with spreading Christianity throughout France and Britain, even before its arrival in Rome. Medieval interest in him centered on two themes, that of Joseph of Arimathea as the founder of British Christianity, and that of Joseph as the original guardian of the Holy Grail.

Accompanied to Gaul by his second wife, Herodias, Antipas died at an unknown date. It is uncertain if Herodias had any children by Antipas. There is an interesting account of St. Martin of Tours, a Gallic saint of the early 4th century. His name, derived from "Mars", means "warring" or "war-like," but it is said that, conscripted as a soldier into the Roman army, he found the duty incompatible with the Christian faith he had adopted and became an early conscientious objector.

St. Martin, the "Roman Soldier," established a monastery in Tours which became the Benedictine Ligugé Abbey, the oldest monastery known in Europe. While Benedict is said to have lived a couple centuries later, it does connect Martin with the origins of the Benedictines. It is said that he travelled and preached through western Gaul (modern-day France): "The memory of these apostolic journeyings survives to our day in the numerous local legends of which Martin is the hero and which indicate roughly the routes that he followed."[149] His life was recorded by a contemporary, the hagiographer Sulpicius Severus. Scholars suggest that some of the accounts of his numerous travels may have been added to his *vita* to validate early sites of his cult.

One folk tale gives that he was drawn to Tours by a ruse: he was urged to come to minister to someone sick, and was brought to the church, where he reluctantly allowed himself to be consecrated bishop. According to one version, he was so reluctant to be made bishop that he hid in a barn full of geese, but their cackling gave him away. This detail may address the rumored complaints by some that his appearance was too disheveled to be commensurate with a bishopric. Again, we must note that the relics of the earliest saints of the church were often represented in stories as living saints.

Peter was connected to Gaul; Joseph of Arimathea, the "rich man", was made wealthy by the tin mines of Cornwall, not far from Gaul.

While St. Martin was a soldier in the Roman army and deployed in Gaul, he experienced a vision, which became the most-repeated story about his life. One day as he was approaching the gates of the city of Amiens in wintry weather, he met a scantily clad beggar. He impulsively cut his military cloak in half to share with the man. That night, Martin dreamed of Jesus wearing the half-cloak he had given away.[150] In his dream, Martin heard Jesus say to the angels: "Martin, who is still but a catechumen, clothed me with this robe." Amiens Cathedral claimed to have the head of John the Baptist.

When Martin woke, he found his cloak restored to wholeness. The dream confirmed Martin in his piety, and he was baptized at the age of 18. His cloak was preserved in the oratory of the Merovingian kings of the Franks at Marmoutier Abbey near Tours. During the Middle Ages, his miraculous cloak was a holy relic upon which oaths were sworn and was even carried by the king into battle. This was a very important cloak, indeed!

The cloak is first acknowledged in records of the royal treasury in 679 CE. The priest who cared for the cloak in its reliquary was called a *cappellanu*, and ultimately all priests who served the military were called *cappellani*. The French translation is *chapelains*, from which the word "chaplain" is derived. Another linguistic development of the term came to refer to the small temporary churches built for the relic; they were called "capella", meaning "a little cloak."

Eventually, such small churches lost their association with the cloak, and all small churches began to be referred to as "chapels". It is significant that the term, chapel, derived from this honoring of an ancient cape! So, who did the early saint, Martin of Tours, really represent? We know that he was not John the Baptist, but I would propose that his true identity was one of the earliest leaders of the church - someone with a long association with France.

THE PENANCE OF ST. JOHN

A story is told, a tall tale, of the "Penance of St. John Chrysostom". John, the "golden-mouthed" of the eastern, Byzantine church – Bishop of Constantinople, a prolific author, whose liturgy is still the common format of masses performed in Eastern Christianity - his "eloquent" writings as prolific and profoundly influential as those of another 4th century saint, Augustine, who wrote treatises on Original Sin. In other words, prior to the machinations of Theophilus of Alexandria which caused his deposition and exile, John Chrysostom was a highly praised, highly revered bishop. Scholars describe his mother Anthusa as a Christian (The *Encyclopedia Judaica*, gives that she was pagan), and his father as a high-ranking military officer.[151]

John, however eloquent and gentle at times, is also is said to have written scathing anti-pagan, anti-Semitic, and anti-homosexual tracts. Were they all his writings, or did other authors creep in, as often happened, satirically, derisively, pseudepigraphically? Were any of them his writings – or was his name usurped by various factions of monk-author-apologist-satirists? He is also said to have led a mob that destroyed the Temple of Artemis, one of the Seven Wonders of the Ancient World. But again, truth - or smear campaign?

In the story of the Penance of John Chrysostom, John shared his cave with a young maiden – a "virgin", you could say. A sin was committed, and the young woman found herself to be with child. In a panic, he threw her over "the cliff". In remorse at his sins, he went to Rome to beg absolution, which was refused. He vowed, as penance, never to rise from the ground again.

In some versions, the young woman was the daughter of an unnamed emperor – a bit of satire? Justinian, perhaps, who built a Temple-like "New Church" for St. Mary at or near the southern end of the Temple Mount in the 5th century, where the drop from the Temple Mount to the valley below was considerable. In the end, John the penitent saint, was forgiven.

The "John or Mary" factions of Christianity debated each other through the centuries, in Folk tales, legends, and hagiography of the saints, as they were wont to do. Martin Luther, Protestant reformer, refuted the tale of the *Penance of St John Chrysostom* in his *Lügend* of the saint. *Lügend* means not legend, but "lies," puns being a common device in Reformation-period satire and polemic as well.

Plate 15 - Penance of St. John Chrysostom-Albrecht Durer

John is hard to see in the middle-ground, in penance for his actions, on all fours – a sly reference to the Bogomils? Critical writers – and painters – could be quite incendiary and crude! Or backlash to Chrysostom's "Sermon on Homosexuality"? – which was considered to be the epitome of homophobia in Christian writings. Or was it simply part of the narrative – that he would, for his sins, never again rise from the ground?

In Campagnola's work (not shown), c. 1482, the kingdom in the distance is clear – with colonnade on the nearest side: much like – yes, much, much like – the eastern portico of the Temple Mount – Solomon's Porch, as it was called, (on the eastern side, adjacent to the Outer Court – the Women's Court) where Jesus often taught. Campagnola's work puts the two figures near the Virgin's cave-tomb which was eastward, across the Cedron Valley from the Temple Mount, near Gethsemane, low on the Mount of Olives. From the southeastern end of the Temple Mount, the cliff dropped off to the Valley beside the Temple Mount, with the lower ground, south of the Temple Mount, leading down to the City of David.

In the work by Lucas Cranach the Elder, John can, again, be seen in the right middle-ground on all fours.

Plate 16 - Penance of St. John Chrysostom - Lucas Cranach the Elder

Were relics actually removed from the Temple Mount at some point, and then discovered and returned to their place of honoring in Justinian's great Temple to Mary in the 6th century, or later? Was this folk tale of the Penance of John Chrysostom a Justinian, pro-Marian, anti-Johannine stance? Was this a re-acknowledgment of relics from being called those of John to being called those of Mary?

* * *

CHAPTER X. SAINTS AND SINNERS

ST. MARINA

In a Greek Orthodox prayer, like other of the virgin saints, Marina is the betrothed of the Lord, "O Glorious Marina, once betrothed to the Logos, you relinquished all worldly concerns and brilliantly gave struggle as a virginal beauty. You soundly trounced the invisible enemy who appeared to you, O Champion, and you are now the world's wellspring of healing grace." Many Mediterranean cultures have a saint with the name of Marina or Marinos: Marina the Monk (or Marina the Syrian), Marina the Martyr of Antioch, Marina of Spain, Marina of Alexandria, Marina of Sicily and Marina the Cistercian.[152]. Most historians give the origin of the tale of 'Marina the Monk" as being related to the Monastery of Qannoubine, Lebanon.

Léon Clugnet posits that, since the most ancient account of the life of Saint Marina is found among the Maronites of Lebanon, that Lebanon must be considered the land of her birth. The Maronites are adamant that Marina's story originated in Lebanon and that as a monk she lived and died in the Monastery of Qannoubine in the Holy Valley of Qadisha in the 5th century.

Clugnet connects her to traditions of Aphrodite, the love goddess of the sea. He states that the confusion pertaining to all of the other saints named Marina is due to the translators and the copyists' attribution of the saint's origins to their own countries or other countries that they felt better fit the Saint's life. This, he proposes, is why we find that the Coptic narrative of Saint Marina's life places her birth in the deserts of Egypt; Latin sources give it as Italy; and the Greek version places her birth in none other than Bethany. In other words, this scholar proposes that the concept of this saint's life was adapted to many regions and cultures. The same may well be true of other saints whose names and stories were altered to suit a purpose, or tell a story.

Like Clugnet, Hermann Usener. and other scholars, have proposed that the legends of St. Pelagia along with St. Marina, St Margaret, and others, are simply a Christian representation of Aphrodite.[153] The legends which have subsequently become connected with her name are often attributed to syncretizations of other historical narratives and folk tales. It would seem that these saints are moreso connected to Mary Magdalene.

Marina's story also has many parallels to the story of St. Mary of

Egypt. However, instead of making Marina a repentant sinner, she is a pious, holy, and falsely accused female monk, who disguised herself as a male, and entered the life of monasticism. The monasteries of the 5th century had small, separate cells where the monks lived, which made it possible for Marina to conceal her identity. With her masculine mode of dress and with her ascetic living, which gave her a gaunt and masculine appearance (much like that of St. Mary of Egypt), Marina was able to live at the monastery undiscovered for many years. In juxtaposing this legend with that of St. Mary of Egypt and other similar storylines, we might begin to see that every sect had their own vision of what Mary's place in the Church was.

Marina's legend states that her father Eugenius (meaning "well-born"), a Bithynian who wanted to become a monk, disguised her as a boy, and brought her with him to the Monastery of Qannoubine. The story goes that Marina, disguised as a male, joined her father in the monastery, where she lived as a monk for seventeen years.

Interestingly, Sophronius, in his *Vita of St. Mary of Egypt*, states that St. Mary went to Alexandria to live her dissolute life for seventeen years. When she traveled to Jerusalem, she was barred by her sinfulness from entering the Church of the Holy Sepulchre. She was only allowed to enter after praying to the Theotokos and dedicating herself to the ascetic lifestyle.

Was there such rancor between Alexandria and Jerusalem at that time as to see those same seventeen years so differently? It seems that the perspective relies on what traditions were used at a given time. While there were ascetic Egyptian monks who rebelled against such customs, Theophilus and Cyril, in the 5th century, seem to have aligned with Byzantine ostentatiousness. Certainly, we can see the contrast in the ideals of Umar, who entered Jerusalem a couple of centuries later in tattered, dirty robes, aligned with the ascetic sentiments of the Syriac-Arab Patriarch, Sophronius.

A Syriac Manuscript dated 778 CE gives many details of Marina's life. It became necessary at one point for Marina/Marinos to lodge at an inn, where the innkeeper's daughter, believing that Marinos was a man, wantonly pursued him (her). At Marinos' rebuff of her advances, she sought revenge by falsely accusing the monk of seducing her and fathering her child. The innkeeper's daughter also wanted to hide the fact that she had, herself, had illicit relations with a soldier and become pregnant.

When we compare this to the narrative of the Virgin birth, it might be seen that this legend does not align with Byzantine traditions at all. Perhaps it is meant to be a refutation. The Roman soldier, in rabbinical satire was the father of Jesus. Here, he is the father of the child of the innkeeper's daughter.

However, the monk, Marina, is a pious virgin who raised the child regardless.

After being accused by the innkeeper's daughter, Marina/Marinos was cast out of the monastery. She did not reveal her identity, and became a beggar at the monastery's gates. Marina/Marinos took custody of the child and was eventually readmitted to the monastery with "his son." There, Marina performed the lowliest tasks and was forced also to perform severe penances. Is this meant to be an illuminating detail? She spent the rest of her life living ascetically and looking after the child. Her gender was only revealed at her death.

Marina is venerated by the Maronite Church. Her legend was sometimes confused with that of Saint Pelagia.

SAINT PELAGIA/PELAGIUS

There is also the story of Pelagius, the saint who lived in an anchorite cave located – where else – but on the Mount of Olives. The narrator of the hagiography goes to visit the holy monk at his cell. "Monks from every monastery and an innumerable multitude of people from throughout the city of Jerusalem, from Jericho, and from the far side of the Jordan gathered to bury his holy remains ..."[154] This was an important saint! "... and after breaking open the window of his cell, they made an opening large enough for a man to enter. Through it, certain pious men went into the cell and removed the precious relics. Then came the Patriarch of Jerusalem with many of the fathers; and when, according to custom, they began to anoint the body with spices, they saw that the saint was a woman. Crying out with tears they said, "O God, Who art wondrous in the saints, glory to Thee! For many are the hidden saints whom Thou hast on earth; not men alone but women as well!"

She was known as "the beardless monk" until her sex was discovered at her death. The story continues, "The clergy and monastics wished to conceal this secret from the people but were unable to do so, for God did not wish that it be hidden but rather desired that it be known, that His handmaiden might be glorified. Many people assembled there, and nuns came forth from their convents with candles and censers, chanting psalms and hymns. They took Pelagia's precious and holy body and with fitting reverence returned it to the cell in which she had labored, burying it there." In the story, the masculine name, Pelagius, becomes the feminine name, Pelagia.

"Pelagia" is, in fact, said to be the Greek equivalent of the Latin-derived name, Marina. To make things more complicated, the Greek *synaxaria* assigns the same feast day to three saints by the name of Pelagia, two of Antioch and the other, known as Pelagia of Tarsus (a city that is significant as the birthplace of St. Paul). While they are said to be different saints, they may well be the same saint from different perspectives.

Pelagia of Tarsus was virtuous and holy, chaste, and pure. Her hagiography states that one night she dreamt of the local Bishop who encouraged her to be baptized Christian, and she was. She sold her clothes to the poor and dressed in very simple clothes; when her mother saw her she was very upset and tried to persuade her to reject the new religion, but Pelagia would not do so. She was engaged to Emperor Diocletian's son, who found out about the baptism and tried to persuade her to reject Christianity and marry him, but she denied his offer, and so, he killed himself. When Diocletian found out, he had Pelagia arrested, tortured, and killed.

In the homily of John Chrysostom, Pelagia of Antioch was also a chaste and honorable virgin of 15 years of age. During the Diocletian persecution, soldiers attempted to force her to publicly offer a heathen sacrifice. To avoid this fate, she went up to the roof of the house and threw herself into the sea. Thus, she died, as St. Chrysostom says, a virgin and martyr, and was honored as such by the Antiochene Church.

There is an opposing legend of Pelagia of Antioch, where she is said to have led the life of a prostitute at Antioch and to have been converted by a bishop named Nonnus. She was also called Margaret, "on account of the magnificence of the pearls for which she had so often sold herself". Well-known for her beauty, her wealth and her dissolute life, she passed Bishop St. Nonnus of Edessa. He had come to Antioch for a synod and was struck by her beauty, which he remarked upon and even defended her beauty to others who judged her.

The legend of this St. Pelagia, from the 4th to 5th century, records that she was a celebrated dancer and courtesan, who, in the full flower of her beauty and wayward behavior, was converted by the influence of the holy bishop St. Nonnus (Nonnus also meaning "saint" – so a double saint!), whom she heard preaching in front of a church which she was passing with her attendants and admirers. Seeking him out, she overcame his pious objection by her tears of genuine penitence, and was baptized.

The *Great Horologion*, also known as the *Book of Hours*, which provides the fixed portions of the Daily Cycle of services in the Eastern Orthodox Church, says of Pelagia, "This Saint was a prominent actress of the city of Antioch, and a pagan, who lived a life of unrestrained prodigality and led many to perdition." Like Hypatia, she was a pagan. "Instructed and baptized by a certain bishop named Nonnus, she renounced material things, including the large fortune she had accumulated as a courtesan, all of which she gave away to the poor upon her conversion."

It goes on, "After her baptism by Nonnus, she departed to the Mount of Olives near Jerusalem, where she lived as a recluse, feigning to be a eunuch called Pelagius. She lived in such holiness and repentance that within three or four years she was deemed worthy to repose in an odour of sanctity, in the middle of the fifth century. Her tomb on the Mount of Olives has been a place of pilgrimage ever since."

Like the stories of the Penitent Magdalene as a reformed prostitute, Pelagia, who is a chaste young virgin in some versions, is in others a wanton sinner, who is only redeemed by her intense penitence. If you distill the meaning of the story, Nonnus rescued Pelagia from, according to his own ascetic sensibilities, the "abominations" of life in Antioch, which included the Byzantine standards of wealth, pomp, and spectacle. Nonnus' example helped restored Pelagia to pious and ascetic sanctity on the Mount of Olives in the Holy City, near the later cave-church of Mary.

The various stories bring to mind a cartoonish image of innumerable figures from various factions of Christianity surreptitiously carrying off relics from one location to another, followed by the promotion of a folktale, a hagiography (she's a saint, she's a sinner, she's a harlot, she's a monk – but how can a woman be a monk?) defending the ideology, the opposing religio-political viewpoints behind the action. Each faction abducting the relics, or, if not that, at least the perspective on the relics for their own purposes. While they cannot be taken as literal truths, they are valuable for pointing out the "truths" of a particular belief system or viewpoint, of a particular religious faction or region.

In the legends of St. Marina and St. Pelagia, we see connections to the Midrashic writings on the "Roman soldier." Pelagia chose death rather than be dishonored by soldiers. Marina, accused of wanton behavior by someone who had, actually, consorted with "a soldier," suffered silently. The legends paint these saints as ascetics, living, after their conversion, like the Desert Fathers, in a cave, or grotto.

The depiction of Pelagia, of Mary of Egypt, and even of the Penitent Magdalene, may have some basis in the Augustine teachings on Original Sin. Painting Mary Magdalene as a repentant sinner, may be nothing more than the insistence on the idea that we are all sinners – that no human is born spotless and immaculate – that only Jesus was without sin.

There is an interesting detail in one story of the courtesan, Pelagia. In the *Life of St. Pelagia the Harlot*, it states that, "suddenly there passed by in front of us the foremost actress of Antioch, the star of the local theatre. She was seated on a donkey and accompanied by a great and fanciful procession. She seemed to be clothed in nothing but gold and pearls and other precious stones. Even her feet were covered with gold and pearls." One is reminded of the bejewelled relics of the catacomb saints, or of the bejewelled head of St. Euphemia, highly honored by the Templars.

In a similar story of Pelagia/Margarita, written by James (Jacob) of the Church of Heliopolis, it states that perfumed and "immodestly bareheaded", the outlines of her body were "clearly visible" beneath her gold cloth, pearls, and precious stones, which ran from her bare shoulders to her feet.[155] She was surrounded by a "worldly crowd", as judged by the clergy.

What image does this description bring to mind? What were the religious customs of Byzantine Christianity at the time? Certainly, the Imperials were often involved in great, opulent and regular processions through the city, they, themselves, dressed in royal robes and carrying gold-filigreed icons, as well as pearl-and-gold-covered relics. Was this the gold and the pearls for which the ascetic monks accused her of "selling herself"?

It continues, "The worldly crowd could not get enough of their beauty and attractiveness. As they passed by us the air was filled with the scent of musk and other most delicious perfumes, but when the bishops saw her passing by so immodestly, with her head bare, and the outlines of her body clearly visible, nothing over her shoulders as well as her head, and yet the object of such adulation, they all fell silent, groaned and sighed, and averted their eyes as if being forced to witness some grave sin." A bare-headed, female – shocking to them! And perhaps even moreso with this particular woman. According to Paul, a woman dishonors her head if she prays or prophesies without a covering on her head. What woman is always depicted with a veil over her head - "The Living Ark of God"?

It is not a great stretch to interpret this as a Byzantine-style ceremony, complete with finery and jewels, as well as perfumes, perhaps of frankincense and myrhh, such as were used in Byzantine religious rites. The rich and regal ceremony was a reflection of Imperial glory, and was known to be the practice with certain relics in Constantinople and elsewhere. The austere and strict sensibilities of the ascetic monks would, of course, have been offended and their persons quite horrified at the lavish and unseemly display of the Byzantine Churches. It is noted in this story, that Pelagia's conversion required the giving up of gold, and jewels, and the adornments of other costly things, considered to be "riches gained by sin."

After her baptism by Nonnus, it states that, while Pelagia slept "at the house of Romana, her spiritual mother, the devil came and awoke her and began to say to her, 'My lady Margarita (another name for the saint), what evil have I done you? Did I not adorn you with precious stones and with ornaments and beautiful robes? I beg you, tell me how I have offended you, and I shall immediately do whatever you command. Only turn not away from me, and do not make me a laughingstock.' Pelagia guarded herself with the sign of the Cross and said, 'My Lord Jesus Christ has snatched me out of your teeth and has prepared me to be His bride in His heavenly bridal chamber. He it is Who shall drive you away from me.' And the devil immediately vanished."

Her mother, *Romana*, which means "Roman woman," (to be read, perhaps, as "Empress" or, at least, a noble-woman) could not understand why Margarita should have to give up her rich adornments. This ostentation is the focus of Tertullian's chastisements in his treatise, *On the Apparel of Woman.* It is he who, early on, calls such things sinful, and the "preoccupation of harlots."

There are details in the story that bring to mind another female saint. When Pelagia begged St. Nonnus for forgiveness, and his permission for her to enter the Church, and be baptised, he said, "The holy canons say that a harlot may not be baptised unless she has sponsors who will guarantee that she will not return to her old way of life. When she heard this ruling of the bishops she threw herself on the floor again and seized the feet of Nonnus, washing them with her tears and wiping them with the hair of her head (as the woman does in *Luke* 7.38) saying that he must take her confession and help her to put away her evil deeds, "Unless you give me rebirth as a bride of Christ and present me to God, you are no more than an apostate and idolater."

After her baptism, she removed her white robes and put on the tunic of the monastics, and was not seen again in Antioch (where Chrysostom was from). "The holy lady Romana wept bitterly, but the holy bishop Nonnus said to her, 'Do not weep, my daughter, but rejoice with great joy, for Pelagia has chosen the better part (*Luke* 10.42) like Mary whom the Lord preferred to Martha in the Gospel.' Now Pelagia went to Jerusalem and built herself a cell on the mount of Olives and there she prayed to the Lord."

In the *Golden Legend*, there is a corollary story about Mary Magdalene delighting in material things. It tells of Lazarus' ownership of Jerusalem, Martha's ownership of Bethany, and Mary's ownership of the Palace of Magdalen. "Then when Magdalene abounded in riches, and because delight is fellow to riches and abundance of things; and for so much as she shone in beauty greatly, and in riches, so much the more she submitted her body to delight, and therefore she lost her right name, and was called customably a sinner." In this commentary, the riches, which gave her delight, were the source of her sin! But were the excesses of the Church being mocked in this legend?

It is not an overstatement to say that many of the tales of the Virgin saints made some reference to the life and hagiography of Mary Magdalene.

The heresy of Pelagianism, caused quite an uproar in the 4th to 5th century, when these stories were developing. Even Jerome felt the need to address the issue with his refutation of the beliefs. Pelagius opposed the teachings of Augustine, which taught that human nature was tainted by original sin and that mortal will is incapable of choosing between good or evil without special Divine aid. In Pelagianism, there was no "Original Sin", which according to Augustine, in the 4th century, made every new-born baby a sinner from birth.

Pelagianism was given the polemical slant of "Limited Depravity." (Who could possibly stand up for that?) Pelagianism views the role of Jesus as "setting a good example" for humanity (thus counteracting Adam's bad example) as well as providing an atonement for our sins. In short, humanity has full control, and thus full responsibility, for obeying the Gospel, in addition to full responsibility for every sin (the latter insisted upon by both proponents and opponents of Pelagianism). According to Pelagian doctrine, because humans are sinners by choice, sinners are therefore criminals – not victims –who need pardon, who need the atonement of Jesus Christ. Pelagianism did not impose a label of "sinner" on infants, or on those who had not committed sin through their own choices. It goes hand-in-hand with the later Islamic teachings about the Free Will of Jesus – which insisted that even Jesus was subject to free will choice and freely chose the higher path.

The Pelagians accused Augustine of departing from the accepted teaching of the Apostles and the Bible, charging that the doctrine of original sin amounted to Manichaeism, which taught that the flesh was, in itself, sinful. Certainly, Augustine had been a Manichaean before converting to mainstream Christianity. Unfortunately, Augustine's theological stance prevailed.

Thus, Pelagianism relates very directly to the story of Pelagia, whose tomb was originally high up on the Mount of Olives, where the Ascension of Jesus was also commemorated. This very interesting story calls Pelagia/Pelagius "His handmaiden," reflecting Mary's statement at the Annunciation, "Here I am, the handmaiden of the Lord." The story speaks of the removal of "precious relics" and the idea that women are also shown to be "hidden saints."

The stories of the Protomartyr, Thecla, found in "The Acts of St. Paul and Thecla", are believed to have been written in the 1st century. As the first female martyr of the faith, Thecla decisively rebuffed the advances of an admirer who thought she was a courtesan, effacing her beauty by cutting off her own hair. Thecla then donned the long, woolen *chiton* before going off to seek after Paul: "[S]he sewed her *chiton* into a cloak after the fashion of men." When she was pursued by wicked men, God protected her, and the rock opened a hiding place for her, and then closed up again to conceal her. Does this relate to the story of Pelagia?

"The blessed Thecla observing, saw the rock opened to as large a degree as that a man might enter in; she did as she was commanded, bravely fled from the vile crew, and went into the rock, which instantly so closed, that there was not any crack visible where it had opened."[156]

The title of Thecla's *vita* includes the phrase, "Equal to the Apostles". This is a title used for saints whose work in advancing the spread and assertion of Christianity to the world was outstanding. One of these saints, for whom the title is also used, is Mary Magdalene.

St. Thais appears in the *Vita Thaisis* ["Life of Thaïs"] by Dionysius Exiguus during the sixth or seventh century, and in medieval Latin text from Marbod of Rennes (d. 1123). Thaïs also appears in Greek martyrologies by Maurolychus and Greven. St. Thaïs the Repentant Harlot of the 4th century CE, lived in Alexandria, where her own mother placed her in a brothel at 17 years of age. Due to her great beauty she became wealthy from her sins. Saint Serapion (March 21), hearing about Thaïs' immoral way of life, was moved by God to try to convert her. He dressed as a soldier, gave her a gold piece, and followed her to her room. There, he took off his tunic, revealing his monastic robe. He counseled her earnestly on the awful consequences of sin, and the infinite mercy of God, who desires that all should be saved. Thaïs, moved by his words, ran to the town square, and much like the harlot, Pelagia, burned all the fine clothes and possessions that she had acquired through sin.

St. Thaïs went with Serapion to a women's monastery, where she remained secluded in her cell, beseeching God's mercy constantly, and only eating every other day. She lived in this way for three years, with a zeal that amazed all her monastic sisters. Serapion went to St. Anthony the Great to ask him if God had accepted Thaïs' repentance. Is this a figurative comment regarding relics? Since Anthony may well be a representation of Athanasius, who wrote Anthony's life story, one wonders what this narrative represents. Anthony and his brethren spent a night in prayer and received a vision in which they were assured that Thaïs had been found worthy of God's mercy. Which "brethren" might have held a council on whether to accept the penitence of the Harlot of Alexandria?

At the monastery, Serapion made the repentant saint leave her cell, though now she was dedicated to a life of repentant prayer. After spending only fifteen days in the common life of the monastery, the holy Thaïs "reposed in peace." Here, again, as with many stories of the virgin saints, the soldier finds his way into the story. The monk, dressed as a soldier redeems the sinner. How does this relate to stories of Yeshua ben Pantera, the illegitimate son of a Roman soldier?

What is the common thread in all of these stories? Were each of these stories skewed to a specific viewpoint, essentially, fictional rhetoric on doctrinal issues such as Free Will and Original Sin? Is it the same woman, inserted into doctrinal frameworks such as the penitent one (Original Sin), "the spotless one" (Immaculate Conception), the accused, but innocent and pious one (Grace), the reformed harlot (the ascetics speaking against the Byzantines), the redeemed one (who, in Pelagianism had the free will to turn from the sinfulness of the physical to the spiritual)?

What is the meaning of the metaphor of the dancing woman, the courtesan, the actress, the harlot? The original image of the woman dancing in celebration was Miriam, the highly honored sister of Moses. With the spectacle of Roman games and theatre, as well as pageantry of religious display, the dancing woman came to mean something else entirely. The very mention of dancing brought with it the image of paganism and harlotry.

The *Gospel of James* includes a notable early comment on dancing, from the priest, Simeon, on the presentation of Mary to the Temple, "The Lord hath magnified thy name among all generations: in thee in the latter days shall the Lord make manifest his redemption unto the children of Israel. And he made her to sit upon the third step of the altar. And the Lord put grace upon her and she danced with her feet and all tile house of Israel loved her ..."

THE PENITENT MAGDALENE

The concept of a Penitent Mary Magdalene became popularized in the western Church when Pope Gregory I (Gregory the Great) officially, in the 6th century, connected the stories of Mary Magdalene to Mary of Bethany, who anointed Jesus' feet, and the adulteress, who washed his feet with her tears and dried them with her unbound hair. (*Luke* 7:38) Gregory was, of course, an ascetic, and he certainly espoused a belief in the need for penance and penitence in overcoming the sins of the flesh, and especially, a belief in the idea of Original Sin as put forth by St. Augustine.

Eastern Christianity has always taught that Mary Magdalene was a virtuous, saintly woman her entire life. They never embraced the idea that she was a penitent sinner, as was proposed in the West from Gregory's time. The Byzantines also held Mary, the Mother of Jesus in highest regard - their liturgy and kontakions (hymn/prayer) elevating her to a level beyond all other saints. Did this create a backlash in the Western Church towards Mary Magdalene?

The Magdalene has traditionally, and consistently, been honored as a "Myrrh-bearer" (the women who brought funeral spices, perfumes, and ointments to Jesus' tomb after his death. They gave her the title of honor of "Equal to the Apostles".

She is given a higher title by certain theologians, including Rabanus Maurus and Saint Thomas Aquinas who called her *apostolorum apostola,* that is the "Apostle to the Apostles", because she announces to the apostles what in turn they will announce to the whole world – the miracle of the risen Christ.[157]

The mystical poems of *Song of Songs* 8:5 proclaim, "How worthy she is who rises from the desert bearing Torah and His Presence, clinging to her beloved." This woman is a type, often associated with Mary Magdalene as the Beloved Disciple.

Hippolytus, 3rd century Christian theologian, in his treatise *Commentary on the Song of Songs* quotes the poem, "I am black, but comely, O ye daughters of Jerusalem, as the tents of Kedar, as the curtains of Solomon. Look not upon me, because I am black, because the sun hath looked upon me: my mother's children [my brothers] were angry with me; they made me the keeper of the vineyards; but mine own vineyard have I not kept."

He writes, "Do not look (or gaze) upon me, because I have become dark, nor concerning this, that the sun despised me." He goes on to interpret, " 'He despised' on account of this, because she believed in him that she might be reconciled through repentance. For 'the sons of my mother have become enemies to me.' The prophets invited me without weariness, 'Return to the law of Moses.'"

Hippolytus continues, "He made me keeper of the vine, thinking to ruin (or corrupt) me concerning the acceptance of the coming ones. I have not cared for my own vine[yard]." And because I did [not take care of my own people, for the people] of Israel is said to be a vine, come, Isaiah, testify and say, "The house of Israel is a vine of the Lord Sabaoth. I *stood* and was hoping that it would bear grape(s), and it produced thorns instead."

He states that the "she" in question was disappointed by Israel, which, instead of bearing grapes, "produced thorns." This line brings to mind the line "...a lily among thorns." This line seems to mean that Mary was holy amongst all other women. It also is reminiscent of Theophilus, after all his Anti-Origenist antics, suddenly letting the issue go by saying that he could "cull the roses from the thorns."

Hippolytus explains, "Do not look (or gaze) upon me, because I anointed Jesus' feet, and the adulteress, who washed his feet with her tears and dried them with her unbound hair." Who does "she" refer to? This would seem to be commentary on the shift from the teachings of John the Baptist, in accordance with Mosaic Law, to the teachings of one who called such laws unnecessary, and even a hindrance to salvation.

The statement that her brothers were angry with her is reminiscent of a very interesting comment in the *Gospel of Philip*, "Mary is the virgin whom no power defiled. She is a great anathema to the Hebrews, who are the apostles and the apostolic men."

Nowhere in the canonical gospels is there any hint of discord towards Mother Mary. However, many of the Gnostic texts make no bones about the fact that Mary Magdalene was at odds with Peter and other of the Apostles. We might note that Paul was also a great anathema to the Hebrews, and to the Jewish-Christians. Peter and James had little interest in inviting the Gentiles into their fold, or in lessening the strictures for Gentiles' conversion to the faith. When the Jews tried to stone him, Paul devoted himself to a ministry to the Gentiles.

In the 6th century, Pope Gregory, paints the Magdalene as a sinner, saved only by her penitence. It appears that he held a belief in Original Sin, but not in the Immaculate Conception, a doctrine which developed as a response to the concept of Original Sin.

Thus, in *Homilia in Nativitate*, he maintained, "For He (Christ) alone was born holy, who, in order that He might overcome 'this condition of corruptible nature', was not conceived after the manner of men." (That is, in a supernatural conception, and not a human one.) He does not speak of the Virgin Mary in these terms, as being spotless or sinless.

Gregory lived in retirement in the monastery of St. Andrew, before being elected pope, and his great austerities during this time are recorded by biographers, many of whom attribute his poor health to the strict penances that he practiced early on in the monastic life. His depiction of Mary Magdalene as a penitent sinner, reflected his own harshly penitent lifestyle and would, strangely, go hand in hand with his ideas of the appropriate lifestyle of his own office as the head of the church. It is Pope Gregory who connected her with the adulteress in *John*, Chapter 8. Was it necessary, in his theological methodology, to give a concrete example of her being subject to sin, and needful of forgiveness and penitence?

Gregory's papacy was during a period of great upheaval in Italy. In 542 the so-called "Plague of Justinian" swept through the provinces of the empire, including Italy, devastating the region. During Gregory's childhood, Emperor Justinian had built a glorious edifice in Jerusalem for Mary, "the Mother of God."

It seems that the more grandiose the celebration of Mary by Byzantine emperors and Christian clergy, the more Gregory found it necessary to propose the sinful humanity of Mary Magdalene, seemingly, in proportion to the praise of Mary in the East. His accusations toward Mary influenced later texts, such as Voragine's *Golden Legend.*

In the 13th century texts of the *Golden Legend*, Mary's sinfulness was described by Voragine, "... and for so much as she shone in beauty greatly, and in riches, so much the more she submitted her body to delight, and therefore she lost her right name, and was called customably a sinner." Her sinfulness, in this tract, is attributed to her enjoyment of the material realm, and not, particularly, to wanton behavior. Here, bodily pleasure and even beauty are equated with sinfulness!

Byzantine practices involved honoring Jesus and Mary as they would honor royalty – with rich, sumptuous clothing and jewels, perfumes, music and fanfare. Is this story in the *Golden Legend* the perspective of ascetics, criticizing Byzantine pageantry? Or since the *Golden Legend* also makes Mary Magdalene royalty, perhaps it is meant to indict her early enjoyment of rich living – like the Imperials?

The story mentions that Mary Magdalene was named for the castle of Magdalo, where she lived with her brother Lazarus, and her sister, Martha. This indicates that Voragine considered Mary Magdalene and Mary of Bethany to be one and the same. He states, "For tofore her conversion she was abiding guilty by obligation to everlasting pain. In the conversion she was garnished by armour of penance..."

Mary Magdalene's "conversion" is not commonly mentioned elsewhere. What are the details of her conversion – or are they given elsewhere, under a different name? After her conversion, "she was praised by overabundance of grace." This is a telling statement. The Magdalene was human and therefore must be guilty of sin, but, as this medieval legend proposes, through penance, she was forgiven and became filled with grace. (The Virgin, in the Ave Maria prayer, is said to be "full of Grace.")

Within this story, is, perhaps, the key to one of the many great confusions and obfuscations of the faith. According to Augustine, the human form was intrinsically sinful. His teaching on Original Sin necessitated a new doctrine of Mary's Immaculate Conception. She must be made to be the only human being who was without sin.

Mary Magdalene, on the other hand was clearly described as a sinner, from the time of Pope Gregory. The loosened hair of Mary Magdalene is so often seen as an emblem of her wanton character. Some theologians consider the woman in the *Gospel of Luke*, who weeps on Jesus' feet and wipes them with her hair to be a prostitute, because her hair was loose in public. Jewish culture in Jesus' day considered a woman's loose hair in public to have sexual connotations, according to the *Journal of Biblical Literature*.

Certainly, if Mary Magdalene was John, then she would have dressed as a man in that role (for example: as depicted in Da Vinci's "Last Supper"). To wear a veil would have revealed her to be a woman.

Ignoring the testimony of the other three Gospels, the Church has allowed Mary Magdalene to be slandered as a prostitute for nearly two millennia, thereby stealing her power and silencing her voice. In 1969 the Roman Catholic calendar of Saints' feast days was revised, separating Mary of Bethany from Mary "Magdalene"--thereby splitting the role of the anointing woman in two.

The rabbinical satire in the story of Mary M'gaddla painted her as a hairdresser, seen to be one step above prostitution. Often, in paintings, her long tresses barely cover her nakedness, which is also given to indicate her unholy nature, though some narratives state that her hair, miraculously grew long to cover her in modesty and piousness. The depiction of the "Hairy Man" of legend, is said to be an indication of his holiness – the hairs representing rays of light. He is a representation of the Sun God or of enlightenment, as with Elijah, John the Baptist, Iron John, and others. Some scholars equate the "hairy" depictions of the Magdalene as related to this legend.

There was no significant contradiction to Pope Gregory's claims until 1517, when, on the brink of the Protestant Reformation, the leading French Renaissance humanist Jacques Lefèvre d'Étaples published a treatise entitled, *De Maria Magdalena et triduo Christi disceptatio* (Disputation on Mary Magdalene and the Three Days of Christ), in which he argued against the conflation of Mary Magdalene, Mary of Bethany (who would seem to be Mary Magdalene in many texts), and the unnamed sinner in *Luke*.

This book stirred a flurry of books and pamphlets in response, the vast majority of which opposed d'Étaples. In 1521, the theology faculty of the Sorbonne formally condemned the ideas of his book as heretical, and debate died down, overtaken by the larger issues raised by Martin Luther. Pope

Gregory's ideas won out in the end.

Did Augustine's teachings lead to the dividing of one into two Mary's - a split necessitated by the uniting of the human form (sinful, as Augustine taught), with the divine? Was it at this point that division of identities was needed? When Mary was called the holy and blessed one? The bare-headed tresses would, necessarily, become covered by the veil (necessary, just as when the Holy Spirit was in the Tabernacle), when the Blessed Virgin was described as "The Godbearer".

When Moses was transfigured on Mt. Sinai and came down from the mountain, having witnessed God in the "burning bush", he had a need to cover his head, for his radiant face frightened his Jewish followers. The Apostle Paul said that a woman should have her head covered when prophesying. As the Ark of the New Covenant, the Blessed Mother's head is always covered – like the Ark in the Temple – necessarily "veiling" the indwelling light of God from the view of humans.

MARY OF EGYPT, HARLOT-SAINT

The *Vita of St. Mary of Egypt*, purportedly written by Sophronius, Bishop of Jerusalem, begins, "It is good to hide the secret of a king, but it is glorious to reveal and preach the works of God" (*Tobit* 12:7) So said the Archangel Raphael to Tobit when he performed the wonderful healing of his blindness. Actually, not to keep the secret of a king is perilous and a terrible risk, but to be silent about the works of God is a great loss for the soul. And I (says St. Sophronius), in writing the life of St. Mary of Egypt, am afraid to hide the works of God by silence".[158]

This is an interesting introduction that makes one wonder if, indeed, it was written by Sophronius. Had he been silent? Might it perhaps have been written by one who wanted to reveal something that Sophronius had not?

The Egyptian monks were descended from the early "Desert Fathers," whose practices were extremely ascetic, and denying of the pleasures of the flesh. There was a sect in Egypt that revered a very ascetic "St. Mary of Egypt." There is a church and following, in modern times, that still honors her.

The icons of St. Mary from the Church of St. Mary of Egypt, greatly resemble an only slightly-feminized version of John the Baptist. She appears wild-eyed, wild-haired, with a gaunt face, wrapped in a cloak leaving her legs and arms bare; often her flat chest as well. She looks like a man. Adding to that her extremely ascetic lifestyle, her story is very much like that of St.

John the Baptist. Though there was no such term during his time, this is the classic image of the "Desert Fathers," the ascetic monks who lived in great poverty and deprivation during the 2nd to 3rd centuries CE.

In *Acts of Philip VIII*, Jesus tells Mary to change her clothes, because the summer dress she is wearing is feminine. She is to wear the clothing of an ascetic, like Philip, remove the signs of her femininity, and take the appearance of a man, as it would be dangerous to travel and complete her mission in feminine dress.

Robert Graves speculates in *The White Goddess* (1948) that Mary of Egypt can be identified with "Mary Gipsy",[159] a virgin with a blue robe and a pearl necklace, also known as Marina, Marian or "Maria Stellis"(Star of the Sea). He connects her to traditions of Aphrodite, the love goddess from the sea.

Could the reformed sinner of the Church of St. Mary of Egypt possibly be related to the highly praised Mary of the Eastern Church? Could this be a representation of the same woman, the virgin, who is honored in the Gospels? It was the Egyptian monks who had the confrontation with other monks at the Second Council of Ephesus. These monks were at odds with Theodoret and others on the subject of the nature of Christ, as well as the nature of Mary (downgrading her title to Christotokos, and not Theotokos). It would make sense that they would want to humanize her, perhaps, even to the point of degrading her from Mother of God, or God-bearer, to a sinful and very human woman who was redeemed only by her penitence and humility. St. Mary of Egypt's nature seems closer to that of the Penitent Magdalene.

Was there metaphor involved? Could the narrative of the life of St. Mary of Egypt be an allusion to relics that were kept in a cave? Could it be an allegory of an earlier saint who disguised herself as a man in order to follow a holy path?

From one of the Dormition narrative's we have only the grave wrappings left behind after the Virgin Mary "falls asleep", or in other words, dies. "Having opened the grave, they found in it only the grave wrappings and were thus convinced of the bodily ascent of the Most Holy Virgin Mary to Heaven." This story seems to say that Mary, like Jesus, bodily ascended.

What is the meaning of depictions of Mary of Egypt as being naked, prompting Zosimus to cover her nakedness with his cloak? Is this the beginning of the traditions of The Penitent Magdalene, also depicted as naked in representations of her as the penitent?

In a pair of panels painted by Quentin Metsys/Massys, in the early 16th century, he gives us almost a mirror image of two female figures – but one painting is of the Magdalene and the other is of Mary of Egypt. One can only distinguish them by their accoutrements of the alabaster jar and the three loaves of bread. We might, first of all, question the connection of the *Penitent Mary Magdalene* and *Penitent Mary of Egypt*.

Certainly, we cannot miss the artist's meaning in these very similar paintings. Yes, Mary Magdalene has her alabaster jar, and Mary of Egypt has her three loaves of bread, but otherwise one would be inclined to think that these are paintings of the same person. Some art historians have suggested that these may have been side panels to a major work, forming an altarpiece triptych, which would make sense. One wonders what the central image would have been? Almost certainly another "Mary image". Perhaps, to match the side panel's background, Mary in her grotto-cave, a Metsys "Madonna of the Rocks" destroyed, plastered over, or otherwise hidden during the iconoclastic period?

Interestingly, there is an opulently dressed Virgin, with the same long wavy hair in Metsys' *Virgin with Child and Three Angels*, at the Museum of Fine Arts of Lyon, France. It is displayed as a central triptych panel with the side panels missing.

A 14th century manuscript of the life of St. Mary Magdalen in Magdalen College, Oxford, rejects the story that she, like Mary of Egypt, lived out her years as a desert ascetic. The manuscript is attributed to the 9th century archbishop of Mainz, Rabanus Maurus (an attribution now largely rejected, but the 9th century dating still supported). It states regarding the Magdalene: "That after Our Savior's Ascension she should have fled at once into the Arabian desert, should have lived there unknown to all, without clothing, in a cave, and that she should have seen no one; that, visited by a priest, she should have asked him for his garments, and suchlike details, are as many false stories, borrowed by fable-mongers from the story of the Egyptian penitent."[160]

In Giotto's painting of *The Hermit Zosimus Giving a Cloak to Magdalene*, a fresco from Magdalene Chapel, the Magdalene, in the nakedness of the penitent, is shown living in an anchorite cave. Giotto's Zosimus gives his cloak to *this* Mary – no mistake, no confusion – a purposeful co-mingling of identities.

Above the monumental tombs of the Kings that still stand on the eastern side of the Cedron Valley of Jerusalem, there is also one higher up the mountain, from 9 to 7 BCE - a cube-like tomb which once had a pyramidal top (like that atop the tomb of Zechariah) that was cut away by the Romans. This tomb was known as the "Tomb of the Daughter of Pharaoh".

There is an interesting addition to the idea of a mingling of the resting place of both Pelagia and St. Mary of Egypt, in *The Travels of Sir*

John Mandeville. Mandeville, also known as John de Long, writing of the holy places of Jerusalem in the late 14th century, speaks of the place of the ascension of Jesus, on the Mount of Olives, with the nearby chapel of the *Pater Noster* (the Lord's Prayer), and a little further on, "there is nigh a church of Saint Mary Egyptian, and there she lieth in a tomb." [161]

ST. ZOSIMUS

What we know of St. Zosimus comes from the hagiography in the *Vita of St. Mary of Egyp*t, written by Sophronius of Jerusalem. Zosimus tells the hermit, St. Mary, "A hidden wisdom and a secret treasure -- what profit is there in them? Tell me all, I implore you, for not out of vanity or for self-display will you speak but to reveal the truth to me, an unworthy sinner. I believe in God, for whom you live and whom you serve. I believe that He led me into this desert so as to show me His ways in regard to you." [162]

The story, according to Sophronius, gives that St. Zosimus was born in the second half of the 5th century, in the reign of Emperor Theodosius the Younger. Zosimus joined a monastery in Palestine at a very young age, eventually, earning a reputation as a great elder and ascetic (much like the life of Sophronius). At the age of fifty-three, by then a *hieromonk*, he moved to a very strict monastery located in the wilderness close to the Jordan River, where he spent the remainder of his life. The wilderness, near the Jordan River has connections to John the Baptist.

Zosimas' life story is detailed by Sophronius. The account focuses mostly on the monk's encounter with St. Mary of Egypt. It was customary for all of the monks in his monastery to go out into the desert for the forty days of Great Lent, devoting themselves to fasting and prayer, until Palm Sunday. While wandering in the desert, Zosimas encountered a woman who was living a life of extreme ascetism as penance. This woman, St. Mary of Egypt, was withered, sunburned, and naked until Zosimus gave her his cloak. After something of a contest of who could be more humble, she told him her life story and asked him to meet her the next year on Holy Thursday on the banks of the Jordan, in order to bring her Holy Communion, which promise he fulfilled. In the third year, he went again to the desert, but discovering that she had died, he buried her.

St. Sophronius claimed to have based his work on oral traditions he had heard from monks in Israel. His *Vita on St. Mary of Egypt* is traditionally read as a part of the Matins of the Great Canon of St. Andrew of Crete; both Catholic and Eastern Orthodox Churches honor her as a saint on the fifth

Thursday of Great Lent.

In a similar way, we might say, Athanasius, "the Immortal One", wrote a biography of St. Anthony, whose beliefs and lifestyle aligned very closely with his own. Was "Saint Zosimas" a glorified version of Sophronius, himself?

Jerome found it important to clarify that Paul of Thebes (and not Anthony, as Athanasius claimed) was "The First Hermit." This debate may well have represented the earliest division within the Church, the two "trophies" of the earliest saints in Rome (with Anthony as the Petrine leader, and Paul, of course, as the Pauline). According to Jerome, this first "Desert Father", Paul of Thebes, fled to the Theban desert at the age of 16, during the persecution of Decius and Valerianus (around 250 CE), taking refuge in a cave at the foot of a rocky mountain. There was also a palm tree, and a nearby spring, hidden amongst the rocks. St. Paul purportedly remained in that cave for the rest of his life - almost a hundred years. Jerome cites stories that circulated claiming that Paul "was a man living in an underground cave with flowing hair down to his feet," and other fabulous tales.

Like Zosimas, who was born in the latter half of the 6th century, Sophronius, who was of Arab descent, was born in 560 CE, in Damascus. (Sophronius' dear friend, St. John Moschus was said to have been born in 550 CE, also in Damascus.) Sophronius was the Patriarch of Jerusalem from 634 until his death in Jerusalem in 638. It gets even more interesting when you add that Zosimas and Sophronius (and Moschus) were contemporaries of Muhammad, whose birth is given as 570 CE, and whose ascension is recorded as occurring in 632 CE, two years before Sophronius turned Jerusalem over to the conquering Saracens.

A teacher of rhetoric, Sophronius became an ascetic in Egypt in about 580 and then entered the monastery of St. Theodosius near Bethlehem. Traveling to monastic centers in Asia Minor, Egypt, and Rome, he accompanied the Byzantine chronicler, St. John Moschus, who dedicated to him his celebrated tract on the religious life, *Leimõn ho Leimõnon,* "The Spiritual Meadow" (and whose feast day in the Eastern Orthodox Church, is shared with Sophronius'). On the death of St. John Moschus in Rome in 619, Sophronius accompanied the saint's body back to Jerusalem for monastic burial.

LILITH AND THE ANCIENT GODDESSES

In *Acts* 19:35, it speaks of an object of interest, "Men of Ephesus, what man is there after all who does not know that the city of the Ephesians is guardian of the temple of the great Artemis and of the image which fell down from heaven? [ie. a meteor]" This was the response in *Acts* 19, which speaks of an Ephesian mob attacking Saint Paul's traveling companions after merchants became fearful that Paul's preaching would harm the sale of religious icons related to the temple. A significant disturbance ensued, with Ephesians chanting, "Great is Artemis of the Ephesians!"

Meteoric rocks were often given a place of honoring in ancient temples. In this case, the temple of Artemis became an oracle-temple, where prophecy and divination were practiced, which seems to have a connection to a meteoric "prophecy stone", like the one in the Phyrgianum of Cybele, in Rome. These stones were connected to cults of the Goddess in the Roman Empire.

The Temple of Artemis (also known as the Temple of Diana) appears in a narrative in the 2nd century apocryphal *Acts of John,* considered to refer to John of Zebedee (the Apostle), though probably written by one of his followers, where John's prayers for the exorcism of demons at the Temple of Artemis caused the altar stone to crack, "Of a sudden the altar of Artemis split in many pieces... and half the temple fell down," instantly converting the Ephesians, who were awe-struck at the sight, and wept, prayed or took flight.[163]

In the *Syriac History of John* it is, again, John the Apostle and Evangelist who brought down the Temple of Artemis. However, in an *encomium* on the Virgin, Cyril of Alexandria accuses none other than John Chrysostom of having destroyed the Artemision - a very interesting addition to this set of Christian figures that were mingled in this same accusation. Was this a second, much later occurance?

The temple was burned or partially destroyed a number of times over the centuries, but its final destruction was brought about in 401 CE by a mob, led by none other than St. John Chrysostom, who was the new archbishop in the city of Ephesus at that time. This signified the end of pagan worship at the temple, and the victory of Judeo-Christian beliefs in the city. Stones from the destroyed temple were used to build other Christian churches, and eight of its green marble columns were, eventually, used in the Hagia Sophia in Constantinople, one of the largest Christian cathedrals at that time.

Goddesses were part of the ancient Jewish traditions, long before the time of the One Father God. Lilith is often described as a kind of "she-devil", but in the more positive portrayals of Lilith, she was previously viewed as the embodiment of the Goddess, a designation shared with other Goddesses that some consider to be her counterparts: Inanna, Ishtar, Asherah, Anath and Isis.

Asherah was a goddess of ancient worship by Semitic tribes which included Akkadians, Phoenicians, Hebrews, and Arabs. She was the "mother of the Gods" in Ugaritic texts. Her son, Yam was the God of the Sea. Asherah was known as "she who walks on the sea." She was connected to trees in stories and images. Many see the use of wood in the Holy of Holies of the Temple, and the decoration of carved fruits, and the pomegranates embroidered on the hems of priestly garments to be a nod to her ancient honoring. She was spoken of in *Jeremiah* as "the queen of heaven". *(Jeremiah* 44:19).

Lilith's role within medieval Jewish literature makes her not a goddess, but the first wife of Adam. There seem to be two different creation stories in Jewish writings. In *Genesis*, Chapter 2, verse 21, we are familiar with the story of God creating Eve from one of Adam's ribs. "And the LORD God caused a deep sleep to fall upon Adam, and he slept: and he took one of his ribs, and closed up the flesh instead thereof; Then the rib which the LORD God had taken from man He made into a woman, and He brought her to the man."

However, in Chapter 1, verse 27, it states that "So God created man in his own image, in the image of God he created him, male and female he created them." Some interpret this to refer to the creation of Adam and his first wife, Lilith, who was created in the same way that Adam was - that is, from the dust, and not from Adam's rib or side. The expansion on the story of Lilith seems to have developed not in biblical texts, but centuries later.

Eliezer Segal proposes that the Lilith myth originated in the *Alphabet of Ben Sira (or Sirach)*, written somewhere between 700 and 1000 CE.[164] This treatise is undoubtedly a satire, perhaps written in response to the *Alphabet of Rabbi Akiva*, which met with some opposition by the 10th century due to issues of anthropomorphism (giving human qualities to God) in that text.

Segal considers the Alphabet of Ben Sira to be a satire of the customs of the Jewish people, though it came to be an accepted text by the Jewish mystics of medieval Germany. This text is a highly complex and sophisticated writing with lots of hidden meanings.[165] In the satirical slant of *Ben Sira*, the woman who wished to be honored as an equal to her husband is conflated with the "*Ardat Lili*" – vampire-like spirits (resembling the *succubus*) that were said to seduce men and bear them demonic children. This was a deliberate intertwining of the two stories to demonize women who sought equality with men. (It also demonizes, in a sense, the natural sexual impulses and experiences of men's fantasies, arousal, and "nocturnal emissions".

Though Lilith's story points to Sumerian origins, she is more likely created from Sumerian beliefs combined with Jewish folk legend, and perhaps satire of Jewish culture. Some sources connect her to the Assyrian storm demon, Lilitu.

Istahar is derived from the Babylonian Goddess, Ishtar – the Queen of Heaven – sometimes identified with Virgo (the Virgin). The Greek writer Aratus, from the early third century BCE, tells how Justice, a daughter of Dawn, ruled mankind virtuously in the Golden Age; but when the Silver and Bronze ages brought greed and slaughter among them, she exclaimed: "Alas, for this evil race!" and mounted into Heaven, where she became the constellation Virgo. Apollodorus recounts the story of Orion's advances on the seven virgin Pleaides, who escaped his embraces by transforming into stars. Popular Egyptian belief identified Orion, the constellation which became Shemhazai, with the "soul of Osiris."

In the *Legends of the Jews*, the maiden, Istehar, uses the Ineffable name of God to escape sexual oppression: "When the angels came to earth, and beheld the daughters of men in all their grace and beauty, they could not restrain their passion. Shemhazai saw a maiden named Istehar, and he lost his heart to her. She promised to surrender herself to him, if first he taught her the Ineffable Name, by means of which he raised himself to heaven. He assented to her condition. But once she knew it, she pronounced the Name, and herself ascended to heaven, without fulfilling her promise to the angel. God said, "Because she kept herself aloof from sin, we will place her among the seven stars, that men may never forget her," and she was put in the constellation of the Pleiades." In *The Jewish Gates*, it was Istahar, who was set in the constellation of Draco (which is to say, the Pleiades.

There is a similar myth about the Goddess, Astraea. "For the Semites, for example, [Virgo] was Ishtar, Queen of the Stars, a concept that migrated through Greece to become attached to the brightest of the planets known as Aphrodite to the Greeks and Venus to the Romans. But the Greeks knew Virgo as Astraea, daughter of Zeus and Themis. She was Goddess of Justice, living on earth with the other gods during the Golden Age. As time went on and men grew wicked, Astraea fled to the starry zodiac where she still resides right next to the Scales of Justice, the constellation Libra." -- (Astro Utah)

There is an interesting connection to a tale of Lady Wisdom, summarized in a poem in an old apocalyptic text, the *Similitudes of Enoch* from the 1st century BCE:

"*Wisdom could not find a place in*
which she could dwell,
but a place was found in the heavens.

Then Wisdom went out to dwell with
the children of the people,
but she found no dwelling place.
Wisdom returned to her place
and she settled among the angels."

Mary is often called the Queen of the Angels, or the Queen of Heaven, which may have been intended to connect her with Lady Wisdom.

In the Orthodox Church and the Roman Catholic Church, the feminine personification of divine wisdom as Holy Wisdom (Hagía Sophía) can refer either to Jesus Christ the Word of God (as in the dedication of the church of Hagia Sophia in Constantinople) or to the Holy Spirit. References to Sophia in *Koine* Greek translations of the Hebrew Bible translate to the Hebrew term *Chokmah*.

It seems that Lilith may be a less sympathetic version, from the Orthodox Jewish perspective, a rebuttal, perhaps, of the many narratives of the woman/Goddess that was lusted after by any number of the Gods, and who evaded their advances by escaping to the heavens, where she is, rather, cast out and vilified.

Charles Leland associated Aradia with Lilith: Aradia, says Leland, is Herodias, who was regarded in *stregheria* (witchcraft) folklore as being associated with Diana as chief of the witches. Leland further notes that Herodias is a name that comes from West Asia, where it denoted an early form of Lilith.

This makes for a complicated picture, because it was Herodias (daughter of Herodias) that asked for the head of John the Baptist. Is the entire story about the beheading of John the Baptist an allegory? If so, the allegation could indicate the "demotion" of the Baptist ("I must decrease, but he must increase") through his beheading at the request of a wanton woman. If this is an allegory, then who does it represent? Who caused John to no longer be the "head" of the radical sect?

Some Rabbinical teachings propose that there were two Eves, one that was not suitable for Adam and another that was. This later became the basis of the story of Lilith, Adam's first wife, who was not obedient enough for him. Other newer interpretations depict her as powerful and beautiful – the true "first woman," an independent and free virgin who would not submit to Adam's (man's/patriarchy's) attempts at sexual domination. After leaving both the first male and Eden, she was replaced by a more dependent and less equal Eve (correlating to a more dependent and less equal Mary?). Eve was not "made" from the Earth like Adam (and like Lilith) but from a rib of the man Adam.

Lilith is said to be but one of twenty names by which the first woman was known, each name containing a "secret of sexual mysticism". These "secrets" most likely represent the erotic teachings and sexual techniques that were taught to initiates and worshippers in the temples of Inanna, Ishtar and Astarte, in matriarchal times. The women were temple virgins, or *hierodules*, which meant, not that they were non-sexual, or conversely, that they were prostitutes, but simply that they were independent of men. Their practices and teachings would, in later times, have been seen as a threat to patriarchal leaders who wished to make woman into a dependent, monogamous servant of their households.

Jewish folk tradition associates Lilith with long hair, which is a symbol of dangerous feminine seductive power in both Jewish and Islamic cultures. Some later traditions associate Lilith with witchcraft. The *ben Sirach* text (c. 700 – 1000 CE) asserts that Lilith is given access to possessing women by entering them through mirrors, long associated with Venus and Aphrodite, Iaso, the healer, and other Goddesses from more matriarchal times. This would have made women afraid of mirrors.

It is possible that the story took a negative turn after the time of Christ, the first accounts of the ministry of Mary Magdalene, and the growing veneration of the Holy Virgin. Lilith was described as having no milk in her breasts and as unable to bear any children - a horrifying status within Judaic culture. Could this be a satire of the Ever-Virgin maiden?

The 13th Century Kabbalistic writings of Rabbi Isaac ben Jacob Alfasi ha-Cohen, state that Lilith refused to be subservient to Adam. She left the Garden of Eden, and, after she mated with archangel Samael (who is given a demonic nature), would not return. What is the greater meaning of this mystical narrative? From the Jewish perspective, was this a reference to the merging of the "Holy Spirit" with a woman, a beautiful young maiden? If they didn't believe in the story of this union of divinity and humanity, would they propose that the spirit was a satanic demon?

The earliest writings about Lilith come from around the 5th to the 8th century CE, and the incantation bowls from around the 6th century CE, which was, coincidentally, the time period of Islam's origins. Is Lilith a demonization of the one who was highly honored in many sects, including the Islamic faith, which began to flourish soon after the first stories of Lilith were being told?

In the Goddess religions, the snake was seen as the embodiment of wisdom, often symbolizing the awakening energies of the higher bodies of an initiate on the path to divine consciousness. In modern times, this is still the symbolism used within Hindu teachings on the awakening and rising of the “kundalini,” sacred life force, through serpentine channels from the sacrum to the crown, connecting one to the celestial realms. The kundalini is often described as “liquid fire” or “liquid light,” which, in these teachings, represents the energy of the Goddess and enlightenment. Many religions seem to try to suppress this spiritual life force energy, which is the doorway to enlightenment.

In the narrative of Moses, leading the Israelites through the desert, he is instructed by God to, “Make thee a fiery serpent, and set it upon a pole: and it shall come to pass, that every one that is bitten, when he looketh upon it, shall live.”

The *Companion Bible* states that the Hebrew word rendered "serpent" in *Genesis* 3:1 is *Nachash* meaning “a shining one.” In Chaldee it means brass or copper, because of its shining surface. In the same way *Seraph*, in Isaiah 6:2,6, means a burning one; because the serpents mentioned in Numbers 21 were burning, in the poison of their bite, they were called *Seraphim* (*Saraphim*). But when the LORD said unto Moses, "Make thee a fiery serpent" (*Numbers* 21:8), He said, "Make thee a *Seraph*", and, in obeying this command, we read in verse 9, "Moses made a *Nachash* of brass". *Nachash* is thus used as being interchangeable with *Seraph*."

The word *seraph*, is related to *seraphim*, the beings closest to the throne of God, in Christian teachings. They are described as “the burning ones,” and are considered the highest rank of angels within Christian angelic hierarchy (in Judaism, the fifth rank). They continually sing praises to the Lord God of Hosts.

Combining the fiery presence of the *seraphim* and the coiling, fiery energies of the *kundalini*, some connect the symbolism of the serpent in the Garden of Eden to the teachings of the Goddess traditions, which was, originally, a teaching of awakening one’s own inherent God connections (becoming immortal). However, by the time of the writing of the *Book of Genesis*, there were seen to be penalties for accessing the serpent wisdom, that is, Divine Consciousness, enlightenment, and immortality.

This seems to be related to the initial movement within Hebrew teachings, away from the “matriarchal” inclusive and communal sharing of wisdom to the “patristic” seeking of individual or hierarchical power, where only the priestly caste was privy to higher wisdom, and, thus, maintained power over the people.

The snake was connected with Goddess wisdom, and so, when patriarchy took hold, it became demonized, along with all matriarchal ideals. The narrative in the *Book of Genesis* demonizes the snake, “the shining one” as representing evil, and Eve as embodying an unforgivable hubris, that of wanting to share in the wisdom of the Divine. It may be more complicated than that, since the phrase "the fruit of the tree of the knowledge of good and evil" seems to represent judgment, with judgment begetting judgment: "Judge not lest ye be judged."

In any case, her punishment, and that of all women, was to have her wisdom, or *gnosis*, disregarded, even suppressed and demonized – how many women were burned as witches over the centuries, simply for sharing their intuitive gifts? Mary Magdalene was described as "the woman who knew the all," seemingly an honored status in Gnostic teachings. But her all=knowingness was diminished in the 6th century by the pope, Gregory the Great, who made her a prostitute and a sinner.

Because of Eve's sinfulness (as viewed by men), women would become second-class citizens, subject to the dictates of men: father, brother, husband, son, and, not least of all, priest.

In the popular 19th century painting by John Collier, Lilith, the demonized first wife of Adam, is depicted with a snake spiraling around her body. (With her long, reddish tresses, and naked body, this depiction resembles many earlier images of the Penitent Magdalene.) Both snakes and Lilith are represented as symbolic of great evil, when, prior to Judaism and patriarchy, snakes were seen in matriarchal teachings as a symbol of wisdom. It isn't hard to see why such an image and concept is often embraced by modern-day women as an emblem of woman's wisdom, and especially, of her independence from men.

Tertullian accused Eve of being the "unsealer of that tree." He declared that, for her audacity, even the Son of God had to die. Does he refer to the tree of the Knowledge of Good and Evil (dualistic beliefs), or of the tree of life, and the higher wisdoms, to which Mary Magdalene had access?

In the Slavonic translation of *Josephus*, there is a line quoted from John the Baptist, when asked who he was: "I am a man had hither the spirit of God hath called me, and I live on the cane and roots and fruits of the tree." His words indicate that he was a vegetarian, which is also given in the New Testament, but the wording here is interesting. The text goes on, "For even as a fleshless spirit, so lived he. His mouth knew no bread, nor even at the Passover feast did he taste of unleavened bread, saying: "In remembrance of God, who redeemed the people from bondage, is (this) given to eat, and for the flight (only), since the journey was in haste. But wine and strong drink he would not so much as allow to be brought nigh him; and every beast he abhorred (for food); and every injustice he exposed; and fruits of the trees served him for (his) needs." (*The Jewish War*, vol 3 of 9, Books IV-VII)

In many early treatises on the subject of Jesus and Mary, they are compared with Adam and Eve. There is also a parallel between the stories of Eve and Lilith, and the stories of the two Mary's. The Mary that is first honored in the traditions of the church is Mary Magdalene – her importance as the Beloved Disciple is hinted at in the canonical Gospels, and more fully acknowledged in the Nag Hammadi texts. Later traditions of the church diminished Mary Magdalene (eventually making her a fallen woman, and repentant sinner). As Mother Mary rose to prominence, later traditions would also contrast the wayward, sinful one, with the chaste and pure spotless Virgin, "Holy Mary, Mother of God."

Arabs and Jews had a common ancestor in Abraham, whose first child, Ishmael, came from his concubine, Hagar, the Arab handmaiden of his wife, Sarah. When Sarah finally bore a child, Hagar and Ishmael were cast out, like Lilith – to "wander in the desert." They were destined to become the ancestors of the nomadic Arab tribes.

The wailing cry of the desert-dwelling Lilith brings to mind the words of the desert-dweller, St. John the Baptist, "I am a voice crying in the wilderness."

Is the connection to desert-dwellers a reference to John the Baptist, or is it, perhaps a reference to the Arabic nomadic tribes? Were they seen to be "consorting with Lilith"? But who was Lilith? From the perspective of Orthodox Jews, associating with Lilith was the same as "being led astray." Was the story of Lilith a polemic against Christianity? Was it a polemic against Islam? Since Lilith was demonized by the Jews, then it stands to reason that they were associating her, in medieval Jewish texts, with either Christianity or Islam (or both?).

GODDESS OF THE NIGHT

Ancient tales of *lilit* – Lady Wind – air,
the owl, the night bird, symbol of wisdom.
Creature of the night, she who finds safety in desert
wastelands. A feminine form, aspect of Nature,
when Nature was honored and respected.
Like the winged Goddess, Inanna, when
matriarchy ruled the land. In her honored image,
Flanked by owls, Maiden Goddess,
Archetypal Beloved, Protector of the Land.

Inanna who descended to the

Underworld (as Jesus did in the "harrowing
of hell"). Inanna, Mother Goddess of Life.
In Tyre it was said that the goddess
Astarte fell from the heavens in the
form of a star – a meteor, thus worship
of the star-goddesses – the Greek, Aster,
the Akkadian, Ishtar, the Hebrew, Ashteroth,
from which came the Hellenized, Astarte, and
the German, Ostara, and Eastre the namesake
of Easter, (to appease the people and their
ancient vernal customs). The feminine,
honored as the Goddess of the Spring:
return of life, renewal, rebirth –
life, not death – The Great Mother.

As also Aphrodite, Persephone, Venus,
Goddess of Love, abundance, fertility.
Istehar, who took umbrage at the advances of
Shemhazai, "When the angels came to earth, and
beheld the daughters of men in all their grace and
beauty, they could not restrain their passion."
She, through her cleverness, discovered and
pronounced the name of God, and rose up,
"aloof from sin", to be set in the heavens as
an honored constellation, no longer subject to the
lustful desires of men, or angels, or the dictates of
patriarchy. Until matriarchy was no more.

Asherah, the Jewish Mother-Goddess, indeed, yes!
Long before the One, the male, the jealous Father God –
did you not know? – there was a Lady-Consort
of El/Yahweh, the Hebrew "wife of God."
In ancient times, the Hebrews highly esteemed
mother-goddess, too. The Queen of Heaven,
for whom the Hebrew women burned incense,
poured "drink offerings" and baked little cakes
in her honor. As did the later Collyridians, the feminine-
worshippers, decried as heretics, by Epiphanius,
an Early Christian Father, of Romaniote
Jewish descent. Despite his claims of heresy,
"little cakes" and incense were incorporated into

Eastern Christian rites – and libations, too.
Syncretization of traditions that happened
throughout Christian history.

Asherah, a Goddess connected with trees
and groves, vines, pomegranates, and wood.
The "robe of the ephod" worn by the Jewish
high priest, dictated by God to have pomegranates
embroidered on its hem – a symbol of Judaism,
of prosperity and mystery, in *Song of Songs*,
the great "mystery teachings" – pomegranates
representing love, beauty, and fertility.
Hundreds of pomegranates adorned Solomon's temple –
carved into the temple walls, and its pillars.
Later a Christian symbol of Mary –
fruitfulness, abundance, and blessing.
Pomegranates and wood – remnant of
Asherah's goddess-reign.

Pronounced use of wood, the Cedars of Lebanon
in the Palace of Solomon, and Solomon's Temple,
Noted in the wood-lined, gold-covered walls
of the Jewish Holy of Holies, the wooden "creche",
of the Christians, the wooden shrine of Umar.
Asherah, who walks on the sea, revered Goddess –
until the exile of the Jews in 586 BC,
whereupon, Yahweh became a jealous God,
the One-God, in early patriarchy – ordering
destruction of Asherah's shrines.
Did the priestly ones blame the woman-goddess
in this exile also? Josiah, cutting down the
Asherah poles in Solomon's Temple, the Holy Place
where she had been honored since
Solomon's reign – idols toppled
for a new God, and new beliefs.

Lilith, after the 2nd century diaspora,
made into the woman-demon, Queen of the
desolate places. The demonized woman?
After the Jewish Independence,
Hadrian's second century razing of the Holy City,
the Temple, the Holy of Holies…even as Jesus

had prophesied, "Not one stone standing on another..."
After the destruction of Jewish life.
What woman, once honored,
in a sacred place in a sacred city,
on the Mount of Olives, from which
Jesus ascended to heaven?

The dispersing of the people to the four winds.
But now a new enemy of the Jews was rising.
Twists and turns: Moreso than Eve, Lilith,
the first wife of Adam – no longer
even a woman – but an evil spirit – ostracized,
condemned, banished to the desert, the wasteland,
living in caves, with the owls, and the howling
winds. The story of Lilith – wisdom figure of the
night made into succubus – stealing the sexual
life-force of men. Stealing man's semen while he slept,
(what complex doctrine therein vilified?) making
demon-offspring as befit her now wicked nature.
Shrieking banshee and baby-killer.

Rabbinical satire: Stories of Mary M'gaddla,
the hairdresser, a step above prostitution,
and her "illegitimate son of a Roman soldier".
Alternately, a sniggering satire of the
young Jewish woman who bathed
in the same water as her father, and became pregnant.
Perhaps, not so much to denigrate the saint,
but rather the exegesis – ridiculing the metaphors,
the formulas of the faith, a faith which
originally sprang from Jewish teachings.
The "Virgin Mother", who had not "known" man,
Overshadowed by the Holy Spirit, "conceiving
by ear", *conceptus ex auditu*, indeed!
A doctrinal teaching of the faith – by listening,
by submitting to the Word – the Will of God.

The Jewish faith, before Christianity, taught of
the "Indwelling Presence" without the metaphors –
not as a child in the womb, but the *Shekinah*,
divine feminine Spirit, embodied, carried in the heart.
Akiva had warned the priests, against separation –

to no avail. Bitterness of the exiles:
a retraction of Rabbi Akiva's endorsement –
the Messiah, the Christ, the Anointed One certainly
had NOT yet come – still hasn't.
Messianism, itself, vilified.

Conquest of the Holy City by the Saracens,
new usurpers of the Temple Mount.
They were Christians first – however heretical –
For 18 months before *qiblah* changed
from the Temple Mount to Mecca,
before Hadith, before creating their own
separate traditions (and history?).
The Quran, said to come straight
from the Angel's lips to the Prophet –
undeniably teaches Judeo-Christian beliefs.

The woman as co-redemptrix?
The All-Praised Mother of God? No –
to some rabbis, in the aftermath of the diaspora
and now the rise of Islam – demon!
Devastator and devourer of her own children.
The worst – the most demonized of all creatures.
Perhaps, after Umar's conquest of the Holy City,
a two-fold cynicism toward Judaism's own offspring -
Christianity and the Muslim faith.
Patriarchy twisted the tale of women's power and divine
knowledge, her access, in three personas, to the
Orchard, Pardes, paradise – her mission, her legacy –
into the bringer not only of Jewish destruction,
but of mankind's demise, Eve and the Forbidden Fruit.
How dared she to enter that Holy Place – as
Tertullian said, becoming the "unsealer of the tree"!

Lilith, the night-spirit invading the Holy City.
The Praiseworthy woman no longer praised,
but demonized. Not for wanting the superior
position (Imperial, Byzantine traditions)
But for walking beside him as his companion,
as His Love. The Beloved Disciple, the two as one –
carrying him in her heart, as each of us may do,
becoming anointed by the Christ light,

the Holy Spirit, the *Shekinah*. *Song of Songs* –
the metaphorical expression of mystical revelation:
"A bundle of myrrh is *my* beloved to me, that lies
all night *between my breasts*." (In my heart.)

* * *

CHAPTER XI. THE BIRTH OF ISLAM

THE PARACLETE

In *John* 14:15, Jesus says, "If ye love me, keep my commandments. And I will pray the Father, and he shall give you another Comforter that he may abide with you forever; *Even* the Spirit of truth; whom the world cannot receive, because it seeth him not, neither knoweth him: but ye know him; for he dwelleth with you, and shall be in you."

He ends this chapter with more words of comfort, "Peace I leave with you, my peace I give unto you: not as the world giveth, give I unto you. Let not your heart be troubled, neither let it be afraid. Ye have heard how I said unto you, I go away, and come again unto you." (*John* 14:27-28) This may be seen as reference to his resurrection, but could also be interpreted to equate himself with the "Comforter" of the Godhead known, in Christian teachings, as the Holy Spirit, who came to those in the Upper Room on Pentecost.

When John first saw Jesus and pointed him out to the other disciples, the narrative states that "he knew him not." Perhaps this was not a literal, but rather, a symbolic statement. When John baptized Jesus, and the dove descended, to rest upon Jesus' head, it is said to signify the descent of the Holy Spirit – the moment when the heavens opened and God spoke, "This is my Beloved Son, in whom I am well-pleased."

The Paraclete is mentioned by Jesus prior to his death and resurrection, when he prophesied the coming of the Comforter, the Holy Spirit which came to those gathered in the Upper Room on Pentecost, "for he dwelleth with you, and shall be in you." This is not the interpretation of the Paraclete in Islamic belief, which states that Muhammad was the coming Comforter/Paraclete of whom Jesus spoke.

It is said that Muhammad received the revelations from the Angel Gabriel in a series of 114 visions in a cave on Mt. Hira near Mecca.[166] It is said that the revelations were received over a period of some 23 years, beginning in the month of Ramadan, when Muhammad was 40; and concluding in 632, the year of his death.

The teachings of the Quran, which were divinely revealed to Muhammad, absolutely reflect Judeo-Christian stories and teachings. Islam proclaims that these revelations were the final, most pure and true revelations from God, through His angel, Gabriel. In a sense, they propose that these teachings were transferred from the mouth of the Angel of God, Gabriel, to Muhammad.

Muhammad's death was said to be in 632 CE, just five years before the Saracen (Arab) conquest of Jerusalem in 637 CE. The historical writings of Islamic *hadith* were written well after the period given as Muhammad's lifetime, and well after the writing of the Quran. According to Herbert Berg, the earliest historical resources for information on early Islam are from one hundred and fifty to two hundred years after the events took place (compared to Biblical sources written twenty to sixty years after the ascension of Christ).[167]

Add to this the great likelihood, as in Christian texts, of later deletions, or alterations attested by Suliman Bashear: "There is difficulty in finding facts of early Islam due to the fact that nearly all the material we have comes from Islam compilations of which their goal was to write history to reflect a more sacred history."[168]

It is notable that the cousin of Muhammad's wife, Khadijah, was a Christian monk named *Waraqah ibn Nawfal ibn Asad ibn 'Abdu'l-'Uzza.* He had translated into Arabic the *Gospel of the Hebrews* (which included no nativity, and no genealogy of Jesus). Like Muhammad and Khadija, Waraqah lived amongst the Quraysh (or Quraish) tribe. The Encyclopedia of Islam states that, “It is said that Waraqah had been engaged to be married to Khadija, but the marriage never took place. Islamic sources affirm that portions of the Bible were translated into Arabic during the time of Muhammad, and Waraqah is cited as being one of those translators.

Aisha, Muhammad's third and youngest wife, states that Waraqah bin Naufal was a Christian convert, who used to recite the Gospels in Arabic. In *Sahih al-Bukhari,* she also states that: "...Waraqah had been converted to Christianity in the Pre-lslamic Period and used to write Arabic and write of the Gospel in Arabic as much as Allah wished him to write.”

Whatever Waraqah's role in the early development of Islam, there is said to be an earlier connection between Muhammad and the Syriac Christian monk, Bahira. The story goes that Muhammad, when he was just 12 years old, met Bahira, who lived in Sham (Syria). It is believed that the monk was expelled from the monastery for certain offenses, in expiation of which, he set out on a mission to Arabia. What monastery, and what offenses?

Bahira, it seems, was expecting a prophet, basing his expectation on old books and manuscripts from generations of monks before him. Some stories say that there was a mark or birthmark on the prophet that would indicate his identity.

Both Ibn Sa'd and al-Tabari write that Bahira found the

announcement of the coming of Muhammad in the original, unadulterated gospels, which he possessed. In them was Jesus' promise that the Paraclete (the Comforter) would come after him: "if I go not away, the Comforter will not come unto you; but if I depart, I will send him unto you." This identification of the Paraclete as predicting the coming of a Prophet is not an idea that is found in mainstream Christianity. Bahira's leanings have been described as, perhaps, Nestorian, or Nazorean, or Arian, but even in these sects, it isn't clear that such a teaching was embraced. The idea of Muhammad as the Paraclete seems to be a later addition within Islamic hadith.

When the merchant caravan that included the twelve-year-old Muhammad was passing by Bahira's cell, the monk invited the merchants to a feast. The young Muhammad was left to watch over the camels, however, Bahira insisted that all should attend. He noted a cloud that was constantly over the head of Muhammad, wherever he went, anytime of day (much like the cloud of the *Shekinah* that came to rest on the Mercy Seat in the Jewish "Holy of Holies." Bahira revealed his visions of Muhammad's future to the boy's uncle (Abu Talib), warning him to preserve Muhammad, the Praiseworthy One, from the Jews (in Ibn Sa'd's version)[169] or from the Byzantines (in al-Tabari's version).[170] Why should he be "preserved" from both the Jews and the Christians? What was their interest in him?

We have, again, in this narrative, the theme of a Christian monk, living in a cave-cell, giving important wisdom teachings and prophecy.

Jesus says of the Paraclete, "Howbeit when he, the Spirit of truth, is come, he will guide you into all truth: for he shall not speak of himself; but whatsoever he shall hear, that shall he speak: and he will shew you things to come." (*John* 16:13) In Christian belief, the Paraclete is generally seen to represent the Holy Spirit. The coming of the Paraclete is seen to have occurred when the Holy Spirit descended in tongues of flame upon the heads of the disciples in the Upper Room on Pentecost, just after Jesus' death, resurrection and ascension into heaven. Jesus clearly calls the Paraclete "the Spirit of truth" and the idea of speaking "whatsoever he shall hear," seems related to speaking in tongues – in languages unintelligible to those speaking.

Many of the Persian depictions of Muhammad show him, and various of his family and companions, with flames surrounding them or their heads, in a manner consistent with that of the fire of the Holy Spirit emanating from them, much like the light of the halo surrounding the head in Christian depictions of the saints, or the tongues of flame over their heads at Pentecost.

In the New Testament, Jesus must ascend to the father, so that the Holy Spirit may descend upon those gathered in the Upper Room. "I will not leave you comfortless: I will come to you. Yet a little while, and the world seeth me no more; but ye see me: because I live, ye shall live also. At that day ye shall know that I *am* in my Father, and ye in me, and I in you."

As Cyril confirms, the Spirit, indwelling in the saints, signifies the presence of Christ: "He reveals to the saints the divine mysteries...The perfect knowledge then is begotten in the saints by the Spirit...For in the revelation of these things by the Spirit working in us in an unspeakable way, we see the deep meaning of the incarnation and the power of the hidden mystery. His Spirit, indwelling in the saints, accomplishes the presence and the power of Christ Himself ..." Cyril relates the indwelling of the Holy Spirit with Christhood, the Incarnation within Mary, which is not only available to the saints, but also to those devoted to the faith.

In Christianity, the Paraclete brings the gift of prophecy, however, Bahira interprets the term as a reference and foretelling of "a prophet." From the Christian perspective, Bahira was considered to be a heretical monk. Some scholars outside of Islam propose that it was Bahira's errant views that inspired the Quran. The names and religious affiliations of Bahira vary in different Christian sources. Some propose that Bahira was an Arian, some that he was a Jacobite, or Nestorian. The Muslim writer, al-Kindi, calls him "Sergius," going so far as to claim that he later called himself Nestorius. Others equate Bahira with "George."

Arianism decrees that the divine spirit of the Trinity was not of the same substance as the Father. It also insists that the spirit of Jesus was created at the beginning of time, which, problematically, would mean there was a time when Jesus did not exist. Therefore, although he has been given all authority in heaven and earth as God's mediator, Jesus is not God in substance. This is a sticking point in Islam – that Jesus (Isa) is acknowledged as a prophet and a teacher, but not as the Son of God, or in any way containing the essence of God.

According to the Quran, a Muslim should not see Jesus as God nor Son of God. "God is only one, has no partner or son, and neither gives birth, nor is He born. He is eternally besought by all and has no beginning or end, and none is equal to Him." (*Surah Al-Ikhlas* 112:1-5)

Certainly, if Bahira was Nestorius, who was condemned at the Council of Ephesus, and his writings anathematized, many pieces of the puzzle fall into place. Nestorius broke away from the mainstream Church and formed the Nestorian Church, which was considered heretical by the Emperor. Nestorius insisted that there must be two persons of Christ, one human, the other divine. He proposed that though Jesus had one substance (*ousia*), he had two persons *(dyoprosopism),* the divine Logos and the human Jesus. He argued that the title of *Theotokos* denied Christ's full humanity, and thus

Mary could not be called the *Theotokos*, "the one who gives birth to God".

A brief definition of Nestorian Christology, which developed from Nestorius' teachings, can be given as: "Jesus Christ, who is not identical with the Son but personally united with the Son, *who lives in him*, is one hypostasis and one nature: human." (This seems to be a simplified version of Nestorius' writings, which taught that the Word, which is eternal, and the Flesh, which is not, came together in a hypostatic union, 'Jesus Christ'.) Jesus thus being both fully man and God, of two *ousia* but of one *prosopon*. The teaching of Nestorianism aligns quite well with Islamic beliefs that Mary was not divine, nor was her son.

Abdiyah Akbar Abdul-Haqq also makes George [Bahira] an early contributor to Quranic writings, "George, a bishop of the Arabs of Mesopotamia, ... wrote a *Scholia* on the Scripture around the sixth century A.D." It is notable that the timeline of Bahira's translation was *before* Muhammad began teaching the Quran in 632 CE. The writing of the Quran, which took 23 years, had a 7th century beginning (23 years before he died, in 632).

He goes on, "But it appears that Christian teaching and preaching in the sixth century Arabia was done mainly by quoting from the Syriac or Ethiopic scripture and then giving a free rendering of it in Arabic ..."[171] Essentially, this was a "recitation" of the texts in Arabic. There are strong Syriac connections to the early writings of Islam.

The very first words of the Quran are: "In the name of God, the Merciful, the Compassionate," said to have been written by the Christian monk, Bahira. [172]

The Encyclopedia of Islam states that "Certain Arabist authors maintain that Bahira's works were the basis of those parts of the Quran that conform to the principles of Christianity, while the rest was introduced either by subsequent compilers like Uthman Ibn Affan or contemporary Jews and Arabs".[173] Khadija's cousin, the Syriac monk, Waraqah, through his translations of Old and New Testament texts, was also likely to have been an important contributor to the foundations of the faith.

Al-Baidhawi and other Muslim commentators state that Muhammad received instruction from learned Christians like Waraqah ibn Naufal, Jubra and Yasara. Also, traditions relate how the Prophet used to stop and listen to these men as they read aloud the Books of Moses and the Gospels. An Arabic translation of portions of the New Testament was circulating in Mecca during the rise of Islam.

Abdul-Haqq points out that, in Muhammad's time: "In addition to translations of the canonical Gospels, there were numerous Arabic translations of the New Testament apocrypha. Some of the better known of these, like *Protoevangelion of James, Gospel of the Infancy, Apocalypse of Paul,* and the *Apocryphal Acts of the Apostles* were available in Arabic translation before the Koran..." This is a reasonable source of the apocryphal Christian stories that are not included in the bible, but ended up in the Quran. Along with these translations, were also full versions of the Syriac New Testament and Syriac Lectionaries.

The infant Jesus speaking from the cradle (or before his birth, from Mary's womb) is one of six miracles attributed to him in the Quran. This theme is also found in the *Syriac Infancy Gospel*, a pre-Islamic 6th -century work, which brings questions about the source of this story in the Quran.

Ibn Arabi, Andalusian scholar, Sufi mystic, poet and philosopher, gives a broader, more mystical description of the birth/nature of Jesus, in the *Bezels of Wisdom*:

> *From the water of Mary*
> *[implying: as a child in the womb]*
> *or from the breath of Gabriel,*
> *In the form of a mortal fashioned of clay,*
> *The Spirit came into existence in an essence*
> *Purged of Nature's taint, which*
> *is called Sijjin (prison)...*
> *A spirit from none other than God,*
> *So that he might raise the dead and*
> *bring forth birds from clay.*

The story of creating birds from clay relates to a story in the 2nd century apocryphal *Infancy Gospel of Thomas,* considered by early Church authorities as inauthentic and heretical. It contains stories of Jesus fashioning a bird out of clay and breathing life into it, along with more disturbing stories of Jesus killing a child and blinding its parents, then reversing his actions and resurrecting the child.

On the mystery of the virgin birth, the Quran states that God need only say, “Be,” and it is. This can be seen to not only contradict the biblical narratives of the Annunciation, but might also be connected to the meaning of Jesus’ name (*yesh* root of Yeshua means “being”).

In Islam, Jesus was neither crucified nor raised from the dead, though “it was made to appear so,” but was rather saved from such a fate by God, and raised alive to heaven. In Islamic eschatology, Jesus has an important role in the Day of Judgment, when he will return in a “Second Coming” to fight the "False Messiah" and establish peace on earth.

In Chapter 74, *Al-Muddaththir* (The Encloaked One), Muhammad's youngest wife, Aisha, covers Muhammad with a cloak, when he came from his first revelation from Gabriel, and was shivering, or trembling from the experience. In the *Bukhari Sahih Muhammad*, Aisha speaks of Muhammad's reaction to his first revelation: "...The Prophet returned to Khadija while his heart was beating rapidly. She took him to Waraqah bin Naufal who was a Christian convert and used to read the Gospel in Arabic. Waraqah asked (the Prophet), "What do you see?" When he told him, Waraqah said, "That is the same angel whom Allah sent to the Prophet Moses. Should I live till you receive the Divine Message, I will support you strongly."

Waraqah essentially substantiates that this message came directly from God, and confirms the Prophet's interaction with the Angel Gabriel of Christianity, who also announced the conception of Jesus to Mary. Here, it is Waraqah, a Christian convert (in some Islamic accounts, he was an Ebionite Christian monk), who confirms and supports Muhammad's Prophethood.

Waraqah, Khadija's cousin, a respected man of his time and a well-known scholar, was an elderly Christian convert who was known to have made a translation of Christian teachings, which he shared in both written and oral form with the Quraysh tribe of Arabs, Muhammad's tribe. If Waraqah's background was aligned with the Syrian *Miaphysites*, then it would also explain the incorporation of such ideas as that Jesus was not the Son of God, and that he did not suffer and die on the cross.

In another part of the narrative by Aisha, it states, "Khadija then accompanied him to her cousin Waraqah bin Naufal bin Asad bin 'Abdul 'Uzza, who, during the pre-Islamic Period, became a Christian and used to write the writing with Hebrew letters." He wished to support Muhammad strongly in his prophethood, "...But after a few days Waraqah died." (*Sahih al-Bukhari*, *Revelation* 1, Chapter 3) It was important to establish that this occured between Muhammad's first revelation and Waraqah's death, since Waraqah is used as proof for the beginnings of Islam.

Waraqah is a direct connection to Christian ideals within the tribe in which Muhammad was believed to have later shared his own revelations! Since he translated "as much as Allah wished him to write," he probably made translations of more than just this Gospel. This could explain the incorporation of apocryphal lore into the Quranic accounts of Christian teachings.

While the demonization of Muhammad by Christian camps was the exception early on, the polarizing effect of skirmishes and war brought a more widespread condemnation by the Church. By the time of the Crusades of the High Middle Ages, and war against the Ottoman Empire in the Late

Middle Ages, the usual war-time propaganda would begin to be directed toward "the enemy." Out of xenophobia, or a deepening hatred of the "infidels," Christian polemics against Muhammad shifted from the early depiction of the teachings as simply heretical to an image of Muhammad as a servant of Satan. Even in the 8th century, Christian monk, John of Damascus and 8th century theologian, Alvarus of Cordoba, among others, actually proclaimed him to be the Anti-Christ.

John of Damascus was an 8th century monk and theologian, a polymath whose fields of interest and contribution included law, theology, philosophy, and music. He was one of the earliest Christians to write of Muhammad, and the most famous writer on the subject of the Assumption of Mary, who claimed that: "a false prophet named Mohammed...after having chanced upon the Old and New Testaments and likewise, it seems, having conversed with an Arian monk, devised his own heresy. Then, having insinuated himself into the good graces of the people by a show of seeming piety, he gave out that a certain book had been sent down to him from heaven."[174]

The Damascene is said by some sources to have served as a Chief Administrator to the Muslim caliph of Damascus before his ordination as a Christian priest. In 746, he wrote the *Fount of Knowledge,* part two of which is entitled *Heresies in Epitome: How They Began and Whence They Drew Their Origin.* In this work on heresy in general, he makes many references to the Quran and, in his opinion, its failure to live up to even the most basic scrutiny. He refers to several *surahs* with apparent incredulity. His commentary is overtly polemical in nature, intended to stir up opposition to Islam. This doesn't mean that his comments are lies – that is something that we must consider carefully – but they may be exaggerations and they also may contain hidden truths. The Damascene writes disparagingly of Muhammad: "He had set down some ridiculous compositions in this book of his and he gave it to them as an object of veneration."

He goes on to say, "There are many other extraordinary and quite ridiculous things in this book which he boasts was sent down to him from God. But when we ask: 'And who is there to testify that God gave him the book? And which of the prophets foretold that such a prophet would rise up?'—they are at a loss. And we remark that Moses received the Law on Mount Sinai, with God appearing in the sight of all the people in cloud, and fire, and darkness, and storm. And we say that all the Prophets from Moses on down foretold the coming of Christ and how Christ God (and incarnate Son of God) was to come and to be crucified and die and rise again, and how He was to be the judge of the living and dead."

He cites ample prophecy of the Messiah's coming, versus no prophecy of Muhammad's coming: "Then, when we say: 'How is it that this prophet of yours did not come in the same way, with others bearing witness to him?" So, of course there was need for the "foreseeing" of his prophethood by Bahira, and confirmation of his prophethood by Waraqah.

He goes on, "And how is it that God did not in your presence present this man with the book to which you refer, even as He gave the Law to Moses, with the people looking on and the mountain smoking, so that you, too, might have certainty?'—they answer that God does as He pleases. 'This,' we say, 'We know, but we are asking how the book came down to your prophet.' Then they reply that the book came down to him while he was asleep."

These questions and ridicule from John of Damascus, in the early 8th century may well have prompted the nascent Islamic faith to claim the prophesied Paraclete of Christian texts as their own prophecy, referring to the Prophet Muhammad. It may also have initiated the narrative of Muhammad receiving the revelation in a mountain cave, and prompted the writing of *hadith* (historical stories of Islam), documenting how every portion of the Quran was related by the Prophet to his circle of followers. According to British historian Alfred Guillaume, it is "certain" that "several small collections" of hadith were "assembled in Umayyad times" (by the mid-8th century).[175]

The *Sahih Bukhari* confirms that a Christian wrote parts of the Quran, said to be the Christian writer, *ibn Qumta*. The name Qumta is thought to come from *komta* ("qomta" in Bashkir Turkish) which means "box" or "frame." This brings images of the Ark of the Covenant or of the Holy of Holies in the Temple of Solomon, or even the cube of the Kaaba.

Those who are commonly cited as being involved in the creation of the Quran include: Imrul Qays, Zayd b. Amr, Hasan b. Thabit, Salman, Bahira, ibn Qumta, Waraqah and Ubayy b. Ka'b. One of the most influential of these was Zayd b. Amr, who preached *Hanifism* – which maintained the pure monotheistic beliefs of the patriarch Ibrahim. In the Pre-Islamic period or Age of Ignorance, the *Hanifs* were seen to have rejected idolatry and retained some or all of the tenets of the religion of Abraham, which is to say, Judaism.

In *Sharing Your Faith with a Muslim*, Abdiyah Akbar Abdul-Haqq describes both a tradition of written translations of the Gospels into Arabic, as well as oral transmissions. He writes, "The Gospels were translated into Arabic from the original Greek as well as Coptic and Syrian versions. Barhebraeus writes of an Arabic translation made by a Monophysite named Johannes, by the order of an Arab prince in 640 CE. Oldest extant fragments of Arabic translations from the Greek date from the early ninth century. The oldest extant translation in the Syriac also dates back to the same time." He also writes, "A Coptic version of the New Testament was current toward the end of the third century...The Gospels were translated into Arabic from the Greek, Syriac, and Coptic versions. Barhebraeus speaks of such a translation made between 631 – 640", which *scholia* might well be the biggest founding work of Islam."[176]

ISLAM

Like Judaism and Christianity, Islam is one of the Abrahamic religions. The word 'Islam' is derived from the Arabic root 'SLM' which can have several meanings. It is often described as equating to the word, "submission", or "surrender", even "obedience", but some also give the meaning of "peace", from the word *salaam* (Jewish *shalom*), which is used in the greeting of Islam, *Salaam alaikam* or, more correctly *As-salaamu Alaikum* meaning "Peace be upon you." It resembles the words of Jesus, "Peace I leave with you, my peace I give unto you..." (*John* 14:27) In Islamic writings, the name of Muhammad and other Islamic prophets is followed by the honorific phrase, "peace be upon him", often abbreviated to "PBUH".

Islamic author, Hammudah Abdalati, states, "Islam is the religion of peace: its meaning is peace; one of God's names is peace; the daily greetings of Muslims and angels are peace; paradise is the house of peace; the adjective 'Muslim' means Peaceful. Peace is the nature, the meaning, the emblem, and the objective of lslam." [177]

Muslims claim a direct descendancy from Abraham through his Arab concubine, Hagar. His wife Sarah encouraged Hagar to have a child with her husband when she, herself, could not. In the *Book of Genesis* in the Bible, when Hagar conceived, "Sarai said unto Abram: 'My wrong be upon thee: I gave my handmaid into thy bosom; and when she saw that she had conceived, I was despised in her eyes: the LORD judge between me and thee.' But Abram said unto Sarai: 'Behold, thy maid is in thy hand; do to her that which is good in thine eyes.' And Sarai dealt harshly with her, and she fled from her face." (*Genesis* 16:5) Hagar was cast out with her child, into the wilderness.

It goes on, "And the angel of the LORD found her by a fountain of water in the wilderness, by the fountain in the way to Shur. And the angel of the LORD said unto her: 'Return to thy mistress, and submit thyself under her hands.'." Even in this early moment, submission to God was required. "And the angel of the LORD said unto her: 'I will greatly multiply thy seed, that it shall not be numbered for multitude." Hagar afterward called the Lord *El Roi*, one of the names of God in Judaism. Hagar returned to Sarah, and Ishmael was born.

When Sarah (miraculously) became pregnant herself, in her old age, and her son Isaac was born, discord again arose between her and her maidservant. When Sarah found Ishmael mocking her son, she convinced her husband to cast Hagar and the young Ishmael into the desert once again.

In the Islamic narrative, when food and water ran out, and Hagar was desperately crying out to God for help for herself and her child, an angel again appeared to her saying that her son would be the "Father of a great nation", and a well appeared in the desert for them to drink from. The *zamzam* well in Mecca, visited by *Hajj* pilgrims, is said to be the very well of this story of Ishmael, the ancestor of the faith. Thus unfolded the beginning of Islam, long before the name of Islam was used.

In none of the writings of Sophronius, the Patriarch of Jerusalem in the 7th century, or other Christian writings of his time, was there mention of Muhammad or of Muslims - only of the Arabs/Saracens. The term, "Hagarenes" (derived from the name of Abraham's Arab concubine), was widely used by early Syriac, Greek, Coptic and Armenian sources to describe the early Arab conquerors of Mesopotamia, Syria and Egypt. The term, "Ishmaelites" (derived from Ishmael, Arab son of Abraham), was used interchangeably with "Hagarenes".

Some scholars, from the explanation of Jerome, have claimed that these nomadic people, unwilling to call themselves by the name of a slave-woman, or her son, chose the term "Saracen" to align themselves with Abraham's wife, Sarah, but this is more Christian folk-tale than anything. The name "Saracen" was not used among the populations so described but rather was given to them by Greco-Roman historians based on Greek place names.[178] Some etymologies suggest that the word comes from the Arabic noun *sāriq* (pl. *sariqīn),* meaning "thief, marauder, plunderer", which would make sense coming from those who were targeted in Saracen attacks.

There may be connection to “Sirachen” (from ben Sirach), or from the term “Syriacen”, which would denote their connection to Syria. In the 17th century, they became known as "Mohammedans" (followers of Mohammed - in the early spelling of his name), less commonly as “Musselmans”, and finally, "Muslims" (followers of Islam, which means, "submission.") While some historians give accounts of "Muslim conquests" in the 7th century onward, the term "Muslim" was not actually used until some 1000 years later.

Often, in early writings, the Arab conquerors of the Holy Land were called by the reigning Caliph/ruler or clan of the time period, that is, the *Umayyads* (from the *Banu Umayya* tribe), the Ottomans (from the leader, *Osman*) and the *Abbasids* (from Muhammad's uncle, *ʿAbbās ibn ʿAbd al-Muṭṭalib* a strange mix: "Father", son and servant of the seeker/desirer). He was also given the name "Shaybah" meaning 'the ancient one' or 'white-haired', which brings to mind Bahira.

The beliefs of early Islam were based on *sunnah*, which is to say the teachings of the Prophet found in the Quran, the Holy Book of Islam. The term *Quran* is said to derive either from the Syriac word, *qeryānā*, which means 'scripture reading' or from the Arabic word *qaraa*, meaning "to read". The literal translation of the Arabic phrase, *al-Qur'ān* is "the recitation" which might reinforce that it was first recited to the Arabs, or recited by them as an oral tradition.

To be clear, Muslims insist that the writings in the Quran were revelations that came directly to the Prophet Muhammad from the Angel Gabriel, forming an oral tradition that was later written down. However, it is also true that various Christian monks were known to recite biblical texts, some in Syriac and later in Arabic translations, to the Arab tribes.

It should be noted that, if a heretical monk, such as Bahira (George, Sergius), or Waraqah or others, did have an influence on the faith, it would have been according to their own heretical beliefs, thus, with notable differences from orthodox Christian teachings - such differences as are found in the Quran.

Many religious scholars have suggested that Muhammad brought no new concepts in his teachings, no new ethical or theological formulas. Ignaz Goldhizer writes that, "The Arab Prophet's message was an eclectic composite of religious ideas and regulations. The ideas were suggested to him by contacts, which had stirred him deeply, with Jewish, Christian, and other elements."[179]

Many people outside the faith do not realize that, along with the honoring of many of the ancient prophets of the Old Testament - and Jesus, John and Mary of the New Testament (Isa, Yahya, and Maryam), the teachings of the Quran are parallel teachings to the Old (Judaic) and New (Christian) Testament teachings, with some apocryphal stories thrown in for good measure. However, these teachings are considered by Muslims to be the final, most pure revelations of the faith, from the Angel Gabriel (*Jibril*).

Islamic traditions mention a *Gospel of Jesus*, called the *Injil*, which is said to have been given to Jesus from God. Interestingly, this gospel is no longer extant. Such a holy text just completely disappeared without a trace – without a scrap left behind. What would early Muslims have called the texts that were translated for them by the Syriac monks? Would a *Gospel of Jesus* be considered problematic once skirmishes began between Muslims and Christians? Would it hamper the development of an independent faith, which necessarily was moving away from its earliest expression as a form of (heretical) Christian belief? Would such a gospel text be the earliest form of Quranic teachings, before the divisions deepened among Muslims, Jews and Christians?

Early on, after the death of Muhammad and disagreements on the rightful succession of the leadership of the faith, there was a branching off from the original, *Sunni*, beliefs into a second belief system of the *Shi'a*. From these two major sects (as in Christianity), many belief systems emerged, including the mystic branch known as Sufism. Some, reflecting Christian divisions, developed around differences in belief about Islamic jurisprudence (Law), and ideas such as metaphorical versus literal interpretation, questions around anthropomorphism, and Divine Will, versus free will, etc.

Early Islam set up the foundations of the Five Pillars of the Faith, still embraced by *Sunni* Muslims:

> *1)Shahadah* - The profession of faith: "There is no God but Allah, and Muhammad is the messenger of Allah."
> *2) Salat* - The practice of the act of supplication (prayer and prostration).
> *3) Zakat* - Almsgiving, the practice of charitable giving to the poor.
> *4) Sawm* - Fasting and ritual purification
> *5) Hajj* - The obligatory Islamic pilgrimage, called the *Hajj* must be performed during the first weeks of the twelfth Islamic month of *Dhu al-Hijjah* in the city of Mecca. Every able-bodied Muslim who can afford it must make the pilgrimage to Mecca at least once in his or her lifetime.

Shi'a and other sects of Islam also embrace additional foundational beliefs or pillars of the faith. These practices reflect many of the foundational aspects of Judaism and Christianity as well, both of which insist on the belief in One God (though Christianity claims three persons in the One Godhead), charitable giving (the *zakah* of Judaism, and the almsgiving encouraged by the desert monks), fasting and purification (the *mikvah* bath and rituals of Judaism, and the fasting and vigils of the desert monks), and pilgrimage to Jerusalem and the Temple Mount by both faiths (desirable, but not required by either faith). In many ways, Islam reflects close ties to the practices of the ascetic monks, who often taught Christian ideals to the nomadic Arab tribes before the rise of Islam, including their vows of poverty, ascetic lifestyle, prayer, prostrations, night-long vigils, and charity for the poor.

PERSIAN INFLUENCES

Waraqah, who had converted to, and had a strong belief in the Christian faith (though with unorthodox beliefs), was an early supporter of Muhammad's status as prophet – a Nestorian Christian monk who was one of the first to support Muhammads prophethood. When Nestorius was excommunicated for heresy, many of his followers fled to Persia for safety and religious freedom. But Nestorians were, essentially, Christians who had broken away from the Church.

In a Persian painting of two figures in the desert, there is an old man with white hair and beard, and a young man being anointed from above by an angel, leaning down through the parted clouds of the heavens. The younger is said to be Muhammad, the Praiseworthy One, the elder, *Bahira*, a name that means "shining and bright." Could this name represent a halo, perhaps even a saint?

There may be some connection of Bahira to *Bahir*, the "Book of Brightness" or "Book of Illumination", anonymously written, but attributed to a 1st-century rabbinic sage, Nehunya ben HaKanah (a contemporary of Yochanan ben Zakai). It is an early work of esoteric Jewish mysticism which eventually became known as *Kabbalah*.

Bahira, the Arab holy man was said to have witnessed a very young Muhammad, on caravan. He was first to acknowledge him as Prophet. It brings to mind the story of the 12-year-old Jesus, who, on caravan with his parents, was somehow left behind at the Temple, where he was found preaching to the Jewish elders.

In some stories of Muhammad's beginnings, it was Waraqah ibn Nawfal, the knowledgeable Nestorian priest and the relative of Muhammad's first wife, Arab merchantess, Khadijah, that gave Muhammad clarity on his mission. Waraqah is revered in Islamic tradition for being one of the first *hanifs* to believe in the prophecy of Muhammad. (A *hanif* is an Arabic designation for true monotheists who were not Jews, Christians, or worshipers of idols.) In fact, in some stories, it was Waraqah, and not Bahira, who told Muhammad that he was destined to be the final prophet of the world.

Hadith states that Muhammad spent a great deal of time in the cave of Hira (note the similarity to Bahira), a mountain cave near Mecca. And here, after much meditation, Muhammad was given the first revelations from the angel Gabriel (*Jibril*).

Abū Bakr, Muhammad's closest companion, factors greatly in the early history of the Prophet. According to some claims, Abū Bakr was the first male convert to Islam, but this view is doubted by a majority of Muslim historians. Bakr means "servant," and sometimes *'Abd Allah* was also attached to his name making it, "Servant of God". One of his early titles, preceding his conversion to Islam, was *siddiq*, meaning "the upright, or noble one." It has a great phonetic similarity, and perhaps, derivation from the Hebrew word "Tzadik", which means "righteous", and which appears in the New Testament in reference to Jesus (*John* 2:1) or the followers of Jesus, the *tzaddikim*, who "shall live by faith" (*Hab*. 2:4, *Rom*. 1:17, Gal. 3:11).

Another title given to al-Bakr was *atiqe (ateeq)*, which has various meanings: "the old or ancient one", again, like Bahira, or "the special one", and also "the saved one".[180] He was already saved, before converting to Islam - which seems to indicate that he was considered holy or saintly prior to his conversion; combined with the idea of salvation, most likely, this would indicate Christian sainthood. He was also thought to be as the "second of the two in the cave" mentioned in the Quran in reference to the event of *hijra*, the migration of Muhammad and his followers from Mecca to Medina, where with Muhammad, al-Bakr hid in the cave at Jabal Thawr from the Meccan party that was sent to capture them.[181]

It is said that these two were fleeing from the Quraysh, the Arabic tribe to which Muhammad belonged, who vehemently opposed Muhammad and his early community. They hid in a desert cave in Medina for three days, a number of years before the Saracens conquered Jerusalem. Did Muhammad and al-Bakr, hide in a cave during the early Quraysh opposition to the prophet's teachings, or were they hidden in a cave, as perhaps they had been hidden before? Semantics, but it makes a difference.

Islamic Hadith states that Muhammad emigrated to Yathrib/Medina in 622, only a few years after Sophronius brought to the holy land the relics of his friend, John Moschus, said to have died in Rome in 619 – a tumultuous period of time in Jerusalem. Where were the holy relics of Christianity in this time period, only a few years after the Persian conquest and sacking of Jerusalem in 614 CE (the Persian army aided by some 20,000 Jewish soldiers)? Were they hidden in a desert cave by the Persians, or from the Persians? Were they honored in secret by some Jewish-Christian-Arab tribe, in Mecca, and later in Medina? Did the relics of two of the most important saints of Christianity somehow end up in the care of a Nestorian priest? Nestorians had fled to Persia for safety, and Persia conquered Jerusalem a decade or so before the rise of Islam.

The hidden truths of Christianity would become confused in the stories of Islam – how could it be otherwise? Murkiness begets murkiness.

Many of the Persian paintings of Muhammad seem to correlate to Christian narratives. Images of the Prophet in a room with his companions, all with their heads being ignited by holy flames. Muhammad lying on a rock platform, resembling the Dormition paintings of Christianity. Bahira meeting Muhammad: what comes to mind, what momentous Christian occasion – what Christian figures might be represented in Nestorian/Persian artworks as an old man with a white beard, and a younger one, anointed (Messiah, Christ) by an angel that leans down from the heavens? Could this be a Persian-Christian depiction of a moment when the heavens opened and God declared, "This is my beloved son, in whom I am well-pleased"? Could this be the Transfiguration on the Mount?

THE ECTHESIS

Flavius Phocas (547 – 5 October 610) was the Eastern Roman emperor from 602 to 610 CE. to gain this status, in 602, he led a revolt against Emperor Maurice. Phocas captured Constantinople, overthrew Maurice, and declared himself emperor on the same day. Phocas brutally purged his opponents and installed his relatives in high military positions.

Under his administration, and likely, due to the instability caused by his revolt, the Byzantine Empire was threatened by multiple enemies, with frequent raids in the Balkans from the Avars and Slavs, and particularly, the Sassanid invasion of the eastern provinces.

The Sassanid Persians had formerly been at peace with Maurice as a result of a treaty they made with him in 591. After Phocas killed Maurice and usurped his title, the Persians invaded the empire in 603. The Sassanids soon occupied the eastern provinces, leading the military leader, Narses, to defect to their side. Phocas swiftly and brutally dealt with him, by inviting him to Constantinople under the promise of safe conduct, then had him burnt alive when he arrived. By 607, the Sassanids occupied Mesopotamia, Syria, and much of Asia Minor. Phocas' incompetence and brutality led the Exarch of Africa, Heraclius the Elder, to rebel against him.

Heraclius the Elder's son, also named Heraclius, succeeded in taking Constantinople in October of 610, and executed Phocas on the same day, before declaring himself the emperor.

In this setting of great upheaval, Patriarch Sergius I of Constantinople and emperor Heraclius sought to form an agreement between the Chalcedonians and non-Chalcedonians to resolve the schism that occurred after the Council of Chalcedon, and its resulting "Chalcedonian Definition". Their efforts began with the promotion of a new concept of *Monoenergism*, which states that Jesus Christ had two natures but only one energy.

At a synod held in 622 the concept of *Monoenergism* was used to attempt to reconcile the non-Chalcedonian Church of Armenia. This is the same year that Muhammad is said to have embraced his prophethood and begun his teaching.

For several years afterwards, the doctrine of *Monoenergism* enjoyed support in the Churches of Constantinople, Alexandria, and Antioch. However, the monk Sophronius did not find the doctrine to be an acceptable belief, and championed the doctrine of *Dyoenergism*, that is, that Jesus Christ had two energies. When he became patriarch of Jerusalem in 634, Sophronius used the authority of his office, prolific writings, and much effort to challenge the validity of the doctrine of *Monoenergism* promoted by the Byzantines.

Patriarch Sergius, in 635, received the endorsement of Pope Honorius I of Rome agreeing with the doctrine of *Monoenergism*, and declaring that all discussions concerning one or two energies should cease. Meanwhile, Sophronius, in his *Synodical Letter*, put forth the position that *Monoenergism* was inconsistent with orthodoxy, and that it was a thinly veiled form of *Monophysitism*, which had been declared heretical at the Council of Chalcedon in 451 CE. Beyond his Synodical Letter, the extensive writings of Sophronius on the subject seem to have been lost. However, under his influence, former supporters of *Monoenergism* began to find inconsistencies in the doctrine. Due to Sophronius' efforts, Sergius and Emperor Heraclius finally abandoned the doctrine, but, undeterred, they soon proposed another new doctrine called *Monothelitism* or the "One Will" of Jesus, as a means to reconcile the *Monophysite* position in the Christological debates.

In response to this new effort, Sophronius composed a *Florilegium* ("Anthology") of some 600 texts from the Early Church Fathers in favor of the concept of *Dyothelitism* (positing both human and divine wills in Christ). This document also is lost.

The proposals of Emperor Heraclius and Patriarch Sergius were seen by many as efforts to strong-arm a reconciliation between Chalcedonians and non-Chalcedonians, which instead, led to great resistance, especially from Sophronius. Eventually, long after Sophronius' death, the Sixth

Ecumenical Council at Constantinople in 680-681 adopted Sophronius' concept of *Dyoenergism* as church doctrine and rejected *Monoenergism*.

One must consider why such ongoing efforts were made towards describing the relationship of Divine to human in the figure of Jesus Christ.

SOPHRONIUS AND UMAR

Sophronius, the exceedingly influential Christian monk and theologian of Arab-Syriac descent was born in Damascus, Syria in 560 CE. He was a teacher of rhetoric, the art of persuasion through speaking. Sophronius became an ascetic in Egypt about 580 CE and entered the Monastery of St. Theodosius near Bethlehem. In his late teens and early twenties, he traveled throughout the greatest monastic centers in Asia Minor, Egypt, and Rome, accompanied by his revered friend, the Byzantine monk, St. John Moschus, reportedly also born in Damascus, Syria.

In 605 CE, Sophronius and Moschus fled to Alexandria before the Persians invaded Palestine. Then in 616, they fled from Alexandria to Rome ahead of the Persian invasion of Egypt. Their flight became a kind of spiritual quest, taking them to many monasteries throughout the Middle East. Moschus dedicated his memoir of their travels, entitled *The Spiritual Meadow*, to Sophronius, his devoted friend. It is a compilation of more than 300 tales about religious practices of the 6th and 7th century written in simple language. Topics include monasticism, devotion to the Virgin Mary, political affairs (including accounts of Persian and Arabic invasions), and criticism of prevailing heresies.

The timing of Sophronius' travels with his friend, John Moschus, is quite interesting. According to Sophronius' account, upon Moschus' death in Rome in 619, he accompanied the body of St. John Moschus back to Jerusalem for burial at a nearby monastery, as the saint had requested. (Muhammad was said to have made his "flight" to Medina in 622 CE, where his prophethood and active teaching began.)

Muhammad would have been the contemporary of Sophronius, but Sophronius' writings give no indication of any knowledge of Muhammad, or of a separate faith led by him. This is an intriguing point to keep in mind. Like Sophronius, many other sources from that time period also make no mention of the Saracens having their own prophet or faith, and only remark, as Sophronius did, that the Saracen attacks must be a punishment for Christian sins.

Certainly, it was a time of great upheaval in the Holy Land. By the time that Emperor Phocas' brutal reign ended in 610, with its merciless internal executions of enemies, and raids and invasions on outside enemies, the Persians had already taken advantage of the volatile situation, crossed the Euphrates and overtaken Zenobia (which may indicate some part of Palmyra, ruled by Queen Zenobia centuries earlier). The Holy City of Jerusalem was conquered by the Persians in 614 CE, and remained under Persian control until the spring of 630, when the new Emperor, Heraclius marched triumphantly into Jerusalem with the "True Cross" which he had recovered from Persia. What was the True Cross that Heraclius returned to the Holy City? We know the story of the three crosses found by Helena, one of which cured people of their illness, but could the phrase mean something else?

As a young man, Sophronius traveled the region for years with Moschus, promoting the Chalcedonian Definition of the "Two Natures". After Moschus' body was safely returned to the monastery of St. Theodosius, Sophronius traveled to Alexandria, Egypt, and Constantinople in 633 CE, to persuade the respective patriarchs to renounce *Monothelitism,* the teaching proposed by Patriarch Sergius of Constantinople (with the approval of Emperor Heraclius), that espoused a single, divine will in Christ to the exclusion of a human capacity for choice. Sophronius was the chief protagonist for orthodox teaching in the doctrinal controversy on the essential nature of Jesus and his volitional acts - standing against the Imperially endorsed *Ecthesis*.

Sophronius was elected patriarch of Jerusalem in 634. Soon after his instatement he forwarded his noted synodical letter to Pope Honorius I and to the Eastern patriarchs, explaining the Orthodox belief in the two natures of Christ, human and divine, rather than *Monothelitism* (the single will of Christ).

Of utmost importance during the time of Islam's origin, were questions, as defined in various Christian sects, on the nature of God: *Monoenergism*, *Monothelitism*, *Monophysitism*, *Dyophysitism*, and other theologically debated positions. It must be noted that one of the great distinctions between Islam and Christianity is that Christianity proposes a Trinitarian formula (that incorporates the Oneness of God), while Islam denies the idea of a Holy Trinity.

Along with his writings on the role of free will and choice in Jesus' mission, Sophronius also wrote 23 *Anacreontic* (classical meter) poems on such themes as the Saracen siege of Jerusalem, and on various liturgical celebrations. If you invert the order of Sophronius' two poems about the Holy City, they describe a complete circuit of the most important sites of Jerusalem. This was in the late 6th /early7^{th} century, "the golden age of

Christianity in the Holy Land."

Subjects of *Anacreonticon* 20 include the gates of Jerusalem (or *Solyma*), the Anastasis, the Rock of the Cross, the Constantinian Basilica (the Holy Sepulchre), Mount Sion, the Praetorium, St. Mary at the Probatica, and Gethsemane. The Mount of Olives, Bethany, and Bethlehem are given in *Anacreonticon 19*. This circuit seems to refer to the recommended route for pilgrims to Jerusalem. Notably, he does not mention the *Nea Ekklesia,* which appears to have still been standing in this time, though it may have been damaged by earthquake and/or the Persian conquest of Jerusalem.

Sophronius' *Anacreontica 19* and *20* are said to be an expression of the longing he had for returning to the Holy City – some believe it was written when he was absent from Jerusalem during one of his many journeys. However, combining the subject matter with his accompaniment of a body of a "St. John" from Rome to the Holy City, one wonders who was actually being described as longing to return to Jerusalem. Who was John Moschus, really?

Sophronius' writings also included an encomium on the Alexandrian martyrs Cyrus and John in gratitude for an extraordinary cure of his failing vision. The Coptics of Alexandria were non-Chalcedonian, as were the Syriac Orthodox Church in Sophronius' home territory. He is considered a saint by the Eastern Orthodox (Chalcedonian) and Catholic Churches.

In his Christmas sermon of 634, Sophronius, as the new Patriarch of Jerusalem wrote about the Chalcedonian issue, giving what seems a rather casual mention of the Saracen advance on Palestine, commenting that they already controlled Bethlehem. Sophronius saw the Arabs as "unwitting representatives of God's inevitable chastisement of weak and wavering Christians." He did speak against the Saracens, at various times calling them cruel, mad, and vile, and against their leader "who is the devil", but one wonders if there might have been "behind the scenes" intrigues involved, and that these derogatory statements might simply have been a cover for his true political-religious alignments.

In 634 CE, Damascus, far to the north of the Holy City, was conquered by the Rashidun Caliphate army during the Muslim conquest of Syria. In some stories it is a Syriac-*Monophysite* priest named Jonah (in others, a Greek Muslim named Jonah) who informed the Saracens about festivities in the city. The priest's collusion offered the Saracen commander, Khalid, the opportunity to capture the city in a surprise attack on the lightly defended walls.

The following pact was drawn up by the commander of the Saracen armies:

In the name of Allah, the Beneficent, the Merciful. This is given by Khalid bin Al Waleed to the people of Damascus. When the Muslims enter, they (the people) shall have safety for themselves, their property, their temples and the walls of their city, of which nothing shall be destroyed. They have this guarantee on behalf of Allah, the Messenger of Allah, the Caliph and the Muslims, from whom they shall receive nothing but good so long as they pay the Jizya."

We must keep in mind that the Syriac monks had close ties to the Arab populations of the region, and so, the amicable terms of this pact are not too surprising.

After the Arab conquest of Damascus in 634 CE, the Basilica of John the Baptist that was located in that city, was transformed into a mosque - now called the Umayyad Mosque or the Great Mosque. It is one of the oldest (that is to say, one of the first) and largest mosques in the world. Ibn al-Faqih relays the story that during the construction of the mosque, workers found a cave-chapel which had a box containing the head of St. John the Baptist, or *Yaḥyā ibn Zakarīyā* in Arabic translation, who was also revered as a prophet by the Saracens. Upon its discovery, al-Walid I ordered the head buried in the mosque under a pillar that was later inlaid with marble.

The given etymology of the Arab word, *mosque* seems to lead down some very strange paths. Some early etymologies claimed a connection to the Spanish: *moskito* - meaning what it sounds like. This connection has since been debunked. It has also been claimed to come from the Arabic *masjid* (place of prayer), none of which seem to give a satisfying or meaningful derivation. Perhaps even a ridiculous etymology is preferable to people understanding the true root of the word. A connection that you don't find in dictionary etymologies is: a certain John from Damascus (soft "a's"), John Moschus (Sophronius' holy companion, St. John), to *mosques.* A simple and reasonable etymology of the term, named for the first conversion of a Christian basilica of St. John the Baptist into a Muslim religious edifice?

In this time period, the Patriarch Sophronius wrote extensively on the most pressing doctrinal issues of the Church. He stood in opposition to the Imperial Byzantine arm-twisting of the *Ecthesis* - both to the first effort of Heraclius' promotion of *monoenergism*, and when that failed, the follow-up proposition of *monothelytism.*

It is notable that, at the time of Islam's beginnings, the Patriarch of Jerusalem was a man of Syriac-Arabic descent, who was opposed to the Imperial/Byzantine doctrinal stance of Constantinople, and who had traveled the entire region for years for political reasons.

He showed little concern for the advancing armies of the Saracens, possibly explained by his own Arabic heritage, and the connection of Syriac monks to the Arabic world, but also in that Arab rulership might be considered preferable by Sophronius to that of the Byzantine hierarchy. If so, then the events that unfolded in Jerusalem would have involved an intrigue of monumental proportions.

In his capacity as Patriarch of Jerusalem, it was Sophronius who surrendered the Holy City to the Saracens in about 637 CE. It is said that the Rashidun army, under the command of Abu Ubaydah, had besieged Jerusalem for four months. According to Sophronius' own writings, surrender was necessary, to save the starving people of Jerusalem whose food supply had been cut off by the Saracens. In these circumstances, Sophronius agreed to surrender, but, oddly, only to the Caliph Umar. According to Muslim sources, Sophronius insisted that no Muslim was to enter the city before the "Prince of the Faithful", Umar al-Khattab.

When an impostor, who looked similar to Umar, was sent in his stead, it is said that Sophronius, privy to certain knowledge about the physical description of Umar, was not fooled, and he insisted on the real Umar being sent to meet with him. Who was this impostor, and what details made Sophronius realize that it was not Umar? How would Sophronius even know details of the physical description of the Saracen leader? Was Umar, perhaps, famous in the Christian world, as well as in Islam? Was Sophronius, in fact, *very* familiar with the physical attributes of Umar? Are we talking about a real – a living person? Or are we talking about the very relics that Sophronius had, perhaps, traveled the region with for many years and not just for the return of his body to Jerusalem) – the relics of his dear friend, St. John Moschus?

Islamic sources, which generally speak well of Sophronius, state that the bishop, leading up to the Arab conquest of the city, made some interesting statements to the people of the Holy City, such as, "I swear on the gospel that, if their prince is here, it signals your destruction". And also, "From the knowledge we have of prophesy, he who conquers the length and breadth of the land, including Palestine, is the dark, tall man, whose eyes have a black iris and a very white cornea. If he has come, there will be no way to fight him, so surrender yourselves to him."[182] In these statements, Sophronius is clearly promoting surrender to the Saracens.

In one version of the story, Sophronius went before the Muslims to meet the Prince of the Faithful, thinking it was Umar. When he realized it was not, he went back to his people and told them to continue fighting. Four months later, he again requested to negotiate with the leader of the Saracens. Finally, Sophronius went to meet the caliph, outside the city gates. Umar, who disdained the finery, the pomp of Eastern Christianity – "coincidentally", as Sophronius did, as did the ascetic monks, the desert monks, the Simple Monks, all of whom unsuccessfully fought Byzantine metaphor and complicated theology. Now the ascetic values would be honored in the Holy City – by the conquering Saracens.

It is said that the Caliph, Umar, journeyed to Jerusalem with one servant. It is made to sound as if no other retinue accompanied the great Umar ibn al-Khattab. According to Islamic tradition, Ka'b al-Ahbar accompanied Umar in his trip from Medina to Jerusalem. Could it be possible that he would finalize the conquest of the Holy City with one servant?

Umar rode into the city in victory, much like Jesus on Palm Sunday, with the Christian Bishop of Arab descent at his side – to the applause and accolades of the admiring crowds (was this surrender or celebration?). The populace, like Sophronius, welcomed the Saracens into Jerusalem. Was this spin-doctoring at some later point in time? These were the same people who had been starving in the supposed months-long siege of the city. Umar arrived, in worn and tattered tunic: the people approved! Not the silks and satins, the gold and pearls of the "simpering Byzantines." High priests wore tunics? Indeed. As did the savior himself: In 9th century Constantinople, Robert of Clari wrote of the Pharos Chapel where important relics of the faith had been sent and were on display. Here "was found the tunic that He wore, which was stripped from Him when He had been led to the Mount of Calvary."

The interaction between Sophronius and Umar certainly seems to have been incredibly cooperative. The patriarch took the Caliph to the Church of the Holy Sepulchre, where he went so far as to invite Caliph Umar to pray, indicating a very amicable relationship, indeed. However, Umar declined, fearing that, in the future, Muslims might say that Umar prayed here and follow suit, altering the Church's status as a Christian temple. The story goes that Sophronius, in appreciation of the caliph's great wisdom, gave the keys of the church to him - certainly an amicable gesture. Tradition says that, unable to refuse, the caliph graciously accepted the keys, giving them into the care of two noble Saracens, who took on the responsibility of opening and closing the church. Though other parts of the holy sites of Jerusalem reverted eventually to the Jews and Christians, the keys of the Church of the Holy Sepulchre remain with the Muslims to this very day.

It is surprising how little attention Sophronius receives in the annals of Christian history. He was exceedingly influential before, during, and after his time as Bishop of Jerusalem. How do we know the truth about Sophronius' religio-political alignments and allegiances, or his possible behind-the-scenes influences in the Holy Land in the 7th century?

One hint is given as to the political intrigues that Sophronius may have engaged in. It is said that he was so gifted as a rhetoricist that he was called Sophronius "the Sophist", a term used in ancient Greece for a person skilled in various studies such as, philosophy, rhetoric, music, mathematics, and athletics. The root word was *sophos*, meaning "a wise man" and is related to the noun *sophia*, or wisdom. Since the times of Homer, it commonly referred to an expert in his profession. Sophists taught *arete* –"virtue" or "excellence"– predominantly to young Greek statesmen and nobility, for which many were paid. This became a contentious issue to Socrates and later philosophers.

Long before Sophronius' time, the term had gained an air of negativity, with connotations of "clever, cunning, and deceptive, or fallacious." Something to keep in mind when considering the details of this influential monk's story - especially his side of the story.

Perhaps in the same way that Sophronius, for his own anti-Byzantine reasons, ignored the extravagant Byzantine "Temple of Mary", known as the *Nea Ekklesia* in Jerusalem, Byzantine Christianity ignored (or buried the record of?) the power and influence, historical actions and significance, of this Syrian monk/bishop of Arab descent.

It is said that Sophronius died about a year after the fall of Jerusalem to the Caliph Umar in 637 CE - some claim that he died of a broken heart (though perhaps that was simply more "spin") - but, not before negotiating the recognition, by the Arab conquerors, of civil and religious liberty for Christians. Their safety was secured in exchange for the required "tribute" money in the form of the *jizya* tax. (This was very much like the agreement that had been made in Damascus, when the Rashidun army overtook that city.) One wonders if he may have adopted an Arabic name and blended into the new governors of the city?

This new agreement between Umar and the people of Jerusalem was known as the "Umari Treaty". The generosity of the conditions for the Christians and Jews of the city indicates a surprisingly close and respectful relationship between Umar and Sophronius. This treaty was also called the "Covenant of Umar", or the Umari Pact.

The name, Umar, has been under our noses for centuries, very present, but somehow, invisible. While "Umari" is generally seen as meaning "related to Umar", it is notable that *ummah* means the community of Muslims, while *umm* means "mother". The Umari covenant was said to cover the people with the "cloak" of the Prophet, like the mantle of Mary covering the faithful: vestige of Christian traditions? – protecting not only Muslims, but Jews and

Christians alike as the "People of the Book". One people...One book?

Muhammad's cloak was preserved and honored as a holy relic in the Ottoman heyday. From the Quran: *Surah al-Muddathir*, "The Encloaked One", is understood to be Muhammad. "O thou wrapped up (in the mantle)! Arise and deliver thy warning! And thy Lord do thou magnify!" For a year and a half, *qiblah*, the direction of prayer was toward the Temple Mount, the Holiest Place of Christians and Jews. Only later was *qiblah* changed to Mecca, with no explanation. Was something moved?

The location of the Holy Place of the Temple was pointed out to Umar by an "early Jewish convert to Islam", Ka'b al-Ahbar, who directed Umar to the southern end of the Temple Mount, where Umar built his first Holy Place.

However, most historians say the Holy of Holies once stood further north on the Temple Mount, where the Dome of the Rock, built by the later caliph 'Abd al-Malik ibn Marwan, now stands, with the Foundation Stone and the cave of the "well of souls" beneath it. Was this a mistaken identification of the Holy Place of the Jews, or did this early Jewish convert to Islam, Ka'b, intend to direct Umar away from the site of the Jewish Temple?

Umar built his first shrine of Islam, described as a "small wooden shrine", on the southeastern end of the Temple Mount. Beneath the southeastern corner of the platform of the Temple Mount, from the Saracen conquest of Jerusalem until now, sanctuaries have stood, the *mihrab* of Maryam, and the Nativity of Jesus. The Temple Mount was in ruins in Umar's time. Did these shrines exist in Sophronius' time, evidenced by his sermon on the Nativity?

Botticelli's painting of the *Adoration of the Magi* in 1475, depicts pillars standing in the background of the wooden "stable" of the Nativity scene - the ruins of the Royal Stoa on the southern end or more likely, Solomon's Porch on the eastern side of the Temple. This structure would not have been in ruins in the time of the Nativity, though perhaps in Botticelli's time these were the columns of the ruined *Nea Ekklesia*, which happened long after the Nativity.

Plate 17 - The Adoration of the Magi - Sandro Botticelli

Does this painting indicate the location of the first humble wooden shrine of Umar? A sort of canopy-ciborium-baldachin-creche? But that wouldn't have been still standing in Botticelli's time. Ah, those cheeky Renaissance masters!

If Sophronius only knew – how simple and ascetic the conquerors of the city would choose to be. Ultimately, there would be no acceptance of "two natures" – so much for the Chalcedonian Creed! (Or was that also his intention?) Too challenging a concept for this nascent Christian heresy – such argument, at that time, in the Christian faith, such confusing and contradictory exegetics. How could it not then be so in Islam also? The Great Heresy – the Great *Christian* Heresy.

Despite all the Bishop's *purported* efforts, the "one nature" would win in the end in Islamic teachings. Jesus would be a holy man, but man only – not "son of God" – Maryam a holy woman, but not the "Mother of God", as the ostentatious Imperialism of the Byzantines insisted.

THE CLOAK

"O thou wrapped up (in the mantle)! Arise and deliver thy warning! And thy Lord do thou magnify!" (*Surah al-Muddathir, 74:1-7*). Does this verse, bring to mind any connection to Christian writings? This phrase which describes Muhammad, the Praiseworthy, echoes Mary's *Song of Praise* (*The Magnificat*): "My soul doth magnify the Lord: and my spirit hath rejoiced in God my Savior. For he hath regarded the lowliness of his handmaiden (servant). For behold, from henceforth: all generations shall call me blessed. For he that is mighty hath magnified me: and holy is his Name." (*Luke* 1:46-48)

Umar was known for his pious and just nature, which earned him the epithet *Al-Farooq,* "the one who distinguishes (between right and wrong)". When Umar learned that Sophronius would surrender the city to no one but himself, he set forth to Jerusalem. According to the story, Umar ibn al-Khattab "left Madinah, travelling alone with one donkey and one servant. When he arrived in Jerusalem, he was greeted by Sophronius, who undoubtedly must have been amazed that the caliph of the Muslims, one of the most powerful people in the world at that point, was dressed in no more than simple robes and was indistinguishable from his servant."[183]

He came to Jerusalem from Medina, where Muhammad and his followers were located at that time. *Ibn* means "son of". Some of the meanings given for *al-Khattab* are, speaker, orator, reciter, and sermon-giver. How and why would a Saracen military leader be given this name? Sermon-giving and reciting were Christian concepts. One is reminded of the name of the 5th century St. John - the eloquent and prolific writer and developer of the liturgy of the eastern Church, Byzantine archbishop, Chrysostom, the "golden-mouthed".

Another version states that, "Umar was wearing a dress with 14 patches, in order to teach Abu Ubaidah that Allah will put our honor in our hearts. If we try to honor ourselves in any superficial fashion, Allah will take it away. And Umar was right. When the people of Jerusalem saw him in that fashion, they started crying. The people were standing on the roofs of their houses, looking at him. They had heard of Umar, but they had never seen him. They couldn't believe their eyes at the simplicity of Islam. They gave the keys to Umar ibn Al Khattab." It continues, "It is mentioned in the book of Ibn Kathir, that they had in their books the signs of the one who would take the keys of Jerusalem, and one of the signs was that he would have 14 patches in his clothes."[184]

The first two successors to Muhammad, Abu Bakr and Umar, were noted for their voluntary poverty. Umar was noted for wearing his frequently patched cloak, rather than a new one – a simple camel's-hair cloak. His modest attire perplexed those who were used to Byzantine splendor, but it was said to be an indication of his support of the common man, and to promote poverty as virtue, which aligned with Syrian asceticism and which would be embraced in the teachings of Islam. Is there a greater significance to the cloak or the mantle? We know that the mantle was, traditionally, associated with Mary. But there are other connotations to consider.

The garments of the Jewish priesthood were seen to be sanctified. As the *Talmud* states, *"While they are clothed in the priestly garments, they are clothed in the priesthood; but when they are not wearing the garments, the priesthood is not upon them"* (BT Zevachim 17:B). Byzantine velvet, silk and satin would not do for Umar, this Saracen (Syriacen) leader.

The garment's holy quality elevates the wearers – that is, Aaron and all his descendants – to the high levels of sanctity required for those who come to serve before God in the "Holy Place." As we read in the Prophets: "And when they go forth into the utter court, *even* into the utter court to the people, they shall put off their garments wherein they ministered, and lay them in the holy chambers, and they shall put on other garments; and they shall not sanctify the people with their garments." (*Ezekiel* 44:19). These garments themselves possess a certain holiness; powerful enough to sanctify all those who merely come in contact with them.

The "Encloaked One" has many connotations, going back to stories of the early Desert Fathers. In the *Acts of Paul*, we read of the Protomartyr, the first female martyr, who, in essence, became the companion of Paul, that "...Thecla yearned after Paul and sought him...and sewed her mantle into a cloak after the fashion of a man...and went to him." In the hagiography of St. Paul of Thebes, the first Desert Father, at his death, his body was wrapped in the cloak given to St. Anthony by St. Athanasius, bishop of Alexandria (who called Anthony the first desert father).

The camel's-hair cloak appears in many contexts in the early traditions of the church. In the eleventh book of the *Ecclesiastical History* it states that Herodias had John's head buried close to Herod's palace (at the Temple Mount in Jerusalem). In the mid-5th century, legend was that John the Baptist revealed the whereabouts of his head to two monks who had come to Jerusalem. They found the head rolled up in haircloth sacks – purportedly, made from the cloak that he once wore in the desert.

In the 6th century, Jacob Baradaeus, the mysterious legendary figure, was said to have disguised himself in old clothes in order to perform his swift and secret journeys throughout Syria and Mesopotamia. His surname, Baradaeus (from the Syriac word *Bara-dai* meaning "horse blanket") or "*al-Barda`I*," so like the *Poem of al-Burda (the Mantle)*, is said to be derived from the ragged mendicant's garb, patched up out of old saddle blankets.

It is recorded that, weary of the bloodshed which was raging in the holy land, Jacobus (James) Baradaeus set out for Alexandria. Apparently, he never reached it; his party got as far as the monastery of Cassianus or Mar-Romanus on the Egyptian frontier, when a deadly sickness came over them, claiming the life of Jacobus, in 578. Interestingly, it is said that Sophronius became an ascetic in Egypt about 580 and then entered the monastery of St. Theodosius near Bethlehem. Can we connect the historically authentic Sophronius with the Syriac Orthodox monk, Jacob Baradaeus? Was he simply the inheritor of the role of Baradaeus? Sophronius, like his predecessor, traveled all the region in efforts to influence the many factions of Christianity.

While the various churches of Syria were well-educated in Greek teachings and texts, the Syriac Churches of both the East and the West arose and developed largely in reaction to and against the Hellenizing influences of Byzantium and Rome. Both the Syriac factions of Jacobitism and Nestorianism, while professing different Christologies, were united in opposing the foreign intrusion and the syncretism that was turning Christianity into a Greco-Roman institution.

The story of Mary of Egypt, which is attributed to Sophronius in the 7th century, may hold some clues about the Syrian perspective on the saint. He wrote that Mary, who had been sinful and a harlot in Alexandria, then repented and became an ascetic, living naked in the desert, until Zosimus gave her his "cloak." It seems that Sophronius highly honored Mary. But Mary of Egypt, the repentant sinner, was far removed from the Mary of the Byzantines. Was he highly honoring her, according to his beliefs, by making her a penitent, ascetic "Desert Father", and by having Zosimus give her his own cloak to cover her nakedness?

Cotterell wrote of the meeting of Umar and Sophronius on the Mount of Olives, "Taken aback by Umar's shabby appearance, Sophronius lent the caliph a cloak until his dirty camel-hair garment could be washed..."[185] According to Cotterell, Sophronius gave Umar his own cloak to wear. Was this Sophronius' own priestly garment? It is hard to imagine that the patriarch of the enemy camp would willingly and so easily make such an offer to someone who was not of the priestly caste, much less to an enemy "invader". Or was this, in fact, veneration for a long-lost and now returning, highly prized, holy and priestly, relic of Christianity?

In the mid-5th century Emperor Leo I, built the Hagion Lousma ("Sacred Bath"), which enclosed the sacred spring, and a circular *parekklesion* (*chapel*), called *Hagia Soros* ("The Holy Reliquary "). In this case, the term *chapel* did relate to a cape. The holy robe (or mantle) and girdle of the Virgin

Mary, were brought from Palestine to Constantinople, to be housed in the Reliquary, which was also known as the "chapel of the Virgin's robe." The mantle was a hugely important relic at this time.

In Islam, a cloak appears in the narrative of the setting of the Black Stone in place, after certain renovations of the Ka'aba. Muhammad settled the dispute of the Arabic tribal leaders, each wanting the honor of setting the stone in place, by wisely putting the stone in the middle of a long cloak and having each of the tribal leaders hold a corner or edge of the cloak, lifting it into place as the cornerstone of the Ka'aba.

In Islam, the *Poem of the Mantle* is a widely known poem composed by the Imam al-Busiri in praise of Muhammad and his miraculous mantle. Tavernier described it as a white coat made of goat's hair with large sleeves, or a cream fabric with black wool lines. Located in modern-day Kandahar, Afghanistan is the "Shrine of the Cloak," located next to the Friday Mosque - one of the holiest Islamic sites in Afghanistan. It holds a cloak that was said to have been worn by Muhammad, the Praiseworthy One, on his Night Journey to the Temple Mount and his ascension to heaven.

The most genuine relics of Islam are believed to be those housed in Istanbul's Topkapı Palace, in a section known as *Hirkai Serif Odasi* (Chamber of the Holy Mantle). The Holy Mantle, *Hırka-i Şerif*, or *Burda* was, reportedly, given as a gift by Muhammad to Ka'b ibn Zuhayr. His children sold it to Muawiyah I, the founder of the Umayyad dynasty. After the fall of the Umayyads, the Mantle went to Baghdad under the Abbasids, to Cairo under the Mamluks, and finally. in 1595, to Topkapi Palace under the Ottomans, which is located in what is now Istanbul, Turkey...which was once called... Constantinople!

Al-Muddaththir, as a reference to Muhammad, is often translated as, "The Enshrouded One," or "The Encloaked One." *Surah* 74:1 states, "O thou shrouded in thy mantle, arise, and warn!" Can we extrapolate this into being a reference to certain relics? And, if so, how do we interpret – how do we practice "reverse engineering" to understand the origins of Islam?

Imam Zuhri gives the following tradition of The Surah *Al-Muddaththir*, "The Encloaked One" (Muhammad), *Surah* 74, based on the authority of Hadrat Jabir bin Abdullah: "The Holy Messenger of Allah describing the period of *falrat al-wahi* (break in revelation) said: One day when I was passing on the way, I suddenly heard a call from heaven. I raised my head and saw that the same Angel who had visited me in the Cave of Hira was sitting on a throne between heaven and earth. This struck terror in my heart, and reaching home quickly, I said: 'Cover me up, cover me up'. So the people of the house covered me up with a blanket. At that time Allah sent down the Revelation: *Ya ayyuhal-Muddaththiru...* From then on revelation became intense and continuous." (Bukhari, Muslim Musnad Ahmad, Ibn Jarir).

Can we step back from a literal narrative of *hadith* (Islamic history) and see the bigger picture here? Is this narrative meant to explain away the early poem of the "one wrapped up in the mantle"? Do we choose to accept a narrative that diverts attention away from any direct connections, or do we choose to see the obvious relationship?

This revelation addresses Muhammad as "the Encloaked One" - one translation gives the verse's meaning as, "O My dear Servant, why have you lain down thus enwrapped? You have been put under the burden of a great mission: you must now arise from your solitude to perform this mission with resolution and courage!"[186] This is said to refer to Muhammad covering up with a blanket, in shock and fear, but beneath the story is an only slightly hidden meaning. The Encloaked One is needed, and cannot remain hidden away, in retreat from the world, but must arise (if only figuratively), to fulfill a great mission.

Muhammad was said to have engaged in eight major battles, some against other Arab tribes. Did this one, in the Christian world, go into battle as talisman, as guardian, as protector of the Christian armies?

Jean-Baptiste Tavernier wrote of a curious 17th century ritual in Istanbul, Turkey, involving a revered cloak, "The Grand Seignor having taken it out of the Coffer, kisses it with much respect, and puts it into the hands of the Capi-Aga, who is come into the Room by his Order, after they had taken the Impressions of the Seal. The Officer sends to the Overseer of the Treasury, for a large golden Cauldron, which is brought in thither by some of the Senior-Pages. It is so capacious, according to the description which they gave me of it, as to contain the sixth part of a Tun, and the outside of it is garnish'd, in some places, with Emeralds, and Turquezes."[187]

So far, we might be discussing a Byzantine ceremony! There is even some resemblance to the "Brazen Sea", the huge ceremonial *mikvah* basin of the Jewish Temple. But this is a 17th century Turkish rite of Islam, "This Vessel is fill'd with water within six fingers breadth of the brink, and the Capi-Aga, having put Mahomet's Garment into it, and left it to soak a little while, takes it out again, and wrings it hard, to get out the water it has imbib'd, which falls into the Cauldron, taking great care that there falls not any of it to the ground. That done, with the said water he fills a great number of Venice-Chrystl Bottles, containing about half a pint, and when he has stopp'd them, he Seals them with the Grand Seignor's Seal. They afterwards set the Garment a drying, till the twentieth day of the Ratnazan, and then his

Highness comes to see them put [it] up again in the Coffer."

This is the cloak of Muhammad (Mahomet), which was housed at the Topkapi Palace in Istanbul, (which was once called Constantinople – the old capitol of the Byzantines, the center of Christianity for hundreds of years). It is the very location that the relics of Mary – the grave-wrappings requested by Emperor Marcian and his wife Pulcheria – were housed for centuries, before the Ottoman's captured the city in the 16th century.

Would this not be the Islamic practice of the Ottoman Turks in Istanbul, following the practice of the Christians, from whom they learned it? Why is the water that the cloak was washed in special – in essence, "holy water"? It was not just that this was the robe of a Jewish high priest – otherwise there would be many robes being washed in similar manner, and the water reverently collected. In Christian practice of the Byzantines, it was because the cloak had once covered the human vessel in which God, himself, had dwelled!

KA'B

Ka'b (or Kaab) al-Ahbar is another important figure in early Islam. Aḥbār is derived from the Hebrew *hābir*, a rank just below rabbi, as used by Babylonian Jews. Thus, Ka'b is said to be a Jewish teacher who was an early convert to Islam. Ka'b means "cube." Ka'b al-Ahbar came to (was brought to?) Medina during the reign of Caliph Umar, and was the "one servant" who accompanied the caliph in his initial journey to Jerusalem, at Umar's conquest of the city.

Ka'b was greatly honored in early Islam and is counted among the Tabi'in (or Tabi'un), the early followers of Muhammad. In one Hadith canon (Islamic historical writing), it states that Umar made Ka'b an *emir*, or king, over Muslims, which seems like high honor, indeed.

When Umar entered Jerusalem, he ordered the building of a mosque on the site of Solomon's temple. [188] It was Ka'b who directed Umar to the Temple Mount, when the caliph asked him, "Where do you advise me to build a place of worship?" We can see that Ka'b was an important advisor to the caliph – one whose guidance was sought for important matters. Ka'b indicated the Temple Rock, which was said to be a heap of ruins from the temple of Jupiter, buried under garbage, where Al-Aksa Mosque now stands. (But the Temple of Jupiter was built in Hadrian's time, in 135 CE or later, and would not have been standing in the 7th century. Though the same location, these would seem to have been the ruins of the Nea Ekklesia – Justinian's 5th century "Temple of Mary"). Abd al-Malik ibn Marwan later built a Holy Place to the north of this – the Dome of the Rock, over the Foundation Stone, which many believe was the location of the Jewish Temple.

It has been argued that Ka'b may be simply a legendary figure. Accounts of his life and influence on Islam have been referred to as myths.[189] Or perhaps there is another explanation for this early "figure" crossing from Judeo-Christian stories into those of Islam. Certainly there is record of his influence in early Islam, both positive and negative, but what is the nature of Ka'b's involvement in the three faiths?

Ka'b narrated many of the honored *Isra'iliyat* (stories from Jewish traditions and other sources outside the Islamic faith). He was very influential in the reigns of caliphs Umar and Uthman, and is associated with the development of the Sunni tradition of Islam. Ibn *Hajar* Asqalani proclaimed that, "Ka'b al-Ahbar is trustworthy." Al-Tabari quoted Ka'b often in his *History of the Prophets and Kings.* On the other hand, Ibn Abbas disputed Ka'b's idea that "on the day of the judgment, the sun and the moon will be brought forth like two stupefied bulls and thrown to hell". Ibn Abbas rebuked him, saying three times, "Ka'b has uttered an untruth!" and quoted the Quran's position, that the sun and moon are obedient to Allah. He accused Ka'b of trying to bring Jewish myths into Islam. Muhammad Jawad Chirri wrote of Ka'b, "He was a Jew from Yemen who claimed to have embraced Islam..."

Ka'b predicted the death of Umar using the *Torah* – you might even say he was a prophet, of sorts, or did his name simply represent a kind of prophetic tool? A Jewish convert to Islam – a trusted Jewish resource now accessed by Islam? His standing with some Muslims became greatly tarnished. Muhammad Jawad Chirri accused Ka'b of deception, of trying to influence Islam through Satanic suggestion. Ali, Imam of the early Shia faction said of Ka'b: "Certainly he is a professional liar!" Ka'b is seen as unreliable within the Shiite community.[190]

Another Ka'b appears in early Islam, Ubayy ibn Ka'b. Ubayy means, "Servant of God", ibn Ka'b is "son of the Cube". He was also known as Abu Mundhir, meaning "Father of the warner or cautioner," terms used for Muhammad in the Quran.

This second Ka'b was also a companion of the Prophet, (how confusing!) and a figure of high esteem in the early Muslim community. Born in Medina, he was, likewise, one of the first to accept Islam and pledge allegiance to Muhammad before the migration to Medina. He came to Medina with Muhammad. How interesting! He became one of the *Ansar*, the "helpers" who supported Muhammad and his followers in their homes (much like early "house-churches" in Rome). Ubayy ibn Ka'b was present at the battle of Badr, and other following engagements – a living person or a talisman, of sorts, like the relics of saints, or even the Ark of the Covenant, carried into battle for protection? It is said that Muhammad, himself, often led the charge, in some of the notable Muslim military confrontations. Does one take this at face value, or does it carry a hidden meaning?

A third Ka'b from the early days of Islam, was Ka'b al-Ashraf, of the *Banu Nadir*, a Jewish tribe who lived in northern Arabia until the 7th century at the oasis of Medina, where Muhammad fled, after persecution of him and his followers by the Quraysh tribe of Mecca. Along with our other two Ka'bs, al-Ashraf, a poet and a chief of the *Banu Nadir* tribe, is said to have, at one time, confessed Islam, and even turned his face in prayer toward Mecca.

When the two Arabian tribes of the *Aws* and *Khazraj* went to war against each other in the Battle of Bu'ath in 617, three Jewish tribes backed both sides and sold weapons to both for profit. The *Banu Nadir,* led by Ka'b ibn al-Ashraf and Huyayy ibn Akhtab, and the *Banu Qurayza* fought alongside the Aws, while the *Banu Qaynuqa* were allied with the tribe of *Khazraj*. The latter were defeated after a long and arduous battle.

Muhammad emigrated to Yathrib (later renamed Medina) in September 622, with a group of his followers, who were given shelter by members of the indigenous community known as the *Ansar*. Amongst his first actions were the construction of the first mosque in Medina, as well as obtaining residence with Abu Ayyub al-Ansari. He then set about the establishment of a pact, known as the *Constitution of Medina*, between the Muslims, the *Ansar*, and the various Jewish tribes of Medina to regulate the governing of the city, as well as the extent and nature of inter-community relations. The conditions of the pact included boycotting the *Quraysh*, abstinence from "extending any support to them", assistance of one another if attacked by a third party, and "defending Medina, in case of a foreign attack."

The *Quraysh* were a mercantile Arab tribe that historically inhabited and controlled Mecca and its sacred Ka'aba. Muhammad was said to have been born into the Hashemite clan of the Quraysh tribe. However, Muhammad and his companion, Abu Bakr, hid from the Quraysh in a cave in Medina, when early on, many of the Quraysh staunchly opposed Muhammad, before converting to Islam *en masse* in c. 630.

Though no explanation is given, after Muhammad's victory over the Meccans at Badr in 624, Ka'b al-Ashraf is said to have composed poems bewailing the defeat of the Meccans by Muhammad, and inciting the *Quraysh* to revenge, though these poems are not properly authenticated. It is related in some accounts that Muhammad said: "He (Ka'b) has openly assumed enmity to us and speaks evil of us and he has gone over to the polytheists [who were at war with Muslims] and has made them gather against us for fighting". This was in contravention of the Constitution of Medina, of which Ka'b's tribe, the *Banu Nadir* were signatories, which prohibited them from "extending any support" to the tribes of Mecca, namely the *Quraysh*.

The Jewish *Banu Nadir* challenged Muhammad as the leader of Medina, and planned, along with allied nomads to attack Muhammad, which led to their expulsion from Medina. Muhammad called for the death of Ka'b al-Ashraf. *Hadith* made clear this intention, saying, "Who is willing to kill Ka'b bin Al-Ashraf who has hurt Allah and His Apostle?" (*Sahih al-Bukhari*, 4:52:270) Muhammad ibn Maslama volunteered along with four others. By pretending to have turned against Muhammad, Maslama and the others enticed Ka'b out of his fortress on a moonlit night, and killed him in spite of his "vigorous resistance".[191] Ka'b al-Ashraf clearly was very important to the Jews, who were horrified at his assassination, and as the historian ibn Ishaq put it "...there was not a Jew who did not fear for his life".[192] The details of his "assassination" are not given.

Though it may be challenging to see these stories as puzzles, as clues to who - or what - "Ka'b" was, with some reflection, it may become apparent.

And, surprisingly, there is a final figure, Ka'b ibn Asad, who was the chief of the *Qurayza*, a Jewish tribe (not the Arab *Quraysh*) that lived in Medina until 627. A tribesman, Al-Zabir ibn Bata, curiously, claimed that this Ka'b's face "was like a Chinese mirror, in which the girls of the tribe could see themselves".[193] Some assumed this to mean that he had a youthful and innocent appearance, but perhaps a more literal interpretation is indicated. Perhaps, none of the Ka'bs mentioned were actual living people, but rather, their prophetic abilities, their importance and/or leadership in the Jewish Arab community indicated something else entirely.

KABBALAH

Kabbalah is a complicated esoteric discipline, and school of thought in Jewish mysticism, whose ideas also became incorporated into mystical Christian and Islamic teachings. Its Jewish followers believe Kabbalah to be an integral part of the study of *Torah*, the *Tanakh* and rabbinic literature, which is seen as an inherent duty of observant Jews.

Though there are ancient teachings of Merkabah-based mystical concepts, modern scholarship generally defines "Kabbalah" as the tradition which flourished from the late Middle Ages onward. According to this categorization, the medieval-Zoharic and the early-modern Lurianic Kabbalah together comprise the Theosophical tradition in Kabbalah. The Meditative-Ecstatic Kabbalah incorporates a parallel inter-related Medieval tradition. And Practical Kabbalah, often deemed unacceptable by the other traditions, involves the magical arts.

It is said that Kabbalistic knowledge was an integral part of the Oral Torah, given by God to Moses on Mount Sinai around the 13th century BCE; although some believe that Kabbalah began with Adam. The knowledge was transmitted orally by the Patriarchs, prophets, and sages (the *hakhamim*) of Judaism. Eventually it was incorporated into Jewish religious writings and culture. It is believed that early Kabbalah, circa the 10th century BCE, was openly practiced by over a million people in ancient Israel. Certainly, in the story of Moses in *Exodus*, magic was practiced in Egypt in his time. When Moses tells his brother Aaron to cast down his rod in the presence of Pharaoh and his courtiers, he did so, and "it turned into a serpent." It may be that the difference between magic and miracles is in the degree of its outcomes! "Then Pharaoh, for his part, summoned the wise men and the sorcerers; and the Egyptian magicians, in turn, did the same with their spells; each cast down his rod, and they turned into serpents. But Aaron's rod swallowed their rods." (*Exodus* 7:8-13)

Invasions of the Holy Land caused the Jewish priesthood and spiritual leadership (the Sanhedrin) to hide the knowledge from non-Jews and make it secret, fearing that it might be misused if it fell into the wrong hands.

Unlike the rational focus of Maimonides' Kabbalah, which incorporates the teachings of Aristotle, those intuitive teachings proposed by the *Zohar*, and later by Rabbi Isaac Luria, became the central stream of Kabbalah, and are, presently, the usual reference of the term "Kabbalah". The theosophy of Luria portrays man as a divine microcosm, within the spiritual realms, the divine macrocosm. Luria taught that human conduct had the effect of redeeming or damaging the spiritual realms. The purpose of traditional theosophical *kabbalah* was to give all of Jewish religious practice this mystical metaphysical meaning.

The Meditative tradition of Ecstatic Kabbalah, exemplified by Abraham Abulafia and others, strives to achieve a mystical union with God, which might be seen as the concept of the "Indwelling Presence" (the *Shekinah),* and may also be related to similar concepts of the "*hypostatic* union with God" of Christian teachings. The "Prophetic Kabbalah" of Abraham Abulafia was the supreme example of this, though marginal in Kabbalistic development. Abulafian meditation was built upon the philosophy of Maimonides, whose following remained the rationalist alternative to the more mystical Theosophical Kabbalists

According to the traditional understanding, Kabbalah was passed down as a revelation to elect *Tzadikim* (righteous people), and, for the most part, and from the time of the Second Temple, was preserved only by a privileged few, that is to say, the high priests of the Temple. Talmudic Judaism records its view of the proper protocol for teaching this wisdom, as well as many of its concepts, in the Talmud. For instance, in *Tractate Hagigah*, 11b-13a, "One should not teach ... the *Act of Creation* in pairs, nor the *Act of the Chariot* to an individual, unless he is wise and can understand the implications himself."

From the 5th century BCE, when the works of the *Tanakh* were edited and canonized and the secret knowledge was encrypted within the various writings and scrolls ("*Megilot*"), esoteric knowledge became referred to as *Ma'aseh Merkavah* and *Ma'aseh B'reshit* respectively "the act of the Chariot" and "the act of Creation". *Merkabah* mysticism alluded to the encrypted knowledge, and meditation methods within the book of the prophet Ezekiel describing his vision of the "Divine Chariot". *B'reshit* mysticism was a reference to the first chapter of *Genesis* (*Bereishit*) in the *Torah* that is believed to contain secrets of the creation of the universe.

The branch of Theosophical Kabbalah proposed a redemptive role for mankind, in the form of harmonizing heavenly forces, while Practical Kabbalah involved white-magical acts, and endeavors to alter both the Divine realms and the World. The latter was censored by Kabbalists for the inherent dangers in its practice - encouraged only for those of completely pure intent. Thus, it was shunned by mainstream Kabbalah. Practical Kabbalah was prohibited by the Arizal until the Temple in Jerusalem is rebuilt and the required state of ritual purity is attainable.

For a few centuries the esoteric knowledge of Ecstatic Kabbalah was referred to by its practice of meditation, *Hitbonenut*, translated as "being alone" or "isolating oneself". It was also sometimes called by its desired goal of the practice, *NeVu'a,* which is to say, prophecy. Kabbalistic scholar Aryeh Kaplan traces the origins of medieval Kabbalistic meditative methods to oral traditions of Biblical Prophecy. This eremitic tradition might be seen in the life of the last of the Jewish Prophets, John the Baptist, who, from childhood, "grew, and waxed strong in spirit, and was in the deserts till the day of his shewing unto Israel" (*Luke* 1:80), and the parallel practices of Christian "desert fathers", who were, essentially, ascetic hermits of the early centuries after Jesus' lifetime.

Rabbi Moshe Cordovero, eminent Kabbalist of the 16th century, who was known as "the Ramak", explains the Zoharic "tree of life" teaching in his *Pardes Rimonim* ("Orchard of Pomegranates"). This title refers to the Pardes mystical ascent (ascension) of the dedicated initiate. The meaning of the ascent is understood through Rabbi Akiva's warning, where the danger concerns interjecting anthropomorphic (human) qualities into definitions of Divinity, introducing corporeal notions into descriptions of the Divine Transcendence or Deity, which is not human but, rather, is ineffable and indefinable.[194]

However, it is a delicate theological line, for in Kabbalah, emanations bridge the Divine Unity of the *Ein Sof* and the plurality of Creation, both of which are essentially, one. And so, as Akiva said, it is a fundamental error to separate Divine transcendence and Divine immanence, as if they were a duality. Is this the error of Eve (and presumably Adam), who gained the "knowledge of good and evil", which represents a divisive, dualistic belief? It is important to bear in mind that the *sephirot* and their interactions involve highly abstract concepts that, at best, can only be understood intuitively.

In Kabbalah, "emanations" have no being of their own, but are dependent on God for their source of life. Dualistic concepts create a false division of above/below, heaven/earth, Spirit/body, and man/woman. Kabbalah maintains that God is revealed through the life of His emanations, man interacting with Divinity in a mutual flow of "Direct Light" from Above to Below and "Returning Light" from Below to Above. Similar concepts would be debated in Christian discussion of the relationships within the Holy Trinity and also in the *hypostatic* union. Such ideas might also be found in modern day quantum physics: at the quantum level, matter and antimatter particles are constantly moving in and out of existence.

Another interesting point in the *Bahir,* the "Book of Brightness" or "Book of Illumination", one of the earliest known works of Jewish mysticism, is the emphasis laid upon a celestial trinity, which became even more accentuated in the later kabbalistic writings ("Bahir," § 48). The *Bahir*, was foundational to the esoteric discipline which eventually became known as *Kabbalah*. The *Bahir* proposes that the world is not the product of an act of creation. Like God, it existed from all eternity. The *Bahir* gives a complicated pattern of connection, the Creation consisted merely in the appearance of that which was dormant or hidden in the first *Sefirah*, known as *Keter 'Elyon*, which emanated from God. This *Sefirah* gave birth to *Ḥokmah or Chokmah* (Wisdom), from which emanated *Binah* (Intelligence). These three, *Keter, Hokmah,* and *Binah*, which are the superior *Sefirot,* form the primary principles of the universe. This might be seen as a kind of Trinity. From these three emanated, one after another, the seven inferior *Sefirot* from which all material beings are formed.

All the ten *Sefirot* are linked to each other, and every one of them has an active and a passive quality—emanating and receiving, which can be described as masculine and feminine. All the *sefirot* are laid out in three columns. Though there is not a direct correlation to the chakras of Hindu teachings, there are some similarities, including the Hindu spiraling feminine channel (*Ida*) and a spiraling masculine (*Pingala*) channel, with a central channel (Sushumna) which is activated in the process of Kundalini Awakening or "enlightenment". The ten *Sefirot* are the energy of God, the forms in which His being manifests itself.

Although the *Bahir* is a difficult work, full of contradictions and obscure ideas, it is very important for the history of the development of Jewish mysticism; being a rough outline of what the *Zohar* would become. The titles of both works are synonyms—one from *Job* (xxxvii. 21), "which is bright ['*bahir*'] in the skies"; the other, from *Daniel* (xii. 3), "And they that be wise shall shine as the brightness ['*ke-zohar*'] of the firmament".

In the *Zohar*, the sin of Adam and Eve took place in the spiritual realms. Their sin was that they separated the Tree of knowledge (10 sefirot within *Malkuth*, representing Divine immanence), from the Tree of life within it (10 sefirot within *Tiferet*, representing Divine transcendence). This introduced the false perception of duality into lower creation, an external Tree of Death nurtured from holiness, and an Adam Belial "fallen" human of impurity.

The first *sefirah*, *Keter*, describes the divine Superconscious Will that is beyond conscious intellect. The next three *sefirot* (*Chokhmah, Binah* and *Da'at*) describe three levels of conscious divine intellect. The seven subsequent *sefirot* (*Chesed, Gevurah, Tiferet, Netzach, Hod, Yesod and Malkuth*) describe the primary and secondary conscious divine emotions. Two *sefirot* (*Binah and Malkuth*) are feminine, as the female principle in Kabbalah describes a vessel that receives the outward male light, then inwardly nurtures and gives birth to lower *sefirot*. Corresponding to this is the female divine presence (the *Shekhinah*).

Kabbalah proposes the human soul as mirroring the divine (after *Genesis* 1:27, "God created man in His own image, in the image of God He created him, male and female He created them"), and more widely, all creations as reflections of their life source in the *sefirot*. Therefore, the *sefirot* also describe the spiritual life of man, and constitute the conceptual paradigm in Kabbalah for understanding everything. One is reminded of Mary Magdalene being described as "the woman who knew the All."

In Lurianic Kabbalah, evil originates from a primordial shattering of the *sephirot* of God's Persona before creation of the stable spiritual worlds. In *Hasidic Panentheism,* from the divine view from above, the appearance (illusion) of duality and pluralism below dissolves into the absolute Monism of God. What appears as evil (below) derives from a divine blessing too high to be contained. One is reminded of The Virgin, who was called "the container of the uncontainable". The mystical task of the righteous in the Zohar is to reveal this concealed Divine Oneness and absolute good, to "convert bitterness into sweetness, darkness into light".

Kabbalists equated the final *Sephirah Malkuth* (Kingdom) with the indwelling Feminine Divine Presence of God throughout Creation, adapting for it the previous Rabbinic term *Shekhinah* (Divine Presence), but lending the concept new *hypostatic* and sexual interpretation (Earlier Biblical Wisdom literature describes Wisdom as a feminine manifestation of God). The fallen, exiled state of Creation by man exiles the *Shekhinah* into captivity among the forces of impurity, awaiting redemption Above by man Below. The Kabbalistic tales of Nachman of Breslov rearrange the archetypal symbols from fairy tales of the world to free the Divine Queen for reunion with "The Holy One Blessed Be He".[195]

The *Zohar* makes reference to *hypostatic* male and female *Partzufim* (Divine Personas) displacing the *Sephirot*. Lurianic Kabbalah places these at the center of our existence, rather than earlier Kabbalah's *Sephirot*, which Luria saw as shattered. In contemporary Kabbalah, cognitive understanding of the *Partzuf* symbols relates them to Jungian archetypes of the collective unconscious, reflecting a progression from youth to sage in therapeutic healing back to the infinite *Ein Sof*/Unconscious, with Kabbalah as both theology and psychology.

Some rabbis had concern that Kabbalist ideas led to the conversion of Jews to Christianity. Perhaps the stories of redeeming the *Shekinah* or the Divine Queen may have resonated with Christian traditions of Mary as the "God-bearer". The Kabbalist ideas of hypostatic union of male and female, might have translated well to the narrative of Mary and Jesus in the New Testament. Certainly the reverse was also happening - the theology of Kabbalism was spreading into segments of both Christianity and Islam. There was a wave of conversions of Jews that swept through Spain in 1391, but it is considered moreso a response to the greatest anti-Jewish violence in medieval history, as well as the engagement of Spanish Jews with Greek rationalism.

Famed 17th century Kabbalist Rav Abraham Azulai wrote a treatise on Kabbalah entitled *The Mercy of Abraham*. Azulai wrote in this treatise, that "a significant spiritual transformation will begin to take hold beginning with the year 2000. It will be an age where Kabbalah will spread to the four corners of the globe, a period when time and space shrink, a time when the secrets of immortality will begin to unravel before the world's eyes."[196]

The Rabbinic ban on studying Kabbalah in Jewish society was lifted by the efforts of Azulai (1570–1643): "I have found it written that all that has been decreed Above forbidding open involvement in the Wisdom of Truth [*Kabbalah*] was [only meant for] the limited time period until the year 5,250 (1490 C.E.). From then on after is called the "Last Generation", and what was forbidden is [now] allowed." He goes on, "And from the year 5,300 (1540 C.E.) it is most desirable that the masses both those great and small [in *Torah*], should occupy themselves [in the study of Kabbalah], as it says in the *Raya M'hemna* [a section of the *Zohar*]."

Azulai puts it succinctly in this statement about the importance of Kabbalist teachings, "From the year 1540 and onward, the basic levels of Kabbalah must be taught publicly to everyone, young and old. Only through Kabbalah will we forever eliminate war, destruction, and man's inhumanity to his fellow man."[197]

TIKKUN OLAM

Another story – allegory?
Another metaphor for the Fall from Grace?
Mystic Kabbalistic sage, Luria,
spoke in the 16th century, of
God light poured into vessels
that could not contain it – they shattered,
scattered throughout the Universe
(like the Jewish people in the *diaspora).*
Shards that trapped God light in matter.

The goal: to gather, collect the light
of the broken shards, reconnect,
return soul light to God.
Release the *Shekinah* – dissolving matter?
"Disappearance of the Universe"?
Or *Tikkun Olam* as "Repair the world."
Rebuild, and renew, on a higher plane?

Return to paradise, back to the Garden.
Restore – resurrect? Not destroy or dissolve –

but repair "With Divine sovereignty".
Not to separate, but to reunite,
what was only separate in belief:
The waters and the waters.
Heaven and Earth, Nature and its Creator,
Spirit and Body, Church and Science,
Masculine and feminine?
Raise the matter, honor the *Shekinah*,
the Holy Spirit in all things.
Restore the Feminine, restore matter,
Restore the woman, restore the world.

* * *

CHAPTER XII. A HOLY PLACE

THE DOME OF THE ROCK

In the *Itinerarium Burdigalense*, written in the early 4th century (after Christianity was made legal), an early Christian source noted the devotion of the Jewish to the sacred rock on the Temple Mount. Jerusalem was then under Roman rule; the Jews had been expelled from the city, and been scattered in the diaspora.

They were allowed to enter the old Temple precincts, one day per year, to perform, according to the author, a ritual at a "perforated stone to which the Jews come every year and anoint it, bewail themselves with groans, rend their garments, and so depart." Was the anointing done upon the Foundation Stone itself, or perhaps, the perforation where once a sacred object may have rested?

Though the Quran attests to a kind of ascension of Jesus, it is not clearly stated, as it is for Muhammad's ascension. Muslims don't, generally, believe in the crucifixion, and resurrection of Jesus' body after three days – they believe that these things were only "made to appear so". The Quran puts forth that Allah said: "O Jesus! I will take thee and raise thee to Myself and clear thee (of the falsehoods) of those who blaspheme." (*Sūrat āl ʿIm'rān* -The Family of Imrān, 3:55)

While the New Testament gives that Jesus ascended from the Mount of Olives, the Quran describes the ascension site of Muhammad as being from al-Aqsa Mosque, said to mean, "the farthest mosque", which is located on the Temple Mount (far from Mecca).

Al-Aqsa is the name of the mosque, but also in the time of early Islam, was generally used to describe the entire Temple Mount, thus the exact place of the Prophet's ascension is debated. However, in *hadith*, the recorded sayings of Muhammad specify that the site of his ascension is not the mosque, but indeed, the Foundation Stone, beneath the Dome of the Rock on the Temple Mount in Jerusalem.[198] Jerusalem, and its holy sites, was the first "holy place" of Islam. After 18 months of the Temple Mount being the center of Islamic devotion, the Holiest Place of Islam was changed to Mecca.

THE KAABA

Kaaba, like Ka'b (or Kaab), means "cube". The *Kaaba* of Mecca is a cube-like structure, now considered to be the holiest place in the Islamic faith, which resides within the "Sacred Mosque", the Great Mosque of Mecca. It is the greatest pilgrimage site in Islam, with over 2.5 million Muslims making the *Hajj* pilgrimage in 2019.

There seems to be a connection of this cube-like structure to another such structure within Christian records. Sophronius, in his review of the major holy sites of Jerusalem, in his *Anacreontic* 20, "The Anastasis (The Resurrection)", writes,

"Let me walk thy pavements and go inside the Anastasis, where the King of All rose again, trampling down the power of death.

I will venerate the sweet floor, and gaze on *the holy Cube*, Through the divine sanctuary, I will penetrate the divine Tomb,and with deep reverence will venerate that Rock.

And as I venerate that worthy Tomb, surrounded by itsconches and columns surmounted by golden lilies, I shall be overcome with joy."

This verse seems to speak of the Church of the Resurrection (Church of the Holy Sepulchre), and the tomb of Jesus, though some references bring questions. What is the "Holy Cube" in the context of the Christian faith, and what is its connection to the Kaaba (the Cube) of Islam? One might consider the connection to Jewish Kabbalah – Ka'b-Allah – cube of God? The "conches and columns, surmounted by golden lilies" is reminiscent of descriptions of the Holy of Holies on the Temple Mount.

In *The Tristoon and the Rock of the Cross*, Sophronius speaks of a "Tristoon", which is a three-sided structure, open on one side, like the Royal Stoa on the Temple Mount,

"Let me pass on to the Tristoon,
all covered with pearls and gold,
and go on into the lovely building
of the Place of a Skull. Ocean of life
ever living and of the true oblivion.
Tomb that gives light!
And prostrate I will venerate the
Navel-point of the earth, that divine Rock
in which was fixed the wood which

undid the curse of the tree.
How great thy glory, noble Rock,
in which was fixed the Cross,
the Redemption of mankind!"

The "divine Rock", the "Navel-point of the earth" is the Foundation Stone of the Temple, but this is not a description of Calvary where the crucifixion was said to have happened. Was the Rock of the Cross that place where the "cross" was hidden, in the Well of Souls - the "wood of the Lord" that gave healing to those who reached into the hole and touched it?

Was the cross always a figure of speech, representing the "Navel-point" of the earth, where heaven (the divine) crossed down into the material plane of the earth? But why would this place be the crossing point of Heaven and Earth? What was special about this particular spot? Did it represent the holy bones which had been the crossing point of Divinity and humanity, and which had perhaps once been hidden within the Well of Souls beneath the Foundation Stone? Or was it another object which may have rested on the hole of the "pierced stone" – a place where Divine inspiration came through into human experience and wisdom?

Since Jewish tradition views the Holy of Holies as the spiritual junction of Heaven and Earth, the *axis mundi* – the center of the world, where spirit crosses into matter, it is therefore the direction faced by those of the Jewish faith when praying the *Amidah.* Notably, this was also the first direction of prayer for the followers of Muhammad – the Foundation Stone (*even ha shetiyah*?) of the Jewish Holy of Holies. The Kaaba is now considered to be the *qiblah* of Islam, the accepted Muslim direction of prayer.

In the eastern corner of the Kaaba, there is a portal or hole that pierces through the corner of the cube-like structure – the hole, itself, surrounded by a huge silver setting, in which rests the sacred Black Stone. During the civil war between the caliph Abd al-Malik and Ibn Zubayr, who controlled Mecca, the Kaaba was set on fire in 683 CE. Reportedly, the Black Stone was damaged at this time – broken into three pieces which were reassembled by Ibn Zubayr in an aggregate material and set in a silver frame. He rebuilt the Kaaba, according to Ibrahim's original dimensions. These renovations cannot be confirmed through archaeological evidence; they are only described in later writings.

Some say that the Black Stone was broken in later time periods. It may be that the stone was broken more than once. One story tells that it was broken into several pieces when the Qarmations, a branch of Ismaili-Shia Islam sacked Mecca. The Muslims of Mecca, generally Sunni Muslims, were outraged at this tribe's theft of the Black Stone, as well as desecration of the holy *Zamzam* well with the corpses of pilgrims in the 930 CE *Hajj* season. The tribe eventually ransomed the stone to the Abbasids for a huge sum in 952, after which it was reinstalled in the Kaaba.

Acts 19:35, makes reference to "... the image [meteor] which fell down from heaven?" Another tradition tells of the sacred stone of the *Magna Mater*, "The Great Mother" - the Goddess Cybele, that was transferred from her Phyrgian Temple to her Palatine Temple in Rome in 204 BCE – a black meteoric stone, which at some point was used in place of a face in her statue, the site which is now the Christian church of Santa Maria Maggiore.

The Foundation Stone, the "Pierced Stone", was the Jewish "Holy Place", the *axis mundi,* the center of the world, where heaven and earth meet, or "cross".

In Islamic belief, the Kaaba now marks the location where the sacred world intersects with the earthly one, and the embedded Black Stone, like Jacob's pillow, is now seen to be a link between heaven and earth. In his vision, while sleeping on his stone "pillow", Jacob saw a ladder upon which angels ascended and descended. (In certain paintings of Muhammad, ladders extend between the levels of the seven heavens.) When Jacob woke, he anointed the stone with oil and said, "How dreadful is this place! this is none other but the house of God, and this is the gate of heaven." One might also say, the gate of paradise, Pardes, or the Orchard, in rabbinical terms.

In the Hebrew language, meteorites were called "betyls", an equivalent to the Greek "baitylia", meaning "the residence of God". From Jacob's account, it would seem that the stone, itself, created the gateway, which caused him to call that place Beth El (the House of God).

Present-day caretakers of the Kaaba anoint the marble cladding of the Mosque walls with the same scented oil used to anoint the Black Stone of the Kaaba. Was this ritual derived from Judeo-Christian customs at the Holy of Holies in Jerusalem, known as the Place of the White Marble? The Kaaba is also known as *Bayt Allah*. Like *Beth El,* where Jacob set up his sacred stone as a pillar at the Jewish Holy Place, the Arabic Holy Place, *Bayt Allah,* also means "House of God."

THE SACRED STONE

A story in Ibn Ishaq's Sirah *Rasul Allah* tells how the clans of Mecca renovated the Kaaba following a fire. The sacred Black Stone was removed for safekeeping during the rebuilding, but the clans argued over who should have the honor of setting the Black Stone back in its place. They agreed that the next man to come through the gate should make the decision – and who should this be but the 35-year-old Muhammad, five years before his prophethood officially began. These stories are not found in the Quran, but in later historical writings of the *hadith.*

In his wisdom, Muhammad put the Black Stone in the center of a cloak, and had each of the clan leaders hold the corners of the cloak, and carry the Black Stone to the eastern corner of the Kaaba. Then Muhammad set the stone in place, while satisfying the honor of all of the clans.

The Black Stone, in Arabic, is known as *Yamin Allah*, meaning "the right hand of God". Tradition says that this stone is a *betyl*, a meteorite that was given to Abraham by the archangel Gabriel.

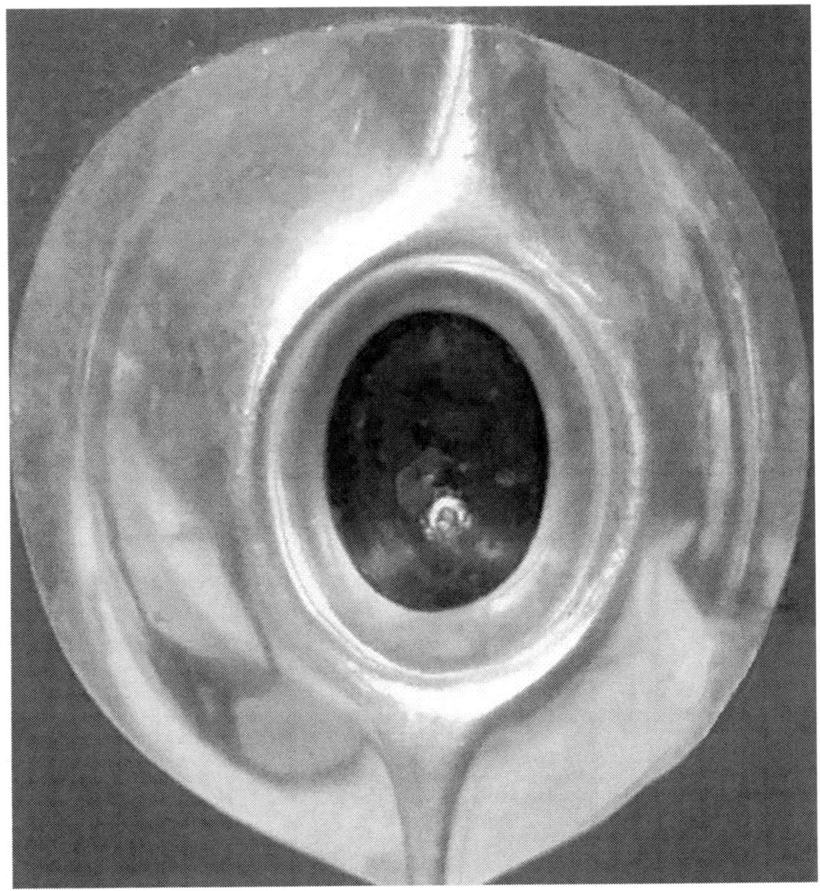

Plate 19 - The Black Stone

In its current form, it is known to contain several pieces of a dark, greenish stone in an aggregate material, which is dark on the outer surface. During the Umayyad Caliphate's siege of Mecca in 683 – the Black Stone was struck and smashed to pieces by a stone fired from a catapult, the fragments then rejoined by Abd Allah ibn al-Zubayr using some kind of aggregate material, bound by a silver ligament.

Regarding the heavenly origin of the Black Stone, Prophet Muhammad once said: "The Black stone descended from paradise, and it was whiter than milk, then it was blacked by these sins of the children of Adam." (Tirmidhi)

The Black Stone has been described as being white with the exception of the shiny black outer face, seemingly, attributable to the fact that the exposed face has been touched by hundreds of thousands of pilgrims over the years. The back or inner side of the stone is, indeed, white.

The silver frame, in the shape of the *Vesica Piscis*, a symbol for the Divine Feminine, with the Black Stone inside, also somewhat resembles an eye. When Sophronius spoke of the coming conquest of Jerusalem, he mentioned the tall, dark man, notable for a black iris, and a very white cornea. According to prophecy known by Sophronius, this was the signal that the conqueror of Jerusalem had come.

In *Pilgrimage*, Davidson and Gitlitz write that the black stone is "the remains of what Muslims believe is the altar that Abraham built. Popular legends say that the black stone is a meteorite that was worshiped by pre-Muslims." (Might that mean Jews and/or Christians?) The authors go on to say that, "Some believe that the ancient stone was brought from a nearby mountain by the archangel Gabriel and that it was originally white; its black color comes from it having absorbed people's sins."[199]

Jewish traditions say that the Foundation Stone was where Abraham bound Isaac for sacrifice to God. While there is scholarly debate on the issue, Muslims proclaim Ibrahim's/Abraham's presence at the Kaaba, and even that he built the Kaaba, many centuries before the Quraysh rebuilt it in 608 CE.

Muhammad was driven out of Mecca in 620 CE to Yathrib (now Medina). Upon his return to Mecca in 629/30 CE, the shrine became the focal point for Muslim worship and pilgrimage. The pre-Islamic Kaaba is said to have housed the Black Stone as well as statues/stone idols of pagan gods. Muhammad reportedly cleansed the Kaaba of idols upon his victorious return to Mecca, returning the shrine to the monotheism of Ibrahim (Abraham). This "cleansing" involved the destruction of the stone idols of the Kaaba. Up until this time, shrines and temples dedicated to Meccan deities still existed there. There were goddesses honored among them as well: the three chief goddesses of Meccan religion were al-Lat, Al-'Uzzá, and Manāt, who were called the daughters of Allah.

Sykes proposed that *Al-lāt* was the female counterpart of Allah while *Uzza* was a name given to the planet Venus. *Manāt* was the most ancient of the three goddesses – highly honored in Mecca up until Muhammad's time.

According to Ibn al-Kalbi, when pre-Islamic worshipers circumambulated the Kaaba, they would chant the names of *Manat, al-Lat* and *al-Uzza*, seeking their blessings and their Goddess intercession with Allah.

The verses in the Quran that referred favorably to these three Arabic goddesses, were called the "Satanic verses" by early Islamic historians, suggesting that Satan somehow was testing the Prophet by giving him these false ideas.

In the pre-Islamic era al-Lat ("The Goddess") was worshipped in the shape of a square stone, al-Uzzah ("The Mighty") a goddess identified with the morning star was worshipped as a thigh-bone-shaped slab of granite between al-Taid and Mecca; Manat, the goddess of destiny, worshipped as a black stone on the road between Mecca and Medina; and the moon god, Hubal, whose worship was connected with the Black Stone of the Kaaba.

One tradition proposes that it was Muhammad himself who toppled the idols at Mecca – 360 stones that represented the many Gods of the polytheistic Arab people. One wonders at the idea that the stone idols of the Kaaba were toppled by Muhammad, while the Black Stone was given a place of highest reverence in Islam. Was the stone truly present in Mecca before Muhammad's time, or was it somehow inherited, along with Judeo-Christian teachings? Was it moved from the Holy of Holies in Jerusalem to Mecca 18 months after the Saracens conquered Jerusalem in 637 CE?

The timing doesn't seem to line up. It is said that Muhammad made a final pilgrimage in 632 CE, the year of his death, and thereby established the rites of pilgrimage. Hadith states that, after his Conquest of Mecca in 630, Muhammad circled the Kaaba seven times on his camel, touching the Black Stone with his stick in reverence, as pilgrims now seek to touch it with their hands, or with their lips, on one of their seven revolutions around the shrine. However, the timing might be meant to prove its location in Mecca before the shifting of *qiblah* to Mecca.

Tradition has it that the Black Stone is revered by Muslims because it was given to Ibrahim by the angel Gabriel. Ibrahim was the grandfather of Jacob, the one who laid his head to rest on a stone pillow and had visions of angels. This puts distance between the stone of Beth El and the stone of Bayt Allah, does it not? Seemingly, this is meant to confirm that it was always in the possession of the Muslims. However, since Muslims didn't follow the Abrahamic teachings until the 7th century, it makes more sense that this stone (which may be Jacob's Pillow) was "inherited" from Judeo-Christian sacred tradition.

If we go back to Da Vinci's paintings of the Madonna of the Rocks, where the Angel Gabriel sits next to Mary, and the infant John and Jesus, what do we see? What does Mary look down at, cradled in the darkness of the folds of her robes?

Did the tradition of honoring the Black Stone begin, not with Islam, but with Judaism, and then Christianity? Why was John the last prophet of the Jews? He is considered an honored prophet of Islam, with Muhammad as the final prophet of their faith. Jesus was, in the end, not accepted in Judaism as the Messiah that his followers claimed him to be. In rabbinical satire, after the suppression of the Bar Kochba Revolt, it would seem that he was seen as a false prophet.

The destruction of the Temple, and the diaspora of the Jews meant that the Jewish priesthood, as such, no longer existed. There was no longer access to the Holy Place, and the gifts of prophecy that it gave to the Jews. Was the stone hidden at this time? Did it only work at the Holy Place of the Temple Mount, with the purification rites of the Judaic priesthood? Was its prophetic usefulness damaged when the stone was broken by the stone fired from a catapult during the Umayyad Caliphate's siege of Mecca in 683? (One is reminded of the strange death of Jesus ben Ananus in the writings of Josephus, "there came a stone out of one of the engines, and smote him, and killed him immediately.")

Or did this happen when it was broken in its capture and ransom by the Qarmations in 930 CE? Or, even, in the attack on the Jewish tribe of the Banu Nadir of Medina, soon after the Battle of Badr (in 624) by the followers of Muhammad. In the 14th century artwork entitled, "Submission of Banu Nadir to the Muslim troops", the people of the fortress are seen surrendering to Muhammad and his troops. One of the figures holds a round dark object. Is it just a shield, or is it something else? IDoes this represent their "assassination" of Ka'b al-Ashraf – the Ka'b whose poems and exhortations had, according to Muhammad, spoken against him and hurt Allah?

Why did the Jewish high priests have to purify themselves with sacred ritual in order to enter the Holy of Holies? Was it necessary to be in the highest states of purity, wisdom, and love to safely access the prophetic capabilities of *even HaShetiyah*? How deeply are we willing to look into the optical illusions of repeating patterns and see the image within the image?

In this painting of Mary and Martha of Bethany, by Italian Baroque master Michelangelo Merisi da Caravaggio called *The Conversion of Mary*, Mary has her hand on what is said to be a mirror. The Church gives a certain meaning to this painting – which art historians continue to glibly disseminate in modern times – that this is the moment of Mary of Bethany's "renunciation of the vanities."

On a number of websites, art historians discuss this painting in just such terms – Mary of Bethany (whom many say is not Mary Magdalene), standing before the mirror, dressed like royalty – being convinced by her sister, Martha, to put aside all worldly goods and pleasures in order to follow the Lord.

Plate 19 - The Conversion of Mary

But the moment that comes to mind here is not one of renunciation – it is another moment altogether: the famous story in scripture about Mary and Martha – the moment of Martha complaining of Mary sitting idle while she, herself, worked, "...Lord, dost thou not care that my sister hath left me to serve alone? bid her therefore that she help me." Why would Martha have complained that Mary was sitting at the Lord's feet, listening to the Word of the Lord? Was this not a rude and unthinking remark for Martha to make?

"And Jesus answered and said unto her, Martha, Martha, thou art careful and troubled about many things: But one thing is needful: and Mary hath chosen that good part, which shall not be taken away from her." (*Luke* 10:39-42) Mary was engaged in the divine art of prophecy. She was speaking to, and listening to the Lord.

The mirror has an intriguing form, but we might assume that mirrors were different in those times. One can look at this painting so many times without seeing it - the object she rests her hand upon is not a mirror at all! Caravaggio, that bold artist, gives us the blatant truth, in his 16th century painting of Mary and Martha of Bethany, hidden in terms that were acceptable to the Church, "Mary renouncing the vanities."

This is the "Ka'b ibn Asad", from the Jewish tribe of the *Qurayza,* who lived in Medina until 627 and whose face "was like a Chinese mirror, in which the girls of the tribe could see themselves".

The truth is there, for those "with eyes that see." Where once the stone itself was the gate to paradise, Mary had become that gate. The presence of God, which once descended onto the Ark of the Covenant in the Temple, had taken up residence within the handmaiden of the Lord. She had become the Ark of the New Covenant, just as had been prophesied.

THE ANGEL GABRIEL

The Angel Gabriel, the messenger of God at the Annunciation to Mary, plays an important role in Islam, as well as Christianity. In Islam, the initial, and ongoing, revelation from Gabriel (*Jibril* in the Quran), occurred in a desert cave to Muhammad, who, like Mary, also submitted to the Will of God, personally receiving the writings of the Quran – did you know? – the stories of the Old and the New Testament, with a few apocryphal tales for good measure. Such texts as the Christian Syriac monks held in high esteem – the wandering monks, like Waraqah ibn Nawfal, the Nestorian monk, who spent years among the nomadic Arab tribes teaching them about the Christian faith and writings, from a Nestorian perspective, seen as heretical in mainstream Christianity. Just so would the Islamic teachings be seen by initially by Christianity – heretical teachings of Christian concepts.

The "Blessed Night" is the name given to the night that Gabriel received the revelation of the Quran from God. In Arabic, it is the *Lailatul Qadr* or *Laylat Qadr.* Muslims propose that revelation of the Quran occurred in two phases: the first phase involved the revelation of the Quran in its entirety on *Lailatul Qadr'* to Gabriel/Jibril in the lowest heaven. Subsequently it was revealed to Muhammad, in a verse-by-verse revelation to Muhammad from Gabriel.

One might see a correlation between *Lailatul* and *Lilitu* (from which "Lilith" is said to derive), or between *Laylat* and Lilit. Not to say that there are etymological connections, only that, in satire, everything is fair game.

The revelation from Gabriel began while Muhammad was in meditation at the Hira cave on Mount Nur in Mecca in 610. The first Surah that was revealed was *Surah Al-Alaq* which is also commonly referred to as *Surah Al-Iqra.*

The Quran states that the angel said, "Take up and read" – read what?

Was it not still to be written? Indeed, say the believers – revelation dictated directly from the lips of the Angel, to the Prophet, like the Word of God to the ear of Mary – the corrected, the pure, the Final Dispensation of the truest Divine Truth – Judeo-Christian stories none-the-less. Abrahamic brothers all.

Islam means "Submission" – like the submission of Mary to God's will, a doctrine also of the Desert monks, who slept little, who lived in poverty, who wore sack-cloth, who practiced all-night vigils – the prayers, the prostrations, the fasting. According to Islamic tradition, on the "Night of Power", in a desert cave in Hira, where Muhammad often sat in meditation, the Angel Gabriel appeared to him, speaking revelation. Truths pronounced by the Angel of God, the self-same one who once "announced" to the All-praised woman, to which she replied, "Here am I, handmaiden (servant) of the Lord, Let it be with me according to thy will." A moment captured by many Christian artists over the centuries, of the "Annunciation to Mary".

Muslims see Islam as the complete and universal version of a primordial faith that was revealed previously through prophets including Adam, Noah, Abraham, Moses from the Old Testament and St. John the Baptist, Joseph, and Jesus from the New Testament. However, Muslims believe the Quran to be the most perfect and complete, the unaltered and final revelation of God, given to the Prophet Muhammad over a couple of decades, directly from the inspiration of the Angel Gabriel (*Jibril*).

One is reminded of early antagonism from such Christian writers as John of Damascus, "And who is there to testify that God gave him the book? And which of the prophets foretold that such a prophet would rise up?—they are at a loss."

In Martini's "Annunciation" (cover image), the moment is depicted: Gabriel and the woman, lily in her hand, the holy dove in the center of a group of angels above them – the words of Gabriel in a line from the angel's lips directly to her ear: *Ave Maria, dominus tecum gratia plena,* "Hail, Mary, full of Grace." The painting depicts the overshadowing by the Holy Spirit and Mary, *conceptus ex auditu,* "conceiving by ear", an actual doctrine of the Church! – a metaphor that got out of hand? A special, a supernatural, a virgin birth, as prophecy had dictated. Mary, submitting to the Word and the Will of God, and "carrying these things/words in her heart".

Church tradition states that the Annunciation (the moment of conception) took place in a grotto or cave that was said to be Mary's home, specified as Nazareth. We find recurring themes of deserts, caves, grottos, as well as other meaningful symbols.

The Quran speaks of Mary veiling herself, before the Angel appeared

"And remember Mary in the Book, when she withdrew from her family to an eastern place. And she veiled herself from them." Does this indicate that she was preparing to prophesy? Or does it indicate that she went through the veil and into the Holy Place? "Then We [God] sent unto her Our Spirit [the angel Gabriel], and it assumed for her the likeness of a perfect man. She said, 'I seek refuge from thee in the Compassionate [i.e., God], if you are reverent." He said, 'I am but a messenger of thy Lord, to bestow upon thee a pure boy.' "

In the Holy Place of the Jewish Temple, there were carvings of palm trees. Here, where Jacob's stone allowed him to see "angels ascending and descending," here in the Holy of Holies, where the Four Tana'im ascended to Pardes. Here, where Muhammad magically flew to on the flying creature, *Buraq*, in order to be able to ascend to the heavenly realms. Here, an important Christian narrative unfolded, and it connects to tales of the first desert hermit, Paul of Thebes, living in a cave with palm tree and springs nearby, and stories of such a location related to Mary, in both the Quran and in apocryphal Christian texts.

In the Quranic narrative of Maryam's travails in childbirth, in her distress, a palm tree was provided to give her dates to eat, and a river beneath her for water to drink. This is a more literal interpretation of an earlier Christian story.

A similar, more expanded and, perhaps, more metaphorical story is found in the *Gospel of Pseudo-Matthew*, when Mary and Joseph are walking through the desert – she, apparently, "with child" and both of them feeling hunger and thirst. "Then the child Jesus, with a joyful countenance, reposing in the *bosom* of His mother, said to the palm: O tree, bend thy branches, and refresh my mother with thy fruit. And immediately at these words the palm bent its top down to the very feet of the blessed Mary; and they gathered from it fruit, with which they were all refreshed." Is this the Orchard of Pardes, the Judaic teaching, perhaps a Christian reconfiguration of the story of "Eve" in the garden, the fruit of her wisdom enjoyed by them both, without judgment?

It goes on to mention paradise, "Then Jesus said to it: Raise thyself, O palm tree, and be strong, and be the companion of my trees, which are in the paradise of my Father; and open from thy roots a vein of water which has been hid in the earth, and let the waters flow, so that we may be satisfied from thee. And it rose up immediately, and at its root there began to come forth a spring of water exceedingly clear and cool and sparkling. And when they saw the spring of water, they rejoiced with great joy, and were satisfied, themselves and all their cattle and their beasts. Wherefore they gave thanks to God."

This apocryphal narrative reflects the idea of a paradise-place, with a kind of "tree of life" with fruit for nourishment, and flowing waters like the "river of life" in Pardes. Here, in this Holy Place, Jesus resides in Mary's bosom, and speaks from there as "the Word" within her, creating miracles in the world around her in acts of Divine Providence. It is a rough outline in folk-tale form, of Judaic ideas, related to Christian beliefs, perhaps not fully understood in Arabic translation, of this place, "the center of the world," the gateway, in a Christian text that was not accepted as canonical by the Church. Is this the Holy Place where the Angel Gabriel came to Mary and the Holy Spirit "overshadowed" her and she conceived the "Word of God" - the entrance to paradise?

The *Sira* and *Miraj* are the two parts of a Night Journey that, according to Islam, the Islamic prophet Muhammad took during a single night around the year 621. In the Quranic narrative of the Night Journey, Muhammad is first carried on a magical flying burro, *Buraq* to the location of the Christian Holy Place – seen to be the site of the later building of the Dome of the Rock. (One might also see connections of the Night Journey to the night-time Transfiguration on the Mount, experienced by Jesus.) Here on the site of the Foundation Stone, the Jewish "center of the world" a ladder *(Miraj)* appears, and Muhammad ascends to heaven and speaks with the prophets.

It was necessary first to go the place of the Sacred Stone, even if in a magical manner inspired by Persian fables and magic - a stone which gave Jacob his vision of angels "ascending and descending" on a ladder to the heavens. Was the stone still at the Temple Mount at this time?

According to the Oxford Online Islamic Studies website, during the Night Journey, "Muhammad traveled with Gabriel to see everything in heaven and earth and then to the Temple in Jerusalem, where he met with Abraham, Moses, Jesus, and other prophets there and led them in prayer." Then he was shown a ladder, in some accounts, a "ladder of light" which he ascended with Gabriel to heaven, where he met with the prophets, including: Jesus, John the Baptist, Joseph, Idris, Aaron, Moses, and Abraham. Muslim scholars debate whether this is to be taken as a physical or mystical journey, just as Jewish scholars debated whether the Four Tanna'im actually ascended to the Orchard or whether the ascent was figurative.

"Then Gabriel brought a horse (Burraq) to me, which resembled lightning in swiftness and lustre, was of clear white color, medium in size, smaller than a mule and taller than a (donkey), quick in movement that it put its feet on the farthest limit of the sight. He made me ride it and carried me to Jerusalem. He tethered the Burraq to the ring of that Temple to which all the Prophets in Jerusalem used to tether their beasts..."

There is an illustrated manuscript in the Library of Paris from the 15th century called the *Miraj Nameh of Mirheydar* (*Book of Muhammad's Ascension* compiled by Mirheydar). His illustration of the Night Journey on the magical flying Buraq, depicts the Prophet soaring through the sky, surrounded by golden bolts of lightning. When he reaches the Holy Place, the Temple Mount, Muhammad ascends, much like Jesus ascended from the nearby Mount of Olives. When he meets with the ancient prophets (as Jesus did in his Transfiguration on the Mount), they have fiery halos around their heads, but Muhammad is surrounded by a fiery gold light, indicating his most superior holiness.

At the Annunciation, when called upon by God, Mary answered, "Here I am", as the prophets of the Jews and the Christians answered, when called on by God – *El* of the Hebrews, and *Allah* of the Muslims. Islam was the "Great Heresy," which the Church called a corruption of Christian ideals, but none-the-less Christian, first...Christian. *This* was the danger – *this* inspired crusades. The problem was in the connection: to Abraham, the ancient Jewish patriarch – to Abraham's sons, Isaac and Ishmael – brothers from ancient times on. But especially, to the woman, whose role had been so successfully hidden in the scriptures of Christianity.

In Islam, the *Hajj*, the pilgrimage to Mecca has its own traditional prayer, the *talbiyah*, first spoken by Thumamah ibn Uthal, an at first reluctant and then ardent convert to the faith: "Here I am at Your service O Allah, here I am...", the prayer of the *Hajj*, the Islamic pilgrimage – to Mecca, Holy Place of the Muslims, (which had first been the Temple Mount); performing the ablutions, circling the Ka'aba, touching the Black Stone, devout pilgrims reciting the prayer: "Here I am at Your service..." The *Hajj* Prayer to Allah ends with what might be seen as complete contradiction to the idea of *hypostatic* union, the "two natures" formula, "Here I am at Your service, You have no partner, here I am. Yours alone is All Praise and All Bounty, and Yours Alone is The Sovereignty, You have no partner [companion]". Maryam, however holy, however worthy of praise, is not divine, is not God's partner or the Queen of Heaven, or the Ark of the New Covenant, she is simply Jesus' mother.

And so, we come full circle in the relationship of the three faiths to each other, of the woman at the heart of Christianity, of truths hidden in plain sight. In the words of the Apostle Paul, "Prove all things, we are exhorted, hold fast that which is good." Do we choose to keep the blinders on for the sake of tradition, and hold tight "in blind faith" to an ancient story-line that has twisted and turned, through hidden truths and hidden identities, morphed and changed in innumerable ways over centuries, according to the leanings and the whims of the powers-that-be at any given moment?

Does our truth, our belief, our understanding of the Divine evolve? Is it meant to evolve? What does your heart say? A question for the times.

JUDGMENT

Jewish prophecy states that the Messiah will come through the Golden Gate of Jerusalem on Judgment Day (*Yawm ad-din*), after the coming of the Messiah. Zechariah 14:4-5 clearly states that the Messiah of Israel will return to Jerusalem from the summit of the Mount of Olives and then surely proceed into Jerusalem from the East, in the direction of the Golden Gate. Christians believe that Jesus Christ will conduct that final judgment. Muslims also expect Jesus to return at the end of the age to participate in the final judgment.

John 12:48 pronounces: "The one who rejects me and does not receive my words has a judge; the word that I have spoken will judge him on the last day."

The Apostle Paul, in *Corinthians* 4:5 states, "Therefore judge nothing before the time, until the Lord come, who both will bring to light the hidden things of darkness, and will make manifest the counsels of the hearts: and then shall every man have praise of God."

The various gospels give a cautionary warning. *Matthew* 7:2 states: "For with the judgment you pronounce you will be judged, and with the measure you use it will be measured to you."

2 *Peter* 3:10-13 paints an apocalyptic Judgment Day: "But the day of the Lord will come like a thief, and then the heavens will pass away with a roar, and the heavenly bodies will be burned up and dissolved, and the earth and the works that are done on it will be exposed." Is this the lie of Ka'b al-Ahbar, regarding the destruction of the sun and the moon? It goes on, "Since all these things are thus to be dissolved, what sort of people ought you to be in lives of holiness and godliness, waiting for and hastening the coming of the day of God, because of which the heavens will be set on fire and dissolved, and the heavenly bodies will melt as they burn! But according to his promise we are waiting for new heavens and a new earth in which righteousness dwells."

The prophecies in Revelations, in the bible, also paint a dark picture of Judgment Day, perhaps, symbolic: of chains and fires, dragons and bottomless pits. But it also says, "He will wipe away every tear from their eyes, and death shall be no more, neither shall there be mourning, nor crying, nor pain anymore, for the former things have passed away."

James 2:12-13 brings to mind the two doors of the Golden Gate in the Holy City: Repentance (John) and Mercy (Mary), "So speak and so act as those who are to be judged under the law of liberty. For judgment is without mercy to one who has shown no mercy. Mercy triumphs over judgment."

Modern Christian theology, generally, avoids ancient images of destruction and eternal damnation, proposing a merciful outcome specifically based in the salvific role of Jesus and Mary.

Pope John Paul II, in *Mulieris Dignitatem*, proposed, "Saint Paul states that the mystery of man's redemption in Jesus Christ, the son of Mary, resumes and renews that which in the mystery of creation corresponded to the eternal design of God the Creator. Precisely for this reason, on the day of the creation of the human being as male and female 'God saw everything that he had made, and behold, it was very good' *(Gen* 1:31). *The Redemption restores,* in a sense, at its very root, *the good* that was essentially "diminished" by sin and its heritage in human history."

Muslims compare the final judgment of mankind to the crossing of a narrow knife blade which stretches from a mountain (the Mount of Olives is often mentioned in Arab legend) to the "gate of heaven." This knife-edged bridge evidently spans the Cedron Valley – as did an ancient stone bridge in Roman times.

On the Day of Resurrection, Muslims say that Paradise will be "brought as a bride to the Holy City, and the Ka'aba also shall come thither with her. So that men will exclaim, 'All hail to those who come as pilgrims. And all hail to her when pilgrimage is made.' And the Black Stone shall be brought, to bridal procession, and the Black Stone on that day shall be greater in size than the Hill of Abu Kubais."

The *Qasidat al Burda* (The Poem of the Mantle) states, "O thou, most generous of mankind, I have no one to take refuge with, except thee, on the occurrence of the universal calamity.' And O Messenger of God! Thy dignity will not grudge my Salvation when the Bountiful God will appear…on the day of judgement."

In a late artwork, which is part of the Reza Abbasi Museum Collection (Iran, unsigned and undated, attributed to the 19th century artist Mohammad Modabber), it is clear that others have followed these ideas to their interesting conclusions.

The prophets of Islam stand on the steps leading to the heavenly realms. Gabriel flies above the crowd blowing his horn. Muhammad, uncharacteristically dressed in black, with a white face-veil, is seated on a camel, in the top right - riding towards Jesus at the top of the steps on the left.

The Arabic term *al-maqam al-mahmud* means “the praised station” and represents Muhammad’s intercession with Allah for the devout and prayerful ones, much like the intercessor within Christianity – the one who intercedes with God for devout followers. The station of mediation (*maqam al-wasila*) is a rank in Paradise that no one but the Prophet shall reach.

MERCY

A famous shabbat hymn of the mystic, kabbalist Rabbi Isaac Luria, speaks of the “Shabbat Bride”:

I sing in hymns to enter the gates
of the Field of holy apples.
A new table we prepare for Her,
a lovely candelabrum sheds its light upon us.
Between right and left the Bride approaches,
in holy jewels and festive garments...

The *Lecha Dodi*, is a Jewish liturgical song that has long preserved the idea of a time of reunion of the Shabbat bride with her King (the Lord). It is recited in synagogues, Fridays at sundown, to welcome Shabbat prior to the *Maariv* (evening services). It is part of the *Kabbalat Shabbat* ("acceptance of Sabbath"), and it suggests not only reunion, but restoration of the Shabbat Bride as a metaphor for the Holy City of Jerusalem:

“Sanctuary of the king, royal city, Arise! Leave from the midst of the turmoil; Long enough have you sat in the valley of tears And He will take great pity upon you compassionately...All my afflicted people will find refuge within you, And the city shall be rebuilt on her hill...”

Mary, the "woman" of the Bible intimately belongs to the salvific mystery of Christ, and is therefore also present in a special way in the mystery of the Church. The *Brevarium in Psalterium* songbook gives an allegorical description, “Christ in Mary, as though the Bridegroom in the bride chamber, and the body of Mary as though the tabernacle.”

The *Lecha Dodi* of Jewish worship on the Sabbath, invites the Sabbath Bride: “Let’s go, my beloved, to meet the bride, and let us welcome the presence of Shabbat...Come in peace, crown of her husband, Both in happiness, in song and in jubilation. Amidst the faithful of the treasured nation, Come O Bride! Shabbat Queen!”

She remains at the center of Jewish worship – the bride, the Queen of Shabbat; Kabbalah's indwelling presence of the Spirit, the *Shekinah*, Holy Wisdom, the Divine Presence, the Light of God.

Sophronius, in his sermon on the Blessed Virgin, said, "You, O Virgin, are like a clear and shining sky, in which God has set his tent. From you he comes forth like a bridegroom leaving his chamber."

She is present in Christianity, beneath the layers of mystery, and of misdirection. Her role debated over and over again by powerful men throughout the centuries of Christian worship: The Beloved Disciple, the Holy Virgin, the Mother of the Church, the Theotokos, the Ark of the New Covenant, the container of the uncontainable, the Bride Unwedded, the Queen of Heaven. In duality, she was divided into the fallen woman and the pure and perfect one. What is her expression in the world when duality merges back into Unity?

"And there appeared a great wonder in heaven; a woman clothed with the sun, and the moon under her feet, and upon her head a crown of twelve stars ... And she brought forth a man child, who was to rule all nations with a rod of iron: and her child was caught up unto God, and *to* his throne. And the woman fled into the wilderness, where she hath a place prepared of God, that they should feed her there a thousand two hundred *and* threescore days." (*Revelation*, 12:1-2)

She is even more disguised, shrouded, veiled, and hidden in Islam – like the veiled Presence of God in the Holy of Holies – that none may look upon her holiness – the veil covering the Divinity. But she is present, none-the-less: the bearer of good tidings, the enwrapped, the enshrouded, the encloaked one, the servant of God, the one who submits, the one who calls [unto God], the light-giving lamp, the light personified, the messenger, the Praiseworthy One. Can you see it? Will you see it? Soften...soften...as the New Era begins, all may now have the eyes to see.

The Age of Pisces was the age of patriarchal rule, of "might makes right," the exploration of masculine principles, rational thought, moral concepts, exclusivity, outward expression of the power and will of the solar plexus, and the dominator model of society. The second millennium after the time of Jesus has continued this exploration of "power over," expanding it to its extreme, before humanity, in the now-dawning Age of Aquarius, is once again able to rise above the power struggles, as well as the ideas of sin, and suffering, and sacrifice - and now experience living from the heart.

Perhaps the metaphor of Mary as the dwelling place of the Lord is meant literally. Perhaps she now supersedes the Black Stone as the Holy of Holies, as this was only preparation for this present time when we might also see that we are able to house the "Indwelling resence," the *Shekinah*, as taught originally in Judaism – the Holy Spirit, the Christ, as taught in Christianity. She demonstrated for us, what Origen and Hippolytus, and other Early Church Fathers suggested, and what is now immanent for all of humanity: the bearing of God, the recognizing of God, in our own human forms – Divinity fully housed within our humanity – the Soul embodied.

The treasures and the objects of power must be used for the good of all people, in order for us to live in the "New Jerusalem." The greatest treasure is to be found in remembering and accepting our own God natures. As Paul asked so many centuries ago, "Know ye not that ye are the temple of God, and that the Spirit of God dwelleth in you?" This is heaven on earth and the new dawn of the New Earth.

And I saw a new heaven and a new earth: for the first heaven and the bnd he said unto me, Write: for these words are true and faithful. And he said unto me, It is done. I am Alpha and Omega, the beginning and the end. I will give unto him[/her] that is athirst of the fountain of the water of life freely." (Revelation 21:1-7)

BOOK PLATES:

Plate 1 – The Aleph – Artwork by B. Waters
Plate 2 – The Tree of Life – Diagram by B. Waters
Plate 3 – The Transfiguration, by Raphael, 1516 - 1520. Public Domain
Plate 4 – The Transfiguration, by Ludovico Carracci, 1594. Public Domain.
Plate 5 – Deposition from the Cross - Peter Paul Rubens, 1612 - 1614. Public Domain
Plate 6 – Descent from the Cross - Peter Paul Rubens, 1612 - 1614. Public Domain.
Plate 7 – Deposition, by Tintoretto, 1602. Public Domain.
Plate 8 – Lamentation, by Peter Paul Rubens, 1618. Public Domain
Plate 9 – Longinus, by Gian Lorenzo Bernini), Public Domain
Plate 10 – The Fall of Simon Magus, by Benozzo Gozzolit. 1461-2. Public Domain.
Plate 15 – Penance of St. John Chrysostom-Albrecht Durer, 1496. Public Domain.
Plate 16 – The Penance of St. John Chrysostom, Lucas Cranach the Elder. 1509. Public Domain.

Plate 17 – The Adoration of the Magi, by Sandro Botticelli. 1475. Public Domain
Plate 18 – Black Stone permission from Amerrycan Muslim, CC BY-SA 3.0 <https://creativecommons.org/licenses/by-sa/3.0>, via Wikimedia Commons (cropped)
Plate 19 – The Conversion of Mary by Carravaggio, 1547. Public Domain

---

[1] *Eve and Adam: Jewish, Christian, and Muslim Readings on Genesis and Gender,* Indiana University Press, Editors:Kristen E. Kvam, Linda S. Schearing, Valarie H Ziegler, 1999, P. 219

[2] "PaRDeS", https://www.ou.org/judaism-101/glossary/pardes/

[3] https://amp.ww.en.freejournal.org/5617860/1/pardes-jewish-exegesis.html

[4] https://www.encyclopedia.com/religion/encyclopedias-almanacs-transcripts-and-maps/aggadah-or-haggadah

[5] Singer, Isidore; et al., eds. (1901–1906). *Akiba ben Joseph, Alphabet of.* The Jewish Encyclopedia. New York: Funk & Wagnalls.

[6] Ibid

[7] "Alpha Bet of Akiba ben Joseph", https://en-academic.com/dic.nsf/enwiki/4520643

[8] *Four Who Entered Paradise* from Rabbi Moshe Cordovero, https://www.chabad.org/kabbalah/article_cdo/aid/380344/jewish/Four-Who-Entered-Paradise.htm

[9] Ibid

[10] *Four Who Entered Paradise* from Rabbi Moshe Cordovero, https://www.chabad.org/kabbalah/article_cdo/aid/380344/jewish/Four-Who-Entered-Paradise.htm

[11] Ibid

[12] Augustine, *The Literal Meaning of Genesis*, VIII, 4, 8 (On Genesis, New City Press, p. 351-353)

[13] Celebration of Palm Sunday of the Passion of our Lord, Homily of His Holiness, Benedict XVI, Saint Peter's Square, XXI World Youth Day, Sunday, 9 April 2006

[14] Tree of Life, https://en.wikipedia.org/wiki/Tree_of_life

[15] Cordovero, Rabbi Moshe, *Pardes Rimonim, Sha'ar Arachei HaKinuim, s.v. Mayim*

[16] Ibid

[17] Ibid

[18] Cooke, G.A., *Ezekiel*, (1936), Bloomsbury Publishing, 2015P. 413

[19] 1 Kings 6:19-38, KJV

[20] Salusinszky, Imre, Criticism & Society, Taylor and Francis, 2013, p. 53

[21] Davila, J (2008). "Aristeas to Philocrates". *Summary of lecture by Davila, February 11, 1999.* Univ. St. Andrews

[22] Joel Kalvesmaki, *The Septuagint.* https://www.kalvesmaki.com/LXX/secondlit.htm 2013.

[23] Eisler, Riane T. (1988). *The chalice and the blade: Our history, our future.* San Francisco: Perennial Library.

[24] Bolen, Jean Shinoda, *Urgent Message from Mother*, Conari Press, 2008

[25] Lapsley, Newsom, Ringe (author/editors),*The Women's Bible Commentary*,
Westminster John Knox Press, [1992] 2012, page 3

[26] Ibid (Lapsley, Newsom, Ringe)

[27] Ginsberg, Louis, *Legends of the Jews*, [1909] Chapter IV, the *Punishment of the Fallen Angels*

[28] Thompson, Thomas L. *The Messiah Myth: The Near Eastern Roots of Jesus and David.* Basic Book Perseus Books, 2005

[29] Tom Harper, *The Pagan Christ,* Thomas Allen Publishers, Toronto Canada, [2004] p. 145

[30] William Barclay, *The Gospel Of John,* 2001, St. Andrew Press, Edinburg, p. 1 (Originally published as *The Daily Study Bible: The Gospel of John*)

[31] Price, R.G., *The Gospel of Mark as Reaction and Allegory,* October 2007

[32] Metzger, Bruce, *A Textual Commentary on the Greek New Testament,* Hendrickson Publishers; 2nd ed. edition (January 3, 2005)

[33] Mournet, Terence C., *Oral Tradition and Literary Dependency: Variability and Stability*
in the Synoptic Tradition and Q, Mohr Siebeck, 2005, pp. 54-99

[34] *Skarsaune, Oskar, "The Ebionites". Skarsaune, Oskar; Hvalvik, Reidar. "Jewish Believers in Jesus" (PDF). Hendrickson Publishers. (2007). pp. 419–62.*

[35] Luomanen, Petri, *Recovering Jewish Christian Sects and Gospels.* Brill. (2012).

[36] Rev. Alexander Roberts, D.D., and James Donaldson, LL.D., *Ante-Nicene Fathers, Vol III: Tertullian: Part II Anti- Marcio.* Wm. B. Eerdmans publishing company, Grand Rapids, MI

[37] Johnson, Luke Timothy, *The Acts of the Apostles.*The Liturgical Press (1992), p. 474-476

[38] Heard, Richard: *An Introduction to the New Testament Chapter 13: The Acts of the Apostles,* Harper & Brothers, 1950

[39] Grant, Robert McQueen, *The Gospel of Luke and the Book of Acts.* A Historical Introduction to the New Testament. Harper & Row. 1963, Ch. 10.

[40] Goodspeed, Edgar J., *An Introduction to the New Testament,* University of Chicago Press, Chicago: IL. Pub. September 1937. Chp. 181

[41] Bart D. Ehrman (2000:43) *The New Testament: a historical introduction to early Christian writings.* Oxford University Press.

[42] Rudolf Steiner, *Esoteric Christianity: The Gospel of St. John and Ancient Mysteries* A lecture delivered in Dusseldorf, on November 27th, 1906

[43] F. W. Beare, *The First Epistle of Peter* (Oxford: Blackwell, 1970). 29. Cited in Grudem, W. A. (1988). *1 Peter: an introduction and commentary* (Vol. 17). Downers Grove, IL: InterVarsity Press.

[44] Rokeah (2002) *Justin Martyr and the Jews*, p. 2, (Leiden, Brill, 2002).

[45] Laing Drake, Susanna, *Sexing the Jew: Early Christian Constructions of Jewishness*, Department of Religion, Duke University, page 155

[46] Drake, Susanna, *Slandering the Jew: Sexuality and Difference in Early Christian Texts*, University of Pennsylvania Press, Incorporated, 2013

[47] *Composition of the Holy Scripture, (Ci nous dit)*, parchment illumination, http://www.mheu.org/en/timeline/holy-scripture.htm

[48] James D. G. Dunn, *The Canon Debate,* L.M. McDonald and J.A. Sanders, editors, 2002, chapter 32, p. 577

[49] A. C. Headlam, *The Clementine Literature in Journ. Theol. Stud.* (1903), III,

41

[50] Chapman, J. (1908). Clementines. In The Catholic Encyclopedia. New York: Robert Appleton Company. http://www.newadvent.org/cathen/04039b.htm

[51] Rhode James, Montague. *The Apocryphal New Testament* (Oxford: Clarendon Press 1924), p. 16-19.

[52] LANGEN, Die Clemensromane; ihre Entstehung u. ihre Tendenzen (Gotha, 1890)

[53] Ibid, (Chapman, J.)

[54] Otto Zwierlein, Bonn, *Has St. Peter ever been in Rome?* https://www.philologie.uni-bonn.de/de/personal/zwierlein/st_peter_in_rome.pdf

[55] *Nicene and Post-Nicene Fathers*, 2nd series, 3: 361

[56] Joseph Priestley, *Corruptions of Christianity*, [1782], New York, Garland Pub., 1974.

[57] F.C. Baur, *Paul, an Apostle of Jesus Christ, his life and his work, his letters and his teaching,* 1845

[58] Ehrman, Bart, "Was Paul a Misogynist", https://ehrmanblog.org/was-paul-a-misogynist, Kirk, J.R. Daniel. "Was Paul a Misogynist?" web

[59] Pope Benedict XVI, *General Audience,* Paul VI Audience Hall, Wednesday, 14 February 2007

[60] Pagels, Elaine. *The Gnostic Gospels.* Vintage Publishers, 1989, p.62

[61] Hyam Maccoby, *The Mythmaker: Paul and the Invention of Christianity*, Chapter 1

[62] James McConkey Robinson, Richard Smith, *Nag Ham. Library, Coptic Gnostic Library Project.* BRILL, 1996. p 524

[63] Ibid (Robinson, Smith)

[64] Karen L. King, "Why All the Controversy? Mary in the Gospel of Mary." in *Which Mary? The Marys of Early Christian Tradition,* F. Stanley Jones, ed. (Brill, 2003), 74.

[65] Ibid (King)

[66] *Midrash Yalkut Shimoni: Torah, Nevi'im, u-Khetuvim.* Machon HaMeor, Jerusalem 2001

[67] Schoeps, Hans-Joachim, *Theologie und Geschichte des Judenchristentums*

[Tubingen: 1949] 441-48

[68] Hemer & Gempf, *The Book of Acts in the Setting of Hellenistic History*, p. 7 (1990). x

[69] Hendrix, Holland L., *Luke/Acts – An Early Christian Romance*, https://www.pbs.org/wgbh/pages/frontline/shows/religion/story/luke.html

[70] "Article 460", *Catechism of the Catholic Church,* New York: Doubleday (1995),

[71] Boyarin, Daniel. *Border Lines The Partition of Judaeo-Christianity.* University of
Pennsylvania Press, 2004, p. 139

[72] Pettegrew, Larry D., *The New Covenant and New Covenant Theology,* https://www.tms.edu/m/tmsj18h.pdf

[73] Albright, William F., *The Archaeology of Palestine: From the Stone Age to Christianity.*
1922–1923, pp. 158–160

[74] Nestle, E., *Philologica Sacra* (1896)

[75] Johann Nepomuk Sepp; Claude-Joseph Drioux; Whittaker, H.A. *Studies in the Gospels,* Biblia Staffordshire 1984, 2nd Ed. 1989 p. 495

[76] Lightfoot, J.B. *Works*, Volume xii, 159-63"

[77] Hahn, Scott, and Mitch, Curtis, *Study Questions for the Ignatius Catholic Study Bible*
The Acts of the Apostles, Ignatius Press , San Francisco, 2001

[78] *The Blackwell Companion to Jesus,* ed. Burkett p. 220, 2010

[79] Schäfer, Peter, *Jesus in the Talmud* Aug 24, 209,) p. 9, 17, 141.

[80] Van Voorst, Robert E (2000). *Jesus Outside the New Testament: An Introduction to the*
Ancient Evidence. Wm B Eerdmans Publishing. p. 122

[81] Dan, Joseph, "Toledot Yeshu" in *Encyclopaedia Judaica*, 2nd ed. (2007)

[82] Flannery, Edward H., *The Anguish of the Jews: Twenty-three centuries of Anti*
Semitism (1965, NY, Macmillan) page 283 (footnote 30 to chapter 2).

[83] Carmilly-Weinberger, Moshe, *Censorship and Freedom of Expression in Jewish History,* Sepher-Hermon Press; First Edition (1977)

[84] Van Voorst, Robert E (2000). *Jesus Outside the New Testament: An Introduction to the Ancient Evidence*. Wm B Eerdmans Publishing. p. 122

[85] Bernard Pick, *Jesus in the Talmud His Personality, His Disciples and His Sayings*, Open Court Publishing Co. Cornell, University, 1913, page 12

[86] Martilla, Marko, *The Figure of Phinehas from Different Perspectives,* The Hero of His People in Num 25:6–13, Ps 106:28–31 and Sir. 45:23–26, Journal of Ancient Judaism, 2014

[87] George A. Kennedy, *Progymnasmata: Greek Textbooks of Prose Composition and Rhetoric*, Brill, 2003

[88] Evans, J. D. G., 1977. *Aristotle's Concept of Dialectic,* Cambridge: Cambridge University Press

[89] Josh McDowell & Bill Wilson, *He Walked Among Us,* Here's Life Publishers (1988), p. 67-68

[90] Cohn-Sherbok, Dan, *Judaism and Other Faiths*, Palgrave Macmillan, 1994, p 48

[91] Baring-Gould, Sabine, *The Lives of the Saints*, vol. III (Edinburgh) 1914, *sub* "March 15: S[aint] Longinus M[artyr]"

[92] Eusebius of Caesarea, *Church History,* Book III, ch. 11.

[93] Epiphanius of Salamis; Williams, Frank (2013). *The Panarion of Epiphanius of Salamis: De fide.* Books II and III, Sect 78:7,5. BRILL. p. 620.

[94] DeConick, April, *Holy Misogyny: Why the Sex and Gender Conflicts in the Early Church Still Matter*, Continuum, 2011

[95] St. Methodius, *Orat. de Simeone et Anna* ii. Patr. Graec. Tom. 18, p. 332.

[96] Ibid

[97] Pope John Paul II, *General Audience*, July 2, 1997

[98] S. Hippolytus, In Dan.vi., Patr. Gr., Tom. 10, p. 648

[99] Orosius, Paulus, *Seven Books of History Against the Pagans*, 7.12.6.

[100] Henderson, Jonathan P., *The Roman-Jewish Wars, Part Two: The Kito War and Bar Kokhba Revolt*, 115 AD – 136 AD, Posted on 17 Dec 2019

[101] Robert Goldenberg. *Review of "Dying for God: Martyrdom and the Making of Christianity and Judaism"* by Daniel Boyarin in The Jewish Quarterly Review, New Series, Vol. 92, No. 3/4 (Jan. - Apr., 2002), pp. 586-588

[102] Boyarin, Daniel, *Review of "Dying for God: Martyrdom and the Making of Christianity and Judaism"*, The Jewish Quarterly Review, New Series, Vol. 92, No. 3/4 (Jan. - Apr., 2002), pp. 586-588

[103] Max I. Dimont *Jews, God and History*, Signet; 2 edition (June 1, 2004)

[104] Brent, Rev. Allen, *Hippolytus and the Roman Church in the Third Century*, Vigiliae Christianae, Supplements, Volume: 31, Brill (1995)

[105] Ibid (Allen)

[106] Livy, Ab Urbe Condita, *History of Rome*, 29.10-1,1 .14 (c. 10 C.E.)

[107] D'Orasio, Masimo, *Meteorite records in the ancient Greek and Latin literature: between history and myth*, https://doczz.net/doc/8099443/meteorite-records-in-the-ancient-greek-and-latin-literature

[108] Nativity, https://www.catholicnewsagency.com/news/46981/first-known-nativity-scene-figurines-can-now-be-seen-in-st-mary-major-basilica

[109] Mitt. 1895, 1-28; 1906

[110] Crotty, Robert, *The Christian Survivor: How Roman Christianity Defeated Its Early Competitors,* Springer, Singapore. 2017, p.265

[111] Severano, *Sette Chiese,* 95

[112] Garder, Helen; et al. (March 17, 2004). *Gardner's Art Through the Ages With Infotrac*. Thomas Wadsworth. p. 619.

[113] Partner, Peter (1972). *The Lands of St. Peter: The Papal State in the Middle Ages and the Early Renaissance,* Volume 10. University of California Press. p. 57

[114] Philip Francis Esler *The Early Christian World, Volume 2*. Taylor & Francis. (2000).

[115] *Neoplatonism*, New Adv. Encyc., https://www.newadvent.org/cathen/10742b.htm

[116] Elizabeth A. Clark, *The Origenist Controversy: The Cultural Construction of an Early Christian Debate*, Princeton University Press, 2014

[117] *Hurlbut, Jesse L., Story of the Christian Church*, Zondervan, 1967, p. 41

[118] Tyson, Joseph B., Publisher's note*, Marcion and Luke-Acts, A Defining Struggle*, 2006

[119] *Hippolytus and His Age*, Volume I, frontispiece, 1852, p. 424.

[120] Price, Robert, *The Evolution of the Pauline Canon* Depts.drew.edu.

[121] Price, Robert, *The Amazing Colossal Apostle: The Search for the Historical Paul,* Signature Books, Salt Lake City

[122] Ibid

[123] Bassett, Paul M. 2013. "Priscillian." pp. 949–50 in *Encyclopedia of Early Christianity* (2nd ed.), edited by E. Ferguson. Routledge.

[124] Jorge, Ana María C. M. (Winter 2006). "The Lusitanian Episcopate in the 4th Century: Priscilian of Ávila and the Tensions Between Bishops". e-Journal of Portuguese History.

[125] Lehmann, H., ed. *Luther's Works, American edition,* vol. 43, p. 40, Fortress, 1968.

[126] McKim, Donald K, *The Cambridge companion to John Calvin* (2004)

[127] St. Methodius, *Orat. de Simeone et Anna ii. Patr. Graec. Tom.* 18, p. 332.

[128] Janin, R. *Eglises* de CP, Paris, 1969, p 177.

[129] Oxford Dictionary of Byzantium (ODB) 1:293; Janin, Eglises CP, 161-71

[130] Cormack, Robin (2000). *Byzantine Art.* Oxford University Press. pp. 199–200

[131] Bernard de Clairvaux, Sermon on "The Song of Songs" (Song of Solomon) http://www.columbia.edu/itc/english/f2003/client_edit/documents/song_of_songs.html, Sermon 1, III.5

[132] Jacobus de Voragine, *The Golden Legend, Readings on the Saints,* Translated by William Granger Ryan, Volume II, Princeton University Press, 1993, page 135

[133] *In Flaccum,* by Philo as published in Vol. IV of The Works of Philo Judaeus translated from the Greek by C. D. Yonge, B.A. London: Henry G. Bohn, 1855

[134] Cameron, Alan; Long, Jacqueline; Sherry, Lee (1993*), Barbarians and Politics at the Court of Arcadius,* Berkeley and Los Angeles: University of California Press,

[135] Deakin, M. A. B. *Hypatia of Alexandria.* Prometheus Books, 2007. p 148

[136] Mangasar Mugurditch Mangasarian, *The Martyrdom of Hypatia,* Sister Projects.sister projects. A speech given at the Majestic Theater in Chicago, May 1915.

[137] Harding, E. M. (2004), "Origenist Crises", *The Westminster Handbook to Origen*, Louisville, Kentucky: Westminster John Knox Press, pp. 162–167

[138] Barry, Jennifer (2016). *Diagnosing Heresy: Ps.- Martyrius's Funerary Speech for John Chrysostom. Journal of Early Christian Studies*. 24

[139] F. Conybeare '*Antiochus Strategos; account of the sack of Jerusalem in AD 614*', English Historical Review 25 (1910), pp.502-16.

[140] Ben-Dov, Meir, *In the Shadow of the Temple: The Discovery of Ancient Jerusalem,* Keter Publishing House, 1985

[141] le Strange, Guy. (1890). *Palestine under the Moslems*, pp. 80–98.

[142] Ibid (Guy) p. 91.

[143] *Commemoratorium*,, translation in J Wilkinson Jerusalem Pilgrims. Before the Crusades, Warminster: Aris and Phillips, 1977, p. 137

[144] J. Pelikan, *The Christian Tradition: A History of the Development of Doctrine*, Vol. 1, Chicago University of Chicago Press, 1971

[145] *Introduction to Book Ten, the 'Spiritual Meadow'* by Benedict Baker, Vitae Patrum. http://www.vitae-patrum.org.uk, p141

[146] Philip Schaff, *Socrates and Sozomenus Ecclesiastical Histories*, Chapter XXI.—Discovery of the Honored Head of the Forerunner of our Lord, and the Events about it.

[147] Ibid (Schaff)

[148] Laurence Gardner, *The Magdalene Legacy: The Jesus and Mary Bloodline Conspiracy* Weiser Books; Reprint edition (March 31, 2007)

[149] *A Select Library of Nicene and Post-Nicene Fathers of the Christian Church*, Second Series, Volume 11, Sulpicius Severus, On the Life of St. Martin New York, 1894

[150] Foley O.F.M., Leonard. *Saint of the Day, Lives, Lessons, and Feast*, (revised by Pat McCloskey O.F.M.)".

[151] *John Chrysostom (The Early Church Fathers)* by Allen, Pauline, Mayer, Wendy (1999)

[152] Clugnet, Leon, Bibliotecque Hagiagraphique Orientale, Kessinger Pub., USA, 1904

[153] H. Usener, *Legenden der heiligen Pelagia* (Bonn, 1879)

[154] *The Life of St. Pelagia the Harlot*, Translated by Sr. Benedicta Ward, S.L.G., “Pelagia, Beauty Riding By” Cistercian Publications, Inc., Kalamazoo, (1986): Latin PL 73, 663-672)

[155] Jacobus Diaconus (James, or Jacob, the Deacon), *"22: The Life of Saint Pelagia the Harlot translated into Latin from the Greek by Eustochius"*, Vol. I, Antwerp. (1628)

[156] *The Acts of Paul and Thecla: The Life of the Holy Martyr Thecla of Iconium, Equal to the Apostles*, Translated by Jeremiah Jones, (1693 - 1724)

[157] Maurus, Rabanus, *De vita beatae Mariae Magdalenae,* XXVII; Saint Thomas Aquinas, In Ioannem Evangelistam Expositio, c. XX, L. III, 6

[158] *The Life of our Holy Mother Mary of Egypt,* From The Great Canon, the Work of St. Andrew of Crete, Holy Trinity Monastery, Jordanville, NY, USA

[159] Graves, Robert, *The White Goddess*, Faber & Faber, UK, 1948

[160] Pseudo-Rabanus Maurus' *Life of Mary Magdalene and her sister Martha*

[161] *The Travels of Sir John Mandeville,* The Version of the Cotton Manuscript in Modern Spelling, with Three Narratives, in Illustration of It, from Hakluyt's "Navigations, Voyages & Discoveries." MacMillan and Company Limited, 1923, p 64

[162] *The Life of our Holy Mother Mary of Egypt,* The Great Canon, the Work of Saint Andrew of Crete, Holy Trinity Monastery, Jordanville, NY, USA, January 2021

[163] MacMullen, Ramsay, *Christianizing the Roman Empire A.D. 100-400,* 1984, p. 26.

[164] Segal, Eliezer. *Looking for Lilith*. First publication: Jewish Free Press Feb. 6 1995.

[165] The Alphabet of Ben Sira, Jewish Virtual Library, https://www.jewishvirtuallibrary.org/alphabet-of-ben-sira

[166] W. Wilson Cash, *Christendom and Islam: Their Contacts and Cultures Down the Centuries* (New York: Harper and Bros., 1937), 8

[167] Herbert Berg, cd. *Method and Memory in the Study of Islamic Origins* (Boston: Brill, 2003), 22.

[168] Suliman Bashear, *Arabs and Others in Early Islam* (Princeton, NJ: The Darwin Press, Inc., 1997), 24.

[169] Omar Ibn Said Collection (Library of Congress) - Bird, Isaac - Dukur, Muḥammad

Date: 1850

[170] al-Tabari , Muhammad ibn Jarir AD *Tafsir al-Tabari, (History of the Prophets and Kings)*, (225-310 A.H., 838-923)

[171] Abdul-Haqq, Abdiyah *Akbar, Sharing Your Faith with a Muslim*, Baker Publishing Group, 1980

[172] David Thomas, *Syrian Christians Under Islam: The First Thousand Years* (Boston: Brill, 2001), 57

[173] Abel, A. *"Baḥīrā"*. Encyclopaedia of Islam. Brill. Brill Online, 2007

[174] John of Damascus, *Fount of Knowledge, part two - Heresies in Epitome: How They Began and Whence They Drew Their Origin*, 749

[175] Guillame, Alfred, *The traditions of Islam : an introduction to the study of the Hadith literature,* Oxford: Clarendon Press, 1924

[176] Abdul-Haqq, Abdiyah *Akbar, Sharing Your Faith with a Muslim*, Baker Publishing Group, 1980

[177] Hammudah Abdalati, *Islam in Focus* (Indianapolis: International Islamic Pub. House, 1975), 141.

[178] Retsö, Jan (4 July 2003). T*he Arabs in Antiquity: Their History from the Assyrians to the Umayyads*. Routledge. p. 50-5506. ISBN 978-0-7007-1679-1.

[179] Ignaz Goldziher, I*ntroduction to Islamic Theology and Law* trans. Andras and Ruth Hamori. (Princeton, NJ: The Darwin Press, 1981), 4-5

[180] Abi Na'eem, "Ma'arifat al-sahaba", no. 60

[181] Glassé, Cyril (15 April 2003). The New Encyclopedia of Islam. Rowman Altamira.

[182] Suwaidan, Dr. Tareq M. *Palestine Yesterday, today and tomorrow, Yesterday, today and tomorrow*. Ebdaa Fekry Publishing, Jan 1, 2006 p. 61

[183] Umar, http://islam.ru/en/content/story/jerusalem-and-umar-ibn-al-khattab-ra 2013

[184] Al Awlaqi, Anwar. *The Hereafter.* Lulu.com. 2017

[185] *Asia: A Concise History,* By Arthur Cotterell, John Wiley and Sons, Pte. Ltd. Chapter (The Umayyad and Abassid Caliphates)

[186] Maududi, Sayyid Abul Ala - *Tafhim al-Quran - The Meaning of the Quran, 1942 - 1972*

[187] Tavernier, Jean-Baptiste. *Nouvelle Relation de l'Intérieur du Sérail du*

Grand Seigneur, 1675

[188] D. R. Hill, *The Termination of Hostilities in the Early Arab Conquests: AD 634-656* (London: Luzac and Co. Ltd., 1971), 59.

[189] Frank, Daniel H. The Jews of Medieval Islam: Community, Society, and identity. London England: Institute of Jewish Studies. p. 182.

[190] *The Shi'a: The Real Followers of the Sunnah* by Muhammad al-Tijani on Al-Islam.org

[191] Ibn Hisham (1955). *Al-Sira al-Nabawiyya. vol. 2. Cairo.* pp. 51–57. English translation from Stillman (1979), p. 125–126.

[192] Ibn Hisham (1955) p. 127.

[193] Guillaume, A. (1955). Translation of Ibn Ishaq's Sirat Rasoolallah, p. 465.

[194] Moses ben Jacob Cordovero, *Pardes Rimonim* (*Orchard of Pomegranates*) a primary text of Kabbalah, composed by the Jewish mystic in Safed, Galilee, in 1548.

[195] Sippurei Ma'asiyot, *Tales of Rabbi Nachman or Rabbi Nachman's Stories* (p. 1816)

[196] *Rav Avraham Azulai, Kabbalah Centre, https://kabbalah.com/en/articles/rav-avraham-azulai/ FEBRUARY 7, 2012*

[197] Azulai, Rav Avraham, *The Mercy of Abraham*, (*Sefer Chesed L'Avraham*), Publisher: Machon Shaarei Ziv

[198] *Sahih Bukhari Hadith* Volume 5, Book 58, Number 226

[199] Davidson, Linda Kay and Gitlitz, David M., *Pilgrimage: From the Ganges to Graceland : An Encyclopedia Two-Volume Edition,* Santa Barbara, CA, 2002, p.222

Made in the USA
Middletown, DE
22 June 2023